INDEPENDENCE

WITHOUT FREEDOM

Independence without Freedom

IRAN'S FOREIGN POLICY

R. K. RAMAZANI

UNIVERSITY OF VIRGINIA PRESS

Charlottesville and London

To my wife, my children, and my grandchildren, wishing for them a better world

University of Virginia Press

Printed in the United States of America on acid-free paper

First published 2013

9 8 7 6 5 4 3 2 1

Library of Congress Cataloging-in-Publication Data

Ramazani, Rouhollah K., 1928–

    Independence without freedom : Iran's foreign policy / R. K. Ramazani.

        pages   cm

    Includes bibliographical references and index.

    ISBN 978-0-8139-3498-3 (cloth : alk. paper) — ISBN 978-0-8139-3499-0 (e-book)

    1. Iran—Foreign relations. I. Title.

    DS274.R338 2013

    327.55—dc23

                                                                    2013012019

There can be no durable political order without equitable

justice under the law and no justice without liberty.

— The author's address to President Mohammad Khatami

at the United Nations, September 4, 2000

CONTENTS

PART V. THE SHAH AND ISRAEL, KHATAMI AND BUSH

ACKNOWLEDGMENTS

I would like to thank Ms. Lillian Frost, a scholar in her own right, for her unstinting and indispensable help in preparing this volume. It has been an enormously challenging task, particularly considering the condition of my health, which has limited my ability to contribute to the publication process, and she has performed it with flying colors. I thank Ms. Carah Ong, also a scholar in her own right, for recommending Lillian to me. I am grateful for the research assistance of W. Scott Harrop, a lecturer on the Middle East at the University of Virginia, who first inspired me to compile a collection of my essays into a new book. There is no appropriate way for me to thank Nesta Ramazani, my beloved wife and an author in her own right. She has read and edited selflessly and tirelessly everything I have written for publication over the past sixty years. I am indebted to my son, Jahan, a world-renowned scholar in English literature, for helping me every step of the way in the course of preparing this volume. He has made sure that I got it right. Finally, I thank heartily Ms. Penelope J. Kaiserlian, director of the University of Virginia Press from 2001 to 2012, for taking an extraordinary interest in the publication of this volume, as well as everyone else at the University of Virginia Press who has helped transform this manuscript into a book, including special thanks to Mark Mones, assistant managing editor, Joanne Allen, manuscript copy editor, and Richard K. Holway, history and social sciences acquisitions editor.

INDEPENDENCE

WITHOUT FREEDOM

INTRODUCTION

The concluding essay in this volume points out that since its revolution in 1979 Iran has effectively resisted any major power intrusion into its decision-making process. Ayatollah Ruhollah Khomeini, the leader of the Islamic Republic of Iran, felt the need to declare to the world the ideals of the Iranian Revolution. They are independence, freedom, and Islam. This study argues, however, that Iran has failed so far to combine the "inseparable" independence and freedom that the Iranian Constitution calls for.

The germ of my interest in Iran's international role can be traced to the crushing effects of World War II on Iran and to Iran's historic decision to free its oil industry from the age-old clutches of the British Empire. I witnessed these momentous developments in Iran at an early age (1941–51), and I relate them here briefly, since they provide the foundational backdrop to all my writing about Iran, including the essays collected in this volume.

First, Britain and the Soviet Union invaded Iran in 1941. I saw the Soviet planes over the skies of Tehran dropping propaganda leaflets; the ominous sight drove me and my family to take refuge in the basement of our house out of fear of Soviet bombing. I understood later that the invasion was primarily to secure routes through Iran for transporting American arms and ammunition to the Soviet Union in the fight against Nazi Germany. In 1942 some 40,000 American troops (the Persian Gulf Command) arrived in Iran for the same strategic and logistical purpose.

Second, the Allied Powers' occupation of the country over five tumultuous years led to a shortage of food, hoarding, and inflation. Complaints against the government often led to demonstrations, including the so-called bread riots, in one of which I and some of my classmates participated. The Allied Powers promised to respect Iran's political independence and territorial integrity and pledged to withdraw their troops from Iran six months after the cessation of hostilities. But when the war ended, the Soviet troops not only failed to withdraw at the legally appointed time but also supported by military force puppet communist regimes in Azerbaijan and Kurdistan. Iran's complaint to the nascent U.N. Security Council got nowhere until 1946, when the United States pressured the Soviet Union to withdraw. I, along with millions of other Iranians, rejoiced over the departure of the Soviet troops. We all felt that Iran had regained its independence.

Third, in 1941, under Anglo-Soviet pressure, the Iranian ruler, Reza Shah Pahlavi, abdicated the throne in favor of his son, a momentous event that threw

Iranian society wide open to unprecedented political activities. Although chaos reigned, I, like most Iranians, felt that freedom had finally arrived after some twenty years of the Shah's dictatorship. In the following years, hundreds of newspapers exploded onto the scene, numerous rival parties competed for power, and political factions and groups of all stripes mushroomed in Tehran and the provinces. They included liberal nationalist, pan-Iranist, socialist, communist, and Islamic activists, and some resorted to acts of violence. The new ruler, Mohammad Reza Shah, escaped an assassination attempt, whereas the dean of my school at the University of Tehran was murdered on the spot. I joined a liberal nationalist group at the university where at one time my life was threatened by communist ruffians who had been brought to the campus by student sympathizers to intimidate their student rivals.

Fourth, the liberal National Front, led by Mohammad Mosaddegh, pressed vigorously for the nationalization of the Anglo-Iranian Oil Company (AIOC). Inspired by my professor of civil law, Dr. Ali Shayegan, I participated in the National Front–sponsored demonstrations.[1] The nationwide demand for nationalization aimed at wresting from Britain the age-old control of the company, and most Iranians, including myself, viewed the passage of the relevant law by the Parliament (Majlis) in 1951 as a profound symbol of the country's assertion of self-determination and independence, just as globally the peoples of the Third World were struggling for independence from colonial powers. Although Iran had never been colonized, it had enjoyed only nominal independence since the turn of the nineteenth century, when it was sucked into the whirlwind of international politics, including economic and political domination by Britain and Russia, world powers that invaded and occupied Iran in World War I, as they would again in World War II.

Fifth, I left Iran for the United States in 1952 in search of liberty and a doctorate in international politics and law. In 1952–54, when writing my doctoral dissertation at the University of Virginia on the legal and political aspects of Iran's oil-nationalization dispute with Britain, I discovered, to my great surprise, that there was no systematic study of the foreign policy of Iran to be found anywhere. I worked for an entire decade, from 1954 to 1964, to gather information for a book on Iran's foreign policy in a historical context, published in 1966 as *The Foreign Policy of Iran, 1500–1941: A Developing Nation in World Affairs.*[2]

In continuing to work on Iran's foreign policy, I have been struck by the persistent poor understanding in the United States of Iran's international role. The problem has not been limited to the era of hostile relations between the United States and Iran since the Iranian Revolution in 1979. It also existed during the decades of the Shah's friendly relations with the United States. Washington failed to understand that its massive sales of arms to the Shah in support of his unrealistic goal of making Iran the world's leading conventional military power constituted a recipe for disaster. And except for the Kennedy administration, all other administrations failed to pressure the Shah to uphold human-rights standards and open up the Iranian political system.

America has had an even poorer understanding of revolutionary Iran. Washington failed at the dawn of the revolution to understand that it reflected alienation of the Iranian people not only from the dictatorial Shah but also from his greatest single supporter, the United States. Moreover, the United States failed to reach out to Ayatollah Ruhollah Khomeini, the revolutionary leader and founder of the Islamic Republic of Iran. More importantly, it failed to listen to the American ambassador to Iran, Bruce Laingen, who warned U.S. officials that Iranian militants might take American diplomats hostage if Washington allowed the ailing Shah to come to the United States for treatment. They took fifty-two Americans hostage, including Laingen himself, after the Shah entered America. Few Iranians believed the Shah was ill, as the condition of his health had been kept secret. Many feared that the United States would try to return the Shah to power, as it had done in 1953.

Now, more than three decades after the Iranian Revolution, Americans still do not really understand Iran. Pundits characterize Iran simplistically as opaque or paradoxical. Some American leaders, such as former secretary of state Condoleezza Rice, admit that they do not understand Iran. President Barack Obama wants to understand how Iran works, and Admiral Mike Mullen, former chairman of the Joint Chiefs of Staff, warns adroitly that Iran and the United States' failure to understand each other is dangerous. Meanwhile, an absurd debate rages on in Washington and Tel Aviv over whether Iranian leaders are "rational."

This volume aims to help the American public and officials understand Iran better, not the other way around. Yet, the misunderstandings are mutual. Had Ayatollah Khomeini understood America better, he would not have incited and endorsed hostage taking, the crucible of U.S.-Iranian mutual antipathy. Nor would President Mahmoud Ahmadinejad have used threatening words against Israel and denied the Holocaust, which gave Washington and Tel Aviv the best propaganda tool to use against the regime and to cast suspicion on Iran's nuclear program as a cover for making nuclear bombs.

To help America understand Iran better, I include in this volume twenty essays selected from the more than one hundred articles and book chapters I have penned over the past six decades. The essays are divided thematically into five parts, and the volume ends with an afterword.

Part I analyzes three factors that seem to have contributed to the onset of the revolution. The first factor stems from the June 1963 crisis. The Shah's troops brutally attacked the cleric-led demonstrators, killing many unarmed protestors in the holy city of Qom. This event revealed a fundamental problem in the Iranian political culture: the relation between religion and state. To this day Islamists view the uprising as the cause of the revolution. The second factor relates to the Shah's White Revolution, which failed mainly because of draconian suppression of political dissent, which led to the "Black" Revolution, the so-called Islamic Revolution. It was a revolution that was racked in its earliest phase by domestic political chaos, terrorism, and counterterrorism (my American-educated young niece, for example, was falsely charged as a counter-revolutionary and summarily executed). The third factor pertains to the Shah's longtime relations with the United States. The Shah lost America because he depended excessively on the United States, and America lost Iran because it failed to pressure the Shah to open the Iranian political system.

Part II examines the evolution of Iranian foreign policy since the dawn of the revolution. It begins with a close analysis of the impact of Khomeini's ideas and ideals on Iran's foreign policy. It then explains the development of contending orientations in foreign policy because of pervasive factional strife and the revolutionary regime's theory and action with respect to the export of the Islamic Revolution. It also analyzes the shifting premise of Iran's foreign policy during the presidency of Mohammad Khatami. Moreover, three persistent problems in Iranian foreign policy are identified in part II: the all-important issue of defining national interest, the tension between ideology and pragmatism, and the aspiration of Iranian leaders to combine spiritual values and practical realities in making foreign-policy decisions. As early as 1986 I identified pragmatic strands in Iran's foreign policy and suggested tempering the United States' stern containment policy for possible future reconciliation between Washington and Tehran, to no avail.

Part III focuses on the problem of security in the Persian Gulf. Immediately after the eruption of the Iranian Revolution, I proposed in *Foreign Affairs* a regional security scheme that would include both riparian and external powers. One essay analyzes the strategic significance of the Strait of Hormuz to Iran's national security interests. Beyond Iran's Gulf interest, part III treats the social and political changes in Gulf societies after the Iranian Revolution and the growing threat of terrorism. Attention is also paid to the rising demand for better treatment for the traditionally disenfranchised Shii minority in Saudi Arabia and the politically and economically deprived Shii majority in Bahrain. Part III also includes a detailed analysis of Shii politics in the Persian Gulf based on my interviews in the region.

Part IV treats two of the most important issues of the revolutionary period, with far-reaching implications for the foreign policy of both Iran and the

United States. First, it takes up the Iranian hostage crisis, arguing that Iran must understand that international legitimacy matters to its national interest and prestige, but no such concern has ever been expressed in Tehran. I proposed to President Jimmy Carter in person on December 9, 1979, that he send a mission of Muslim scholars to Tehran to try to express to Khomeini the Muslim world's concern over the captivity of fifty-two Americans. After the mission was organized, I understand, Khomeini declined to receive it. Second, a fundamental question about the Iran-Iraq War (1980–88) is, who started the war? I analyze this question critically, arguing that the U.N. Security Council could be blamed for tardiness in calling upon Iraq to desist promptly from hostilities, although politically speaking, Iran enjoyed little sympathy in much of the world in the wake of the hostage crisis. The controversial statement of the U.N. secretary-general about Iraq's "aggression" is also considered.

Part V starts with an analysis of the Shah's policy toward the Arab-Israeli conflict, especially his friendly relations with Israel in contrast to the hostile policy of the revolutionary regime. The main essay in part V, however, discusses in detail the quest of the Iranian people for representative democratic governance during the Constitutional Movement (1905–11) and the Nationalist Movement, which began in earnest in 1949 and continued until the CIA's overthrow of the democratically elected government of Mosaddegh in 1953, a period known in Iranian history as the "era of constitutional revival." Many Iranians hoped that such an era would return after the election of President Khatami, but his "Islamic democracy" failed to accentuate political and social freedom. This failure should be blamed primarily on the opposition of the die-hard conservative factions. And President George W. Bush's hostile portrayal of Iran as a member of the "axis of evil" had a significant negative effect on Khatami's conciliatory policy toward the United States. A deeper question, however, persists to date. Could Khatami's goal of Islamic democracy ever be realized under the Constitution of the Islamic Republic of Iran, which gives the lion's share of power to the *faqih*?

The afterword points out the reasons for America's poor understanding of Iranian foreign-policy behavior and outlines the fundamentals of my approach to the study of Iranian foreign policy. I call this approach "diplomatic culture," defined as those values, norms, mores, modes of thinking, and ways of acting that have developed over centuries as a result of Iran's diplomatic interaction with other nations. The afterword also identifies the factors and forces that drive Iranian behavior in world politics, outlines the major instruments of Iran's foreign policy, and briefly places the nuclear dispute in the context of my approach.

NOTES

1. Shayegan was a close confidant of Prime Minister Mosaddegh. They were both victims of the CIA-engineered coup in 1953. The pro-Shah army officers captured and imprisoned them. A military court summarily sentenced Shayegan to life imprisonment; the sentence was later reduced to ten years. However, after three years he was exiled to Europe, and he later came to the United States, where he died in 1981.

2. The American Association of Middle East Studies honored me by giving the book manuscript its award for "the most distinguished contribution to Middle East Scholarship in 1964," and in 1966 *Foreign Affairs* called the book "the only work in any language, which gives an objective and detailed account of Iran's international role during this entire period."

I

THE SHAH

AND KHOMEINI

REVOLUTIONS

"CHURCH" AND STATE IN

MODERNIZING SOCIETY

The Case of Iran

After nearly ten years of political quietism and apparent political stability, antigovernment riots broke out in Iran early in June 1963. The riots were not incited by the supporters of Dr. Mohammad Mosaddegh, whose government had been overthrown by the "Royalists" nearly ten years before. Rather, the government charged, they were instigated by "the elements of Black Reaction." In retaliation, therefore, the religious figures who led the riots, Ayatollah Khomeini of Qom, Ayatollah Qumi of Meshed, and Ayatollah Mahallati of Shiraz, were thrown into prison and were subsequently released upon having given their word not to interfere in the affairs of the state. An apparent lull returned to the Iranian political scene after much bloodshed and the destruction of millions of dollars' worth of public and private property. But the fundamental problem that lay at the heart of the riots continues to haunt Iranian society and politics.

This is the problem of the role of the *ulama*, the Islamic clergy, in Iranian society and its relations with the state. While the problem is as old as the modern Iranian state, which rose to power at the turn of the sixteenth century, the developments that led to its reappearance in early June 1963 differed significantly from those of any previous time. The Shah's revolutionary land reforms were the immediate cause of the riots supported by the religious figures mentioned. But the significance of the Iranian experience is that it points out a fundamental problem encountered by most if not all modernizing societies.

Modernization is a multifaceted and complex process, involving every aspect of human life and the relations of the individual to society and the state. It is well known that profound socioeconomic transformation tends to incur opposition from traditional groups, and the *ulama* in the Middle East have faced challenges to their positions of wealth, prestige, and power similar to those faced by the Church in Latin America. The Shii *ulama* in Iran, like the Church in Latin America, have learned from experience that, in practice, official recognition is not quite the sine qua non that it is in theory.

" 'Church' and State in Modernizing Society: The Case of Iran" was originally published by SAGE Publications Inc. (http://online.sagepub.com) in *American Behavioral Scientist* 7, no. 5 (January 1964): 26–28.

A theory of comparative politics requires much research on the relation of "church" to state in modernizing societies. In the Middle East, the relation of the *ulama* to the state in various countries needs to be studied in the context of the unending quest for effective socioeconomic change. To prove fruitful, such research must avoid confusing the role of religion in society with the relation of the *ulama*, as an interest group or institution, to the state. This distinction is analytically necessary not only for the differences obtaining in the subject matter but also for the different methodological problems that each presents. I hope that these preliminary remarks on the relation of the Shii *ulama* to the state of Iran will stimulate interest in research on the impact of revolutionary change on the fortunes and the waning power of the *ulama* and of comparable traditional religious systems in other societies.

THE TRADITIONAL PATTERN

The very establishment of the Iranian state at the turn of the sixteenth century was made possible as the result of the adoption of Shiism as the official creed of Iran and the forcible imposition of the Shii ideology on the population by the monarch in alliance with the *ulama*. Shah Ismail, the founder of the Safavid dynasty, posed as the "Absolute Agent of God" and demanded *sajdah*—that is, prostration before God—from his newly converted subjects. But this basically theocratic characteristic of the state and its close relation with the *ulama* changed gradually during the following century. During the reign of Shah Abbas the Great (1588–1629) the millennial institution of the absolute monarchy at last clearly overshadowed the role of the *ulama* in the affairs of the state, and for the first time since its rise to power Iran concluded a peace treaty with the Ottoman Empire, which in essence embodied something like the principle of *cuius regio eius religio*.

The close identification of the monarch with the state, and the concomitant eclipse of the role of the *ulama* in the affairs of the state, continued in the eighteenth and nineteenth centuries. It is true that during the reign of ineffectual rulers such as Shah Sultan Hussein (1694–1722) the *ulama* played a disproportionately large role. It is also true that in certain policy decisions, such as Fath Ali Shah's second war with Russia (1826–1928), the influence of the *ulama* manifested itself. But these were, in the main, exceptions to the primacy of the role of the absolute monarch in Iranian politics and policymaking. The monarch was the "Sole Executive." His ends and means were those of the state. The Qajar monarchs (1796–1924) not only showed the pomp of their ancient counterparts but surpassed them in their unbridled exercise of power in making both domestic- and foreign-policy decisions in the nineteenth century.

Ever since the last quarter of that century, however, the relations of the *ulama* with the state have fluctuated with the vicissitudes of Iranian politics. These relations have ranged from complete subordination to the monarch to open control of the affairs of the state. Except for a relatively brief period at the beginning of the reign of the present shah, when the *ulama* were allied with rather than subordinate to the monarch because of his faltering control, the *ulama* either have been dominated by the Shah or have defied him in alliance with other groups in Iranian society.

THE *ULAMA*'S DEFIANCE OF THE MONARCH

The *ulama*, in their struggle for power, have often allied themselves with the nationalists. One of the earliest and most successful examples was the tobacco-monopoly incident that signaled the beginning of the events leading to the Constitutional Revolution (1905–11). Haj Mirza Mohammad Hassan of Shiraz, a religious leader, wrote to the Shah that the grant of the monopoly was contrary to Sharia (Islamic law) and issued a *fatwa* (a religious decree) requiring the people to abandon smoking until the monopoly had been cancelled. The cancellation of the concession emboldened the *ulama*, whose role in the affairs of the state had been decreasing. In the Constitutional Revolution itself many of them cast their lot with the moderns, who demanded a constitutional monarchy in which limitations would be placed upon the powers of the absolute monarch. But some of the *ulama* confused constitutionalism (*Mashrotiat*) with the reestablishment of the Sharia (*Mashro'iat*). The Constitution made Shii Islam the official religion of the state, required the Shah to protect and propagate Islam, and provided for the representation of religious leaders. In practice, however, the "legislative review" powers of the *ulama* have never been put into force, and the role of the Shah as the protector and propagator of Islam has been overshadowed by his overriding concern with the more mundane affairs of the state. Nevertheless, at least in theory, the *ulama* reasserted their power in alliance with the nationalists.

Another example of the *ulama*'s attempt to control the affairs of the state was the ever-growing influence of the clergy in the years of the Mosaddegh regime. A distinction may be made between the activities of such fundamentalist groups as the Fedayan Islam (Devotees of Islam) and the Mujahadeen Islam (Fighters of Islam) and the *ulama*. Yet in practice this distinction is of little significance because the actions of the fundamentalists tended to increase the influence of the *ulama* in the affairs of state. The Fedayan Islam terrorized the Shah-supported government of Razmara, and one of the members of the group assassinated the Prime Minister in the Shah Mosque. They demanded strict application of Shii law and the restoration of Shii rule under the *Imam*. Their terrorist tactics were matched by slanderous campaigns against the ruling elite. Like the nationalists, their main target was the Anglo-Iranian Oil Company, but their ultimate goal surpassed that of the moderate nationalists. The Fedayan demanded elimination of all ties with all foreign countries.

However, a rival group, the Mujahadeen Islam, exercised for a time an unprecedented influence in the affairs of the state in alliance with the supporters of the National Front of Dr. Mosaddegh. Sayyid Abolghassem Kashani, the leader of this group, was made Speaker of the Majlis, which immediately voted to pardon Khalil Tahmassebi, the assassin of Razmara. Throughout this period of alliance with the nationalists at least some of the *ulama* were defying the Shah to the extent that they succeeded in enlarging the rift between the Court and Dr. Mosaddegh. This defiance came into the open most graphically in July 1952, when the Shah selected Ahmad Qavam to replace Dr. Mosaddegh as prime minister. A momentous dialogue between Qavam and Kashani took place in which the age-old problem of "church" and state was openly discussed. In his controversial declaration, which is believed to have contributed to his dramatic downfall, Qavam stated in unequivocal terms:

Just as I hate demagoguery in political affairs I detest hypocrisy in religious matters. Those who on the pretext of fighting Red extremists reinforce black reaction strike at freedom and undermine the efforts of the founders of the Constitution. While respecting the sacred tenets of Islam, I divorce religion from politics and will prevent the dissemination of superstitious and retrogressive ideas.

In equally strong terms Kashani rejected Qavam's dictum for separation of religion and politics, alluded to the possibility of declaring a *jihad* (holy war) on Qavam, and proclaimed:

The separation between religion and politics has been for centuries the program of the British. It is by this means that they have kept the Islamic peoples ignorant of their interests. Traitors who have followed British policy for centuries have now, however, overthrown the barrier of the Mosadeq government. They have replaced Mosadeq by a person who was reared in the arms of monarchy and despotism, and whose political life is full of treason, as has been demonstrated on a number of occasions.

But the alliance between the *ulama* and the nationalists was short-lived, as evidenced by the Mosaddegh-Kashani rift, which was probably influenced by the August 1953 overthrow of the government of Dr. Mosaddegh by supporters of the Shah. This triumph of the Royalists marked the beginning of nearly ten years of clerical impotence, which was momentarily interrupted by the riots of

June 1963. Before dealing with the events leading up to the riots, we must discuss the other primary form that the relation of the ulama to the state has taken.

THE ULAMA'S SUBORDINATION TO THE MONARCHY

For the most part the ulama have been impotent during the reign of the Pahlavi dynasty, that is, since 1925. The successful show of strength made by the ulama in 1924 was followed by nearly two decades of complete subordination to the Shah. In that year they triumphantly opposed Reza Khan's bid for a republican form of government. But beginning in 1925, when he ascended the throne of Iran, the Shah, like his Turkish counterpart, Mustafa Kemal, made secularism a cornerstone of his public policy. Until 1941, when he abdicated the throne in favor of his eldest son, he relentlessly pursued an unprecedented program of modernization, which significantly reduced the power of the clergy. But, unlike those of his Turkish counterpart, the Shah's modernization efforts tended to be more apparent than real. Principally for this reason, when his repressive anti-clerical measures were removed as the result of his abdication, the ulama reasserted their power and influence in the affairs of the state with relative ease.

But the renascent role of the ulama in Iranian politics, which reached its peak during the government of Dr. Mosaddegh, was almost completely reversed as the result of the Royalist victory and the subsequent increasing role of the present shah in the affairs of the state. The millennial institution of the monarchy once again overshadowed the institution of the ulama, whose members were suppressed jointly with the nationalists. Nevertheless, it was not until November 1961 that the Shah's revolutionary measures posed a serious challenge to the ulama as well as to the landed aristocracy, the forces in favor of the status quo. The land reform measures seemed to challenge one of the most fundamental bases of clerical power in Iran. Reza Shah's suppressive measures as well as his modernization efforts had made a dent in the power of the ulama, but the land reform measures of his son would seem to have deprived them of most, if not all, of what was left of their waning power.

Before November 1961 the Shah had assumed that his own efforts in land distribution would provide an example to be followed by other owners of large tracts of land. The failure of this approach, together with both internal and external pressures, finally prompted the promulgation of the Farman Sheshganeh (Six-Point Royal Decree), which directed the government of Dr. Ali Amini to enforce laws limiting landholdings, to form agricultural cooperative societies, to set up youth work battalions, and to utilize the Army to build feeder roads and irrigation canals and to instruct farmers. The bill of the Minister of

Agriculture stipulated that landowners could hold one village, that they would repay them in ten installments, and that the government would resell these to the peasants, who would have to pay the government in fifteen installments. The bill also provided for the establishment of cooperatives for the purpose of development and distribution of seeds and husbandry, extension of credits and services, maintenance and improvement of waterways, utilization of agricultural mechanization, and so on.

Although these revolutionary measures are not directed exclusively or even primarily against the *ulama*, the June 1963 riots revealed that they have begun to shake the very fabric of Iranian traditional society. In this society the *ulama* have attempted with varying degrees of success to influence public policy. Even the Shah in the past has relied, at times, on the *ulama* as well as on the army and the bureaucracy. But at present the Shah appears to be taking the risk of ignoring these traditional sources of his support in the hope of luring to his side the hitherto neglected peasantry and the workers. He is simultaneously seeking to gain influence in another traditionally neglected segment of the society, the women of Iran.

In spite of these breaks with tradition, it is interesting to note that the Shah has rather consistently utilized religious symbols in rationalizing, popularizing, and legitimizing his socioeconomic reforms. He has on many occasions invoked the concept of *barakah* (divine blessing), posing as the monarch who has since childhood been mysteriously spared many catastrophes, including a serious attempt against his life. Before the riots of June 1963 he recalled these miraculous escapes when making a major statement concerning land reform at the holy city of Qom. More important was the way in which he tried to justify the revolutionary measures in Islamic terms. He stated:

If the Muslim community adapts itself to the requirements of modern times in the glorious spirit of Islam, it will find new power and victory. Our society continues to be in need of religious and moral principles, and those Ulama who have either cooperated with, or remained unopposed to, the land reform program are indubitably our religious leaders. But those others who have expressed opposition to it would seem to be preoccupied with the appearance rather than the substance of the religion. The land reform put into effect today in this sacred place should be a great lesson to the followers of such Ulama. The Shia as well as the entire Islamic community can no longer drag behind the times. We trust that Allah will guide those in positions of leadership to the Right Path, and that by the blessings of this sacred shrine they will serve Islam, the Shah and their country.

In spite of the June 1963 riots, the land reform program has been pushed with speed. Meanwhile, after a suspension of about two and a half years the Iranian Parliament was opened by the Shah on October 6, 1963. For the first time in Iran's history women voted and ran for the Parliament. In his inaugural address to Parliament the Shah noted that "from now on public policy decisions will truly reflect the interests of the majority of the Iranian people because they have for the first time elected their own representatives." The Shah attributed this "national revolutionary change" not only to the historic emancipation of women but particularly to the land reform measures of his government. He declared that Iran's aims were to raise the people's standard of living, increase agricultural and industrial production, and raise per capita income.

It is difficult to say how revolutionary a revolution decreed from the top can be. It is also hazardous to state how representative the present Parliament really is. Nevertheless, it is clear that there is an unprecedented change in the makeup of the present Parliament. Whether this change will usher in a "democratic" era remains to be seen. But it already is apparent that the government is less aware of the complex nature of social change than it is of its own belief in the possibility of decreeing even psychological change in Iranian society. Religious figures do not dare to speak in opposition, and the government is using many media of communication to tell the masses that religion is a matter of individual belief and should have nothing to do with the affairs of the state.

It seldom seems realized in Iran that the persisting traditional attitude toward the relation of religion to the state cannot be decreed out of existence. Such a change in attitude is essentially bound up with the intellectual and psychological life of the society. The change in these spheres will require of the Iranian people a rethinking of the whole structure of their life and culture, and the rebuilding of their universe and their identity in it. This is the most difficult task confronting all modernizing societies, Islamic or otherwise. It is the most difficult task because it does not lend itself to solutions decreed from above.

Yet it is a task that no modernizing society can afford to ignore, because modernization in one aspect of life tends to reverberate in all others. The process of urbanization reduces the luster of religion as a guide to human conduct. The educated urban classes progressively will seek to find answers to moral and ethical questions elsewhere. If this "elsewhere" is not to be in lectures on Marxist values, the ulama will have to adjust themselves to the demands of a modernizing society. More importantly, they must be encouraged by the state to find, in collaboration with modern intellectuals, answers to moral and ethical questions of the emerging society in the ancient as well as the Islamic heritage of Iran.

IRAN'S "WHITE REVOLUTION"

A Study in Political Development

Iran is entering the second decade of its "White Revolution." The Shah has set forth his own account of it,[1] but the scholarly community has, as yet, made no serious attempt at analyzing it.[2] This omission is glaring regardless of justifications. It is, in fact, an omission that verges on scholarly neglect because, if there is any validity in the propositions of this study, a better understanding of Iran's contemporary achievements and dilemmas would seem to require probing the very meaning of the "White Revolution" by going beyond its official label and the adumbration of its programs. The purpose of this essay is to do exactly that. And toward that end it will seek to utilize concepts of political development as suggested in particular by Professor Gabriel Almond. I prefer these concepts because they facilitate examination of the "White Revolution" within the broad and fundamental framework of the major challenges of Western civilization to Iran.

In theorizing about these challenges to "new nations" in general, Professor Almond identifies four major revolutions. The leaders of these nations, he suggests, confront a *national* revolution, an *authority* revolution, a *participation* revolution, and a *welfare* revolution.[3] Which one, or which combination, of these does Iran's "White Revolution" resemble? In raising this preliminary question in search of the meaning of this phenomenon we are at once struck by the insufficiency of these four concepts of revolution in light of the Iranian experience. The reason for this would seem to be the incremental nature of Iran's winning of independence. The modern political history of Iran, as an "old" and technically sovereign nation, but in many ways a "new" nation, is largely that of a nation in search of its "true" or "complete" independence. This is quite different from the experience of most new nations (such as India, Pakistan, Syria, Lebanon, and numerous others), which "won" their independence at a rather decisive moment of their history. This may well be the reason for Almond's non-inclusion of national independence as a fifth revolution. Even so, it must be pointed out that in the case of all nations, old or new, though particularly more vulnerable new nations, analysis of domestic politics should include foreign-policy considerations, including the all-important concept of what we may call "an *independence* revolution," encompassing both the acts of *winning* and *maintaining* freedom of decision making in international politics. In analyzing Iran's foreign policy over a long span of time I felt impelled to stress the theoretical necessity and empirical demonstrability of domestic- and foreign-policy interaction.[4] Almond's own recent plea for noting the interaction of the domestic society, the international environment, and the political system[5] would certainly seem to indicate that my addition of the concept of an "*independence* revolution" to his previous formulation of four revolutions would be found of general theoretical utility.

The simultaneity of these five revolutionary challenges to the traditional Iranian political culture finds its roots primarily in the nineteenth century, despite the sporadic sixteenth- to eighteenth-century contacts with the West.[6] The principal stimulus for change in the ancient conception of monarchical absolutism, in the autocratic conception of foreign policy, in the provincial, tribal, and communal bases of governmental administration, and in the accumulation of economic wealth in the hands of a few came from outside the political culture, just as in so many historical Western and especially modern non-Western societies. And just as in these societies, in Iran, too, the single most important catalyst for introducing the need for change was external pressure at the beginning. Military defeat in wars with tsarist Russia, the imposition of the humiliating peace treaties of Gulistan (1813) and Turkomanchai (1828) by Russia, the opening of telegraphic communications by Great Britain, the Anglo-Russian rivalry over commercial and economic concessions, and the dissemination of ideas through foreign education, missionary activities, and the printing press marked the processes that forced the traditional political culture open to modern conceptions of society and government. The Constitutional Revolution was simultaneously the product and the cause of this Western penetration. As such it reflected the Iranian response to the fivefold challenge of Western civilization, calling for emancipation from foreign control, integration of diverse linguistic, tribal, and communal groups into a homogeneous political community, centralization of governmental authority, popular participation in politics, and social and economic modernization. The resulting constitutional documents, which are still in force, support the proposition, I submit, that at the time these were adopted simultaneously by the national elite as the basic goals of the "new political order" and have remained so to date. For example, the Majlis was granted major powers in foreign affairs toward the goal of ensuring national independence, it was required to investigate all important matters in the public interest and to assist the Cabinet in reforms toward the goal of "happiness and well-being" of the Iranian people, and the people of Iran were recognized as a source of power in addition to and separate from the monarch in keeping with the goal of participation.[7]

To suggest that ever since the Constitutional Revolution national independence, national integration, centralization of governmental authority, popular participation, and socioeconomic modernization have simultaneously constituted the most fundamental goals of the Iranian political system does not, of course, mean that these objectives have been defined uniformly by various national leaders during different periods. For example, the Constitutional leaders perceived the goal of national independence primarily in terms of the eradication of extensive tsarist Russian and British economic and political control, just as did Reza Shah during most of his rule, but from 1941 to 1946 it was perceived primarily in terms of resistance to foreign, particularly Russian, interference and occupation, from 1947 to 1953 in terms of a crusade against the Anglo-Iranian Oil Company, from 1954 to 1961 in terms of resistance to Soviet psychological pressures, and since 1962 in terms of reduction of dependence on the United States and normalization of relations with the Soviet Union. To take another of the five basic goals, for example, the Constitutional leaders perceived socioeconomic reforms in their time primarily in terms of financial reorganization of the administrative system, toward which end they hired the American financial adviser Morgan Shuster. Reza Khan (and subsequently as Shah) did largely the same from 1922 to 1927 by supporting the employment of Dr. Arthur Millspaugh by the Majlis. Neither Reza Shah nor his predecessors would seem to have perceived the goal of socioeconomic modernization in such basic terms as, for example, the distribution of land among the peasantry. Even Muhammad Reza Shah would not seem to have perceived the requirements of socioeconomic modernization in the same way throughout his rule despite the repeated plea for modernization ever since his accession to the throne in 1941. National independence, socioeconomic modernization, as well as other basic goals of the Iranian political system, in other words, have persisted ever since the Constitutional Revolution, despite the fact that various national leaders have defined them somewhat differently in light of their particular circumstances.

Neither the simultaneity of adoption nor the continuity of execution of these goals alone can take us far in search of the meaning of the "White Revolution." We must also consider the crucial problem of *priority*. In generalizing about this problem as it confronts any given national leader in a developing country, Almond insists that it should be "unambiguously clear that he is not even free to choose the particular mix of revolution or the order which he prefers. Whether he likes it or not he must give a higher priority to the creation of a nation and of effective government authority before giving way fully to demands for participation and welfare."[8] As was suggested earlier, however, in the case of Iran, where the winning of national independence has been an incremental process, this must also be considered as a continuous goal of various national leaders in discussing the problem of priority. More importantly, I submit, from the dawn of the Constitutional Revolution to the early 1960s this goal was most of the time accorded the *highest* priority by Iranian leaders.

Let us illustrate this proposition by some major examples. The Constitutional Revolution itself, although reflecting modernizing, participatory, and nationalistic aspirations, was, according to the testimony of its foremost student, E. G. Browne, more a *nationalistic* than a democratic movement.[9] It aimed in principle at Iran's emancipation from Anglo-Russian control, which it failed to achieve at the time. In fact, that rivalry frustrated Iran's then subordinate goal of modernization as the result of the pressured departure of the American financial adviser Morgan Shuster. Reza Shah, in fact, fulfilled the basic nationalist goal of the Constitutionalists, namely, winning a large measure of political independence for Iran from Great Britain and Russia. For this reason I have elsewhere characterized Reza Shah chiefly as the "architect of independent Iran."[10] This is, I submit, a more appropriate characterization of his accomplishments, during most of his time, despite the more familiar portrayal of the late Shah as a modernizer.[11] He certainly was a modernizer too, but in terms of his highest goal and greatest concerns he was first and foremost a nationalist leader. Given the circumstances of Iran at the time, independence had to take priority over welfare. Let us take two quite different examples of the Shah's major acts of modernization: the construction of the Trans-Iranian Railway and the adoption of the Iranian Civil Code. To be sure, these represented major changes, but modernization in these, as in numerous other instances, was incidental; the Shah's overriding goal was political independence. The choice of the Trans-Iranian Railway's termini was largely dictated by his earnest desire and dogged determination to thwart the Anglo-Russian influence in the south and the north; welfare considerations were only secondary.[12] The Civil Code, to turn to the other example, was rushed through the Majlis primarily as an inducement to Western powers, particularly Great Britain, to accept the consequences of the abolition of capitulations.[13]

To cite some examples from a later period, let us first take Qavam's overnight creation of the "Democratic Party of Iran" and the Supreme Economic Council. The party was to steal the thunder of the Soviet-dominated Democrats of the Azerbaijan Party, and the Council, like some other swift creations, was to placate those in the adamant Tudeh Party and the Soviet Embassy who were pressuring for reforms.[14] His party was not created as a modern political infrastructure toward the goal of popular political participation. Nor were the economic measures designed so much to achieve the goal of economic welfare.

A final example may be cited from the oil nationalization movement. Nationalization of the oil industry in the late 1940s and early 1950s was, to be sure, often paraded in terms of the goal of socioeconomic modernization, but in light of the perception and performance of its most important advocates it was launched primarily as a political act directed toward the goal of Iran's "true independence." Dr. Mosaddegh, for example, in principle favored land reform but did not accord it priority at the time. In a major speech to the Majlis Oil Commission on February 21, 1951, he vehemently argued that the British-dominated oil industry, not the landowning system, was the principal cause of all Iran's misfortunes.[15] In the circumstances of the time this was a widely accepted conception of the primary challenge to the Iranian nation. The overriding concern with this challenge overshadowed not only efforts toward economic modernization but also efforts at political institutionalization, such as the construction of a viable party system during 1951–53. This and similar evidence would seem to support the proposition that although the challenges of nationalism, modernism, and democracy simultaneously burst upon the Iranian political culture, the goal of national independence most often received a higher priority over those of economic modernization and political participation from the dawn of the Constitutional Revolution to the early 1960s.

In light of the above proposition, the goal of socioeconomic modernization was not accorded the highest priority until the early 1960s. If it can now be shown that (1) it has been given first priority since that time and (2) that the "White Revolution" in the last analysis stands for the goal and programs of socioeconomic modernization, or what Almond would call "*welfare* revolution," then it would be possible to suggest that only since the early 1960s has the goal of socioeconomic modernization been accorded the highest priority by the Iranian government in modern times. This is what the "White Revolution" would seem to mean. It would also seem to mean that the priority accorded socioeconomic modernization is bound to have far-reaching implications for Iran's other basic goals.

In essence, the circumstances that would seem to have made it possible for the Shah's regime to begin to give priority to the goal of socioeconomic modernization fall into two major categories, domestic and foreign. To take up the internal circumstances first, as already noted, the Shah aspired to the adoption of the goal of socioeconomic modernization as early as his accession to the throne (1941), but modernization requires concentration of power, which the Shah did not possess sufficiently either during the war or in the early postwar period. Even his triumph over Dr. Muhammad Mosaddegh in 1953 did not mark the end of serious opposition to the Shah's bid for supreme power. It only signaled the beginning of a painful process of consolidation of power between the overthrow of the government of Dr. Mosaddegh and the bloody crushing of the June 1963 uprising. With the effective suppression of the National Front and the Tudeh as well as other sources of opposition, the throne felt secure enough to accord social and economic reforms the highest priority.

External circumstances by the early 1960s also made such a choice possible. Three factors in particular proved important. The destruction of the unpopular monarchical regime in neighboring Iraq in 1958, Iraq's subsequent defection from the Baghdad Pact, and the bellicose attitudes of the new Iraqi military regime were causes for concern. A less pro-Western orientation and a more serious reform program seemed necessary if a similar fate was not to await the regime in Iran. A second external factor was the amelioration of relations between Iran and the Soviet Union subsequent to the crisis of 1958–59 over negotiations for a long-term nonaggression pact. Iran's ability in 1962 to pledge to the Soviet Union that it would not allow rocket or missile bases on its territory ushered in the era of good-neighborliness between the two countries that has lasted to the present time and has been marked by unprecedented commercial, technical, and economic cooperation. Iranian energies could then be channeled toward socioeconomic reforms at home rather than resistance to Soviet pressures. And a third factor in the external circumstances favoring the adoption of socioeconomic modernization as the primary goal of Iran by the early 1960s was the attitude of the Kennedy administration: the United States seemed more interested in aiding those countries that helped themselves. Iran had had its share of generous American economic and military assistance, was deriving increasing revenues from its oil, and yet was at the time gripped by a serious economic crisis. To deserve more American aid Iran had first to put its own house in order by undertaking long-overdue social and economic reforms now that the regime seemed more stable.

The first and single most important "principle" or "point" ('asl) of these reforms was the land-reform program launched in 1962, followed by eleven other points, which all together constitute what is officially labeled the "White Revolution of the Shah and the people" (enqelab sefid Shah va mardom).[16] Detailed description of these points is obviously beyond the scope of this analysis, but their salient features and attendant problems may be swiftly examined in order to indicate that the "White Revolution" is primarily a program of socioeconomic modernization.

Land reform has meant the emergence of millions of peasants as the new owners of land, the development of thousands of rural cooperatives, and increased agricultural productivity despite the migration of the labor force to cities and towns and the inability of existing industry to absorb it. Financial, technical, organizational, marketing, and other problems persist, but generally the distribution of land is now well under way. Attention has also been paid to the lot of the workers: the government claims that some 55 factories and workshops have been sold to laborers and a total of some 150,000 have begun sharing up to 20 percent of net profits in nearly 2,000 factories. Some $2 billion in annual revenues from oil underwrite socioeconomic modernization, as evidenced by the allocation of 80 percent of the oil revenues to the current Fourth Development Plan (March 21, 1968 to March 20, 1973). The oft-quoted GNP achieved an average rate of 9.8 percent per year at current prices between 1963 and 1968 and has reached an average of about 10 percent in more recent years. The regime's accomplishments in these and other respects, such as the increasing proportion of investment to GNP, changes in the composition, direction, and volume of trade, and the expansion of foreign markets, are seldom matched in other areas of modernization.

A major one of these is the field of public administration. The Iranian political system, saddled with an old, established bureaucracy, has so far made little headway in administrative change. Nevertheless, some changes are on the horizon. For example, the quality of personnel has improved considerably in the National Iranian Oil Company (NIOC), the Central Bank, and the Plan Organization. What is called the "Administrative Revolution Conference" met in 1967 and was followed by the creation of the Government Department Evaluation Organization (GDEO). GDEO's primary function is to oversee administrative changes. Two of its guiding principles are use of the merit system in personnel recruitment and the abolition of "unnecessary" rules and regulations. But not much else has been done. The Shah himself has been cited as stating that 95 percent of government institutions were based on "irrational and unsound principles." Informed Tehranis themselves view the shortcomings of the administrative system as stemming not only from overcentralization of authority in Tehran and from overstaffing, inefficiency, and incompetence but also from outworn attitudes.

Administrative problems tend to affect adversely other areas of modernization. For example, the all-important educational reforms are often impeded severely by red tape, by refusal to take responsibility, and by other familiar problems. There is a general tendency in measuring achievements in education, as in other fields, to overemphasize quantitative criteria, such as increases in the number of elementary- and secondary-school students, or the building of educational infrastructures. Ever since the Ramsar Conference of August 1968, however, a degree of sophistication in evaluation is becoming noticeable: the imbalance between academic education and vocational training, the declining quality of education in most secondary schools, and the so-called diploma craze have come under verbal attack. The regime has been justifiably proud of its innovative creation of the well-known "Army of Knowledge," comprising some 74,000 young men and women in the past eight years, who have carried literacy to the far corners of numerous villages. The problems of education in urban centers, however, like those of public administration, are the ones that would seem most troublesome. New universities and schools are constantly emerging, and yet every year many thousands of students are turned away from the University of Tehran, which in the summer of 1971, for example, granted admission to only some 10,000 out of 70,000 anxious applicants. The entrance examination will reportedly come under scrutiny, if it has not already.

If there is any validity to my proposition that the "White Revolution" symbolizes the adoption of socioeconomic modernization by the Shah as the highest goal of his government since 1962, the implications of this preference for the other basic goals of Iran must be sought. First, insofar as the goal of national *independence* is concerned, the Shah's socioeconomic modernization has contributed significantly to Iranian capabilities and has been paralleled by an unusually active foreign policy, officially called the "independent national policy" (*siyasat-i mustaqel-i melli*). The Shah himself envisages Iran's new role in world affairs solely as the product of the "White Revolution," but a favorable international environment has probably been more influential, as I have suggested elsewhere.[17] Given the emerging intense and active role of Iran in the Persian Gulf, the question may be raised whether the regime is not about to accord priority to the goal of its leadership in the Gulf area even at the expense of the current primary objective of socioeconomic modernization. This question is *not* hypothetical insofar as the $6.4 billion budget of the Iranian fiscal year that ended on March 20, 1972, envisaged further increase in military expenditures, namely, an increase of nearly 30 percent over the last year. The familiar problem of "more guns or butter" may have to be faced sooner or later, but at the present time socioeconomic welfare is still accorded the highest priority.

Second, since Iran is blessed with an overriding sense of national identity, the problem of national *integration* would not seem to have posed too serious a problem in the past decade despite the fact that Iran is still a "country of minorities." To be sure, the Azeri and Kurdish rebellions of 1945–46 in part reflected communal uprisings,[18] but there is little doubt that the Soviet Union played the dominant role in the rise of the so-called autonomous republics. Short of massive foreign intervention, no communal group, not even the recently agitated Arabic-speaking minority in Khuzistan, could be expected to pose such a serious threat to the Shah's regime as to require according the goal of national integration priority over any other goal. The socioeconomic processes of modernization are presumed to assist social integration; whether this is indeed taking place requires research.

Third, the implications of the "White Revolution" for the goal of establishing effective *authority* are more difficult to assess. As already noted, the very act of according the goal of socioeconomic modernization the highest priority was influenced in part by the concentration of power by the Shah through the suppression of sources of opposition. The regime's feared and reputedly omniscient security police (SAVAK), backed by the army, is the principal instrument of control, scoring at times extraordinary success. Recently, for example, it destroyed, through infiltration, a vast plot allegedly hatched in Baghdad and supported by a motley group of alienated Iranians. To cite another recent example, the SAVAK faced a much tougher assignment in the *Siah-kal* incident of December 1970, when an allegedly "communist-nihilist" group of young people attacked a gendarme post from their hideout in the Gilan forest. Thirteen of the captured leaders were executed, but the fugitives of the same group reportedly assassinated the Chief of the Military Tribunal and wounded his son in April 1971. But if effective *authority* is not to be equated with *forcible control*, popular attitudes toward the regime must be probed as well. Lacking data on such attitudes, we must rely upon field observation in order to outline our own *impressions* for whatever they are worth.[19]

Observable attitudes may be divided into three major categories: "approbative," "disapprobative," and "selective." First, the peasantry lies at the approbative end of the spectrum at the present time, although it is difficult to predict whether this large bulk of the loyal population will in the near future believe and behave as at present in light of ever-increasing politicization. Similarly allegiant attitudes are to be found among the various strata of the population other than the peasantry, such as segments of the industrial workers and of the urban-based middle class, including poets, writers, teachers, and university professors. Second, the disapprobative attitudes are largely formed among the urban middle class, particularly the intellectuals. But these attitudes are not confined to these groups, as they are also found among the disgruntled former landowners and the exiled clergy, as well as other groups. Third, the selective category of attitudes refers to varying mixes of approbative and disapprobative orientations toward certain objectives or policies of the regime. Unlike the approbative and disapprobative orientations, which refer to attitudes toward the regime as a whole, the selective attitudes are found among those who pick and choose among the features of the regime. For example, there are individuals who show intense disapproval of the methods of the security police, while they simultaneously applaud such features of the "White Revolution" as the Literacy Corps, the Health Corps, and the Extension Corps.

Fourth, the implications of according the goal of socioeconomic modernization the highest priority are probably the most crucial for the goal of popular participation and hence must receive closer attention. In other words, while the Shah is pursuing the "White Revolution," how does he perceive the problem of political participation, and how does his regime respond to the demand for sharing in the decision-making process? As a backdrop to probing this inquiry, it would be helpful to recall our first proposition, namely, that the goal of popular participation in politics, like the other four goals, has been one of the major goals of the Iranian political system most of the time since the Constitutional Revolution, no matter who has happened to be ruling the country. The revolution itself partly aimed at democratic participation. Even Reza Shah paid it lip service insofar as he at least kept alive the parliamentary symbol of participation. The era of the so-called Revival of Constitutionalism (ehya-ye Mashrutiat) after his abdication (1941) witnessed unprecedented freedom of the press, speech, and assembly in spite of the chaos, factionalism, personalism, cliquism, and clientalism that characterized much of party politics and parliamentary practices alongside the rising demands for popular participation during the war and intermittently afterward until the early 1960s. Yet, as has already been suggested, until the early 1960s the winning of independence dominated the scene. In other words, first the primacy of the goal of national independence and subsequently that of modernization has had the effect of suspending the adoption of popular participation as the *primary* goal of the political system. The following discussion further supports this proposition.

Yet, to state that the regime today emphasizes social and economic modernization is by no means to imply its abandonment of the goal of popular participation in politics. The evidence for this is found, we submit, in the regime's "behavior," namely, its words and its deeds. The Shah's own conception of democratic participation may be gleaned from his own writings, policy statements, domestic and foreign interviews, and other sources over a period of some thirty years.[20] The communist conception of democracy is patently rejected, as is the notion of democracy cast in primarily political terms. Social and economic development is regarded as essential for the attainment of a participatory polity, but this does not mean that socioeconomic progress is enough. Political democracy must be developed side by side with socioeconomic democracy, and both developments, in the Shah's conception, must be accompanied by profound changes in the attitudes of individuals. These qualitative changes include the sacrifice of private interests for the public good, the rule of law, a spirit of cooperation, and so on. The most lucid statement so far of the Shah's conception of the relationship between socioeconomic modernization and democratic participation is found in his address to the inaugural session of the

Town and Provincial Councils' Congress of October 1970, in which he stated that the launching of land reform, the enfranchisement of women, and profit sharing by workers "was only a prelude." "We aimed," he declared, "at establishing rule of the people by the people, extending democracy in various fields." "Our aim," he declared elsewhere in the speech, ". . . is the achievement of a true constitutional democracy based on the freedom of free Iranian men and women."[21]

The Shah's conception of the institutional requirements of what he calls "true constitutional democracy" is far more difficult to ascertain. It is obvious that he considers the emergence of popularly based party and parliamentary systems essential, but the implications of this for the role of the monarchy are still unclear. Nevertheless, his own statements could show the general direction of his thoughts at the present time. There is no doubt that he perceives some kind of blending of the principle of parliamentary democracy with the Iranian monarchical tradition. But what kind of a mix is intended? The Shah does not perceive any diminution of what he calls the "moral power" of the monarchy, but he does envisage increasing relinquishment of his "immediate intervention power in every field to the competent people that are being trained for this job."[22] It would be a "pity," he believes, if the moral power of the monarchy should diminish, because the institution is a stabilizing element in the system and because it would allow a "good monarch" to do useful things, while a "bad monarch" would not be able to do harm, since the general powers would be divided and the system would be one of checks and balances. But he considers it "very important" for heads of state such as Iran's to control the armed forces, because, he states, the monarch, as the commander in chief, could prevent the army from entering into politics, or politics into the army.

So much for the perception of the regime. What about its performance in political development? The major trends may be grasped swiftly. Political development being conceived as inseparable from socioeconomic change, the concept of "popular participation" in the present Iranian context embraces not only the construction of a party system but all other efforts resulting in an expansion of the role of the masses in the decision-making process at every level of social and economic as well as political life. For this reason the establishment of such new structures as the Literacy Corps, the Extension Corps, the Health Corps, equity courts, rural cooperatives, or farm corporations and the institutionalization of such social reforms as the enfranchisement of women or profit sharing by workers are viewed by the elite as democratizing processes.

The regime's performance in political development as such, however, falls into only two general categories: (1) party politics and (2) local government. The Iran-Novin Party (Hezb Iran Novin) has dominated the Iranian political scene since its creation. The party was constructed from above out of the former Progressive Center, which had been formed by nine loyal supporters of the Shah in 1962. Although the ruling party survived the assassination of Premier 'Ali Mansur, its lack of widespread social support, its primitive structural features, and its domination by the powerful boss 'Ataollah Khosravani until 1969 impaired the development of the party in two major respects: (1) in its perpetuation of an extremely small and centralized decision-making body within the party and (2) in its lack of any significant degree of success in mobilizing broad support within the various strata of the society at large. Manuchehr Kalali, who succeeded Khosravani in 1969 and is still Iran-Novin's secretary-general, has been considered a representative of the "liberal wing" of this otherwise "elitist and conservative" party. He denies that the technocratic and pragmatic preponderance of the party membership is a serious problem and has shown interest in broadening the decision-making apparatus of the ruling party so that in the future no one man may try to dominate it. Although the Shah would seem to disfavor the single-party system, the universally admitted fact in Iran is the unencumbered rule of the Iran-Novin. In the provincial and township council elections (September 1970) the party captured more than 60 percent of the votes and 300 out of 960 seats. In the national elections of the Twenty-Third Majlis (July 1971) the party won more than 86 percent of the votes cast, thus securing 226 seats in the present 268-seat Majlis. The presumptively opposition Mardom Party is partly blamed for the continuing domination of the political scene by the Iran-Novin. The criticism is often leveled at the Mardom Party's lethargic, belated, and disorganized election campaigns and particularly at its inability to come forward with any viable alternative platform. In January 1971 the new "Iranians' Party" (Hezb Iranian) was founded by Dr. Fazlollah Sadr. The party claims university students as well as guild members, and its central committee is dominated by intellectuals, particularly university professors. In the Twenty-Third Majlis elections, however, the newly formed party won only a single seat. Reportedly, nearly 5 million votes were cast in this election, representing an increase of almost 40 percent over the preceding national election (1967). This marked, according to *Kayhan*, the biggest voting turnout in Iran's constitutional history.[23]

The regime's action in favor of local government took place only in 1970 despite the well-known role of the *anjumans* (provincial and departmental councils) in the Constitutional Revolution and the Supplementary Fundamental Laws of 7 October 1907. The law called for the immediate establishment of the *anjumans*, whose members were to be elected by the people and whose function embodied the "exercise of complete supervision over all reforms."[24] The first provincial and township council elections, however, were held as late as

September 1970 in pursuance of a local elections law enacted by the Twenty-Second Majlis. Despite the shortcomings of this new law, 150 local councils were elected. Their functions range from the construction of schools and other educational facilities, to the creation of experimental farms, to the development of public-health, public-utilities, and social-welfare services. The recency of these councils bars assessment of their performance, but they are expected, in addition to the functions just stated, to act as watchdogs over the provincial departments of the central government.

In light of the foregoing analysis I shall conclude this study with a brief specu-lation about the second decade of the "White Revolution." In all probability the current dynamic tempo of social and economic development will be not only maintained but significantly accelerated during the next decade. The private sector of the economy will probably keep pace with the expansion in the pub-lic sector, consumer goods will increase, GNP and the ratio of investment to it will grow, industry will diversify and expand, agriculture will receive greater attention, and social services will be deepened and broadened. Simultaneously the present trend of concentration of political power at the center will probably continue untrammeled, and the construction of participatory political struc-tures in the next decade, as in the last, will probably lag behind socioeconomic development, while political consciousness and popular demands for uncon-trolled party politics will grow by leaps and bounds. *In other words, the regime's political responsive capability will probably continue to fall ever short of its socioeconomic responsiveness so long as its current snail's pace and shallow depth of constructing viable po-litical infrastructures are maintained.* Conversely, the system's capability to respond to world affairs will grow dynamically both as a substitute reaction to negligible response to domestic political demands and as the result of increased military and economic power in the face of the relatively favorable power position, par-ticularly in the Middle East. The effects of Iran's expansive role in world affairs will be felt most particularly in the general area of the Persian Gulf.

These broad conjectures are based upon extrapolation from past trends, but even that would not make them inevitable. Nor would our attempt to utilize cer-tain broad concepts of political development. To be sure, modern political sci-ence is trying to extricate its approaches from the accidents of time and place, but in all probability it cannot do so totally. In fact, there are signs that modern political science is coming of age, leaving behind the simplicity and brashness of youth. Fortuity plays a large part in human experience, and as such it can aid sober political analysis. In this study, for example, we have noted that the fortuitous conjunction of domestic and international circumstances limited the choice of the national elite to independence as the primary goal of Iran most often during the period from the dawn of the Constitutional Revolution to the early 1960s and has ever since confined it largely to socioeconomic modernization, despite the fact that other goals have been simultaneously pursued.

Given the utility of the concept of fortuity in the analysis of the past and present, it may also be useful in speculating about the future. *Although Iran today aspires to reaching, in less than a dozen years, what is called "the Era of Great Civilization" (daureh tammadon bozorg), emphasizing once again continuous socioeconomic development, we may still hope that fortuitous circumstances, as well as prudent conscious choice, will enable the present elite to try to match recent socioeconomic accomplishments by wholehearted and relentless political institutionalization aimed at deepening and broadening popular participation in the near future.* The universal dilemma of reconciling the requirements of rapid social and economic modernization with the surging demands for popular political participation is basically the same in Iran as in other Third World nations, but the hope is that the task might be within the historically tested integrative capacity of Iranian civilization.

NOTES

1. Muhammad Reza Shah's book *Enqelab Sefid* was published in Tehran in 1965/66 and subsequently appeared in a number of languages, including English (*White Revolution*). It is currently used as a text in Iranian high schools, where students are encouraged to take a course on the "White Revolution." The only extensive commentary on the Shah's book in Persian is the apologetic work of 'Ali Zarrynqalam, *Sayri dar Ketab Enqelab Sefid* [List of books on the White Revolution] (Tehran, 1966/67). English readers may find useful *Points for Progress: A Glimpse into the Far-reaching Effects of Iran's "White Revolution"* (Tehran, 1967), published by the Ministry of Information. Also see n. 3 below.

2. Of course, whoever writes about contemporary Iran deals in one way or another with aspects of problems and programs related to the "White Revolution," but this is not the same as subjecting it specifically to analysis with the special purpose of exploring its meaning and place in Iran's modern political development. For first-hand descriptive accounts of Iran during the 1960s, see, for example, two articles by Peter Avery: "Trends in Iran in the Past Five Years," *World Today* 21, no. 7 (July 1965): 279–90 and "Iran 1964–8: The Mood of Growing Confidence," ibid. 24, no. 2 (November 1968): 354–466.

3. See Gabriel A. Almond, *Political Development: Essays in Heuristic Theory* (Boston, 1970), 223–33. These pages are reprinted from *Stanford Today* 1, no. 10 (Autumn 1964).

4. See R. K. Ramazani, *The Foreign Policy of Iran, 1500–1941: A Developing Nation in World Affairs* (Charlottesville, 1966).

5. See Gabriel A. Almond, "National Politics and International Politics," in *The Search for World Order: Studies by Students and Colleagues of Quincy Wright*, edited by Albert Lepawsky, Edward H. Buehrig, and Harold D. Lasswell (New York, 1971), 283–97.

6. For a succinct social history of Iran from the dawn of the nineteenth century to

1969, see Nikki R. Keddie, "The Iranian Power Structure and Social Change, 1800–1969: An Overview," *International Journal of Middle East Studies* 2, no. 1 (January 1971): 3–20. For an earlier sketch of the Western challenge to Iranian society, see Ann K. S. Lambton, "The Impact of the West on Persia," *International Affairs* 33, no. 1 (January 1957): 12–25.

7. The evidence for the adoption of independence, modernization, and democratization, as well as centralization of authority and national integration, as the fundamental goals of modern Iran is spread throughout early constitutional documents, namely, the Royal Proclamation of 5 August 1906, the Fundamental Laws of 30 December 1906, the Supplementary Fundamental Laws of 7 October 1907, and subsequent amendments. For the texts, see Helen Miller Davis, *Constitutions, Electoral Laws, Treaties of States in the Near and Middle East* (Durham, NC, 1953), 104–30.

8. See Almond, *Political Development*, 229–30.

9. See E. G. Browne, "The Persian Constitutional Movement," in *Proceedings of the British Academy* (London, 1917–18), 223–24.

10. See Ramazani, *Foreign Policy of Iran*, 256–57.

11. This portrayal is perhaps much induced by Amin Banani, *The Modernization of Iran, 1921–1941* (Stanford, 1961), although the author does not seem to suggest that Reza Shah accorded the goal of modernization the highest priority throughout his rule.

12. Reza Shah's own statement published in Iran's *Daily Telegraph* on 5 September 1930 clearly reveals that he believed that the construction of the railway would first and foremost contribute to Iran's political and economic independence. See the text of this statement as reproduced in Persian in Fathullah Nuri Esfandiyari, *Rastakhiz Iran* [Resurgence of Iran] (Tehran, 1956/57), 486–90. Even a leading Western student of Iran regarded the construction of this gigantic railway significant as a sign of Iran's financial independence. L. P. Elwell-Sutton wrote that "perhaps for the first time since the Middle Ages, a major undertaking was carried through in an Oriental country without leaving it indebted to the finances of the West." See his *Modern Iran* (London, 1942), 94.

13. A leading Iranian professor of jurisprudence, 'Ali Pasha Saleh, states that for many years prior to the adoption of the Civil Code several commissions of jurists had been constituted and dispersed, but for the purpose of abolition of capitulations in 1928 the first 955 articles of the Civil Code were presented to the Majlis for approval. See his *Quveh Muqananneh va Quveh Qaza'iyyeh* [Legislative and judicial corps: A glance at Iran's legal history from the earliest times until 1962] (Tehran, 1964), 38. Amin Banani states that Reza Shah's "interest in legal reforms was motivated by nationalistic considerations, for his first objective was to abolish the system of capitulations." See Banani, *Modernization of Iran*, 70. See also Ramazani, *Foreign Policy of Iran*, 243–45.

14. Ahmad Qavam went so far as to decree the distribution of the state lands to peasants at the time in order to blunt the Tudeh and the Azeri communist propaganda campaign for reforms. All observers in Iran at the time noted that Qavam's primary motive was to maintain Iran's national independence; under the circumstances, he had no serious interest in economic welfare or political participation. See, for example, various revealing dispatches in U.S. Department of State, *Foreign Relations of the United States, 1946*, vol. 7, *The Near East and Africa* (Washington, DC, 1969), 490–91, 505.

15. Despite all the evidence accumulated between 1947 and 1951 showing the preponderance of political considerations, the basic law of nationalization of 20 March 1951

stated that the "happiness and prosperity of the Iranian nation" formed Iran's primary purpose in nationalizing the oil industry. But in many moments of frankness Iranian leaders emphasized that "true" political independence was their primary concern. For the text of Dr. Mosaddegh's speech before the Oil Commission mentioned in the text, sees *Ettela'at*, 22 February 1951.

16. The other eleven points were nationalization of forests, shares in state-owned factories to compensate former landowners, profit sharing by factory workers, reform of the electoral law, formation of the Literacy Corps, formation of the Health Corps, formation of the Extension Corps, the establishment of local courts, nationalization of underground water resources, "making anew the countryside," and the "Administrative Revolution." The points may be said to have increased to thirteen with the recent addition of the "Educational Revolution," of which more will be said in the text of this essay.

17. R. K. Ramazani, "Iran's Changing Foreign Policy: A Preliminary Discussion," *Middle East Journal* 24, no. 4 (Autumn 1970): 421–37. For a detailed analysis of Iran's new role in international politics with particular reference to its all-important policy in the Persian Gulf, see Ramazani, *The Persian Gulf: Iran's Role* (Charlottesville, 1972).

18. See R. K. Ramazani, "The Autonomous Republic of Azerbaijan and the Kurdish People's Republic: Their Rise and Fall," *Studies on the Soviet Union*, ser. 2, 16, no. 4 (1971): 401–27.

19. I call these "impressions" because I did not undertake a systematic study of such attitudes: no questionnaires were prepared or *formal* interviews conducted. Yet, as a native Iranian (naturalized and educated in the United States) I was able to mingle freely with individuals from a wide variety of groups in the capital and several provinces during 1968–89, which provided an unusual opportunity to observe the great diversity of attitudes toward the present regime.

20. Quite apart from the Shah's well-known *Mission for My Country* (New York, 1961) and his *White Revolution* (2d ed., Tehran, 1967), recent volumes prepared by the Pahlavi Library can shed much light on his views on a variety of subjects. The library's *Bargozideh-ey az Neveshteh-ha va Sukhanan Shahanshah Aryamehr* [Borgozideh on the writings and lectures of Shahanshah Aryamehr] (n.d.) is quite a convenient collection, but it is not as complete as *Majmu'ah Muntakhab: Nutqha, Payamha, Neveshtehha, va Musahebehha-ye A'ala-hazrat Humayoon, Muhammad Reza Shah Pahlavi, Shahanshah Iran az Shahrivar 1320 ta Mehr Mah 1340* [Collections of lectures, notes, writings, and interviews with His Majesty, Muhammad Reza Shah Pahlavi, the Shahanshah of Iran from August 1941 until September 1966] (n.d.) or as specialized a collection as the two volumes prepared by Ghulamreza Nykpay, *Surat Jalasat Shura-ye Eqtisad dar Pyshgah Shahanshah Aryamehr ya Majmu'ah-ey az Asnad Tarikh Mu'aser Iran* [The list of the Council of Finances at the session of Shahanshah Aryamehr and The collection of his documents related to contemporary Iran] (n.d.).

21. See *Kayhan*, 3 October 1970, international edition.

22. This statement and the rest of this paragraph are based on probably the frankest remarks the Shah has ever made about the monarchy in Iran. These remarks were contained in an extensive interview with NBC's Edwin Newman that was broadcast over the network's program *Speaking Freely*. For the transcript, see *Kayhan*, 28 February 1970, international edition.

23. The editorial also stated: "The main lesson to be learnt from the general election

is that parliamentary democracy is here to stay. . . . This in itself is enough to show that an increasing number of people from all walks of life are beginning to consider parliamentary democracy as the backbone of the nation's political life." See *Kayhan*, 17 July 1971, international edition.

24. See articles 90–93 of the Supplementary Fundamental Laws. The text is in Helen Miller Davis, *Constitutions, Electoral Laws*, 127.

IRAN'S REVOLUTION

Patterns, Problems, and Prospects

The global repercussions of the Iranian Revolution continue. All around the world the revolution produces almost daily headlines referring to the tensions, strains, uncertainties, and conflicts that it exhibits at the local, regional, and international levels. The increasingly polarized domestic politics of Iran, the mounting tensions on its borders with Iraq, and especially the rupture of diplomatic relations and the start of economic warfare between the United States and Iran arouse worldwide concern. Beyond this, the threat of unilateral American military action against Iran over the issue of the American hostages hangs like a storm cloud since few observers believe that the consequences of military intervention in the strategic Persian Gulf and the Strait of Hormuz can be effectively contained. For these and other reasons worldwide interest in the development of the Iranian Revolution has intensified.

The chief purpose of this essay is to consider the nature of this revolution and the prospects for its stabilization. This task can be attempted, obviously, from a variety of perspectives; that which is adopted here is the perspective of Iran's own political history. The paucity of reliable information about current developments and the short existence of the nascent Republic commend such an approach. Moreover, the widespread belief among Iranians themselves in the relevance and importance of historical patterns of behavior for the better understanding of the present and future developments of this revolution also supports this approach. "Underlying patterns of behavior are still the same," or *raval haman ast*, as goes the skeptical Iranian saying.

CYCLES OF CRISIS

Iran's current revolutionary crisis is the third of its kind in the twentieth century. Elsewhere, I have identified five general crises preceding the present one of which account must be taken for purposes of foreign-policy analysis.[1] In this analysis the 1914–21 and the 1941–51 crises are excluded because they were sparked by two world wars and consequent foreign invasions of Iran rather than by domestic convulsion. The 1961–63 crises are also excluded because they did not result in a change of regime. What makes the 1905–11 Con-

"Iran's Revolution: Patterns, Problems, and Prospects" was originally published by Wiley-Blackwell in *International Affairs* (London) 56, no. 3 (Summer 1980): 443–57.

stitutional Revolution and the 1951–53 oil nationalization crisis the most relevant historical precedents for the current revolution is the fact that they both represented popular domestic uprisings leading to the fall of one regime and the rise of another.

Iran's current revolutionary crisis shared, at its inception, four crucial factors with these two precedent crises. Most important, each crisis reflects a revolution of rising alienation from the monarchical regime and perceived foreign domination. This alienation developed essentially from the adverse effects of the previous domestic- and foreign-policy decisions of the ruling elite. In the period of the Constitutional Revolution, the economic policies of the Qajar monarchs dating back to the last quarter of the nineteenth century had resulted in an empty treasury, widespread corruption, financial disorganization, and foreign (British and Russian) economic domination.[2] The Qajar's arbitrary rule, political repression, and, in particular, the maladministration of justice also contributed significantly to the rise and spread of alienation.

Although opposition to the British appeared to be the primary cause of the increasingly nationalist sentiment during the oil nationalization crisis in the early 1950s, dissatisfaction with the Shah's rule was also a major contributory factor.[3] The assassination in 1951 of his strong prime minister, General Ali Razmara, followed after a previous attempt upon the Shah's own life had failed two years earlier. Opposition to foreign powers has been a major factor in all three crises: in the 1950s the principal target was Britain, as contrasted with Russia during the first crisis and the United States in the third. But in the crisis of the 1950s the Anglo-Iranian Oil Company (AIOC) was opposed as much for its close association with the ruling elite as for being an instrument of British interference in Iran's domestic and foreign policies.

In the current revolution popular alienation has displayed the same twofold pattern. Domestically, the adverse social, psychological, cultural, moral, and religious effects of the Shah's modernization policies in the 1970s came to be felt to outweigh whatever material and economic gains had been made in the 1960s.[4] The massive and arbitrary infusion of spectacular new oil revenues into the economy after the explosion of oil prices in 1973–74, coupled with large-scale corruption and rapidly rising rates of inflation, fueled the fires of widespread dissatisfaction. This trend became more and more articulate once the traditional political intolerance of the ruling elite was institutionalized in the single, hated Rastakhiz Party, formed by the Shah in 1975. Externally the principal ingredients of the strong current of anti-American sentiments were Washington's close association with the Shah's regime since engineering the Shah's return to power in August 1953, and what was perceived as the imposition by the Pentagon of a "capitulatory" regime on Iran in 1964—the same year that Ayatollah Khomeini was exiled, following the Shah's bloody suppression in 1963 of a national uprising directed against his American-induced socio-economic reforms (the "White Revolution"). The Ayatollah at the time declared the agreement of the Shah's government to grant the United States exclusive criminal jurisdiction over its military personnel in Iran a "document of the enslavement of Iran."

Like its historical precedents, the current revolution has enjoyed the support of many disparate groups, classes, and individuals. Modern factory workers, traditional shopkeepers, urban and rural street cleaners, snow removers (barfi), kerosene peddlers (nafti), members of various guilds, and artisans, as well as bazaar merchants, dentists, lawyers, teachers, professors, intellectuals, civil servants, and, shortly before the actual seizure of power by the revolutionary forces, even air force technicians and thousands of deserting soldiers—all joined hands in common opposition to the Shah's regime. However, university students, "theological seminarians" (tolab), bazaar merchants, and intellectuals have stood out in the current revolution, as in the two previous uprisings. In terms of leadership too, the role of religious and nationalist figures was paramount in all three uprisings, although both religious and lay leadership were more diffused in the Constitutional Revolution than in the uprisings of the 1950s and the 1970s. Coalitions between religious and nationalist leaders have been a feature of each Iranian crisis. For example, Ayatollah Abolghasem Kashani and Dr. Mohammad Mosaddegh formed an *alliance de convenance* in the second crisis of the century, while Ayatollah Khomeini forged a coalition with Mosaddegh's successor to the National Front leadership, Dr. Karim Sanjabi, in France. They jointly declared that the revolution marked the convergence of the "religious and the national movements." However, in the current revolution religious leadership has predominated from the start.

Ideological diversity has marked the current revolution as it did the previous uprisings. There has at no stage been a monolithic ideological movement. Although the signs of Islamic resurgence are to be seen everywhere, from Mauritania to Malaysia, the current of particularistic Shii Muslim fundamentalism as interpreted by Ayatollah Khomeini[5] and the lay Shii Muslim social and political radicalism expounded by the French-educated Iranian sociologist Doctor Ali Shari'ati (1934–1977), which have been so prominent in the present revolution, have their special Iranian flavor despite their resemblance to the Islamic resurgence elsewhere.[6] Shari'ati, in particular, was attracted to the theories of the Algerian psychoanalyst Franz Fanon—although the similarity between the Shii Muslim–based emphasis of Ayatollah Khomeini on the uplifting of the "down-trodden" (mustaz'afeen) and Fanon's emphasis in Wretched of the Earth is also intriguing.[7] This is perhaps why there has been a widespread, if mistaken, tendency to think of the current revolution as an ideological "monolithic movement," to use the phrase emphasized in Iran's new constitution: the clergy dominated the "Assembly of Experts," which approved this constitution.[8] In fact, in the current revolution, as in the previous ones, modern liberal nationalism has been a primary force. The clash between Muslim fundamentalism and democratic secularist conceptions of society and polity has been as real in this revolution as in the previous crises, although some leading modernists, such as Mehdi Bazargan, have argued persuasively that Islam and modernism can be made compatible.[9] Nevertheless, despite the fact of ideological diversity, the appeal of Islamic symbols to some modern-educated groups in the current revolution has surpassed that in historical uprisings. Alienation from blind Western-style modernization has exposed many students and intellectuals to Islamic ideology as a "third way," rejecting both the Western and Eastern models[10]—although others have embraced Marxism and Maoism instead. For the rural and illiterate masses and their fundamentalist leaders, however, Islam had always been "the way" and the only "right path." In neither of the previous uprisings was the participation of the rural and urban masses as extensive or were they so politically awakened. The intensely egalitarian, anti-establishment, and communitarian aspects of Shii Islam have been marshaled against the tyrannical, agnostic, frivolous, and iniquitous features of the rule of the elite. Sermons on the ancient martyrdom of the "innocent" (mazlum) Imam Hussein—the third Shii Twelver Imam and the grandson of the prophet—at the hands of tyrannical Yazid have reached millions through the widespread use of the tape-recorder cassette, portraying the righteous struggle of the exiled Imam Khomeini against the Shah, who is depicted as the ruthless modern Yazid.

FEATURES OF THE PRESENT REVOLUTION

The forced departure of the Shah on January 16, 1979, and the seizure of power by the revolutionary forces on February 10–11 have been followed by the emergence in Iran of many power centers. Among these must be numbered the many freewheeling revolutionary committees, which have often taken the law into their own hands; the secret Revolutionary Council; and, since the downfall of the Bazargan government, the militant students who have occupied the American Embassy in Tehran. The Islamic Republican Party (IRP), which was formed by nine major clerical associates of Ayatollah Khomeini, must also be regarded as an independent power center under the powerful leadership of Ayatollah Muhammad Beheshti, the secretary of the Revolutionary Council and the new chief of the Supreme Court. Finally, the recently elected president, Banisadr, and his close associates also constitute a center of power.

The seizure of power by the revolutionary forces has been followed—as in previous crises—by the emergence of numerous rival religious and lay political forces.

Shared alienation from the Shah's regime unified the disparate political as well as social forces before the revolution, but as happened in the oil nationalization crisis in the early 1950s the religio-national alliance in the current revolution has largely broken down. The traditionalist-modernist dichotomy is reflected in every major political institution and sphere of activity, including the Revolutionary Council. But neither the traditionalists, nor the modernists, nor the secularists constitute a homogeneous group. For example, the secular communist Tudeh Party has consistently failed to forge a united front with other secular leftist or modern nationalist forces. Even the Marxist Fedayan have defied the overtures of the Tudeh leadership. To cite another example, the two religion-based parties, the IRP and the Muslim People's Republican Party (MPRP), were bitter rivals—until recently the latter was for all practical purposes dissolved.

Another important factor of the revolution has been the resurgence of the efforts of tribal, ethnic, and linguistic groups demanding various degrees of "autonomy." Although some 90 percent of the Iranian population follows Shii Islam, most of the Muslim minorities believe in Sunni Islam of various Hanafi, Shafa'i, and Maliki and Hanbali denominations. Since Iranian Kurds (numbering about 2 million out of a population of approximately 35 million)—as contrasted with the Baluchi tribesmen (600,000), Turkomans (500,000), and a large number of Iranian Arabs in the oil-rich province of Khuzistan—have posed the greatest challenge to the revolutionary authorities so far, their efforts require further attention.

Throughout the centuries the Kurds of Iran have been restless, but their demand for "autonomy" has been revived, as always, in the face of the paralysis of the central government's military forces. The revolutionary authorities have wavered between negotiation and the use of armed force. The leftist orientation of the Kurdish Democratic Party (KDP), the interaction of the Kurds across the hostile frontiers of Iran and Iraq, and charges of Kurdish complicity with Russian, American, Zionist, Savakist, and other alleged supporters of counterrevolution complicate the deep-seated mutual distrust between the Iranian government authorities and the Kurds, who believe that prolonged negotiations are simply being employed by the central government for the purpose of delay.

Some progress, however, appears to have been made in these negotiations, although fighting continues sporadically. The Kurdish Democratic Party (KDP) has presented a new six-point program to President Banisadr, but the decisions have to be made by the Majlis, which has not yet assembled. The secretary of the KDP, Abdolrahman Qasemlu, is reported to have said in March 1980 that the party "firmly believes that Kurdistan is an integral part of Iran and that there is no room for separation in its demand."[11] The Kurdish claims include the right of autonomy of an Iranian Kurdistan to be incorporated in the Iranian Constitution; that Kurdistan should incorporate all Kurdish-inhabited regions; that apart from foreign relations, the army, national defense, and long-term planning, the Kurds themselves should resolve their own problems; that an elected Kurdish "executive committee" should administer the region as an autonomous unit; that the Kurds should be responsible for maintaining their internal security; and that the Kurdish language should be recognized on a par with the Persian language in all official correspondence.[12]

A major, if not a crucial, outcome of the seizure of power by the revolutionary forces has been the paralysis and demoralization of the Iranian military. Consent and coercion are present in any kind of regime in varying proportions, but in the authoritarian traditions of Iran the element of compulsion has most often predominated. The surrender of the military to the revolutionary forces in Tehran did more than effectively destroy the Shah's regime; it undermined the core of the traditional power structure, which was dominated historically by an alliance between the monarchy and the military. In the middle of the revolutionary uprising the deposed Shah could still boast that "nobody can overthrow me. I have the support of 700,000 troops . . . I have the power." Ironically, it was within his favored air force, equipped with some of the world's most sophisticated weapons, that loyalty to the Shah first broke down.

The military has been gravely undermined as a result of mass desertions, the wholesale dismissal of high-ranking officers, and the series of summary trials and executions. The decapitation of the armed forces—partly out of fear of its counterrevolutionary possibilities—has proved to be counterproductive in many ways. It has been difficult to disarm the revolutionary elements that helped themselves to weapons from the Shah's vast arsenal during the seizure of power. Despite such efforts as Ayatollah Khomeini's emphasis on the importance of the army (he declared April 18 "Army Day"), the creation of the Revolutionary Guard (Pasdaran), the extension of amnesty to the security forces, and President Banisadr's planned reconsideration of unjustified past purges, the paralysis largely continues.

Iran's economy is another victim of the revolutionary crisis. The authorities dream of cutting the Iranian economy off from the apron strings of foreigners, and particularly of the Western, industrialized world. This is, of course, a goal of many Third World leaders. But the Iranian revolutionary leaders, particularly President Banisadr, acknowledge that this goal will elude Iran as long as its economy depends upon the sale of oil. In the meantime, the flight of capital and managerial skills, frequent slowdowns and strikes, occasional sabotage, and unmanageable worker intervention in management have reduced the productive capacity of non-oil industries to half of what it was prior to the revolutionary seizure of power; and at least 3 million people—a third of the Iranian labor force—are unemployed. The revolutionary authorities' commitment to the uplifting of the standard of living of the poorer masses, to the increase of Iran's long-neglected agricultural production, particularly in food, and to the overall reduction of the nation's dependency on other countries through the processes of "Islamisation" of the economy remains to be fulfilled.[13]

THE INSTITUTIONALIZATION
OF POWER AND AUTHORITY

Faced with the continuing problems presented by the existence of competing power centers, by the proliferation and polarization of political forces, the demands of ethnic groups for autonomy, and the reconstruction of the military and the economy, the revolutionary forces nevertheless take special pride in their attempts at political institutionalization during the first year of the Islamic Republic.

Establishment of the Republic. After a two-day-long referendum at the end of March 1979, Ayatollah Khomeini proclaimed April 1 to be "Islamic Republican Day"; 97 percent of the electorate had voted for the Islamic Republic, out of the 98 percent eligible to cast ballots. In his official proclamation of the Republic, the Ayatollah said that "such a referendum is unprecedented in history—to establish a government of righteousness and to overthrow and bury the monarchy in the rubbish pile of history."[14] As seen by the Ayatollah, even the referendum was superfluous, since by their uprising against the Shah's regime the people had already shown their desire to establish an Islamic republic.[15]

However, as pointed out by many supporters of the revolution—including the influential Ayatollah Shariatmadari—the government offered the people no other choice than the "Islamic Republic." Although the debate appeared to center around the designation of the new republic, the real divisions went deeper. The National Frontists, for example, believed that their coalition with the religious elements had been based on the prospective establishment of a republic in which liberal democratic and Islamic principles would equally guide and govern the construction of the new political order. They insisted on designating Iran as an "Islamic Democratic Republic," and they characterized the whole revolution as a "great national Islamic movement of the Iranian people" (*jonbesh-e bozorg-e melli-e Irani*). But Ayatollah Khomeini rejected the very concept of "democracy," either of an Eastern (Marxist-Leninist) or Western (liberal-democratic) variety. To him and his supporters, Islam provided the "right way," which, in its insistence on the egalitarian principle and on the normative imperative of the triumph of the "down-trodden" over the "dominant elements" (*mustakbereen*) not only in Iran but throughout the world, included within it the superior principles of "Islamic democracy" (*democracy-e Islami*). In such a democracy, according to the Ayatollah, there is justice for all, and brotherhood, equality, and unity for all strata of the society, founded on the superior value of individual "spiritual righteousness" (*taqva*) rather than material or any other mundane privileges.[16]

Adoption of the Constitution. The failure of the liberal nationalists as well as of other moderate elements, both lay and religious, to persuade the fundamentalist clergy to offer the public a broader choice than the "Islamic Republic" was a foretaste of what was to come. At the time of the official establishment of the Republic, the government promised elections for a "Constituent Assembly" (Majlis-e Muasisan). It was estimated that such an elected body would be made up of some three hundred representatives, providing a genuine opportunity for a representative public debate about the articles of the new constitution. In May 1979, however, the Ayatollah decreed that the Constitution would be considered instead by an Assembly of Experts (Majlis-e Khebregan).

The seventy-five-member Assembly of Experts was elected August 3–4, began its deliberations on August 19, and approved the Constitution on November 15. The document was then ratified in a referendum held December 2–3. A wide variety of groups, including such notably liberal groups as the Bar Association and the National Democratic Party, and others such as the Kurdish and religious minorities, the Marxist Fedayan, the Muslim Mujahadeen, and a number of political parties, expressed serious opposition to this process for both procedural and substantive reasons. For example, the National Front believed that "an assembly of experts cannot be a substitute for a real constituent assembly representing the general will of the people because it lacks democratic character"; and it charged that threats, assaults, and insults directed against the modernist and secularist groups by Muslim zealots created a "stifling political climate." However, the principal procedural reason for the dissatisfaction of the National Democratic Front, led by Dr. Hedayat Matindaftari, and the new Iranian Nation Party, led by Dariush Forouhar—as well as the National Front— was that the difference between electing a Constituent Assembly and an Assembly of Experts was that the latter would be—as it was—a clergy-dominated assembly with far-reaching consequences for the substance of the Constitution.

The controversy centered on the single most fundamental issue of *Velayat-e Faqih* (leadership of the jurisprudent).[17] Although the concept is not specifically mentioned in the Constitution, it is stated that the Twelfth Imam would be represented in his absence by a qualified religious leader enjoying the confidence of the majority of the people.[18] Furthermore, the Constitution places the most extensive powers at the disposal of such a leader—at present, of course, Ayatollah Khomeini.[19] The most eminent and consequential criticism of the extensive powers of the *faqih* was voiced by Ayatollah Shariatmadari. He reasoned that the grant of these powers is in contravention of the principle of the "sovereign right of the nation" acknowledged in the Constitution.[20] The Constitution forbids anyone, including by implication the *faqih*, to "take away this God-given right."[21] In a nutshell, Ayatollah Shariatmadari believes that sovereignty should rest with the people, while some provisions of the Constitution could result in a dictatorial government. He refused to vote for the Constitution and demanded its amendment.

There is little doubt that Ayatollah Shariatmadari's protest partly contributed to the uprising in Azerbaijan, where he commands overwhelming support. To be sure, a variety of factors—ranging from historical grievances against the central government to the revolutionary regime's disregard of the wishes of the Azerbaijanis to have a say in their own affairs (such as the appointment of religious leaders and the governor of Azerbaijan) and including a physical attack on the house of Ayatollah Shariatmadari in Qom—contributed to this upheaval. It is clear that the Ayatollah's position on the Constitution enjoyed widespread support in Azerbaijan, was acknowledged as such by him, and was considered by the pro-Shariatmadari MPRP to be the "principal cause" of the clashes between some Azerbaijanis and government forces and Khomeini supporters.

Ayatollah Khomeini charged that the turmoil in Azerbaijan was anti-Islamic and supported by both "Zionism and imperialism." Ayatollah Shariatmadari publicly disagreed. In the end, however, discussions between the two religious leaders and between the Khomeini and Shariatmadari representatives (such as Hojat ol-Islam Shahabeddin Eshraqi and Hojat ol-Islam Sobhani, respectively) resulted in a negotiated truce. Nevertheless, the MPRP paid a heavy price in the end. Several ayatollahs, such as Rabbani Shirazi and Sayyid Abolhussain Dastghayb, asked Shariatmadari to declare the MPRP dissolved, although he had repeatedly disavowed having sponsored the party. By the middle of December 1979, without any attempt at intervention by Shariatmadari, the party began to dissolve under considerable pressures from pro-Khomeini and pro-Beheshti forces: 6,000 members of the Ardebil branch of the 2- to 3-million-member party resigned en masse, and guilds, bazaar merchants, Muslim students, and others in Tabriz and other cities were induced to demand its dissolution. As a result, the field was largely cleared for the Khomeini-supported and Beheshti-led IRP. It is important to note, however, that besides Ayatollah Shariatmadari, a number of other influential Iranian figures, including Abulhassan Banisadr (subsequently elected president) and even Ayatollah Khomeini himself, have acknowledged the need to amend the Constitution at a later date. For instance, in January 1980 Khomeini approved a proposal to amend Principle 12 of the Constitution.[22] This proposal had been made by the representatives of the Sunni population of Baluchistan and Sistan to Dr. Ibrahim Yazdi, then the Ayatollah's representative to the area, and had been unanimously approved by the Revolutionary Council. The relevant principle provided that Sunni Islamic denominations would enjoy "complete respect," while the Twelver Shii Islam was designated as the only "official religion" of the country. The proposed amendment provided that where the followers of other Islamic religious denominations have a majority, they "also should be official." It is worth noting that Iran's first constitution—that of December 30, 1906—also had to be amended in 1907 and several times subsequently. (Except for the first amendment, however, the others enacted during the authoritarian rule of the Shah and his father were considered of dubious legitimacy.)

Election of the President. The election of the president followed the adoption of the Constitution. The landslide victory of Abulhassan Banisadr, the finance minister, was variously attributed to his own popularity as an "Islamic thinker" (*mutefaker-e Islami*), as the son of a late religious leader, as an economist who could help restore the shattered Iranian economy, and above all, as the candidate who more than any other enjoyed the confidence of Ayatollah Khomeini. His victory was variously viewed, within and outside Iran. The communist Tudeh Party disliked his perceived anticommunist and anti-Soviet attitudes; the Islamic Mujahadeen welcomed his willingness to engage in debate with their leader, Massoud Rajavi; while the Marxist Fedayan were critical of him. He seemed to enjoy the confidence of Ayatollah Shariatmadari as well as Khomeini, while the powerful Ayatollah Beheshti was regarded as his staunch rival. Outside Iran, on the whole, he was considered by some as a political "moderate" economist and by others as a "radical" one. He himself resented the view supposedly held in the United States that his victory was a triumph of French-made, pro-Western liberalism over the Muslim clergy.[23]

THE HOSTAGE CRISIS

The limits to President Banisadr's power have become sharply apparent in the continuing crisis over the American diplomatic hostages. The United States' principal concern was, and still is, the fate of these American hostages. President Banisadr himself from the beginning accorded the resolution of this crisis a high priority, not, so he said, to please Washington but in order to get on with economic and other pressing problems facing the revolutionary regime. In this he was taking on the militant students who have occupied the American Embassy since November 4, 1979. He embarked upon this course with good hope of success because, in addition to being the first popularly elected president of the Republic, he headed the Revolutionary Council and was temporarily appointed (on February 19, 1980) the commander in chief of the Iranian armed forces by Ayatollah Khomeini.

The occupation of the U.S. Embassy had been a major domestic political development, in addition to having far-reaching international repercussions and its adverse impact on relations between Iran and the United States. This international aspect of the crisis was probably of secondary importance to the militant students. Their capture of the embassy was not a spontaneous reaction to the arrival of the Shah in New York—he had, in fact, been admitted to the United States two weeks previously, on October 22, 1979. The takeover seems rather to have been planned to coincide with the anniversary of the most destructive confrontation between the Shah's regime and its opponents at the University of Tehran. This had marked a turning point in the revolutionary uprising, as the opposition then, for the first time, called for the overthrow of the Shah's regime.

To be sure, the militant students demanded that the United States extradite the Shah in return for the release of hostages; but they also had a more important and less widely recognized objective—that of forcing the provisional government of Mehdi Bazargan out of power. This seems clear from the militant students' own statements of November 4 and 8. When first appointed as provisional prime minister eight months earlier, Bazargan had told Ayatollah Khomeini that he would adopt a "gradualist" approach to the performance of his duties. During the entire course of his incumbency he had complained about the multiplicity of power centers, the disarray and chaos that engulfed the nation, the politics of extremism, the summary trials and executions, and the insufficiency of the support given him by the Revolutionary Council and at times even by Ayatollah Khomeini himself.

The talks that took place between Bazargan and his foreign minister, Ibrahim Yazdi, with the American national security adviser, Zbigniew Brzezinski, in Algeria played into the hands of the militant students and their supporters. The meeting was used to attack the Bazargan government, which resigned after the takeover of the American Embassy. The militant students accused Bazargan afterward of lack of "revolutionary decisiveness" and treacherous failure to abrogate diplomatic, military, and economic ties with the United States. He was also accused of leaving open the way for the influence of the United States and Israel by keeping "westernized, liberal intellectuals" at the top of many executive organs of the country.[24] In his first supportive message to the militant students, Ayatollah Khomeini told them that Iran was still in a state of revolution, "a revolution greater than the first one."[25] The fall of the Bazargan government marked a new stage in the radicalization of revolution politics in Iran. Both the extreme Left and the Right welcomed the change.[26]

President Banisadr has in fact been twice rebuffed in attempting to consolidate his authority by resolving the hostage crisis. The first occasion was when the militant students refused to allow the five-man U.N. Commission to visit the American hostages, despite a momentary indication that they might do so.[27] Divided between various shades of traditionalist clergymen and modern lay elements, the Revolutionary Council finally referred the decision to Ayatollah Khomeini, who came down on the side of the militant students on March 10 by saying that if the U.N. Commission issued its report "on the crimes of the deposed Shah and interventions of the invading United States in Tehran, it will be allowed to see the hostages."[28] Faced with such a demand, the Commission finally left Iran after a stay of seventeen days, to the embarrassed disappointment of President Banisadr and the Foreign Minister, who had worked hard to make the necessary arrangements for the Commission's visit.

Banisadr's second rebuffal followed President Carter's decision at Camp David to proceed with economic and political sanctions against Iran if nothing was done to transfer the hostages to the hands of the Iranian government authorities—a decision that was communicated to Iran on March 25 with a deadline for an Iranian decision on the transfer of hostages by March 31. In response to this, President Banisadr stated on "Islamic Republic Day" (April 1) that action would be taken if, in effect, the United States made a broad and binding promise to withhold threats and hostile statements to gain the transfer of American hostages until the yet-to-be-elected Majlis had decided their fate—a solution previously promulgated by Ayatollah Khomeini himself after the arrival of the U.N. Commission in Iran.

Once again, the divided Revolutionary Council failed to reach an agreement, and once again the Council referred the issue to Ayatollah Khomeini, who, as before, came down on the side of the militant students. He ruled on April 7 that the American hostages would remain in the custody of the militant students until a decision could be made by the Majlis. On the same day, President Carter ordered the breaking off of diplomatic relations with Iran, announced the prohibition of American exports to Iran, except for food and medicine (such a sanction had been approved by ten members of the U.N. Security Council on January 13 but had been vetoed by the Soviet Union), gave indications of a plan to use frozen Iranian assets for the payment of outstanding claims of American citizens and corporations against Iran, and instructed the Attorney General to invalidate all visas issued to Iranian citizens and not issue new visas or renew old ones.[29]

Majlis Elections. Yet another attempt to consolidate the revolutionary regime's power and legitimacy has been the Majlis elections. Held during the first half of 1980, the elections to the 270-member Parliament began amid a continuing controversy between supporters of proportional representation, which favored small groups and parties, and their opponents, who advocated election by absolute majority. Except for the Islamic Republican Party and its supporters within and outside the Revolutionary Council, few groups and leading individuals favored the latter method. President Banisadr also opposed it. Nevertheless, a two-stage, or absolute-majority, system was finally adopted, resulting in a clear majority for the clergy-dominated IRP in the elections held in March and May. President Banisadr's so-called Office for the Co-ordination of the People and the President has not yet, therefore, proved a match for the IRP.

PROSPECTS FOR THE FUTURE

Given the brief existence of the revolutionary regime and the pace of events, speculation about its future is hazardous: it is still too early to identify the most significant emerging trends with any degree of confidence. Yet, in light of the historical precedents, it is possible to suggest a few crucial factors relevant to the regime's prospects.

Both the Constitutional and the nationalist regimes survived for only a relatively brief period of time. The Constitutional regime, which was established in 1907, was removed in 1908, reestablished in 1909, and destroyed again in 1911. The life of the nationalist regime of Dr. Mosaddegh was equally brief: it was established in 1951 and brought down by a coup in 1953. These two regimes of the past thus each survived for fewer than three years—and for reasons that were broadly similar. In both cases their leaders were unable to stabilize conditions by consolidating and institutionalizing their power and legitimate authority. They failed to transform charismatic leadership swiftly and successfully into acceptable and workable institutions. Consequently, ideological, factional, personal, and other divisions perpetuated unstable conditions until tranquility was imposed by autocratic and authoritarian rulers. Further, the Constitutional and the nationalist regimes both failed to avoid being trapped in the conjunction between a hostile external environment and internal disarray and chaos. The Constitutionalists could not resist the pressure from both Britain and Russia, which was in turn a consequence of their pursuit of an excessively unrealistic foreign policy. The Mosaddegh government fared hardly better. At first it tried to play the impartial, if not supportive, United States against Britain, but by the end it had lost the American card because of its inability to resolve the protracted oil nationalization crisis. The combination of deteriorating domestic conditions and a hostile external environment paved the way for the American-supported coup that brought down the nationalist regime.

The most fundamental factor underlying the ultimate demise of these two regimes was, however, the inability of the nationalist leadership to temper ideological purity with considerations of pragmatic utility. Ideological preoccupations foreclosed the chances for any compromise settlement in dealing with the pressures of domestic and foreign policy. Seen in this light, the emerging trends in the present Iranian revolution point to a basic fragility in the revolutionary regime—unless they can be reversed. Domestically, the remarkable efforts at institution-building since the establishment of the Islamic Republic are still challenged by a continuing concern with the ultimate shape of the new constitutional order, particularly as it relates to the fundamental contradiction between the idea of the sovereignty of the people and the enormous powers granted to the religious leader or the *faqih*. The nascent institutions are overshadowed by the specter of unbridgeable divisions within the prospective Majlis and between the Parliament and the President. The fear weighs heavy of a monopoly of power in the hands of the fundamentalist and often extremist Muslim clergy in the face of the mounting alienation of modern-educated groups and moderate religious figures, despite Ayatollah Khomeini's own repeated exhortations for the participation of "all strata of the society." It seems to be impossible to settle the Kurdish and other ethnic problems within the framework of Iran's territorial integrity. And there are formidable problems of military reconstruction in the face of the pressing requirements of internal security and national defense, as well as sharpening problems of economic reconstruction in the context of declining productivity, rampant unemployment, and rising expectations for economic betterment.

The external environment of the revolutionary regime also seems to be deteriorating. Despite repeated official denials by the revolutionary authorities, fears regarding the export of the Iranian Revolution continue to haunt Iran's neighbors—conservative and radical alike. The transnational claims of Iran's new foreign policy, reflecting what is perceived as a universal Islamic commitment to the support of all liberation movements, is believed to contradict the revolutionary regime's fierce opposition to foreign interference in Iran's internal affairs. President Banisadr's concern that failure to resolve the hostage crisis would weaken the revolution is justified, not only because, as he believes, it deters the nation from concentrating its energies on coping with mounting domestic economic and political problems, but also, in the view of the author, because it tends to aggravate Iran's relations with an increasing number of states, including the Western European countries, Britain, and Japan. This must make it extremely difficult in the end for Iran to maintain equidistance from the East as well as the West, in keeping with the fundamental premise of its new revolutionary foreign policy.

In light of its own historical experience, Iran must surely note the danger of a convergence between a polarized domestic political process and a hostile external environment. This is a lesson of the past that must be learned if the country is to give itself a decent chance finally to break out of the vicious cycle of the nationalist crises of the past. The failure to do so, historically, has always entailed the return of authoritarian regimes. And the fundamental reason for that failure, it is here submitted, was the inability of the leaders of the anti-autocratic regimes, Constitutionalist or Mosaddeghist, to temper ideological extremism with pragmatic requirements. The friends of Iran hope that the new revolutionary leaders of the Islamic Republic of Iran will recall that the glorious achievements of Islamic civilization were always made possible by the ability of Muslim leaders to wed their faith to an accurate reflection of the real facts of life.

NOTES

1. See my study "Iran's Foreign Policy Perspectives and Projections," in *Economic Consequences of the Revolution in Iran: A Compendium of Papers Submitted to the Joint Economic Committee, Congress of the United States* (Washington, DC, 1980), 65–97, 443.

2. See R. K. Ramazani, *The Foreign Policy of Iran, 1500–1941: A Developing Nation in World Affairs* (Charlottesville, 1966).

3. See R. K. Ramazani, *Iran's Foreign Policy, 1941–1973: A Study of Foreign Policy in Modernizing Nations* (Charlottesville, 1975).

4. For greater details on this theme, see R. K. Ramazani, "Iran's Revolution in Perspective," in *The Impact of the Iranian Events upon Persian Gulf and United States Security*, project director Z. Michael Szaz (Washington, DC, 1979), 19–37.

5. See Ayatollah Ruhollah Khomeini, *Islamic Government* [in Persian] (n.p., n.d.). For a recent compendium of Ayatollah Khomeini's messages, speeches, and interviews in Persian, see *Nedat-e Khalq* [The voice of God], vol. 1 (Paris, 1978).

6. For a translation of samples of Shari'ati's lectures in English, see Ali Shari'ati, *On the Sociology of Islam*, translated by Hamid Algar (Berkeley, 1979). There is a considerable literature by and about Shari'ati in Persian. See, for example, *Haj* [Hajj] (Tehran); *Besar-e Aql Amadan-e Sarmayeh-dari* [The rational instruments of capitalism in Iran] (n.p., n.d.); and the lectures *Alz Tanha ast* [All is unique] (Tehran), *Pedar, Madar, Ma Motahem-mevem* [The father or mother of Motehaven] (Tehran), *Shahadat* [Testimony] (Tehran), *Yadnameh-ye Shahid-e Javid; Ali, Haqiqati bar guneh-ye Asatir; Az Koja Aghaz koneem?* [A letter

from the Eternal Martyr, Ali; Reality of the cloth of Asatir; from where should we start?],
Jahan-biny [Seeing the world], Mazhab Alath-e Mazhab [Religion the greatest of religions],
and Shi'ah, Yek Hezb-e Tamam [Shia, the complete religious tradition].

7. See Franz Fanon, The Wretched of the Earth (New York, 1963).

8. For the phrase "monolithic movement," see the introductory section of the text of
the Constitution of the Islamic Republic of Iran. For the text in English with my introductory note, see Middle East Journal 34, no. 2 (Spring 1980): 181–204.

9. See, for example, Mohandes Mehdih Bazargan, Rah-e Tay Shodeh [The paved path],
published between 1941 and 1953.

10. See, for example, Ali-Reza Nobari, ed., Iran Erupts, (Stanford, 1978). In Persian
see Abolhassan Bani-Sadr, Naft va Solteh, ya Naqsh-e Naft dar Tos'ah-ye Sarmayeh-dars dar
Pahneh-ye Jahan va Zaman [Oil and dominance, or the role of religious capitalism in the
spectrum of the world] (Tehran, 1977).

11. Beijing in English, 7 March 1980, as monitored by the Foreign Broadcast Information Service, in FBIS, Daily Report, vol. 5, Middle East and North Africa (FBIS-MEA), 7 March
1980, 12.

12. See, Tehran Times, 3 March 1980, English ed., in FBIS-MEA, 13 March 1980, 18–19;
and Beijing in English, 7 March 1980, in ibid., 7 March 1980, 12.

13. See Ramazani, Iran's Foreign Policy, 1941–1973.

14. New York Times, 2 April 1979.

15. Ettela'at, 3 April 1979.

16. Ibid.

17. The Shia believe that there were twelve imams (successors of Mohammed)—Ali,
Hasan, Hussein, and nine in line of descent from Hussein—of whom the twelfth, Mohammed, born in AD 873, disappeared mysteriously in AD 939. They believe that the
Imam is only "hidden" and will reappear as the Mahdi (the rightly guided) to establish
a golden age.

18. Principle 5 provides: "During the absence of the Glorious Lord of the Age (the
missing Twelfth Imam of the Shii sect), may God grant him relief, he will be represented
in the Islamic Republic of Iran as religious leader and imam of the people by an honest,
virtuous, well-informed, courageous, efficient administrator and religious jurist, enjoying the confidence of the majority of the people as a leader. Should there be no jurist
endowed with such qualifications, enjoying the confidence of the people, his role will be
undertaken by a leader or council of leaders, consisting of religious jurists meeting the
requirements mentioned above, according to Principle 107."

19. Principle 110 provides: "Duties and powers of leadership: 1. Appointing the jurists on the Council of Guardians; 2. Appointing the highest judicial authorities of the
country; 3. Command of all the armed forces as follows: (A) Appointing and dismissing
the chief of the general staff; (B) Appointing and dismissing the commander-in-chief
of the Islamic Revolutionary Guards Corps; (C) Organizing the High Council for National Defense, which will be composed of the following seven members: president of
the republic, prime minister, minister of defense, chief of the general staff, the commander-in-chief of the Islamic Revolutionary Guards Corps, two advisers specified by
the leader; (D) Naming the commanders-in-chief of the three armed forces at the sug-

gestion of the High Council for National Defense; (E) Declaring war and mobilizing the armed forces at the suggestion of the High Council for National Defense."

20. Principles 6 and 56 are at issue. Principle 6 provides: "The affairs of the country should be administered in the Islamic Republic of Iran by relying upon public opinion expressed through elections, i.e., election of the president of the republic, deputies of the National Assembly, members of councils, and the like, or by plebiscite, anticipated for cases specified in other principles of this Constitution." Principle 56 provides: "The absolute ruler of the world and humanity is God and He alone has determined the social destiny of human beings. No one shall take away this God-given right from another person or make use of it to serve his personal or group's interests. The nation will use this God-given right to act according to the manner determined by the following principles."

21. *Ettela'at*, 1 December 1979.

22. Principle 12 provides: "The official religion of Iran is Islam, and the sect followed is Twelver Shiism (Ithna 'Ashari). This principle is never subject to change. Other Islamic denominations also, such as Hanafi, Shafi'i, Maliki, Hanbali, and Zaydi, enjoy complete respect. The followers of these sects are free to perform their religious rites, based on their religious jurisprudence. They are also officially recognized as such in the courts in connection with lawsuits dealing with religious teachings and personal affairs (such as marriage, divorce, hereditary disputes, wills, etc.). In any area where the majority of the population should consist of the followers of any of these sects, local regulations within the power possessed by the councils will be based on the regulations of that denomination."

23. President Banisadr complained to Eric Rouleau in an interview published in *Le Monde* on 11 February 1980.

24. See Tehran Domestic Service, 5 November 1979, as monitored by FBIS, in FBIS-MEA, 5 November 1979, R3–R4.

25. Ibid., R-2.

26. The communist jubilation is well exemplified by an interview with the Tudeh Party leader, Nuroddin Kianuri. He said on 18 February 1980 that the role of the militant students was "very important" in defeating the attempts of the "liberal bourgeoisie" under the government of Bazargan to divert the revolution from its "anti-imperialist" path. For details of this revealing interview, see FBIS-MEA, 28 February 1980, 24–28.

27. For the text of the militant students' statement, see *New York Times*, 7 March 1980.

28. For the text of Khomeini's statement, see ibid., 11 March 1980.

29. For the text of President Carter's directive, see ibid., 8 April 1980.

WHO LOST AMERICA?

The Case of Iran

Whatever the reason for any puzzlement over the title of this essay may be, I hope to challenge it. We Americans are accustomed to asking, "Who lost Iran?" as in the past we have asked, "Who lost China?," "Who lost Indochina?," "Who lost Nicaragua?," and as in the future we may ask, for example, "Who lost El Salvador?" As long as this thought pattern persists we are apt to repeat similar questions about any country in which a regime friendly to the United States is toppled and American influence collapses as a result.

The reason for this tenacious habit of thought is in part conceptual fallacy. Despite all the dynamic changes in international politics and economics since World War II, including the disappearance of Western colonial empires, the emergence of increasingly assertive new states within and outside the United Nations, and the inescapable realities of the dilemma of increasing interdependence and fierce independence, we have yet to shake off the habit of equating raw power with influence. Most of us still assume that the greater the power of one state relative to another, the greater the influence. In other words, it is simplistically assumed that the more powerful states necessarily control the behavior of the lesser powers.

The corollary to this kind of thinking is twofold. First, it is always the more powerful state that loses its friend, ally, or, to use a more revealing characterization, client. By definition, clients lack influence over their patrons. They are "puppets," "pawns," or, to recall an earlier label, "satellites" within the orbit of a great or superpower. Whatever the label, these hapless and helpless creatures of the international system are wooed, won, and lost, all depending on the success or failure of the policies of their great-power partners. Second, by definition, any setback to the exercise of influence by the greater power must be its own fault. How could it be otherwise? Since the big powers supposedly control the destiny of the little ones, something must be wrong with their decisions, their policy process, or some other factor. This is why self-flagellation is a hallmark of American reaction to perceived failures, especially when a hostile "second-rate" power like Khomeini's Iran, for example, inflicts "humiliation" on America for 444 days by holding "America in captivity."

"Who Lost America? The Case of Iran" was originally published in *Middle East Journal* 37, no. 1 (Winter 1982): 5–21.

Ideological fantasies, no less than conceptual fallacies, also account for misunderstanding the nature of influence in the relations between a large and a small state such as the United States and Iran. The so-called globalists on the right blame the Carter administration's human-rights policy for the fall of the anticommunist Shah's regime and the loss of strategic Iran to the Free World. The former President, the globalists argue, should have used an "iron fist" to save the Shah. President Reagan, for example, said on October 17, 1981, "I don't believe that the Shah's government would have fallen if the United States had made it plain that we would stand by that government and support them in whatever had to be done to curb the revolution and let it be seen that we still felt that we were allied with him." The President might find it difficult to understand that one of the causes of the revolution was indiscriminate American support of the Shah's regime.

The so-called regionalists, ranging from liberal reformers to leftist romantics, in contrast, blame the Shah's downfall on the failure to uphold American democratic ideals in dealing with the Shah. They hold the Nixon administration responsible for failing to press the Shah for the democratization of the Iranian political system and for catering to the Shah's "megalomania" by assigning him the role of the "protector" of Persian Gulf security and by promising him the sale of whatever conventional and sophisticated American weapons he wanted. What is remarkably similar in this and comparable views is that they all seem to share the same fundamental assumption about the unlimited nature of American influence over Iran.

What is even more remarkable is that most Iranians also seem to share that basic assumption. The Muslim fundamentalists, the secular nationalists, the leftist Mujahadeen, the Fedayan, and the communist Tudeh Party too believe in the omnipotence of American influence. Even His Majesty, "The Light of the Aryans," suspected during his fits of depression before his downfall that the United States was involved in a conspiracy against him, and he believed after leaving Iran that General Huyser "threw the Shah out of Iran like a dead mouse," as Air Force General Rabi'ei had said.

This extraordinary combination of American mythology and Iranian demonology leaves little room for either considering empirical evidence or interpreting it in ways other than superimposing the predisposition of the analyst on the actual record. This problem is all the more serious with respect to the Iranian side of U.S.-Iranian relations during the Shah's regime. After all, the Shah was presumably an "American king," so why bother delving into an examination of his foreign policy if it was dictated by Washington anyway? The problem, however, is not only that such an assumption distorts the realities of the Iranian situation; it also exaggerates both the success and the failure of American policy in Iran. American policy was neither formulated nor executed in a vacuum. It interacted with an Iranian foreign policy that either facilitated or complicated the exercise of American influence over the Shah's regime. In other words, without an understanding of the Shah's policy toward the United States, the true limits of American policy can hardly be understood.

An understanding of the Shah's American policy must take note of his domestic politics. The interplay between domestic and foreign policy should be considered in regard to the foreign policy of all countries, but in the case of the Shah's Iran it is particularly important. The fundamental reason for this importance is the fact that the Shah's domestic politics formed the raison d'être of his American policy from start to finish. Bluntly stated, the Shah wooed, won, and eventually lost American support largely because of the way he played the game of domestic politics.

When and how did the Shah win American support for his regime? The question is prompted by the myth that American support was a function of the American covert intervention in Iran in 1953. On the contrary, the Shah decided to induce American involvement as early as 1941, when he acceded to the throne. This important fact is largely overlooked, presumably because the Shah was young and inexperienced, which is true, but that did not preclude his influencing the development of U.S.-Iranian relations. As a matter of fact, he had both the requisite motivation and the capacity.

He was motivated primarily by the desire to withstand the pressures of domestic political forces and foreign powers. He feared popular doubts about the legitimacy of his rule. Reza Shah's abdication was forced on him in effect by the Anglo-Russian invasion of Iran. He had ruled the country as a dictator for nearly twenty years. Muhammad Reza Shah was believed to be the son of a dictator; as expressed by politically awakened Iranians who quoted from the thirteenth-century poet Sa'adi, "A wolf's offspring will always be a wolf" (aghabat gorg-zadeh gorg shavad).

The Shah had a variety of domestic foes and many potential challengers, to say the least. At the end of his father's stern rule, when a more open political atmosphere prevailed, political forces of all shades and colors burst upon the scene. Although the clerics, including Khomeini, did not challenge the rule of the young Shah at the time, the fundamentalists demanded clerical power as envisaged under the 1906–7 constitution (Reza Shah had never granted that power to the clerics in practice). The nationalists, on the other hand, demanded that the Shah reign rather than rule. The communists, for their part, sang nationalistic songs but privately entertained the idea of establishing a people's republic of Iran. The British position added to the Shah's worries. They recognized his rule contingent on his observance of the Iranian Constitution.

Nor was the Shah's external enemy imaginary. He, like his father, hated communism and feared the Russians; Russia was his bête noire too. The firm control of the Russian forces in northern Iran, the Soviet moral and material support of the communist Tudeh Party, Moscow's revival of old tsarist demands for Iranian oil resources in the North, and, above all, the Kremlin's reluctance to pledge firmly the withdrawal of Red Army troops from Iran after the war deeply worried the young Shah.

American involvement in Iran could be used to protect his nascent rule against perceived domestic and foreign foes. The war had breached American isolationism, but that in itself was not enough to induce American involvement in Iran in support of his rule. His father had been not only a dictator but also a friend of Nazi Germany. His own record, however, was clean. On October 8, 1941, less than a month after his accession to the throne, the Shah approached the American Minister in Tehran about an alliance with America. He blamed "bad advisers" for the failures of his father, stated his own intention to "govern constitutionally and look after the welfare of his people," and, above all, declared enthusiastically that he "would be very happy to be an ally of America."

He was not only determined to obtain American support for his rule; he also felt he had the capacity to do so. That was not imaginary either. He inherited loyal supporters within the civilian and military bureaucracy, both the creations of his father. He even enjoyed the support of some members of the aristocracy within and outside the Majlis. At his accession to the throne he was supported loyally by the philosopher-statesman Muhammad Ali Foroughi and a whole succession of other loyal prime ministers. Even the differences between him and his strong prime minister, Ahmad Qavam, were never allowed to result in a serious conflict, as evidenced, for example, by their common strategy, eventually, toward the Soviet Union and the Moscow-supported rebel regimes in Azerbaijan and Kurdistan.

The Shah sought single-mindedly—but not single-handedly—to manipulate American involvement in Iran. He first tried to exploit the uninvited arrival of some 40,000 American troops in 1942 as a basis for American participation in the tripartite alliance between Iran, Britain, and the Soviet Union. Although he failed in that attempt, he managed to gain President Roosevelt's decisive support for an Allied guarantee of Iranian "territorial integrity and political independence" in the 1943 tripartite Tehran Declaration. To the Shah, this first public pledge of American support for Iran at the highest level signaled the beginning of American involvement. Subsequent events seemed to prove him right. In the oil crisis of 1944 and the Azerbaijan crisis of 1945–46 the United States fully supported the Shah's governments against the Soviet Union, despite the Soviet-American wartime alliance. The American involvement was redounding to the Shah's advantage diplomatically even before the end of World War II.

More than anything else, however, the Shah sought American involvement in Iran as a way of strengthening his security forces. He, like his father, regarded military strength as the sine qua non of royal survival. To American officials, however, he presented military strength as the essential prerequisite for social and economic modernization as well as national independence. Despite American reluctance to get involved at the beginning, the Shah managed to acquire U.S. aid to strengthen the Imperial Gendarmerie and the Iranian Army during the war and to receive American military equipment soon after. The American-Iranian military ties that were thus established in the 1940s formed the foundation of most military transactions between the two countries during the subsequent decades.

The advent of Dr. Muhammad Mosaddegh to power disrupted the Shah's decade-long cultivation of American friendship. The nationalist Prime Minister tried at first to exploit the offer of American mediation between Iran and Britain to his own advantage. As long as the attitudes of Washington and London toward his government diverged, the Prime Minister seemed to have a chance to use American influence to extract concessions from Britain, but once the Anglo-American assessments of the Iranian situation converged, Mosaddegh's opportunity to manipulate American influence was lost. That loss redounded to the Shah's advantage in his power struggle with Mosaddegh. The decade-long embryonic American involvement with the Shah—which he himself had largely cultivated—now paid off handsomely. Over a decade he had successfully projected the image of a "pro-Western" monarch. In the conditions of the Cold War that characteristic was good enough for London and Washington to plan the overthrow of the Mosaddegh government in favor of the friendly Shah.

The Shah himself, however, was not an innocent bystander in the campaign against Mosaddegh. He participated surreptitiously in the Anglo-American plan. After all, in order to resist the challenge of the forces of domestic opposition to his rule, he had courted American friendship assiduously from his very accession to the throne. Within this context, the covert CIA intervention was at least in part induced and implemented by the Shah himself. He was thus able to influence the United States to his advantage during the hour of his greatest need. His capacity to do so was partly the function of the Anglo-American belief that he alone could protect the Western oil and strategic interests in Iran, a belief that he had carefully cultivated over a decade.

The Shah had so successfully sold that idea to his American friends that after the coup Washington denied itself any leverage whatsoever over his future conduct. The Shah himself volunteered to the principal CIA agent immediately after his return to power in 1953 that he owed his throne to the United States, but that agent told him emphatically that he had "absolutely no obligation" toward America. Those American observers who have recently found the American "original sin" responsible for the downfall of the Shah's regime to be the Nixon administration's cavalier arms-sales promise to the Shah in 1972 should find this earliest carte blanche to the Shah far more original! They could argue that the Eisenhower administration voluntarily gave up its leverage over the Shah when it was strongest, and when it might have been used to extract from him a pledge to respect the Iranian Constitution. The British had done so, they could say, in 1941, when they made their recognition of the new Shah contingent on his observance of the Constitution.

The Shah exploited the American strategic concerns in the next quarter of a century to deepen the American support for his regime just as he had done in the first decade of his rule to establish that support. His participation in the covert CIA operations brought the Shah closest to his youthful dream of becoming an American ally. President Eisenhower, who regarded the nationalist crusade of Mosaddegh against the British as a "fanatical campaign," believed that, with the Shah as an American ally, "we may really give a serious defeat to Russian intentions" in the Middle East. The Shah lost no time in conveying to the President the idea that, with American help, Iran could become "a significant link in the Free World's defense."

The global and local villains of the Shah and John Foster Dulles were the same—the Soviet Union and Gamal Abdel Nasser. The Shah joined the Washington-sponsored Baghdad Pact (later CENTO), endorsed the Eisenhower Doctrine, involved American interests in the Iranian oil industry for the first time in history, threw the doors of the Iranian economy open to American trade and investment, and received millions of dollars of American military and economic aid.

Never satisfied with the American nonmembership in the CENTO alliance, the Shah complained from the moment he joined the Baghdad Pact. He wished for a NATO-type automatic American defense of Iran, but the United States was unwilling to go beyond consultation in case of aggression against Iran. He tried to use negotiations with Moscow for a fifty-year nonaggression treaty as leverage to extract a more effective defense commitment from the United States, but caught between the Soviet demand for Iran's withdrawal from the American-sponsored alliance and the American offer of a bilateral defense agreement, he opted for the latter. Although this executive agreement did not strengthen the alliance beyond the protection already available to the Shah under the Eisenhower Doctrine, he used the crisis atmosphere after the Iraqi Revolution to seek more economic and military aid.

The Shah's opportunity for the exploitation of American desiderata dramatically improved in the 1960s and 1970s. As a student of power politics, he must have noted what Machiavelli had said about the Shah's own model, Cyrus, and other leaders of ancient times, who "owed nothing to fortune but the opportunity which gave them matter to be shaped into what form they thought fit." The essence of the Shah's opportunity was threefold: the increasing American aversion to committing U.S. forces abroad because of the searing experience of the Vietnam War; the historic withdrawal of British forces from the area east of Suez, including the Persian Gulf region; and the dramatic transformation of the world oil market from a buyer's to a seller's market.

The Shah presented himself as the "ideal" of the Nixon Doctrine by exploiting the American predicament, which years later Secretary Kissinger described in these words: "There was no possibility of assigning any American forces to the Indian Ocean in the midst of the Vietnam War and its attendant trauma. Congress would have tolerated no such commitment; the public would not have supported it. Fortunately, Iran was willing to play this role." In the same year, 1968, when the British announced their decision to withdraw their forces from the Gulf region, the American public was agonizing over involvement in Vietnam, and in 1971, when the American public was more dismayed over the handling of the Vietnam War, as revealed by the Pentagon Papers, the Shah's forces moved to capture the three strategic Gulf islands of Abu Musa and the two Tunbs.

On the oil front too the Shah was on the offensive. He had signed the oil consortium agreement (1954) reluctantly because it did not give him all the oil revenues he needed to strengthen his regime. But he signed it, nevertheless, because the Iranian economy was bankrupt, because the agreement involved American interests in the Iranian oil industry, because it broke the traditional British monopoly, and because the American government pressed the oil companies to make room for the reentry of Iranian oil supplies into the world markets. After years of protracted negotiations and occasional intimidation, he led the Gulf oil producers triumphantly against the Western oil companies in 1971. Two years later he first nationalized the Iranian oil industry at a time when all other Gulf producers except Iraq were willing to gain control of their oil industry gradually through the process of "participation." In the same year he led the unprecedented increase in OPEC oil prices with far-reaching global economic and political repercussions.

Washington resented the Shah's nationalization of the oil industry for its possible spillover effects on the other Gulf producers. His hawkish role in increasing oil prices irritated at least some Washington circles. Only a year earlier the Shah had disingenuously worried about the adverse impact of the Soviet-American detente on the Irano-American alliance. Were the superpowers trying to divide the world between them as Britain and Russia had divided Iran into spheres of influence in 1907? The Shah, of course, knew better, but he put on a show of worrying about the threat of Soviet-American condominium for President Nixon when the latter stopped in Tehran on his way back from the Moscow summit. The President assured the Shah of continuing American support and promised him the sale of whatever sophisticated conventional American arms he wanted.

Despite all his fascination with linkages, Henry Kissinger did not choose to use the arms sales as a leverage to curb the Shah's appetite for ever-higher oil prices. Iran's value to America as a "strategic prize" in the East-West global competition, as a policeman in the Gulf region, and as the second largest oil producer increased as a result of the explosion of oil prices. The Shah's soaring oil revenues, used for massive purchases of American arms, were a major source of petrodollars for the sagging American economy. In 1974 the value of the Shah's arms transaction with the United States amounted to twice the total value of all arms contracted during the previous twenty-two years. Even after 1974, when Iran's oil revenues dropped, Kissinger announced in Tehran (August 7, 1976) that the United States would sell Iran $10 billion worth of military equipment in the next six years. This was out of a total trade figure for the period of $50 billion.

Nor did the Carter administration really discourage the Shah's unbridled arms purchases, despite all the fanfare in the presidential election campaign about future arms-sales limitations. Even after the outbreak of the Iranian Revolution the Shah and the President continued arms deals for nearly nine months, as if the critical uprising in Qom, the widespread disturbances at Tabriz, the tragic fire at Abadan, and the massacre on "Black Friday" in Jaleh Square were not happening at all. The Shah pressed ahead with his plans for a massive naval expansion worth more than $5 billion as late as March 1978, and President Carter approved the sale of nearly $600 million worth of American arms, including thirty-one Phantom jet fighters, as late as July.

Just as the Shah's wooing and winning of American support did not occur overnight, the loss of it did not either. Rather it was the result of a complex process stretched in effect over two decades. In the same statement to the press of October 17, 1981, when President Reagan said that the Shah's government would not have fallen if the United States had made it plain that it would stand by that government's efforts "to curb the revolution," he also said, "I have been told by someone very knowledgeable and involved at that time that there was a point at which the revolution, so-called, could have been headed off with the arrest of 500 individuals, just the arrests. They weren't executing people like they are now and we advised against that."

If that is the kind of advice our president gets, it is no wonder that we do not seem to learn any meaningful lessons from our role in the Iranian Revolution. The President did not specify at what point the arrest of five hundred people would have done the trick, but it must have been sometime during the 1978–79 period. If so, the evidence is that many thousands were involved even in the first uprising at Qom in January 1978, let alone in the February disturbances in Tabriz, which were a citywide insurrection, or the September upheaval at Jaleh Square, which involved over a million protestors, or the massive Ashura demonstrations of November, in which several million people participated. Nor is it clear who the individuals could have been who should have been arrested; the supreme revolutionary leader, Ayatollah Ruhollah Khomeini, was in exile, and other revolutionary figures, such as Bazargan, Sanjabi, Forouhar, and the like, were in and out of the Shah's jails. Their arrests, instead of curbing the revolution, intensified its momentum.

Obviously the revolution destroyed the Shah's regime, and with it American influence in Iran. What concerns us here is not the study of the revolution as such but how the Shah's long-standing wooing and winning of American support for his regime paradoxically contributed to the ultimate loss of this support. Even this limited objective cannot be met in any great detail within the confines of this brief discussion, but I shall give it a try.

As seen, the young Shah single-mindedly initiated, courted, cultivated, and expanded American involvement in Iran primarily for the purpose of protecting his regime against domestic forces of opposition, although he obviously aimed at deterring the perceived threats of external enemies as well. To him Iran was an extension of himself, and so efforts to protect Iranian independence—including, and foremost among them, his efforts to conclude an alliance with the United States—were inseparable from the preservation of his regime and the Pahlavi dynasty. In essence, the Shah, like most Iranian political actors in or out of power, felt the need for foreign friends largely in order to manage a domestic political struggle.

To put it differently, the Shah sought to resolve the basic problems of the political legitimacy and authority of his regime partly with the aid of the United States. From the outset this kind of royal manipulation was bound to set—as it did—his protector as well as himself in potential conflict with the forces of opposition. This is partly why as early as World War II the domestic forces of opposition began to resist American involvement in Iran. For example, the opposition of Mosaddegh to American advisers in general and of Khomeini to Dr. Arthur Millspaugh's American economic mission in particular was directed as much against extensive American involvement in Iran as against the Shah himself.

To be sure, through single-minded manipulation of American aid the Shah increased his power and control over the opposition, but at the same time he also deepened his problems of legitimacy and authority. These basic problems were far more potential than active when he first ascended the throne; the mystique of the Shahanshah initially outweighed whatever popular qualms existed about his being the son of a dictator. In fact, to be fair, the Shah's perceived role in the destruction of the Soviet-communist-supported rebel regimes in Azerbaijan and Kurdistan at least momentarily seemed to help the prestige of the throne and of the military, which had been in ruins since the army's ignominious collapse in the wake of the Anglo-Soviet invasion, and when the first attempt against his life was made in 1949 it was widely believed to have been instigated by the extremists on the left.

In a real sense the Shah's problems of legitimacy and authority took a turn for the worse in 1953, when he participated in the planning and actual implementation of the American covert intervention in his favor. No matter how important the adverse effect of this event on the Shah's legitimacy, however, it should not be exaggerated as the root cause of either the Iranian Revolution or the loss of American influence in Iran about a quarter of a century later. Such a proposition would smack of excessive imagination, because the record shows that the Shah's mystique continued to help his rule, despite the serious blow that it definitely suffered as a result of his role in the American-supported coup.

More important, many other misguided moves by the Shah in connection with his relations with the United States had to occur over the subsequent decades before the twofold process of popular alienation from him and from the United States could transform the 1953 nationalist resentment against the Shah and the United States into the revolution of 1978–79. An understanding of that profound transformation would require an analysis of the entire fabric of the relations between the Shah and the United States over a period of nearly thirty-seven years; that is, of course, impossible to attempt here. Instead, I shall try to summarize my main findings and to indicate the broad trends and approaches of the Shah's policies and tactics that contributed, in my judgment, to the loss of both his throne and American support of his regime.

First, strategic and military considerations dominated the Shah's policy toward the United States from start to finish. From his accession to the throne, he wished to be a full-fledged American ally. Toward this end, he made every effort to establish and deepen American involvement in Iran. Above all, he sought American military assistance and military equipment for the Iranian armed forces. He established the foundations of both in the 1940s, as evidenced by his first military agreement with the United States in 1943, which furnished the basis for the U.S. Military Mission to the Iranian Gendarmerie (GENMISH) until 1976, and the 1947 agreement that set up the U.S. Army Mission Headquarters (ARMISH), which in 1958 was consolidated with the Military Advisory Group (MAAG). Later on, during the Vietnam War, he exploited the American aversion to committing U.S. armed forces to the defense of the Persian Gulf region after the British withdrawal to increase Iranian military power in the region, mainly with the aid of American military equipment and training.

By making security and military ties with the United States the centerpiece of his American policy, the Shah made it the main engine of the twofold popular alienation from his rule and from the American government. The point is not that he had no external enemies, or that Iran needed no deterrent power against potential threats, but that it was widely believed that the Shah's goal of military power had expanded far beyond the requirements of Iranian self-defense; he dreamed of transforming Iran into one of the world's five major conventional military powers. And the vast Iranian military purchases created logistical, maintenance, and training problems that it was beyond the country's capacity to handle.

Contrary to the conventional view, however, nearly a decade before President Nixon's 1972 promise of sophisticated American weapons to the Shah and the 1973 explosion of oil prices that made the Iranian purchases possible, the Shah's handling of the American military presence in Iran deepened his domestic political problems dramatically. Under pressure from the Pentagon, he granted diplomatic privileges and immunities to American military personnel in Iran. This grant coincided with his acceptance of President Johnson's offer of $200 million in credits for the purchase of American military equipment. The Iranian public linked the two and perceived them as the establishment of American "capitulations" in Iran in return for the money. Ayatollah Ruhollah Khomeini characterized the bill for American diplomatic immunities as a "document of the enslavement of Iran" and said acerbically, "I declare that this shameful vote . . . is contrary to Islam and the Koran and hence illegal." "The world must know," he continued, "that all the difficulties faced by the Iranian nation and the Muslim peoples are because of aliens, because of America."

This bold protest led to the exile of Khomeini, but for nearly a whole decade before the Iranian Revolution the American military presence in Iran was the principal target of the underground forces of opposition to the Shah's regime.

We now know from published Mujahadeen sources that the bomb explosions that occurred during President Nixon's visit to Iran in 1972 were part of their "Nixon Operations," which were followed by assassinations of mainly American military personnel as well as the Shah's officials during every subsequent year well into the Iranian Revolution.

Second, the Shah's approach to "economic modernization" contributed to the fall of his regime and the loss of American support in two major ways. In the first place, the Shah's modernization plans were dominated from inception by political considerations. This problem first surfaced in 1947, when the Shah instituted the first Iranian plan for economic development, the so-called Seven Year Development Plan. The primacy of political considerations was noted at the time as an impediment to genuine economic development by Max Thornburg, the president of American Overseas Consultants Incorporated (OCI), which was invited to help the Iranians with their planning. He believed that the plan was doomed to fail because the ruling elite preferred industrial over agricultural development, and over educational and health improvement, and because of the government's "political interference."

The persistence of this twofold problem is evidenced, for example, by the Shah's single most important attempt at economic reforms in the 1960s. The "White Revolution" was prompted, first, partly by the pressures of the Kennedy administration, which withheld military aid to the Shah's regime as leverage for social and economic reforms. But the Shah also had his own political reasons for launching the land-reform program. He was facing a potent twofold threat to his regime. Domestically, the forces of opposition that had been suppressed for a whole decade reemerged on the political scene. National Front leaders such as Baqer Kazemi, Karim Sanjabi, Allahyar Saleh, and others, for example, demanded "liberty and democracy" and "an independent national" foreign policy. Teachers' strikes, mass demonstrations at the University of Tehran, and the like, called for some kind of political maneuver, as did the unprecedented Soviet onslaught against the Shah's regime in the wake of the breakdown of Soviet-Iranian negotiations for a nonaggression pact. The land-reform program, therefore, was not intended simply to woo the peasantry by curbing the power of the large landowners. It was also intended to pull the rug out from under the reformist-nationalist demands, to curb the power of the clergy, and to counter the Soviet propaganda attack on the "rotten monarchical regime" by adopting a "progressive" plan.

In retrospect, the Shah's brutal suppression of the June 1963 uprisings against his land-reform program increased popular alienation from both the regime and the United States. Just as the coup of a decade earlier was perceived as an "American coup," the reform programs of 1963 were regarded as an

"American revolution." More important, the arrest and exile of religious leaders who opposed the land-reform program—not only because of their vested interest but also because of their belief in the sanctity of private property and their need for revenues from *vaqf* lands for religious education—destroyed the kind of religious support that the Shah had enjoyed previously as a result of the cooperation of Ayatollahs Burujerdi and Behbehani. Ayatollah Khomeini symbolized the religious opposition to the Shah's regime from then on. He resented especially the Shah's casting his land reform in Islamic terms in an often neglected speech in the holy city of Qom, in which the Shah said that only those religious leaders who did not oppose his land reform "are indubitably our religious leaders . . . and by the blessings of this sacred shrine they will serve Islam, the Shah and their country."

Furthermore, after that brutal suppression the forces of secular opposition went underground, with far-reaching consequences. The old National Front and the Tudeh Party were significantly discredited in the eyes of the younger generation for their failure to combat effectively the Shah's authoritarian regime. Some of the younger members of Bazargan's Iran Freedom Movement broke away from it to form the Mujahadeen, and others defected from the Tudeh Party to organize the Fedayan group. They both advocated armed struggle against the Shah and the United States as the only effective method of political opposition.

In the second place, the Shah's economic modernization suffered from an obsession with the rate and pace of economic growth. Long before the explosion of oil prices in 1973, the performance of the Iranian economy in terms of GNP was remarkable by any reasonable standards of measurement. This was especially the case under the Third (1962–67) and Fourth (1968–73) Development Plans. The real rate of growth was over 9 percent. It occasioned the termination of American economic aid (1967) and was considered by many Western as well as Iranian observers as indicating that Iran was economically approaching the "take-off" point. But the "black gold" (*talay-e siyah*) turned into a "black blight" (*balay-e siyah*). The way vast oil revenues were used magnified every weakness in the Iranian economy. The grandiose economic and atomic-energy development plans, the massive imports of food and consumer goods, the rapidly rising rate of inflation, the spreading corruption, the shortage of electricity, the infrastructural "bottlenecks," the decline of agricultural productivity, the maldistribution of wealth, and so on, could not be cured by such palliative measures as increasing the workers' shares in factories by up to 49 percent or state subsidization of social idleness in the name of social welfare. By the time the Iranian planners began to talk about a "modest rate of growth" and the Shah admitted (1976) the need for cutbacks, it was too late to do any good.

Yet such a flawed economic modernization was expected to accomplish political miracles as well. Many Iranian planners, not unlike many American social scientists, believed that modernization in the form of increasing industrialization, spreading education, improving communication and transportation, growing urbanization, and so on, would transform a traditional, parochial, multiple, "mosaic," or heterogeneous society such as Iran's into an integrated national community; transform subjects into citizens and communalism and tribalism into nationalism; and change primordial loyalties, values, attitudes, ethnic and linguistic particularities, and other "anachronistic" features of old societies such as Iran's into all the ingredients that are necessary for the creation of a civic polity. In other words, economic modernization would lead to political development. This kind of blunder made the Iranian technocratic elite all the more insensitive to the noneconomic roots of political alienation. Even at the height of the Iranian revolutionary turmoil some Iranian policymakers advised American Embassy personnel, for example, to disregard the agitation on the part of religious and bazaari forces, believing that better economic medicine could take care of all the ills of Iranian society. This kind of insensitivity to the deeper problems of their own society made them really "alien Iranians." And their absolute faith in the miracles of Westernization made them equally questionable modernizers. To use a Persian expression, they were "neither here nor there" (az inja roondeh, azunja moondeh), neither Eastern nor Western.

This brings me to the last, although a most important, problem of the Shah's policy. Those observers who blame the fall of the Shah's regime on American human-rights policy clearly exaggerate the point with respect to both the American and Iranian sides of the ledger. To be sure, there is enough evidence to suggest that President Carter's human-rights campaign emboldened the forces of opposition in Iran. But this should be balanced against the fact that the President's pressure for political liberalization was not ever allowed to override the basic American support for the Shah's regime. To be sure, the administration's two-pronged approach of supporting the Shah and at the same time expecting him to liberalize his politics created ample confusion within both Iran and the United States, but the American support for the Shah's regime continued nevertheless.

More important, however, the Shah's own long-standing attitudes and policies toward the forces of political opposition made political liberalization impossible. Despite economic cooptation, techniques of divide and rule, and other nonviolent methods that the Shah employed in maintaining his regime, coercive instruments dominated his approach to the political opposition. The American-created secret police, SAVAK, used modern methods to inflict ancient cruelties on the opponents of the regime. No matter who helped create the organization, there would have been no guarantee that the regime would not abuse it. Resorting to violence has historically been a potent instrument of Iranian politics. All the fanfare about the piecemeal pardon of political prisoners and the alleged termination of torture—especially after the start of the Iranian Revolution—were widely disbelieved not only because of the public's searing experience with SAVAK over the decades but also because the Shah's regime continued past practices even at the height of the revolution. For example, the U.N.-affiliated International League of Human Rights reported in November 1978 that thousands of political prisoners were still being held, political offenses were still handled by military courts, and, above all, only the accent of torture had changed, from physical to psychological methods.

Nor did the American human-rights campaign produce any significant change in the political attitudes of the Shah's authoritarian regime. For example, the Shah's own tenacious tendency to tar all the forces of opposition with the same brush continued well into the revolutionary period, as evidenced by his equating the nationalist forces with the communists on the occasion of Constitutional Day as late as August 1978. Prime Minister Sharif-Emami's so-called conciliatory government did not do any better. In defending his government's brutal suppression of the demonstrations at Jaleh Square in September of that year, he told the Majlis flatly that they would have led to a "communist rebellion" (shoresh-e komonisti). To cite another example, throughout 1977 and well into 1978 the Shah refused to abandon the Rastakhiz Party—the hated symbol of his political intolerance and his demand for political unanimity in support of his regime. Instead, he orchestrated a campaign to defend the party and enlisted the aid of the members of the royal family and of his officials within and outside the party to tell the story of the Iranian perception of human rights and reject the Western and American model of democracy.

The tactics of the Shah's government also continued to be provocative during the Revolution. Except for Ayatollah Ruhollah Khomeini, no major religious or secular leader demanded the end of the Shah's regime before November 5, 1978, when Bazargan, Sanjabi, and the bazaari leaders all succumbed to the overall leadership of the Ayatollah. During the long and tumultuous ten months before then, the regime's mishandling of the demonstrations and strikes radically transformed even the reformist calls of the more moderate elements of the opposition into revolutionary demands for the destruction of the regime. For example, there is little doubt that the demonstrations at Qom in January 1978—which marked the beginning of major revolutionary disturbances—were peaceful, but the police opened fire anyway. The government was no less provocative in its handling of the Tabriz demonstrations in February, when it locked the peaceful mourners out of the mosque (Masjed-e Jom'ah). The callousness of the government toward popular sentiments was no less evident when, in August 1978, in spite of the already explosive political atmosphere and the religious sensitivity, which was at its height during the month of Ramadan, it chose to celebrate the twenty-eighth of Mordad—the date of the Shah's American-supported coup in 1953—by sending its goose-stepping soldiers to parade in Tehran. The date coincided with the tragic fire at Abadan, and while there is no evidence that the Shah's agents were involved, the attitude represented by the parade lent credibility to rumors spread by the opposition that the fire was SAVAK's doing.

In short, the fall of the Shah's regime, and with it the long-standing American role in Iran, was a by-product of what I may call "the Iranian syndrome." At the heart of that syndrome lay the interplay between the Shah's personality traits—and, eventually, physical ailment—and the deep-rooted problems of social, economic, political, psychological, and cultural continuity and change in Iranian society. That interplay shaped the Shah's policies, strategies, methods, and tactics, which significantly contributed to his own ultimate demise. The main thrust of his policies was threefold: (1) obsession with military prowess, (2) "economic modernization," aimed primarily at internal and external political gains, and (3) "political liberalization," used largely as a tactical device to avoid sharing real power with the forces of opposition, moderate or radical, and to ingratiate the regime with the United States.

To the extent that the American approach to Iran reinforced the main thrust of the Shah's policies, it contributed to the fall of the Shah and the collapse of U.S. influence in Iran. First, the Shah's obsession with military power paralleled America's overemphasis on strategic considerations during every administration. The so-called exceptions of the Kennedy and Carter administrations have been exaggerated. True, President Kennedy at first emphasized social and economic change, but he was too quick to praise the Shah for his planned land reforms. True, also, President Carter talked about political liberalization in Iran, but in fact his human-rights policy toward the Shah's regime had more bark than bite. Like the policies of all other American presidents, his was guided mainly by strategic considerations. Second, in the 1960s in particular, American policymakers, with few exceptions, were no less infatuated than Iranian technocrats with the rate of economic growth as the measure of economic development. And third, while the Shah's "political liberalization" was primarily a tactical device of the kind mentioned above, the record shows that at no time did the American interest in democratization of the political process in Iran override strategic considerations. The Carter administration's two-pronged policy of supporting the Shah and at the same time expecting him to liberalize the Iranian political system was a perfect example of this. This obviously contradictory policy was pursued in the naive hope that a despot could be transformed into a democrat. Too often the critics have inveighed against America for failing to understand Ayatollah Khomeini or the forces of opposition. As contrasted with the American lack of understanding of its oldest friend in the Middle East, that failure looks insignificant.

But all told, on balance we could not have saved the Shah from himself, nor Iranian society from the ancient cycles of tragic convulsions—including the current revolutionary upheaval. The Shah wooed, won, but also lost America.

As an epilogue to the basic theme of this essay, I would like to conclude with one essential point: so far the revolutionary regime has not been able to abandon the ancient Iranian habit of exploiting foreign policy as an escape from the problems of domestic society. Superficially, it may appear that the opposite is true. After all, the Iranian Revolution claims to have destroyed Iran's dependence on the United States. The slogan "Neither West nor East" has been accompanied by constant preachment on the value of Iranian self-reliance. Under the Shah, the revolutionary forces claim, Iran lost not only its political but also its economic and cultural independence. The revolutionary self-reliance, therefore, must be comprehensive, total, and irreversible. It must include complete economic self-sufficiency, total political independence, and absolute cultural autonomy.

In practice, however, the revolutionary potential for a positive search for Iranian identity, dignity, and integrity through the creation of a different order has turned into a foreign and domestic witch hunt in an incessant and destructive struggle for power. Just as the Shah's regime used "American partnership" or "special relationship," for example, to escape from the realities of Iranian domestic disunity, of ideological divisions, and of basic structural flaws in the Iranian society, the revolutionary regime is feeding and exploiting anti-American sentiments toward basically the same end. The arm of the "Great Satan" is seen emerging out of every conceivable sleeve. America is seen as being behind every foreign and domestic threat to the revolutionary regime. The Iraqi war against Iran, attempted coups against the regime, acts of terrorism by "counterrevolutionaries," and the Kurdish armed uprising against the regime, to mention only a few examples, are all considered the handiwork of the "Great Satan and its lackeys."

To illustrate the point, those American observers who believe that the revolutionary regime failed to reach a beneficial hostage settlement with the United States do not recognize this broader problem of Iranian political behavior. True, the revolutionary regime did not succeed in forcing America to return the Shah, but that was hardly the sole basic intent of the militant students in seizing the

American Embassy. The taking of American hostages was a supreme example of the continuity of past Iranian behavioral patterns, namely, to manipulate foreign powers or their nationals in domestic struggles for power. The Shah used American friendship and alliance to that end, and the revolutionary regime is using hostility toward America in the same way. The student militants and their sympathizers feared that the Bazargan government and "liberal" Iranians were about to normalize Iran's relations with the United States to thwart the march of Muslim extremists toward total control of the Revolution. The rupture of any kind of normal relations between the United States and Iran as a result of the ensuing hostage crisis in part insured the process of radicalizing the Iranian political process in favor of the Muslim militants.

The exploitation of friendship with, or hostility toward, foreign powers may buy time for basically unstable regimes, but it will not constructively address the basic problems of the society. The resolution of the problems of monarchical legitimacy and authority was not aided by the Shah's manipulation of friendship with the United States. Nor will the management of similar problems now facing the revolutionary regime be helped by the exploitation of hostility toward America. The fundamental difficulty that underpins both approaches is the tendency to escape the responsibility of facing the deep malaise of Iranian society.

II

REVOLUTIONARY

FOREIGN POLICIES

KHOMEINI'S ISLAM IN

IRAN'S FOREIGN POLICY

The "Islamic Republic of Iran" celebrated its third anniversary on April 1, 1982. The Iranian Revolution has gone through three major stages of development in three years and is still evolving. It has been marked by international crises and war with other states, as well as by domestic political chaos, economic paralysis, acts of terrorism, armed insurrection, ethnic insurgency, summary executions, and generally a basic lack of internal cohesion. It has also been marked by a sensational record of governmental changes; revolutionary Iran has had three presidents, four prime ministers, and seven foreign ministers in the span of only three years.

The primary purpose of this essay is to inquire into the influence of Ayatollah Khomeini's Islam on the foreign policy of revolutionary Iran. This study is not intended to be an analysis, or a survey, of Iran's foreign relations since the seizure of power by revolutionary forces. Nor is it intended to be a complete discussion of Khomeini's theory of international politics. Nevertheless, it is intended to provide a preliminary understanding of both. Toward that end, I begin with a brief inquiry into the interaction between revolutionary politics and foreign policy in Iran since the fall of the Shah's regime in 1979.

DOMESTIC POLITICS AND FOREIGN POLICY

The interaction between domestic politics and foreign policy has been intense throughout the three stages of Iran's revolutionary development. The eruption of the revolution itself significantly reflected the effects of that interaction. It was a "twin revolution."[1] The Shah's foreign policy, particularly his American policy, contributed over the decades to the revolutionary process, as did his misguided domestic politics. Revolutionary forces destroyed his regime as much out of a conviction that he was an "American king" as out of one that he was a tyrant monarch.[2]

The first stage of Iran's revolutionary politics began with the seizure of power by the opponents of the Shah's regime (February 11, 1979) and ended with the fall of the provisional Bazargan government (November 6, 1979). It

"Khomeini's Islam in Iran's Foreign Policy" was originally published in Islam in Foreign Policy, ed. Adeed Dawisha (Cambridge: Cambridge University Press, 1983), 9–32, copyright Cambridge University Press, and is reprinted with permission.

was marked by an incessant struggle for power between his largely secular and technocratic government, with what Bazargan called a "gradualist" policy, and the militant Shii clerics and their lay supporters within and outside the Revolutionary Council. At the beginning it appeared that the important understanding of November 5, 1978, reached in Paris between Ayatollah Khomeini, Bazargan, and Sanjabi would provide a basis for the new political order. They had agreed that the revolution embodied both the "national and Islamic movements."[3] Bazargan was appointed prime minister, and Sanjabi foreign minister, but as Bazargan boldly protested, Iran had a "thousand chiefs." Khomeini sacked Sanjabi from two of his ambassadorial appointments, and Yazdi was appointed foreign minister in his place.

Domestic political divisions were reflected in the different approaches of Bazargan and Khomeini to foreign policy. Bazargan was intent on establishing a semblance of an "equal" relationship with the United States, which Khomeini denounced as the "Great Satan." Khomeini did not see why Iran should have any relationship with the United States. He charged that Iran's relationship with the United States was that of a "tyrant" (zalem) with an "oppressed" (mazlum) people, that of a "plunderer" (ghaarat-gar) with a "ravaged victim" (ghaarat-shodeh), and declared, "We don't need America; it is they who need us. They want our oil."[4] Bazargan's foreign minister, Yazdi, as well as the prime minister himself were suspected by leftist extremists of having pro-American sentiments. Yazdi was pressured by right-wing as well as leftist extremists to reverse his decision on receiving Walter Cutler as the new American ambassador in place of William H. Sullivan. The meeting between Bazargan and Yazdi with the American national security adviser, Brzezinski, played into the hands of militant Muslim students led by Hojatoleslam Khoeiniha, who later became the head of the Foreign Affairs Committee of the Majlis (Parliament). They seized the American Embassy on 4 November 1979, forcing the fall of the Bazargan government, which was accused by the student militants of trying, together with other liberals, to invite the Americans and the Israelis into Iran through the back door. The fall of the Bazargan government put an end to any attempt at normalization of Iran's relations with the United States on an equal footing.

The second stage of Iran's revolutionary politics, having thus begun with the fall of the Bazargan government and the onset of the hostage crisis, lasted until the dismissal in June 1981 of Banisadr, who had been elected in January 1980 as the first president of the Republic. Revolutionary politics during most of this period were marked primarily by a power struggle between Banisadr and Ayatollah Beheshti, the leader of the Islamic Republican Party (IRP) and the head of the Supreme Court. With the fall of the Bazargan government, the Revolutionary Council moved to a central power position. Although Banisadr chaired the Council, he was unable to influence its decision significantly; the Council was dominated by hard-line Khomeini supporters. Furthermore, Banisadr, the romantic and, as Iranians dubbed him, "talkative" (Bani-Harf) leader, was not much helped by either his landslide electoral victory or the earlier support of Khomeini. Above all, his failure to establish a political party made him a poor rival of the shrewd and cunning Beheshti, whose IRP focused the power of the Muslim militants against Banisadr and whose friends Rafsanjani and Rajai formed an informal but powerful triumvirate with him against Banisadr. Fundamentalist clerics and their lay supporters, who had presumably helped establish a "purely" Islamic republic, one that was not contaminated by the "democratic" designation that many had unsuccessfully demanded and which had shaped a constitution that accorded the faqih ("jurisprudent") the leadership of the Republic during the first phase of the Revolution, now established their control through the IRP over the newly elected Majlis.

Banisadr's power struggle with the Beheshti-Rafsanjani-Rajai triumvirate increasingly estranged him from the Muslim fundamentalists. Even his attempted exploitation of Iran's setbacks in the war with Iraq, which he blamed on his opponents, failed to make up for his ineffective leadership. Banisadr's power rivalry with Muslim fundamentalists and their political arm, the IRP, focused at this particular time on an open clash with Prime Minister Rajai, whose appointment had been practically forced on Banisadr. The president and the prime minister attacked each other over a wide variety of issues, including the conduct of the Iran-Iraq War, the hostage crisis, and the appointment of several Cabinet members, especially the foreign minister.

The disturbances at the University of Tehran on March 5, 1981, marked the beginning of the end for Banisadr. The scuffles, assaults, hearings, and knifings between the supporters of Banisadr and Rajai[5] played into the hands of the Muslim militants. They castigated Banisadr and tried to pressure Khomeini to strip him of his position as the commander in chief of the armed forces. Although Khomeini confirmed Banisadr in this position, he appointed a three-man committee to pass judgment on Banisadr's conduct. Meanwhile, his opponents joined in a chorus of denunciation of the beleaguered president. Rajai's minister of state for executive affairs, Behzad Nabavi, for example, accused Banisadr of being involved in a movement to weaken and overthrow the Rajai government; Ayatollah Sadeq Khalkhali urged the Majlis to try and dismiss him on the ground that he had "committed treason against constitutional law"; and 130 judges and prosecutors from all over the country sent a letter to Khomeini asking him to deliver a judgment on Banisadr's behavior, which they claimed had created national disunity. The handwriting was on the wall. The story of Bazargan was repeated. Muslim militants once again managed to outmaneuver their relatively moderate opponents. On June 10, Banisadr was stripped of his post as commander in chief of the Iranian armed forces. While in hiding, he was also dismissed as president on June 22, 1981.

The domestic power struggle and its resolution in favor of right-wing Muslim militants in the second stage, as in the first stage, were also reflected in the overall direction of the Republic's foreign policy. The taking of American hostages, which had brought down the Bazargan government and terminated its attempted policy of normalization of relations with the United States, was now used by the right-wing Muslim militants to consolidate their power and foil any attempt by the United States to forge a new relationship with Iran. The hostage crisis, to use Behzad Nabavi's characterization, had been squeezed dry like an orange and had to be finally discarded once it was no longer useful. Muslim militants held the hostages, while Banisadr unsuccessfully pressed for their release, and once the Muslim militants decided to release them, Banisadr opposed the terms of the hostage settlement. The decision to release the hostages was actually reached before the outbreak of war between Iran and Iraq, as evidenced by the Iranian initiative to approach American officials secretly in Germany before the four-point proposal of Khomeini was declared in his message to the pilgrims to Mecca on September 12, 1980. The Iranians told the Americans in advance to anticipate the Khomeini proposal as a means of indicating to the skeptical American officials that the Iranians meant business this time.[6] The Iran-Iraq War and the prospects of a hard-line position by the United States in the event of the success of Ronald Reagan's candidacy no doubt added impetus to the settlement of the crisis, but they did not cause the Khomeini decision to release the American hostages. That decision was influenced primarily by the felt impact of the Western economic sanctions and the success of the Muslim militants in capturing the seats of power by September 1980.

The prolonged hostage crisis did more than destroy the prospects of normalization of Iran's relations with the United States; it isolated Iran in the international system in general and estranged it from the West in particular. The unanimous Provisional Order (November 29, 1979) and the Judgment (May 15, 1980) of the International Court of Justice; the Security Council's Resolution 457 (December 4, 1979) and Resolution 461 (December 31, 1979); and the resolutions of the Organization of the Islamic Conference in January and May 1980, for example, all disapproved the taking of the American hostages and called for their release. The estrangement of Iran from the United States was intensified as a result of American economic and diplomatic sanctions against Iran. President Carter's imposition of a ban on U.S. imports of Iranian oil on November 12, 1979, and of a freeze on $8 billion of Iranian assets were subsequently followed by such other measures as the American break in diplomatic relations with Iran; the ban on all American exports to Iran, except food and medicine; and the ban on all American imports from Iran.

The Western European decision to impose phased economic and diplomatic sanctions against Iran on April 22, 1980, was, to be sure, half-hearted. The European countries and Britain had larger stakes in Iran as compared with the United States, but the fact still remains that their symbolic actions antagonized Iran. Even the failed American rescue mission on April 24, 1980, which was denounced by most states, failed to engender any real or durable sympathy for Iran. For example, after the Iraqi invasion of Iran on September 22, 1980, there was a clear reluctance on the part of many states, both within and outside the United Nations, to contemplate any serious action against Iraq.

Besides the fall of President Banisadr, the bombings that killed first Beheshti and seventy other IRP leaders in June 1981 and then President Rajai and Prime Minister Bahonar in August 1981, marked the start of the third phase of the Iranian Revolution. The so-called alliance between Banisadr and Rajavi, the leader of the Mujahadeen, in exile in France, has been paralleled by continuous acts of terrorism against the Khomeini regime. The regime's countermeasures have included mass arrests, imprisonment, torture, and executions of many thousands of members of the Mujahadeen organization, their sympathizers, and others suspected of counterrevolutionary activities. There is little doubt that in this violent political process innocent people have also been the victims of terrorist and counterterrorist acts. My own young niece was suspected as a counterrevolutionary and executed in 1981. Furthermore, this latest and most violent phase of the Iranian Revolution has far-reaching implications for domestic policies and foreign policy.

On the domestic level, two implications in particular deserve brief mention. First, the acts of assassination by the opponents of the regime have taken a heavy toll among the more moderate IRP leaders. The new leadership, as a result, is perceived to be more anti-Western. Since October 1981 Hojatoleslam Sayyid Ali Khamenei—formerly the imam of the Friday prayers in Tehran and the victim of an attempted assassination—has been Iran's president.[7] He is reputedly a Turkish-speaking hard-line cleric who is supported by other hard-line anti-Western elements both within and outside the IRP. Second, despite the decimation of IRP leaders, the supporters of Khomeini have continued to consolidate their power. As a matter of fact, a year after the bombing of the IRP headquarters, and despite other acts of terrorism against its leaders ever since, the Khomeini regime appears to have tightened its control on the reins of power. Events have so far disproved the forecasts by its opponents of the regime's imminent demise.

On the international level, the ability of the Khomeini regime to implement

Iran's foreign policy appears to have increased. The regime seems determined to break away from its isolation in international politics that followed the taking of American hostages. It has stepped up its ties with a wide variety of countries, largely by using its oil in barter deals with such Third World countries as Syria, Turkey, Pakistan, North Korea, India, and others. It has expanded its transit, trade, and economic ties with the Soviet Union despite continued political, ideological, and other differences. Above all, the consolidation of power domestically increased the capacity of the regime to successfully defend Iran against Iraq until Tehran blundered into the invasion of Iraq on July 13, 1982. The first real break in the stalemated war in favor of Iran occurred in September 1981, only a few months after the fall of Banisadr. Subsequently, successful Iranian offensives led to the expulsion of the bulk of the Iraqi troops and the recovery of Khorramshahr. Iran's conduct of the war was greatly aided by Khomeini's effective use of Islamic symbols as long as Iran appeared to wage a defensive war against the Iraqi invaders on its own territory, but once Iran repeated the blunder of Iraq by deciding to invade, Khomeini's use of Islamic symbols failed to make up for logistical and other pragmatic problems facing the revolutionary regime.

PROLIFERATION OF IDEOLOGICAL CONFLICTS

Interaction between Iranian domestic politics and foreign policy during all three stages of the Iranian Revolution outlined above has invariably contained ideological factors. The struggles for power between Bazargan and the Muslim fundamentalists in the first stage, between them and Banisadr in the second stage, and between them and the Mujahadeen in the third stage have all included ideological conflicts of various kinds and degrees of intensity: Khomeini's fundamentalist Islam clashed first with Bazargan's liberal interpretation of Islam in the first stage, then with Banisadr's socialist Islam in the second stage, and finally with Rajavi's Marxist Islam in the third stage.

This portrayal, however, reveals only the clash of ideologies between predominant political actors and their supporters. In every stage of the Iranian Revolution other ideological conflicts have also prevailed. Khomeini's interpretation of Islam, for example, has been challenged by the secular liberal democratic ideology of the National Front, by the social democratic ideology of the National Democratic Front, by the Marxist-Leninist ideology of the Fedayan-e Khalq, by the communist ideology of the Tudeh Party, and by the ideologies of myriad other disparate groups and individuals who banded together under the leadership of Khomeini in their common opposition to the Shah's regime but have split up since its fall.

Ideological conflicts exist even among the present supporters of Khomeini both within and outside the IRP. The most prominent example is the division between the *Maktabi* and *Hojati* clerics. Both schools of thought believe in the establishment of a political order shaped by Islam, but the Maktabi school of thought believes in the choice of a single man to succeed Khomeini as the *faqih*, while the Hojati school of thought envisages a collegiate group—not just one man—to exercise religious leadership and leave government in secular, not exclusively religious, hands.[8]

Diversity in ideological perspectives, both religious and secular, is reflected in ideas regarding the shape not only of the polity but also of foreign policy. For example, with respect to the hostage crisis, Khomeini declared: "This is not a struggle between the United States and Iran; it is a struggle between Islam and blasphemy," while Banisadr viewed it as a struggle for Iran's political independence. He considered the taking of hostages as contrary to the law of nations and wished to settle the matter through the United Nations, which Khomeini decried as an instrument of American foreign policy. To cite another example, the current ideological perspectives of the Maktabi and Hojati schools of thought have different foreign-policy implications. The Maktabis believe in the export of the "Islamic Revolution" as a prime goal, while the Hojatis do not. The Maktabi school of thought is, of course, closer to Khomeini's Islam. Rajai made the Maktabi orientation the supreme test of qualification for holding posts in government; merit was only a secondary test.

Granted all these and other ideological differences, we should now turn to Khomeini's Islam and Iran's revolutionary foreign policy. Despite the challenge of all other ideologies, his interpretation of Islam has so far prevailed. This essay, therefore, will first examine his worldview and then consider its practical effects on the conduct of Iran's foreign policy. In attempting the latter, analytical difficulties involved will be pointed out, and three major issues in particular will be closely examined.

KHOMEINI'S WORLDVIEW

Compared with his political thought, Khomeini's world outlook has been remarkably consistent over the decades. There are some observers who seem to have read their own predispositions into Khomeini's view of the desirable political order. One observer, for example, seems to read Khomeini's rejection of the monarchy in the late 1960s and early 1970s into his early criticism of Reza Shah's rule.[9] But my own comparison of Khomeini's political thought during World War II with his view of "Islamic government" (*Hokomat-e Islami*) in the early 1970s reveals that earlier he seemed to accept the idea of limited monarchy but that he rejected it altogether after his long exile in Iraq. He did not at first reject the constitution of 1906–7, which included the institution of monarchy. Rather, in his *Kashf-e Assrar* (Discovery of secrets), published in 1944, he demanded the implementation of the constitutional provision for clerical supervision of all laws enacted by the Majlis.[10]

In any event, compared with his political thought, Khomeini's ideas about the international system have undergone little change. They deserve closer attention than they have received so far. Given the limited scope of this essay, however, only four major aspects of Khomeini's world outlook will be analyzed. The related outlooks of other leaders of the republic will also be examined as a means of showing how Khomeini's precepts and guidance are interpreted by those who use them in practice.

First, Khomeini has consistently rejected the contemporary international system. Given his world outlook, he would find the Westphalia conception of the nation-state and the international system to be flawed. The earliest indication of this strong view is found in his *Kashf-e Assrar*, in which he stated categorically that modern states "are the products of man's limited ideas," and the world is "the home of all the masses of people under the law of God."[11] Populism, millenarianism, Shiism, and revolutionism converge in Khomeini's world outlook. For example, in a statement to Iranian students abroad, he declared:

> Iran's Islamic Revolution, with the support of the gracious Almighty, is spreading on a worldwide scale and, God willing, with its spread the satanical powers will be dragged into isolation and governments of the meek will be established; the way will be opened for the world government of the imam Mahdi [Twelfth Imam], may the exalted God hasten his noble advent and may our lives be sacrificed to the dust of his path.[12]

As applied to revolutionary Iranian foreign policy, the satanical powers are the enemies of Islamic Iran, and the governments of the meek are its true friends. For example, in a meeting with the Lebanese Shii Amal delegation, he said:

> Even if America and Israel were to shout: "There is no god but God," we would not accept it from them, because they wish to deceive us. . . . Do you expect us to be indifferent to America and Israel and the other superpowers that wish to swallow the region? We will not agree to be dominated by America or by the Soviet Union. We are Muslims and wish to live. We want that kind of progress and civilization which would make us reach our hands out to aliens. We want that civilization which is based upon honor and humanity and which would preserve peace upon this basis. The superpowers wish to dominate human beings. We, you and any other Muslim, are duty-bound to remain steadfast against them, not to compromise with them and to reject

plans such as those of As-Sadat and Fahd. It is our duty to condemn these plans which are not in the interest of the oppressed people.[13]

Second, Khomeini's world outlook calls for Islamic universalism. The passages quoted above include this notion, but, it should be emphasized, Khomeini advocates neither pan-Shiism nor pan-Islamism; he calls for the establishment of Islam throughout the world. In the words of Mir-Hossein Mousavi, Iran's former foreign minister and present prime minister, the ultimate goal of Iran's foreign policy is the "liberation of mankind." The context of his statement is important. As Iran's foreign minister, he told the CBS television network:

> The fact is that values have been greatly transformed in Iran and new values have been presented to our society. Correct understanding of the values will show that our nation regards recent events in Iran as salutary, not that our nation is fond of killing. Rather they regard this as a prerequisite to the liberation of mankind in the region and those struggles will continue until the region and the world are rebuilt upon new foundations. . . . All over the world, today, Islam is reviving. What is being formed in the Islamic world now is the return to an Islamic human identity and the Islamic Revolution of Iran is a prerequisite for the transformation of the Islamic countries and the world.[14]

Khomeini's Islamic universalism is sometimes portrayed by his supporters as what is in fact expected of Iran by other Muslim people. For example, one revolutionary reporter claims that during the Hajj rituals, when he met with people of all nationalities and politico-religious personalities from different countries, he learned that "now people expect everything from Iran alone." He then adds that "what is to be said is that the Moslem nation of Iran has risen for the obliteration of tyranny throughout the world and will not seize [sic] its struggle until a global Islamic government is established."[15]

Third, it is more than implicit in Khomeini's own world outlook as well as those of his supporters that Iran is considered uniquely qualified to exert worldwide leadership for the realization of the ultimate goal of the establishment of an Islamic world order. In his own words, "Islam is a sacred trust from God to ourselves and the Iranian nation must grow in power and resolution until it has vouchsafed Islam to the entire world." Khomeini's disciples consider the Iranian leadership as a divine obligation; they also point to the uniqueness of the present form of government in Iran as the special leadership qualification that Iran alone enjoys as compared with all the nations of the world. Only in Iran is the *faqih* the head of the state, and presumably this feature of the Islamic Republic of Iran entitles the followers of Khomeini to expect that other

Muslim-populated states should emulate the same form of Islamic govern-ment. For example, one Khomeini disciple states:

> Today if we want the establishment of Mohammad's Islam, we should en-trust the political leadership of our societies and countries to one who is also a religious leader. And this magnificent fact has only come to reality in the Islamic country of Iran, where Imam Khomeini, as a person who studied Islam for 70 years as the religious Marj'a and the religious leader of the Mus-lims, accepted responsibility for political leadership and for the formation of the Islamic Government, as well as the post of Commander in Chief of the Armed Forces.[16]

Fourth, given the universalist, populist, and millenarian features of Kho-meini's world outlook, the important leadership role of Iran for the export of the Islamic Revolution to the rest of the world becomes self-evident. In a major speech to the Iranian people on the occasion of the Iranian New Year in 1980, Khomeini declared unequivocally:

> We should try hard to export our Revolution to the world. We should set aside the thought that we do not export our Revolution, because Islam does not regard Islamic countries differently and is the supporter of all the op-pressed peoples of the world. On the other hand, all the superpowers and all the powers have risen to destroy us. If we remain in an enclosed environ-ment we shall definitely face defeat.[17]

An important practical question about such an advocacy is how the Islamic Revolution is supposed to be exported. This question has been of great concern to the leaders of most states of the Middle East, especially the Gulf states, as we shall see. At this point, however, it is necessary to consider what policy guide-lines, if any, are provided by the Iranian leaders themselves for the export of the Islamic Revolution. The best way to start is with Khomeini himself. For exam-ple, he told a group of young Iranians going abroad:

> Today we need to strengthen and export Islam everywhere. You need to ex-port Islam to other places, and the same version of Islam which is currently in power in our country. Our way of exporting Islam is through the youth, who go to other countries where a large number of people come to see you and your achievements. You must behave in such a way that these large gath-erings are attracted to Islam by your action. Your deeds, your action, and your behavior should be an example; and through you the Islamic Republic will go to other places, God Willing.[18]

Iranian leaders have taken pains to stress to Iranian foreign-service personnel on numerous occasions that the export of the Islamic Revolution must be accomplished by example and propaganda. For example, Khomeini told a group of ambassadors and chargés d'affaires who had been recalled to Tehran for consultation:

> It does not take swords to export this ideology. The export of ideas by force is not export. We shall have exported Islam only when we have helped Islam and Islamic ethics grow in those countries. This is your responsibility and it is a task which you must fulfill. You should promote this idea by adopting conduct conducive to the propagation of Islam and by publishing the necessary publications in your countries of assignment. This is a must. You must have publications. You must publish journals. Such journals should be promotive and their contents and pictures should be consistent with the Islamic Republic, so that by proper publicity campaigns you may pave the way for the spread of Islam in those areas.[19]

The theme that the export of the Islamic Revolution must be effected by the example of Islamic behavior of Iranians abroad in general and of Iranian diplomats in particular has been taken up by other Iranian leaders as well. For example, Hojatoleslam Ali Khamenei,[20] the president of the republic, stated that the Iranian Foreign Ministry's officials abroad are the apostles of the revolution. The nature of an official dispatched abroad by a government demonstrates the nature of his government. If our diplomatic representative in all his dealings, including with people and government officials of the country to which he is dispatched, adopts an Islamic approach, then he will be utilizing the best method to demonstrate the role of the Islamic Republic of Iran.[21]

Theoretically, subversion as well as armed aggression for exporting the Islamic Revolution seems to be ruled out by Iranian leaders. For example, Mir-Hossein Mousavi asserts, "We have declared time and again that we have no intention of interfering in other countries' internal affairs, but what is shaking the Islamic world is a movement springing from this revolution among the Moslem masses of the world and, naturally, each people will shape their movement according to their own peculiar circumstances. They will force their governments to tread this path and, if not, naturally they will be confronted by the peoples' moves."[22]

KHOMEINI'S ISLAMIC WORLD ORDER
AND IRANIAN FOREIGN POLICY

The effects of ideological influences on the foreign policy of any state present formidable intellectual and methodological challenges, let alone in the foreign policy of a country like Iran, which is caught in the pangs of a revolution. For example, Soviet specialists debate inconclusively the relative weight of communism and the legacy of Russian imperialism in the foreign policy of the Soviet Union. The debate on the relative importance of democratic ideals and pragmatic considerations has never ceased among specialists on American foreign policy either. Former President Carter's human-rights crusade, for example, is still faulted by some observers for the failure of American policy, including the Carter administration's policy toward Iran before, during, and after the seizure of power by revolutionary forces.

Examination of the role of Khomeini's Islamic world order in Iran's foreign policy presents its own particular problems. Two of these must be faced at the outset. First, it is not always possible to say what pronouncements, decisions, and courses of action in foreign affairs unambiguously represent the official policy of the revolutionary regime. For example, in 1979 a cleric's renewal of the Iranian claim of sovereignty to Bahrain aroused a deep and widespread sense of outrage not only in Bahrain but in all other Arab states of the Gulf region. In response, however, Foreign Minister Yazdi and other Iranian officials joined in a chorus of denials. They denied that Ayatollah Ruhani's threats, to the effect that Iran would annex Bahrain unless its rulers adopted an Islamic political order, represented the official position of Iran.

Second, the same revolutionary disarray that underpins the official-unofficial division just mentioned creates another problem that also complicates analysis, namely, the problem of the administration of Iranian forcign policy. The Shah's Ministry of Foreign Affairs, like his military and other institutions, is undergoing drastic changes as a result of repeated purges, resignations, and exile. Furthermore, revolutionary leaders want to overhaul both the ministry and the Iranian diplomatic mission abroad in keeping with the emerging ideological tenets, direction, and priorities of the Islamic Republic. According to former foreign minister Mousavi, for example, the Iranian Foreign Ministry "is disorganized . . . it seems the various units are not working in harmony." It is thus crucial "to create a united and coordinated organization inside the ministry, by making use of devoted people, specialists and others devoted and faithful to the revolution." This and other organizational changes envisaged will include the creation of a committee or a unit that "will determine the basis of the foreign policy from an ideological perspective, and the principle of rule of theocracy."[23]

Despite such general statements about the changing nature of Iran's revolutionary foreign policy, it is still too early to speak with certainty about what it will mean in practice. For example, various Iranian foreign ministers, including the present foreign minister, Ali Akbar Velayati, have said that in establishing relations with other states Iran accords the highest priority to Muslim states, followed by other Third World states and then others. Meanwhile, the present Iranian president, Ali Khamenei, states: "We have divided the world into groups—brotherly countries, friendly countries, neutral countries, and enemy countries. Enemies are governments which launch aggression against us and have an anti-Iranian posture. The rest are either brothers, friends or neutral."[24] Are these revolutionary leaders talking about the same ideas regarding Iran's foreign-policy priorities? It is difficult to say.

In light of the ideological stance of Iranian leaders discussed above, and of their pronouncements, however, the main guiding principles for the conduct of Iranian foreign policy seem to include at the present time: (1) rejection of dependency on either the West or the East; (2) identification of the United States as the principal enemy (doshman-e asli) of the Islamic Revolution; (3) struggle against superpowers and the Zionist power; (4) close relations with all oppressed peoples, especially those in Muslim countries; (5) liberation of Jerusalem and opposition to pro-Israel states; (6) anti-imperialism; and (7) support everywhere for oppressed people (mustaz'afeen). These "principles" represent a total break with those that guided the foreign policy of the Shah's regime. For example, for the first three principles listed above one could easily substitute: (1) reliance on the West, especially the United States, as a means of maintaining the Shah's regime and the territorial integrity and political independence of Iran; (2) identification of the Soviet Union and communism as the main sources of threat; and (3) friendship with pro-Western and anti-Soviet states.[25]

Revolutionary leaders take pains to emphasize a total break not only with the principles and priorities of the Shah's foreign policy but also with those of the former nationalist leader Dr. Muhammad Mosaddegh. Nowhere does this appear more clearly than in their insistence that their overriding principle, "Neither West nor East," is not only a question of negative balance. In other words, they reject the central principle of Mosaddegh's foreign policy, that is, "negative equilibrium" (movazeneh-ye manfi). For example, Mir-Hossein Mousavi says that the slogan "Neither West nor East" should also include the phrase "Islamic Republic," denoting that the people of Iran will not, under any circumstances, allow Iran to slip toward the East or the West. Furthermore, they "want to establish a new system of values, independent of East and West in their own country; to expand it and under the all-round cover of this new system of values—which stems from ideology, Islam—to continue their own way; organize their lives; organize their relations with other countries, nations and liberation movements."[26]

The central analytical difficulty in specifying the weight of Islamic influence in the formulation and execution of Iran's revolutionary foreign policy is not helped by examining Iran's actual practice any more than by analyzing the policy statements of its leaders. The principal reasons for this are two. First, the unreliability and contradictory nature of the available data. Second, the fact that few, if any, decisions, commitments, or courses of action can be said to reflect, purely or predominantly, the influence of Khomeini's Islamic ideology. Even the Iranian policymakers themselves admit that the overriding principle of Neither West nor East only in part reflects the influence of their Islamic ideology; it also derives, they say, from Iran's own unhappy historical experience with the hegemonic policies of the superpowers. Because of this mixture of ideological with non-ideological foreign considerations in Iran's foreign policy, observers may alternatively emphasize pragmatic or ideological influences in Iran's foreign-policy behavior.

A few examples will suffice. It may well be argued that the Iranian decision to settle the hostage crisis was made purely for political and economic or other pragmatic reasons. Ideologically it should have been unacceptable for Muslim leaders to compromise with the "Great Satan." Examples of the controlling effect of pragmatic considerations may be easily cited for other Iranian actions as well. In order to advertise its success Iran did not hesitate to invite the ideologically distasteful "imperialist media and purveyors of Satanic untruth" to visit Iran's war front after the March offensive. Nor did Iran hesitate to charge that the Muslim Brothers who rebelled in Hama and paid with their lives were the agents of Iraq and Zionism. It was expedient to maintain friendship with Syria, the enemy of Iran's enemy, Iraq. Despite vehement denials, there is evidence of Iranian oil sales to the Great Satan (the United States), arranged through a Geneva-based trading company named Gatoil International.[27] Also, despite Iran's ferocious denials, Israeli arms have indirectly arrived in Iran. But any such judgments about the influence of pragmatic considerations on Iran's foreign policy must be balanced against a different interpretation that would emphasize ideological considerations.

Now, it may well be argued that the compromise with the Great Satan over the hostage crisis was a lesser evil than the weakening of the Islamic Revolution that would have resulted from dragging out a crisis that was no longer useful to the Islamic Republic. The indirect oil sale to the United States and roundabout military purchases from Israel, one may argue, were justified by the higher good of defending the interests of Dar al-Islam (the Abode of Islam).

Granted all these and other analytical difficulties, the influence of Islam with respect to several other issue areas deserves closer attention. Three of these issues will be discussed below.

The Gulf War. No matter what personal, historical, racial, political, legal, and other factors are influential in the war between Iraq and Iran, the influence of Khomeini's Islam has been manifest in a variety of ways. First, the universalistic, millenarian, legitimistic, and populist Islamic Revolution was perceived before the war in Baghdad as posing a major threat to the secular Ba'athist ideology and the regime of Saddam Hussein. The Iraqi Revolution did not enjoy, the Iranians claimed, any popular support comparable to that of the Iranian Revolution. Furthermore, the Ba'athist ideology did not possess the same legitimacy as did the Islamic ideology; the authentic indigenous Islam challenged the imported ideas of nationalism and socialism that underpinned the Ba'athist secular ideology, and thus it was inevitable that the Ba'athist regime would be provoked. Saddam Hussein, for example, rejected in an interview with *Al-Mustaqbal* the charge that the Ba'athist ideology was a foreign product. He then claimed that the "Arab Revolution" has the task of effecting "qualitative change in the society in all fields." It also has the task of placing the Arab nation in a position in which it can defend and reconstruct itself, and achieve justice. This is an Arab revolution whose formula is not the same as a religious one; it derives "its central value from its history," and Hussein added that "the Islamic Revolution and any other revolution should be friendly to the Arab Revolution; and any revolution calling itself Islamic should not contradict the Arab Revolution, otherwise it would not be Islamic at all."[28]

Second, Khomeini's Islam has had more than an influence on the outbreak of the war. Ever since Iraq launched its "all-out war" (*harb al-shameleh*) against Iran on 22 September 1980, the Islamic ideology has been a major instrument of military mobilization for the conduct of the war. The decimated and demoralized Iranian armed forces were called on to defend Islam against "Shah Husayn," or Yazid. Islam has also been a ferocious motivating force for the Muslim masses, which form the backbone of the regular and especially the irregular forces. Soldiers of the Revolutionary Guard Corps (Pasdaran) and the Mobilization Force (Basij) are known to be among the youngest and most devoted disciples of Khomeini. Some Basij recruits threw their bodies on minefields to clear the way for the forward march of Iranian forces against the Iraqi troops. After the first successful Iranian thrust in the Shush-Dezful area in March 1982, Khomeini told both these revolutionary forces and the regular forces:

> Our Revolutionary Guards Corps and the Mobilization Force had just been formed from the people and had just been armed with rifles, not having had proper military education and not having proper warfare machinery at their disposal, and with all the signs of weakness apparent in them. Only their faith in God, love of martyrdom for Islam and a spirit of self-sacrifice as-

sisted them in this unequal war. . . . If the army and other armed forces did not enjoy the spiritual divine assistance, how otherwise could this extraordinary affair (miraculous victory) be explained?[29]

Third, Iran's hard-line negotiating stance during the war has been consistently rationalized in terms of Islam as expounded by Khomeini instead of the Charter of the United Nations. In insisting on the withdrawal of Iraqi troops from Iranian territory as the prerequisite for peace negotiations, Iranian leaders invoke Quranic precepts. For example, Khomeini admonishes the representatives of the Organization of the Islamic Conference, who are trying to obtain a cease-fire between the belligerent countries:

> As for the other Islamic countries that also claim to adhere to it [the Quran], whose peoples accept the Qur'an, they should gather here. They should send their representatives. We shall then open the Qur'an, the Al-Jujurat verse, and read only one paragraph of this verse. They ought to come and comply with this verse. This verse tells how two Muslim tribes engaged in war should be treated. It says that if one tribe invades the other then all others are obliged to defend the latter in war, until they obey God. Once they obey God, then make peace with them.[30]

Fourth, and paradoxically, Islamic ideology has been invoked in rationalizing both Iran's defense against and its invasion of Iraq. Since in Khomeini's ideology there is a universal Islamic society, in which international frontiers are presumably of secondary importance, once an aggression against Islam is committed, its defense cannot be stopped at the boundaries of the territorial state. After Iran's first major and successful counteroffensive, in March 1982, Khomeini seemed to promise that Iran would not carry the war into Iraq, but it did despite the fact that Khomeini had declared: "Today Iran is still bound by what it said at the outset: we have no intention of fighting against any country, Islamic or non-Islamic. We desire peace and amity among all; to date we have engaged only in self-defense which is a divine duty and human right enjoined upon all. We have never had an intention of committing aggression against other countries."[31]

Gulf Security. Another major issue area where the influence of Islamic ideology has been at work is the security of the Persian Gulf region. Raymond Aron observes that a small power restricts its ambitions to physical survival and the preservation of its legal independence, while a great power acts to achieve an ill-defined purpose that he calls "the maintenance or creation of a favorable international environment." This author has added that a medium power acts to create and maintain a favorable regional environment while aspiring to global political political stature, a proposition that has been demonstrated in the case of pre-revolutionary Iran.[32] Has the revolution destroyed its validity? Not really, except that Iran, like all revolutionary regimes, big and small, acts to make both the regional and the global environment hospitable to its ideology as well as favorable to its position of power. The Shah's regime acted to make the Persian Gulf region safe for his regime and the Pahlavi dynasty by alliance with the West, particularly the United States. The revolutionary regime acts to make the region safe for its Islamic ideology and its own survival by militantly espousing a policy of nonalignment.

This policy is rationalized in terms of Islamic self-reliance as expounded by Khomeini. His Islam is perceived as a threat not only by Iraq but also by all other Gulf states. As seen in the case of Iraq, it is perceived as a challenge to the secular Ba'athist ideology and regime, but in the other Gulf states it is perceived as a menace to their security and stability partly because in Khomeini's Islam there is no room for monarchical systems. Furthermore, Iran's militant non-alignment policy runs counter to the close ties that exist between conservative Gulf states and the United States. Saudi Arabia is regarded as the arch-agent of the Great Satan, whose Gulf policy is condemned in every respect, including massive arms sales, military facilities in Oman, American operation of AWACS aircraft in Saudi Arabia, the Western naval presence near the Strait of Hormuz, the Rapid Deployment Force, and so on.

As seen, Khomeini advocates the export of the Islamic Revolution as a means of promoting the idea of establishing the rule of God on earth everywhere. "If we remain in an enclosed environment we shall definitely face defeat," he says. And no environment is closer to his Islamic revolutionary abode than the Gulf region. As we have also seen, he instructs his followers that the way to export his revolution is not by the use of the sword but by propaganda and other non-military means. Nevertheless, this has proved unsettling to all conservative Gulf states, where Khomeini's peaceful means are perceived as threatening their internal stability and external security.

The best example of Khomeini's interpretation of Islam being used for making the Gulf region favorable to his revolution is the dispute between him and King Khalid of Saudi Arabia over the behavior of Iranian pilgrims to Mecca. The incident broke out amid growing recriminations between Saudi Arabia and Iran. The facts of the case are difficult to ascertain. Suffice it to say that Iranian pilgrims engaged in political demonstrations against the United States and Israel while carrying portraits of Khomeini. The embittered relations between Riyadh and Tehran finally prompted King Khalid to write to Ayatollah Khomeini on October 10, 1981, to the effect that some of the Iranian pilgrims had indulged "in activities in your name which not only were contrary to your aims but were also contrary to the aims of pilgrimage and the honor of holy places." These pilgrims, the king continued, shouted slogans and demonstrated in the holy precincts, actions that "disturbed and disgusted other pilgrims to the holy house of God and no doubt this action will damage Iran's credibility and prestige."[33]

In his long, stern reply of the same date, Khomeini took exception to the king's view. He argued dogmatically that the purpose of pilgrimage was not religious worship alone. He contended that pilgrimage under all prophets, especially the prophet of Islam, had been "completely linked to politics," the separation of which was the idea of the superpowers. He charged that the king had received a "distorted version and false reports" of the incident, and he admonished the king that if his government made use of "the religiopolitical" ceremony of Hajj, "it would have no need of America, AWACS planes. . . . We know that America has put these planes at the disposal of Saudi Arabia so that America can make use of them in its own interests and in the interests of Israel."[34]

Saudi-Iranian tensions reached a new peak about a month after this exchange between the two Gulf leaders. Iran was accused of having armed and trained a large group of Shii Muslims to carry out a plot in Bahrain. Most members of the group were primarily from Bahrain, and few were from Saudi Arabia. No Iranian national was involved. The group, seventy-four strong, apparently belonged to the "Islamic Front for the Liberation of Bahrain," with its headquarters in Tehran. Significantly, about 35 percent of the group were students, and about 17 percent were unemployed persons.[35] One wonders how effective Khomeini's export of the Islamic Revolution could ever be without such adverse indigenous human conditions within the Gulf states themselves.

The crisis precipitated feverish security arrangements among the Gulf Arab states on various bilateral levels. Furthermore, the emphasis of the members of the newly established Gulf Cooperation Council (GCC) shifted from economic matters to security concerns. The tension between Riyadh and Tehran was intensified. The Saudis signed a security cooperation agreement with Bahrain during a visit there by the Saudi interior minister, Prince Nayif. He asserted that the Iranians had said at the beginning of their revolution that they would not act as the Gulf's policeman; they have now become, he said, "the Gulf's terrorists."[36]

Afghanistan Settlement. With respect to no other foreign-policy issue discussed so far has the influence of Khomeini's Islam been so clearly visible as in the case of Afghanistan. The Soviet invasion has been consistently condemned by Iranian revolutionary leaders; the Marxist puppet regime is viewed with utter contempt; the Afghan Mujahadeen are hailed; and nearly a million Afghan refugees are sheltered in Iran. To be sure, as with respect to the other issues already discussed, the Iranian policy toward Afghanistan is shaped by geographic proximity, historical experience, cultural and religious affinity, as well as Khomeini's ideological stance. But the Iranian position in the case of Afghanistan is the best example of how far the Iranian revolutionary regime is inclined to go on pushing to create a favorable Islamic environment around Iran. In effect, Iran wants to replace the Marxist regime in Kabul with an Islamic government that is significantly modeled on the Iranian one.

The best evidence for this is the Iranian proposal for the solution of the crisis in Afghanistan. On November 10, 1981, the Iranian deputy foreign minister, Ahmad 'Azizi, unveiled an "Islamic solution," admitting clearly that it was "based on the revolutionary experience" of Iran. As a backdrop to announcing the Iranian plan, he denounced numerous plans issued by various international organizations and by governments. "In the opinion of the Government of the Islamic Republic of Iran," he asserted, "most of these plans have been designed to allow European and U.S. forces to intervene in the region." Instead, Iran proposed a plan guided by two principles. These were: (1) unconditional Soviet withdrawal from Afghanistan; and (2) recognition of the right of the Afghan people to decide "their political fate."[37]

The five-point plan, however, amounted in effect to a scheme for the establishment of an Islamic state and government. Although the plan envisaged nationwide elections of the members of a constituent assembly that would draw up a constitution and define the type of government Afghanistan wanted, an Islamic council composed of thirty Muslim clergy was given such vast legislative and executive powers during the transition period that, for all practical purposes, it would be able to determine the outcome of the elections. An assembly and a government would emerge that would definitely be dominated by the clerics, or at least by their close associates. The Iranian experience is indeed pertinent. The Iranian Revolutionary Council ensured during Iran's transition period that the clerics and their associates would rule. Why could not the same be repeated in Afghanistan? The plan proposed a peacekeeping force made up of forces from Iran, Pakistan, and another Muslim country. This force would replace the Soviet troops during a transition period, until Afghanistan, like Iran, was transformed into a theocratic Muslim state.

GENERAL OBSERVATIONS

To sum up, the fluidity, complexity, and confusion of the state of the Iranian Revolution make it impossible to end this study with any customary set of conclusions. There are none. But a number of tentative propositions may be derived from the foregoing discussions.

First, the prolonged revolutionary instability and lack of domestic cohesion over the past three years have at every stage been reflected in Iran's foreign policy. As a result, no stable foreign policy has emerged, although since the settlement of the hostage crisis and the ousting of Banisadr, the regime's domestic capacity for activity in the external environment seems to have increased relative to the two earlier stages of the revolution.

Second, the domestic political instability partly reflects the proliferation of ideologies of both secular and religious varieties, but at present Ayatollah Khomeini's interpretation of Islam prevails on both the domestic and international levels. The challenge of other ideologies, both secular and religious, is silenced more by resort to coercion than by efforts at accommodation.

Third, Khomeini's worldview rejects the very conception of the contemporary international system as it is constituted today. As such, contrary to the characterization of most observers, Khomeini's ideology is neither pan-Shii nor pan-Islamic; it aims at the establishment of what I would call an "Islamic world order." Toward that ultimate end, it advocates the export of the Islamic Revolution to other countries everywhere by pacific means, especially by the example of Islamic behavior and propaganda, and decries in theory both political subversion and armed aggression as instruments of an Islamic foreign policy.

Fourth, because of the vagueness of the ideological precepts and the lack of political cohesion, as well as the determination of revolutionary leaders to make a clean break with the foreign policy of the late Shah and his father, Reza Shah, two problems in particular destabilize Iran's foreign policy: (1) the official-unofficial division in the foreign policy–making process; and (2) the decimation of both skilled diplomats and the organizational structure of the Ministry of Foreign Affairs. The taking of American hostages was the single most far-reaching foreign-policy decision in revolutionary Iran. Although militant students took the initiative to act, Khomeini had incited students, religious and secular, to act, and he also endorsed the taking of hostages after the fact.

Fifth, Khomeini's interpretation of Islam influences Iran's revolutionary foreign policy in a variety of ways. It motivates his own foreign-policy pronouncements, decisions, commitments, and strategies, as well as those of his disciples, who may believe in his line as dogmatically as he does. It also performs other functions, including communicating, rationalizing, and justifying foreign-policy behavior. Above all, it is used to mobilize domestic support for the conduct of diplomacy and the prosecution of war. Once a war is claimed to be waged in defense of Islam, the usual distinction made between a defensive war and an invasion on the basis of the concept of the territorial state is cast to the winds.

Sixth, the overriding goal of Iranian revolutionary foreign policy is proclaimed to be absolute independence from the West and the East. That means self-reliance and freedom from the domination of either power bloc not only politically but also economically, culturally, intellectually, and psychologically. Toward this goal Iran is said to pursue a two-pronged policy: (1) a self-reliant nonalignment policy; and (2) a pro–Third World policy that accords first priority to Muslim countries and second priority to other Third World states.

Movement in these directions is evidenced by Iran's rejection of normal relations with the United States, but America is not the West. Western European countries and Japan are still the principal trade partners of Iran. Relations with the Soviet Union are still strained, largely over ideological and political differences, but otherwise they are what Iranian leaders themselves characterize as good and friendly. Compared with the Shah's days, when considerable economic ties with Moscow also existed, current economic, commercial, and technical relations between Tehran and Moscow are more extensive. Adding this to the rigidly expanding trade and economic relations with Eastern European countries and to the influence of the communist Tudeh Party in Iran, some Western circles are alarmed at the perceived "Iranian tilt" toward the East. However, it is too early to judge.

Movement in the direction of expansion of relations with the Third World states is also discernible, as evidenced by emerging new ties not only with such Muslim states as Syria, Turkey, and Pakistan, which have revived the old notion of a common market among them, but also with such diverse Third World nations as North Korea, Argentina, Brazil, Nicaragua, India, and others. Oil is still the principal commodity in the Iranian economy. It is being used in an ever-increasing number of barter deals with diverse foreign countries. The revolutionary regime has sold Iranian oil to the Soviet Union for the first time in the history of the relations between the two countries.

Finally, whether any of these foreign-policy goals, means, and courses of action are durable, one cannot tell. Beyond Khomeini, the future of the Iranian Revolution is unpredictable, and so is the future of Iran's foreign policy. But what is relatively ponderable is the deep and controlling influence of the political culture on Iran's foreign policy regardless of who rules the country and what is the dominant ideological stance. That is a different subject, which needs separate treatment. It could nevertheless be argued that there is one major aspect of the political culture that the "Islamic Republic of Iran" has not so far been able to escape, namely, the Iranian leaders' ancient habit of setting unrealizable goals and using inappropriate means in both domestic politics and foreign policy.

1. This conception of the "twin revolution" has been used by me elsewhere to suggest that every Middle Eastern revolution has had this external-internal characteristic, as evidenced, for example, by the Egyptian Revolution, which, according to Gamal Abdel Nasser, was launched against "foreign and internal despotism." This characteristic is historically as applicable to Iran's own experience as it is to its 1978–79 revolution. Both the Constitutional Revolution of 1905–11 and the nationalist uprising of 1951–53 aimed simultaneously at independence from foreign control and freedom from domestic tyranny. For details, see R. K. Ramazani, *Beyond the Arab-Israeli Settlement: New Directions for U.S. Policy in the Middle East* (Cambridge, MA, 1977), 36–40. See also "Iran's Revolution: Patterns, Problems, and Prospects," pp. 33–49 in this volume.

2. For a detailed analysis of the cumulative effects of U.S.-Iranian relations during the entire period of the Shah's regime on the Iranian Revolution, see R. K. Ramazani, *The United States and Iran: The Patterns of Influence* (New York, 1982). See also "Who Lost America? The Case of Iran," pp. 50–67 in this volume.

3. Unfortunately, the text of this important document is not available in English. For its text and related materials in Persian, see *Mitch Bray-e Deaf'a Az Howqua-e Bashar va Pishraft-e An dar Iran* [The defense of the right of humanity and its progress in Iran], no. 16 (10 December 1978), 99–100.

4. This was one of the earliest and most bitter attacks on the United States by Khomeini after his return to Iran from exile. For the full text, see *Ettela'at*, 20 May 1979. For numerous other statements against the United States, see subsequent issues of this same source during the years 1979–82.

5. See, for example, *Ettela'at*, 7 March 1981.

6. With the approval of Khomeini, Sadeqh Tabatabai, a relative of the Ayatollah, was authorized to meet secretly with an American counterpart in West Germany. The details of this development are discussed in Pierre Salinger, *America Held Hostage: The Secret Negotiations* (New York, 1981). Salinger's account is reliable. I have checked the information with Warren Christopher, who was President Carter's principal negotiator and who has helpfully provided me with a copy of his *Diplomacy: The Neglected Imperative* (n.p., n.d.).

7. Currently, in 2012, Ayatollah Sayyid Ali Khamenei.

8. See *Christian Science Monitor*, 12 May 1982.

9. See the section authored by Yann Richard in Nikki R. Keddie, *Roots of Revolution: An Interpretive History of Modern Iran* (New Haven, 1981), esp. 205–6.

10. See Haj Ruhollah Musavi Khomeini, *Kashf-e Assrar* [Discovery of secrets] (Tehran, 1944).

11. Ibid., esp. 267.

12. For the text see Foreign Broadcast Information Service, *Daily Report*, vol. 8, *South Asia* (FBIS-SA), 4 November 1981.

13. Ibid., 29 October 1981.

14. *Tehran Journal*, 7 October 1981.

15. Ibid., 25 October 1981.

16. Ibid., 4 November 1981.

17. For the text, see Foreign Broadcast Information Service, *Daily Report*, vol. 5, *Middle East and North Africa* (FBIS-MEA), 24 March 1980.

18. *FBIS-SA*, 9 March 1982.

19. See *Sourush*, March 1981, 4–5.

20. See n. 7.

21. *FBIS-SA*, 11 March 1982.

22. *Tehran Journal*, 7 October 1981.

23. *FBIS-SA*, 8 July 1981.

24. See his interview in *The Middle East*, April 1982, 16–17.

25. These points are based on my *Iran's Foreign Policy, 1941–1973: A Study of Foreign Policy in Modernizing Nations* (Charlottesville, 1975), *The United States and Iran: The Patterns of Influence* (New York, 1982), and other works.

26. See *FBIS-SA*, 8 July 1981.

27. See *Middle East Economic Digest*, 30 April 1982, 8.

28. *Baghdad Observer*, 16 October 1979, 4–5.

29. *FBIS-SA*, 19 April 1982.

30. Ibid., 16 March 1982.

31. Ibid., 1 April 1982.

32. See R. K. Ramazani, "Emerging Patterns of Regional Relations in Iranian Foreign Policy," *Orbis* 18 (1975): 1043–69.

33. *FBIS-SA*, 13 October 1981.

34. Ibid.

35. These percentages are my calculations based on the information contained in *Asharq Al-Awsat*, 16 March 1982.

36. *FBIS-MEA*, 21 December 1981.

37. *FBIS-SA*, 12 November 1981.

IRAN

Burying the Hatchet

Today's wisdom may be tomorrow's folly, unless political leaders are able to combine their current imperatives with foresight. For the past half-dozen years American foreign policy has aimed at containing revolutionary Iran and has been based on the conviction that an Iranian victory in its war with Iraq would shatter the structure of the industrialized democracies' interests in the Persian Gulf region. Startlingly enough, scholars, no less than leaders, who obviously must prepare for the worst, have uncritically accepted the current conventional wisdom about an Iranian victory, even though it is not shared by most NATO members (including Turkey), Japan, or Pakistan.

But emerging changes in Iranian foreign policy indicate that pursuing a stern containment policy alone may create risks of its own, risks arising from a missed chance at reconciliation with the Islamic Revolution. Specifically, America's failure to temper its containment policy as soon as possible could destroy any chance of exploring any opportunity for reconciliation that may already exist. It would in effect make escalating conflict the centerpiece of U.S. policy toward Iran. And it would continue to subject American interests and lives to an ever-expanding hostile environment in the Middle East.

U.S. fears about an Iranian victory revolve around a facile domino theory of Persian Gulf politics that assumes that if Iraq were overrun by the Iranian hordes, all the other Arab states of the region would also fall sooner or later. Even if these states could somehow survive the immediate shock of Iraq's defeat, a decisive Iranian victory would bring economic, military, and political disaster in the Persian Gulf and beyond.

Economically, it is feared, the Iranians would dictate ever-higher oil prices and ever-lower oil production to the rest of the world through the Organization of Petroleum Exporting Countries (OPEC). As the self-appointed champions of such indebted oil producers as Nigeria and Venezuela, have not the Iranians already made life miserable for Saudi Arabia and other rich Persian Gulf sheikdoms? Have not the Iranians gleefully proclaimed in OPEC meetings that "any reduction of Saudi oil production that is added to ours means victory," while adamantly demanding an increase of their own production quota from 2.4 million to 3.2 million barrels per day? And have not the Iranians vociferously advocated

"Iran: Burying the Hatchet" was originally published in Foreign Policy 60 (Fall 1985): 52–72.

at a minimum linking oil prices to the rate of world inflation, or at most raising them to about "$60–$70 per barrel"—presumably the price of substitute forms of energy? What could stop the Iranians from becoming even more hawkish if they won the war?

Militarily, many warn, after an Iraqi defeat, massive waves of Iranians would press on to greater victories in the name of Islam, overrunning the tiny city-state of Kuwait and easily overwhelming the meager ground forces of Saudi Arabia and the other sheikdoms. Having sacrificed nearly 200,000 soldiers in the five-year struggle against Iraq, Iranian leaders would like nothing better than to get revenge against all those countries, especially Kuwait and Saudi Arabia, that repeatedly have failed to heed their warnings to stop aiding the "infidel" Saddam Hussein, Iraq's president.

Politically, would not the Iranian vanguards of the Islamic Revolution proceed from the Iraqi stepping-stone to realize farther afield their dream of an Islamic world order? Given the putative power of this most populous Shii Muslim state in the world, would not the triumph of "Islam over blasphemy" in the Iran-Iraq War incite the poor Shii communities throughout the Persian Gulf to rise up against the United States and the ruling monarchies that have befriended it? Given the Iran-Syria axis, would not such a spectacular success by Middle East radicals threaten the Jordanian monarchy and encourage the pro-Soviet Syrians to push for an even greater hegemony in Lebanon and the rest of the Eastern Mediterranean? And, finally, would not the establishment of an Islamic republic in predominantly Shia-inhabited Iraq embolden the pro-Iranian Lebanese Shii factions Islamic Amal and Hezbollah to try to create yet a third Islamic republic in Lebanon and then to press forward to destroy Israel by replacing it with a Palestinian state, as Iran has urged?

The extent to which such apocalyptic scenarios actually shape America's Iran policy is difficult to say. But clearly, such scenarios have generated unprecedented American commitments and policies in the Persian Gulf. Undoubtedly, the Soviet invasion of Afghanistan prompted the initial U.S. commitment to defend, even by military means, the uninterrupted flow of Persian Gulf oil supplies against "any outside force." But few seem to recall that it was the Iranian Revolution that originally gave rise to the ideas and courses of action that finally led to the Carter Doctrine and to the official formation of the multiservice Rapid Deployment Joint Task Force. It is similarly overlooked that because of the Iran-Iraq War and other regional conflicts, this force has undergone significant changes.

When the Carter Doctrine was declared, there was only a conception of defense; there was no military unit. But on January 1, 1983, Washington established a unified regional command, the United States Central Command, on which the Reagan administration reportedly has spent $14 billion per year. More important, what began as a unilateral declaration of U.S. policy, without any advance consultation with the very friendly regional states that Washington wished to defend against an external threat, has in effect turned into an American deterrent force that supplements local defense efforts directed primarily against a regional, not a Soviet, threat. America's "over the horizon" presence in the Indian Ocean, for example, has been strengthened to cope with the threat of a spread of the Persian Gulf War beyond the belligerents, especially to the Strait of Hormuz.

America's so-called tilt toward Iraq is designed to contain the same perceived threat by nonmilitary means. It flows from the view that an Iraqi defeat would not be in America's interests. Washington maintains a formal policy of neutrality toward the war, refusing to sell arms to either belligerent and discouraging other arms suppliers from doing so. Nevertheless, U.S. trade with Baghdad undoubtedly helps Iraq's war efforts. By crowning nonmilitary aid with the accolade of resumed diplomatic relations with Iraq, the United States probably hopes to further pressure Iran to drop its perilous insistence on fighting to Hussein's finish. To Iranians, all these efforts provide incontestable evidence for their initial charge of American collusion in the original invasion.

The United States is also trying to contain the spread of Iran's Islamic radicalism and to prevent expansion of the war by giving military aid to its Persian Gulf friends. The deployment of American airborne warning and control system (AWACS) aircraft in Saudi Arabia since the start of the war, the sale of these planes and the transfer of naval craft to the six-country Gulf Cooperation Council (GCC), and the emergency military aid provided in late May 1984, at the height of the so-called tanker war, are only the major examples of such assistance. A dogfight is not a battle, let alone a war, but the Saudi downing of an Iranian F-4 fighter plane on June 5, 1984, was no doubt an important show of Saudi political resolve. The restraint that both Iran and Saudi Arabia showed after the incident, however, was even more important; both sides avoided further military escalation.

QUESTIONABLE NOTIONS

Whether all such U.S. containment efforts will ultimately succeed remains to be seen. But at least an equally important question is whether all these American efforts are needed to avert disaster.

No matter how hawkish the Iranians are on oil price and production issues, the belief that they could dictate their tough terms to the rest of the world contradicts OPEC's experience since 1973. Market forces, on balance, have dictated price and production levels more than any other factor, as OPEC's recent weakness clearly demonstrates. Regardless of why oil is currently in surplus and how long this may last, the stark fact is that Iran, no less than other major producers, must adjust to the realities of the international oil market. Despite its tough stances on price and production, Iran has surprised its OPEC partners by complying with the organization's landmark 1982 and 1983 decisions on these matters. Its price discounts aim at compensating its customers for the higher insurance premiums required because of the war.

The assumption that a military disaster is inevitable also is unjustifiably alarmist. The notion that Iran will carry the war into other Arab territories because it has more people and soldiers than the Persian Gulf sheikdoms, because its leaders nurture a deep sense of revenge, and because its militant and universalist ideology so dictates is highly questionable. But even if this analysis is defensible, it totally disregards the disincentives to Iran's expansion of the war. No doubt weighing on the minds of Iranian leaders are the near destruction of the once-powerful Iranian Air Force, the growing war-weariness of the Iranian public, the fear of Soviet counterintervention, and the disappearance of the principal ideological rationale for continuing to fight—to defend true Islam— once Iraq is defeated. Further, President Ronald Reagan seems to have engaged sufficient U.S. credibility in the defense of the House of Saud to give Iran pause.

Finally, projections of political disaster seem even more flawed than warnings of economic and military calamity. The notion that the Shii communities in the Arab states will rise up to embrace the Iranian victors smacks of fantasy. During repeated research visits to the Middle East over the past six years, I have been struck by the great ambivalence of the Shii Muslims toward the Iranian Revolution. From Bahrain to Baalbek, the example of Iran has, to be sure, inspired many Shii Muslims. But only political extremists on the fringes of these societies want to emulate the Iranian form of Islamic government. Most Shia admire only the revolutionary regime's perceived resistance to foreign domination. When Iran carried the war to Iraq in July 1982, the Iranian leader Ayatollah Ruhollah Khomeini called on all Iraqis to rise up against the Ba'athist regime. None responded, even though Shii Muslims make up approximately 60 percent of the Iraqi population.

Farther afield in Lebanon, the Iranian influence has been partly a by-product of the Iran-Syria axis. But this alliance rests largely on the common hostility of Khomeini and Syrian President Hafez al-Assad toward Iraq's Hussein and would no doubt break apart after an Iranian victory. Syria has no interest in seeing Hussein replaced by an Iranian-backed ayatollah in a new Islamic republic next door. Nor will Damascus continue to tolerate in its Lebanese sphere of influence an increase in Iranian influence. The Iranian volunteers and revolutionary guards who have used the Syrian protection in the Bekaa Valley for their own revolutionary ends already have worn out their welcome. Actual and potential rifts between Damascus and Tehran—stemming principally from Assad's desire to see Israeli troops out of southern Lebanon completely, which would remove the common enemy whose presence prompted cooperation in the first place; from the emergence of the mainstream Shii Muslim movement Amal, led by Lebanese Minister of Justice Nabih Berri, as the brawniest new power in Lebanon; and from the Syrian impatience with the pro-Iranian Hezbollah that was revealed by the summertime TWA hijacking crisis—indicate that Syria soon may ask the guards to leave Lebanon. Iran has promised to honor such a request.

But the alarmists' argument also fails completely to allow for other kinds of consequences that might result from an Iranian victory. First, a servile, pro-Iranian regime will not necessarily emerge in Iraq simply because Hussein's regime is ousted. A military regime with or without Hussein's ruling Ba'ath Party is one distinct possibility. But that would hardly produce an Iranian satellite. All the geographic, cultural, social, and political factors that for generations have underlain recurrent conflicts between the two neighbors would continue, as might the conflict itself. Second, Iran's relations with all of its conservative neighbors in the Persian Gulf, especially Kuwait and Saudi Arabia, would improve significantly, for these countries' logistic and financial aid to Iraq during the war has been a principal cause of tension. In spite of the war, Iran has managed to maintain diplomatic representation at various levels with the Persian Gulf states—including, strange as it may seem, Iraq. Further, shortly after the landmark visit of Saudi Foreign Minister Saud al-Faisal al-Saud to Iran in May 1985, Iranian Foreign Minister Ali Akbar Velayati sent a special envoy to Persian Gulf capitals to discuss "the necessity for further cooperation among the regional states." Third, freed from the war in the west, Iran would revert to its historical pattern of focusing on its eastern borders. Only now it would do it with a vengeance because of the Soviet thorn in its side—the Marxist regime in Afghanistan and the accompanying burden of growing numbers of Afghan refugees. In addition, Iran faces an ever-present Soviet threat to the province of Baluchistan. And fourth, after six years Iran would have had its fill of economic disaster and destruction. The regime would finally have to try to fulfill the revolutionary promise of a better life, especially for the politicized masses, which the war has permitted it to postpone for years.

MORE REASON, LESS PASSION

An unconditional Iranian victory would hardly be inconsequential, and U.S. efforts to prevent the spread of the war should continue. But Washington's current assessment of these consequences is so vastly exaggerated that the United States may well fail to temper its containment policy and thus effectively rule out the option of reconciliation with Iran at some future time. This danger is heightened by the widespread sense of victimization at the hands of the Khomeini regime, felt not only by the general public but within the policy community as well. Considering Tehran's virulent anti-American crusade ever since the Iranian hostage crisis, American resentment and frustration are perfectly understandable. But Americans nevertheless should remind themselves of what they tell Iranians—that passion is not policy.

Whatever else the revolution has changed, it certainly has not changed Iran's great strategic significance to the United States. Every American president since Franklin Roosevelt has understood this, for obvious reasons. Despite the toll taken by the revolution and the protracted war, Iran still is putatively the most powerful state in the entire Persian Gulf. It abuts more than 1,000 miles of largely Muslim-inhabited Soviet territory and hundreds of miles of Soviet-occupied Muslim Afghanistan. It also dominates the strategic Strait of Hormuz, the world's oil choke point. Iran is one of the few areas of the world outside Western Europe where U.S.-Soviet conflict could touch off a world war. Moscow's domination of Iran would effectively destroy the only real buffer between the oil-rich Arab countries of the Persian Gulf and the Soviet Union. Assuming that more reason and less passion were to guide U.S. containment policy, the question would still remain whether revolutionary Iran is amenable to any kind of reconciliation with the United States. Former secretary of state Henry Kissinger, like all hard-nosed analysts, subscribes to the current domino theory about the Persian Gulf War, but unlike most others, he has argued—in the February 5, 1985, issue of the *Washington Post*—that "the United States should retain the option of improved relations" with Iran. Yet he thinks that the requisite sense of reality will appear in Iran only "within a decade." He gives no reason why the United States should keep open the option of cooperation. Nor does he explain why Iranian realism would take so long to develop. Kissinger merely refers to an analogy to America's relationship with China in the 1950s and 1960s.

Like most other analysts, Kissinger apparently does not realize that the foreign policy of revolutionary Iran has been undergoing subtle but increasingly significant changes that indicate that the United States need not wait a decade to explore possibilities for a reconciliation that would serve important U.S. interests.

These emerging changes reflect an intricate set of pressures that spring from the combined consequences of the unfinished Iranian Revolution and the unwinnable war with Iraq. Five years of death and destruction have added the problem of public war-weariness to many unsettled problems facing Iranian leaders in their quest for the "Islamization" of Iran's political order and foreign policy. Outside observers see only the fountain of blood at the Behesht-e-Zahra Cemetery, south of Tehran—which spouts a column of crimson-colored water day and night—and surmise that the public is obsessed with martyrdom. But in truth, Iranians are fed up with the war, and the regime knows this. In June 1985, in order to reduce casualties, Khomeini decreed that fewer Iranian troops would take part in future offensives—partly to increase military effectiveness but also to dampen antiwar feelings. Antiwar protests in April and May 1985 were reported in foreign publications such as the *Economist* and impelled the government hastily to organize large prowar rallies in June that allegedly attracted more than 5 million people.

After Khomeini, clerical rule presumably will continue through an authoritarian one-party system, many unbridled revolutionary committees, vast networks of mosques, and hundreds of thousands of ideologically committed revolutionary guards and club-swinging Hezbollah hoodlums, all reputedly supported by the poor masses. But even if these instruments of political control go unchallenged, the overriding problem of leadership succession will continue, despite the existence since 1982 of a mechanism for the selection of one or more clerics to rule. The war has made the resolution of the succession problem not only more urgent but also more critical to the revolution's survival.

The war also has intensified the economic problems of the unfinished revolution. The revolutionary regime blames all of Iran's economic ills on the "imposed war." These include pervasive black-marketeering and corruption, the exodus of half of all Iranian physicians—leaving only 15,000 doctors for more than 40 million people—an unofficial inflation rate of about 35 percent per year, and dwindling foreign reserves. But the fundamental, persistent problem of low productivity can hardly be blamed on the war alone. By its own admission, the regime's overriding socioeconomic goal of equitable distribution of wealth has yet to be met. The revolution has done little to improve the material life of the poor, whom it pampers ideologically. In reality, it cannot do any better for numerous reasons, including management techniques that reportedly try to run the economy "like a rural parish"; heavy government intervention in the economy; the unresolved dispute over priorities among private, public, and cooperative sectors; the glaring failure to reverse the flight of educated, skilled workers and capital from an anti-intellectual and anti-entrepreneurial climate; mounting imports of food and consumer goods; and growing demands for wages and salaries to pay for an apparently chaotic and ever-expanding bureaucracy.

To these and other major problems have been added an estimated $150 billion in total war damages and about $5 billion a year in war costs—the latter figure representing one-third of all government expenditures. And no quick recovery is in sight, even after the war. Each year of postwar reconstruction might cost as much as a year of conducting the war. Still worse, funds to meet the country's social and economic needs will surely be scarce. Further, the war's end might well reduce oil revenues even more, as resurgent Iranian and Iraqi production adds to the current oversupply of oil.

ENDING IRAN'S ISOLATION

External problems also exert pressure for change in Iranian foreign policy. Paradoxically, the principal external difficulty, Iran's isolation in world affairs, has been created by the Khomeini regime itself. The seizure of American hostages on November 4, 1979, not only plunged Iran into a protracted and agonizing dispute with the United States but also transformed the very character of revolutionary Iran's foreign relations. In the words of its first prime minister, Mehdi Bazargan, the Khomeini regime's stance changed from "defensive" to "confrontational." Before the takeover of the U.S. Embassy, Bazargan had tried to build Iran's new relationship with the United States on the basis of the principle of "equality." After the downfall of his government on November 6, 1979, the perpetrators of the so-called second revolution substituted hostility for equality as the touchstone of relations with Washington.

Yet, though the ideological crusade against the United States, the "Great Satan," has continued unabated since the hostage crisis, the emerging direction of Iranian foreign policy may well contain potential for ultimate reconciliation between Washington and Tehran. The Khomeini regime is now determined to terminate Iran's pariah status in world affairs. This new commitment is considered necessary precisely because the Islamic Revolution is threatened by so many social, economic, and political problems. An increasingly influential leader in foreign affairs, President Ali Khamenei, who also is chairman of the powerful Supreme Defense Council and general secretary of the ruling Islamic Republican Party (IRP), calls Iran's new look in world affairs an "Open Door Foreign Policy" that calls for greater interaction between the Islamic ideology of Iran and the "ideologies and cultures" of other countries. Iran's new posture also seeks a much better balance between what he calls Iran's "needs" and its "message"—that is, between its national interest and its Islamic ideology.

Khomeini himself also has emphasized the importance of this new open-door foreign policy. He has already called for the establishment of diplomatic relations with nearly all governments in the world. He states categorically that expanding relations with other countries is compatible not only with the Islamic Prophetic Tradition but with the Iranian national interest as well. Failure to do so, he warns, will mean "defeat and annihilation" for Iran. Although he omits relations with Israel, South Africa, and the United States from these declarations, he draws a significant distinction among the three. He says enigmatically that Tehran possibly could establish new relations with Washington if the United States "behaves itself." Even this little opening toward the United States by Khomeini would have been unthinkable only a few years ago. Finally, for the first time since the seizure of the U.S. Embassy, an Iranian leader, Speaker of the Parliament Hojatoleslam Hashemi Rafsanjani, has publicly raised with Washington the question of restoring diplomatic relations. On July 3, 1985, according to the *Washington Post*, he called on the United States to take the initiative in resuming relations with Iran. He was quoted as stating, "We have no intention to keep our diplomatic relations severed forever but it will be difficult to restore relations under the present administration." What Rafsanjani was really saying, in a characteristically Persian style, was that diplomatic relations can be restored even under the Reagan administration, if the administration changes its flagrantly bellicose attitude toward Iran. If reports of this landmark invitation are confirmed, it would be completely in keeping with Khomeini's first hint on the subject.

Even more encouraging than these emerging changes in Iran's declaratory policy are the nascent patterns of its actual foreign policy. Three features of this policy require special mention. First, the Khomeini regime has moved decisively to balance Iran's relations between the East and the West. As soon as the Western European powers lifted economic sanctions against Iran after the settlement of the hostage dispute, mutual economic and commercial relations expanded swiftly. Today, Japan and West Germany are again Iran's main trading partners. More than 70 percent of Iran's total imports in 1983–84 came from Canada, Japan, and Western Europe, and more than 50 percent of its total exports went to these same areas. By comparison, in the same year only 10 percent of Iran's imports came from Eastern Europe and the Soviet Union, and only 26 percent of its exports went to the Soviet bloc.

Iranian revolutionary leaders make no secret of their continuing dependence on Western economies. They rationalize their predicament by blaming the ousted Shah Mohammed Reza Pahlavi's "enslaving" economic policies. They insist that their recognition of the continued dependence on foreign economic relations does not signal flagging interest in their long-standing goal of economic self-sufficiency, which they maintain will be reached as soon as possible. Under any circumstances, however, they unabashedly prefer the superior technology of the West to that of the East—not because they favor the West but because they claim to deal with each country or bloc of states as it serves their "national interests" and "Islamic ideology."

Efforts also have been made to redress the earlier imbalance in political relations between the East and the West. Once the Soviet Union increased large-scale arms supplies to Baghdad in spring 1982, when the tide of war definitely turned against Iraq, the relations between Tehran and Moscow deteriorated rapidly. The disappointed Soviets, who had tried unsuccessfully to woo the Khomeini regime, accused it of "anti-Sovietism." The regime's destruction of the pro-Soviet, communist Tudeh Party and the expulsion of eighteen Soviet diplomats on espionage charges in 1983 hardened Moscow's attitude toward Tehran. The Iranian leaders disavowed any link between their relations with the Soviets and the fate of the Tudeh Party, insisting that the latter was an internal affair.

The Soviet occupation of Afghanistan is a far more important source of Soviet-Iranian tensions. Repeatedly invaded over the centuries by the Russians from the north, Iran now also feels menaced by Moscow on its eastern flank. Ideology makes this increased strategic threat all the more ominous to the Khomeini regime. In contrast with America, the Soviet Union is characterized as the "Lesser Satan," but there is no doubt that ideologically the Soviet "atheists" are regarded as the greater Satans.

Second, Iran's open-door foreign policy emphasizes the priority of expanding relations with Muslim and Third World countries, most of whose foreign-policy interests need not conflict with Western interests. Nowhere else in the Third World is Iran's preference for such countries more clearly demonstrated than in the so-called Northern Tier, that strip of western Asia bordering the Soviet Union. And nowhere else in the world does Iran's foreign policy show more realism, as Iran enjoys increasingly friendly relations with decidedly pro-Western Turkey and Pakistan. This rapprochement in part reflects the fact that Turkey and Pakistan are relatively large powers, provide cheap overland transportation routes for Iranian exports, and, as oil-poor countries, have economies that complement Iran's.

Yet, probably more than any other single factor, it is the imperative of geopolitical realities that underlies Iran's close relations with Turkey and Pakistan. Because of the Soviet occupation of Afghanistan, Iran has even more reason than during the Shah's days to cultivate friendships with these two countries. Pakistan and Iran have in effect become the confrontation states of the Northern Tier with respect to Soviet-occupied Afghanistan. They share a fear of Soviet penetration into Baluchistan, which straddles their common border; they share the burden of the Afghan refugees (about 1 million in Iran and 3 million in Pakistan); and they feel, as does Turkey, that the Soviet Union itself is too close for comfort. Iran has used its increasing economic, commercial, and transportation ties with Turkey and Pakistan to forge closer political relations with these countries. Trade with Turkey has expanded tenfold since the revolution, making Turkey Iran's largest Third World trade partner. In fact, Turkey has replaced the United States in Iran's overall commercial life.

The same geopolitical imperatives also have prompted the three neighbors to form the new Economic Cooperation Organization (ECO). Iranian leaders insist that this venture, launched in January 1985 to encourage trade, technology transfer, and other economic exchanges, differs greatly from the Regional Cooperation for Development organization of the Shah's era. But both arrangements reflect longtime Iranian concerns about becoming too dependent on the Soviets for trade, transit, and technical ties. Nor is this consideration incompatible with the desire of these countries ultimately to reduce dependence on the United States. But for Iran, at least, that economic consideration is not the issue right now; U.S.-Iranian economic flows have dwindled to a trickle.

The third dimension of Iranian diplomacy, encompassing the Persian Gulf and Lebanon, has not featured such encouraging developments. In particular, Iran's refusal to negotiate a peace settlement with Iraq; its insistence on identifying Iraq as the "aggressor"; and its uncompromising demand for the punishment of the Ba'athist regime have all needlessly prolonged the war. Tehran wants a kind of peace that it cannot impose. For its part, Baghdad is responsible for escalating border skirmishes to a full-scale war; creating an oil spill in the Gulf waters; using chemical weapons; and initiating strikes on civilian targets and oil tankers, all in the hope of ending a war that it started but lacks the power to end. The Persian Gulf War is already the longest, bloodiest, and costliest conflict seen by the contemporary Middle East.

Nor has Iran done much in the Persian Gulf or Lebanon to live down its reputation as a renegade state. Ever since the eruption of the Iranian Revolution, the Khomeini regime has been accused of complicity in acts of terrorism—in Bahrain and Kuwait in the Persian Gulf region since 1981 and in Lebanon since the bombing of the American Embassy in Beirut in April 1983. In spite of official Iranian denials, the suspicion of Iran's terrorist involvement has grown by leaps and bounds, largely on the basis of circumstantial evidence. Inferences have been drawn from the fact that since at least 1981 Iran has supported a multitude of Islamic "liberation fronts" opposed to the incumbent governments in countries from the Philippines to the Persian Gulf. Tehran has adamantly advocated the export of the Islamic Revolution; has housed, indoctrinated, and trained political opponents of various countries in the region; and has sent many hundreds of revolutionary guards to Lebanon.

Yet there are encouraging signs that Iran's new open-door foreign policy might begin to moderate its attitudes toward the war with Iraq and the export of the revolution. In this light, the Saudi foreign minister's May 1985 visit was a milestone in the relations of the two principal Persian Gulf countries, for several reasons. First, Iran took the initiative to invite Saud. Second, his visit represented the consensus of the GCC, whose ministerial council launched an unprecedented peace campaign in March 1985. Third, the visit is to be reciprocated by the Iranian side and possibly followed up with the dispatch of a three-man GCC delegation to Tehran. Fourth, and most important, the improvement in Iranian–Saudi Arabian relations might not only help reduce suspicions about Iranian-supported acts of subversion and terrorism in the area but also, perhaps, aid new efforts to end the war.

The single most important thing that Iran can do to reduce suspicions about its complicity in terrorism is to match its antiterrorist rhetoric with concrete action. Iranian officials have condemned all acts of terrorism, and Khomeini has complained—notably, during the mining of the Suez Canal and the Red Sea in 1984—that "whatever incident or crime . . . happens throughout the world, [we] are said to have had a hand in it."

On that occasion Khomeini added: "How is it possible that we can support an issue which is against the sentiments of the world, against Islam, and against common sense? Laying mines in a place is tantamount to wiping out a group of innocent people. How can Islam allow such a thing? How can Iran permit this?" When it was discovered that the mysterious mining was not Iran's fault, Egyptian President Hosni Mubarak backpedaled on his original charges.

Iran was once again blamed for terrorism during the TWA hijacking crisis. Senator Jesse Helms (R-NC) was one of many who pointed a finger directly at Tehran. The accusations came in spite of the fact that the day after the hijacking Iran closed all its airports to the hijacked plane, and the Iranian civil aviation organization declared that it "would not be absolutely permitted to land at any Iranian airport." On June 24 Rafsanjani condemned the hijacking while on a visit to Damascus, stating unequivocally that "if we had such knowledge, we would have prevented it."

Even more critically, Rafsanjani was instrumental in creating a consensus on the need to help free the thirty-nine American hostages the day before Assad sought Washington's reaction to his proposal to give the hijackers his own guarantee that Israel would release its Lebanese prisoners. Rafsanjani met in Damascus not only with officials of Hezbollah but also with some Amal officials and with a group of leading Shii and Sunni Muslim Lebanese clerics, including Sheikh Mohammad Hussein Fadallah, reputedly the "supreme spiritual guide" of Hezbollah and a close friend of Khomeini's and of many other Iranian clerical leaders. No less important, on June 29, while in China, Rafsanjani again denounced the hijacking, probably as a message to Hezbollah holdouts still refusing to turn over four hostages to Amal. They did so the following day.

This apparently constructive Iranian role in freeing the American hostages was completely in line with its emerging open-door foreign policy. It will no doubt help remove the blemish of terrorism from Iran's reputation. Iran can further improve its image by trying the hijackers of a Kuwaiti airliner who have been in Iranian custody since December 1984. They should be punished not only for the crime of hijacking but also for the cold-blooded murder of two innocent American passengers.

In order to retain the option of improving relations with Iran in the future, the United States should temper its containment policy now. If America is willing to listen; if America is willing to forgive and forget; and if America is willing to harness the passions of the moment, it will see that potential for reconciliation can already be discerned in the theory and practice of Iran's new open-door foreign policy. No matter how virulent much of their rhetoric still is, the Iranian leaders finally have come to believe that the very survival of their revolution is at stake and that mounting domestic problems can be eased only by breaking down the walls of Iran's international isolation. They also have come to realize that the excesses of their ideological crusade, their courtship of uncontrollable Shii and other extremists, and the image of Iran as a renegade country militate against expanding their international ties.

AN AMERICAN PEACE STRATEGY

Washington should pursue a two-track strategy, at the regional and bilateral levels. At the regional level, the United States should now pursue an active peace strategy. It is high time to go beyond the current "tilt" toward Iraq in the Persian Gulf War. No matter how useful this fence-sitting has been to date, it is fast becoming a rancid formula, for the situation has been changing rapidly. The same domestic and external pressures that have produced Iran's new open-door policy are now helping to create a more flexible Iranian position on ending the war. Although still demanding the punishment of Iraq's Ba'athist regime, Rafsanjani, in his address to Islamic ambassadors on June 19, 1985, seemed to make more room than usual for the role of third-party judgments, including an "international court." Other straws in the wind—and there still are only a few—include the earnest peacemaking efforts of the GCC; the visit of Saud to Iran for talks on peace as well as on improving bilateral relations; more frequent statements by Iranian leaders about ending the war rather than fighting to the finish, as well as Khomeini's new order to conduct a "defensive holy war"; and the growing confidence of the combatants in the role of the U.N. secretary-general as a potential mediator.

Consequently, America's peace strategy should now encourage the role of the United Nations more than before. Given the belligerents' confidence in the secretary-general, his office probably would be the best medium for that purpose. That office, in fact, played an important role in the settlement of the 1970 dispute between Iran and Great Britain over the Persian Gulf island of Bahrain, now an independent state. Aspects of this precedent provide some useful guidelines for resolving today's conflict.

Yet moving Tehran toward the negotiating table will require some kind of conciliatory gesture toward Iran by the United Nations itself. Ever since the start of the war, the Khomeini regime has felt deeply aggrieved by the attitude of the Security Council, for two reasons. The first concerns what it calls the Council's failure at the outset of the war to condemn the Iraqi invasion. The second concerns the Council's adoption on June 1, 1984, of Resolution 552, which Iran considers one-sided. Without mentioning it by name, the resolution criticized Iran for attacking oil tankers traveling to and from Kuwaiti and Saudi ports but made no reference to Iraqi attacks on tankers traveling to and from Iranian terminals. Nor is Iran impressed with the argument that the distinction was required by legal technicalities.

Some ways must be found to redress these grievances as a means of regaining Iran's trust. The Security Council could rectify its failure to condemn the Iraqi invasion by working out a resolution deploring both Iraq's escalation of armed hostilities on September 22, 1980, when the war assumed major proportions, and Iran's extension of the war into Iraqi territory for the first time on July 13, 1982. Regarding the tankers, the Council could reaffirm its more evenhanded Resolution 540, of October 31, 1983, on the principle of the freedom of navigation. It should add, however, that the same principle must be observed by Iran by granting Iraq unimpeded access to its terminals, ports, and other facilities, through the Persian Gulf.

Washington's intensified diplomatic efforts through the United Nations, or through any other medium, should insist on the recognition of one fundamental point. The belligerents cannot simply return to the status quo ante. It is imperative either to renegotiate the 1975 Algiers Agreement, which sought to resolve Iran-Iraq border disputes, or to conclude a new one. Either solution should establish a third-party peacekeeping force on the ground between the two neighboring countries. The lack of any such mechanism, in spite of elaborate security provisions, was the greatest flaw in the previous agreement.

In addition to intensifying its own diplomacy, the United States should encourage one other regional development. Iraq and every other Persian Gulf state consider the adoption of the principle of nonintervention the single most important agreement they seek from Iran. Iran's strident ideological crusade and its alleged complicity in acts of political violence lie at the heart of the Arab states' concern. The inclusion of this principle in any future agreement between Iran and Iraq must be matched by its adoption in the relations between Iran and other Gulf states too. The best way to accomplish this is to work through the GCC. No Iranian leader has ever denounced the GCC, and its image has improved in Iranian eyes since its ministerial council launched an earnest and genuine peace initiative in March 1985. The excellent relations between Iran and the United Arab Emirates—largely because of the traditional friendship of Dubai and Sharjah with Iran—could greatly aid the GCC's efforts.

Iran should endorse in theory a Gulf-wide adoption of the principle of non-intervention. It is a cardinal principle of Iran's own constitution, and it has been increasingly emphasized by its leaders. Khomeini has unequivocally ruled out the use of force or interference in the internal affairs of other countries as an acceptable means of exporting the Islamic revolution; setting an example of ethical "Islamic behavior," he says, is the preferred means. And Rafsanjani has denounced intervention in the internal affairs of other countries as a violation of the Quranic precept that "there is no compulsion in religion." Iran's new open-door foreign policy will amount to nothing but empty rhetoric if Iran fails to observe in practice the principle of nonintervention.

Although progress on peace and nonintervention issues at the regional level will perforce aid the improvement of America's relations with Iran, that is not enough. The United States must first and foremost try to regain Iran's confidence. The Khomeini regime's perception that America is determined to isolate and destroy the Iranian Revolution lies at the heart of the problem. The Iranian revolutionary leaders rode the tide of anti-Americanism into power. The militant revolutionaries took over the U.S. Embassy and forced out of office the moderate provisional government of Bazargan for fear that the "liberals" might otherwise invite the Americans back into Iran and continue the Shah's servile policies and the U.S. domination of Iran.

The ideological crusade that was first launched against U.S. diplomats and the embassy in Tehran was then extended to the rest of the Middle East. To the militant revolutionaries, an all-out struggle against American interests was the only way to ensure the new regime's survival. Thus, any and every American move to promote and protect its interests in the Middle East has been seen as targeting the Iranian Revolution. Americans should realize that this view, paranoid or not, significantly shapes Iranian policy toward the United States and its friends in the region.

Realistically, therefore, Washington can temper its containment policy only gradually and patiently. Regaining Iran's confidence will not be easy during Khomeini's lifetime.

During Khomeini's lifetime, however, Washington should take up Rafsanjani's invitation and take the initiative to explore an improvement in bilateral relations. The United States should ask Iran in private what it means by asking in public for changes in the American attitude. Rafsanjani's election as the next president of the Republic would make it even easier to take up his public overture in spite of its caveat about the difficulty of working things out with the Reagan administration. President or not, Rafsanjani is the most influential leader after Khomeini, and he played the central role in the 1981 hostage settlement between the United States and Iran.

Second, during Khomeini's lifetime the United States should at least try to preserve this longer-term option by limiting further damage. Washington should avoid unnecessarily provocative acts and statements, such as Reagan's warning that a "new danger in Central America" had arisen simply because Prime Minister Mir-Hossein Mousavi visited Nicaragua in January 1985. This warning no doubt was intended to increase pressure on the Sandinistas and to shore up support in Congress for Nicaraguan rebel forces. As such, it might have been a good exercise in power politics. But the president overlooked the fact that the Iranian prime minister had just signed the most important economic agreements that Iran has reached recently with Turkey, America's NATO ally. Washington should note and encourage Tehran's establishment of important relations with U.S. friends and allies instead of exaggerating the importance of its inconsequential relationship with Nicaragua, the Reagan administration's current bête noire.

Moreover, Reagan's July 8, 1985, denunciation of Iran as a terrorist country, which came right after Iran helped release the TWA hostages and after Rafsanjani's call for restoring relations, might have pleased the American Right but amounted to an entirely gratuitous and particularly ill-timed provocation.

After Khomeini, the prospects for reconciliation with Iran will improve substantially. The domestic and international pressures that have finally produced the beginnings of a more pragmatic Iranian foreign policy will in all probability continue regardless of the successor regime's makeup. The emerging open-door foreign policy will mean even greater expansion of relations between Iran and China, Japan, and the Western European countries. It also will mean the strengthening of greater regional cooperation through the nascent ECO. If the Iran-Iraq War is ended, the current tensions between Iran and its Arab neighbors also will decrease significantly. Within such an improved regional environment, the United States will be in an even better position to start establishing a new relationship with Iran, beginning with nonstrategic trade and with technical assistance for Iran's postwar reconstruction.

It has taken the Iranian Revolution a fraction of the time it took the revolution in China to launch an open-door foreign policy. In both cases, external threats sped up the process. And in the modern, interdependent world, neither revolution could maintain isolation for long. But the force of this reality hit Iranian leaders much faster than it hit the Chinese. The United States need not wait as long to seek to improve relations with Iran as it did with China. Opportunities for better relations with Iran are just around the corner and should be seized now, with an eye to future cooperation based on mutual interests and respect.

IRAN'S FOREIGN POLICY

Contending Orientations

Weight not the seat of power with your grandeur
Unless by deeds you've made the seat secure.
—*Hafiz*

An entire decade of cold war and nearly a year of sporadic armed skirmishes between Tehran and Washington have not led to a better U.S. understanding of revolutionary Iran's foreign policy. Academic discussion has helped, but not enough. Two dominant analytical tendencies have impeded a fuller comprehension. One views Iran's foreign policy as though it were a mirror image of its "domestic politics." The other sees Iran's foreign policy mainly in terms of geopolitics. An examination of Iran's words and deeds and its theories and practices make clear that Tehran's foreign policy has been shaped largely by an acute interplay between its domestic situation, not merely factional politics, and its external environment, not merely superpower behavior.

By taking such a look, this essay attempts to enhance the understanding of Iran's foreign policy by identifying, in broad strokes, its main orientations. In doing so, it also endeavors to shed fresh light on some older interpretations about such momentous decisions as to why Iran took U.S. hostages and then took the initiative to free them, or why it continued the war with Iraq when it could have ended it and then did end it. Finally, this essay broaches the central implications of all this for Iran and the United States.

The eruption of the Iranian Revolution in 1978 reflected as much a nationwide opposition to the Shah's foreign policy as to his domestic policy. The opposition's attack on his foreign policy centered on his de facto alliance with the United States; hence the revolutionary epithet "the American King." Whether the "roots" of the revolution are traceable back to 1953, when the government of Mohammad Mosaddegh was destroyed, or to 1963, when the opposition to the Shah's regime led by Ayatollah Ruhollah Khomeini was suppressed, or to the society, culture, and politics of an Iran of earlier times, the immediate causes of the revolution lay in the unprecedented ferment of the 1972–77 period, or in what can be described as the "twin revolution of rising alienation" from the Shah's regime and from the United States.[1]

"Iran's Foreign Policy: Contending Orientations" was originally published in *Middle East Journal* 43, no. 2 (Spring 1989): 202–18.

Although as early as 1941, when he ascended the throne, the Shah had longed to become an "ally" of the United States, and although after the fall of Mosaddegh he forged unprecedented economic, political, and military ties with Washington, his de facto alliance with the United States was the by-product of the 1972–77 era. In 1972 President Richard Nixon promised the Shah that he could buy any and every category of U.S. conventional military equipment he wanted. The explosion of oil revenues the following year enabled the Shah to buy large quantities of arms; by 1977 he had purchased over $6 billion's worth from the United States and had more than $12 billion's worth on order. The Shah dreamed of making Iran one of the five conventional military powers of the world, and Washington fueled his ambitions to some extent by anointing his regime the policeman of the Persian Gulf.[2] Many Iranians saw this surrogacy of the Shah's regime as a sign of Iran's complete subservience to the United States and its loss of independence. This popular perception developed into a profound source of alienation.[3]

Yet such alienation alone would not have triggered the revolution; there developed an even greater source. The colossal oil-revenue earnings of 1973–74 were accompanied by a spectacular rate of economic growth—43 percent in 1974—an unprecedented budget surplus of $2 billion in the same year, and rising expectations. But almost immediately thereafter the GNP rate fell drastically to 14 percent in 1975, the budget deficit rose dramatically to nearly $6 billion by 1977, and the revolution of rising expectations developed into a revolution of rising alienation. As if the tumultuous social, economic, and psychological dislocations that all this financial boom and bust entailed were not enough, the Shah's regime in 1975 destroyed even the appearance of competitive politics by creating the Rastakhiz Party and demanding allegiance to it. Instead of mobilizing mass support for his regime, this hated party helped provide the mass support base for the disparate sociopolitical forces that finally coalesced in opposition to the Shah. Thanks to his modernization efforts of the previous decade, by 1978 half of the Iranian population was urban, and mostly poor. The Shah's repressive rule also intensified the underground campaign of assassination against his officials and U.S. military personnel. During this time, while in exile in Najaf, Iraq, Ayatollah Khomeini taught about the anti-Islamic nature of monarchy and the virtues of the rule of the *faqih*.

NATIONALIST NONALIGNMENT

When Khomeini appointed Mehdi Bazargan as the provisional prime minister on February 5, 1979, the first priority of his government was to terminate the subservient de facto alliance of the Shah's regime with the United States and place the relations of the two countries on a plane of "equality." He plotted his foreign policy on the basis of "equilibrium" (*tavazon*), a principle dating back to 1848–51, when it was first introduced in earnest into Iranian foreign-policy thinking and practice by Mirza Taqi Khan, better known as Amir Kabir, during his short-lived premiership.[4] This principle was the inverse of the European balance-of-power principle. It aimed at maintaining Iran's independence vis-à-vis Britain and Russia—the imperial rivals of greatest concern to Iran at the time—by adopting a policy of "impartiality" (*bitarafi*), or nonalignment. In his book on Amir Kabir, Majlis Speaker Ali Akbar Hashemi Rafsanjani characterizes him as "the champion of the struggle against colonialism."[5]

Bazargan adopted a nonalignment policy. He believed that Iran's policy toward the great powers, to use his words, "should be the same as the policy of [Mosaddegh]."[6] Better known as the policy of "negative equilibrium" (*movazeneh-ye manfi*), Mosaddegh's nonalignment policy had aimed at maintaining Iran's independence by terminating British domination. Bazargan sought similarly to end America's dominant influence by undoing the Shah's de facto alliance with the United States. According to revolutionary Iran's first foreign minister, Karim Sanjabi, Iran's nonalignment policy was based on four pillars: "history, the country's geographic position, the spiritual and humanist ideals of Islam, and the principle of complete reciprocity in relations with other countries."[7]

The reference to Islamic ideals did not mean that either Sanjabi or Bazargan believed, as Khomeini did, that the prime unit of loyalty in the Iranian polity should be Islam. Sanjabi's National Front and Bazargan's Iran Liberation Front were both secular, nationalist, and democratic in nature, drawing their social support largely from the middle classes and the modern-educated intellectuals. For both of them the prime unit of the people's loyalty to polity was considered to be the Iranian nation-state. Bazargan claimed that his movement was a bridge between the secular National Front and the religious movement led by Khomeini. Yet, he knew that he was what could be called an "Iran firster," while Khomeini was an "Islam firster." In Bazargan's own words, "I believe in the service of Iran by means of Islam," while Khomeini "believes in the service of Islam by means of Iran."[8] This profound difference between the two leaders, which exists to date, surfaced in a dramatic way at the outbreak of the hostage crisis.

Despite his deep-felt resentment of the Carter administration's continuing support of the Shah's regime, Bazargan tried to pursue a nonhostile, nonalignment policy toward the United States. To end the Shah's de facto alliance with the United States, on March 12, 1979, Sanjabi withdrew Iran's membership from the Central Treaty Organization (CENTO). More consequentially, on November 3 Foreign Minister Ibrahim Yazdi canceled the Iranian-U.S. defense agreement of March 5, 1959. To overturn the Shah's de facto alliance more substantively required the overhauling of a complex web of military relationships with the United States built up over the years by the Shah. This overhauling involved such issues as the disposition of the $12 billion's worth of arms on order, the security of some eighty American-built F-14s, and the disbanding of two secret U.S. listening bases near the Soviet border.

On the same day that the Bazargan government canceled Iran's defense agreement with the United States, it also abrogated Articles 5 and 6 of Iran's 1921 treaty with the Soviet Union. After the November 6, 1979, resignation of Bazargan, this cancellation was affirmed on November 10 by the Revolutionary Council. The Soviet Union claims that these articles give it the unilateral right to intervene in Iran militarily whenever it judges that its security is threatened from Iranian territory.[9] These nefarious articles have been repeatedly invoked by the Soviet Union as a means of pressuring Tehran whenever Moscow believed that Iran was tilting toward the West. Reza Shah secretly tried to cancel them in 1935, and his son did the same in 1958–59, but to date the Soviet Union refuses to do so.

Sanjabi told the Soviet Union in no uncertain terms that Iran had "bad memories" of its relations with its northern neighbor. He said that "our country genuinely wants friendly relations with the USSR, and it will refuse to be [the base] for attack or propaganda against it. . . . On the other hand, we will not allow recurrence of disturbing precedents such as requests for oil concessions, territorial demands or proclamation of the Kurdish Republic at Mahabad. We will defend Iran's independence, integrity and unity whatever the cost."[10]

IDEALISTIC CONFRONTATION

The seizure of the U.S. Embassy on November 4, 1979, and the 444-day hostage dispute that followed became the crucible of an idealistic revolutionary foreign policy that set Iran against much of the rest of the world. Bazargan's nonalignment policy was nationalistic and accommodational, based on the historic principle of equilibrium. As such, it sought to maintain Iran's independence within the context of the existing international system of nation-states. The new idealistic revolutionary orientation in essence defied that system, its norms of diplomatic behavior, and its international law. It was based on a radical interpretation of Khomeini's transnational ideal of what this author terms an "Islamic world order." The "student-captors" of the U.S. hostages were the original architects of this confrontational foreign policy, an orientation that continues to date within the ruling political elite and certain nonelite factions of Iranian political culture.

The takeover of the U.S. Embassy in part reflected the culmination of the opposition of extremist factions to the moderates at the center. Extremists at opposite poles of the political spectrum attacked Bazargan's policy of non-alignment, accusing him and his foreign ministers of pro-Americanism. It was no coincidence that only three days after the seizure of power by revolutionary forces, the U.S. Embassy was attacked for the first time. The common bond of opposition to the Shah that had held the disparate sociopolitical forces together, however, became unglued during the seizure of power from the Shah on February 11, 1979. After a couple of days, U.S. Ambassador William Sullivan and some other Americans were freed as a result of intervention by Ibrahim Yazdi and others in Khomeini's entourage. The Carter administration's admission of the Shah to the United States on October 22, 1979, triggered a massive anti-American demonstration, whose goal of attacking the U.S. Embassy was averted. But on November 4 the anti-Bazargan government forces used the excuse of a meeting held in Algiers between Bazargan and Yazdi with the then–U.S. national security adviser Zbigniew Brzezinski as a pretext finally to attack and occupy the embassy.

Khomeini's endorsement of the embassy seizure after the fact reflected both internal and external concerns. The creation of a *faqih*-ruled Islamic republic being his overriding goal, he calculated that his support of the students' action would ensure the realization of his vision. At the time, their action was emotionally popular and seemed to have a mass support base. Concerned with the Carter administration's antirevolutionary attitude and its scrambling to find a substitute U.S. surrogate for the Shah's regime in the Persian Gulf, Khomeini was suspicious of every move Washington made in the realm of Gulf security and stability. These moves included Secretary of Defense Harold Brown's visit to the Middle East (February 9–19, 1979), which took place at the time of the revolutionary seizure of power, and his unprecedented statement that the U.S. would itself defend its vital interests in Gulf oil supplies by military force "if appropriate." They also included the U.S. negotiations with Oman, Somalia, and Kenya for military facilities and the dispatch of the USS *Constellation* and several supporting warships to the Indian Ocean and the Arabian Sea, as well as the strengthening of the small U.S. naval force in the Gulf itself.[11]

Contrary to conventional wisdom, the kind of nationalist and realistic nonalignment policy that Bazargan had been pursuing did not disappear with his resignation in November 1979. Iran's foreign policy split down the middle between two major orientations. Both Abulhassan Banisadr, first as acting foreign minister and then as the first president of revolutionary Iran, and Sadeq Qotbzadeh, Iran's foreign minister, hewed to a foreign-policy line that was close to the nationalist nonalignment policy of Mosaddegh and Bazargan. Although Banisadr rationalized his "equidistance" policy in Islamic terms, he would rely on Western Europe or France as a counterbalance to the superpowers.[12] Qotbzadeh, no less than his archrival, Banisadr, believed in a non-alignment policy, using the Mosaddeghist term "negative equilibrium" with what he called "honesty in word and in deed."[13] They, therefore, like their predecessors—Mosaddegh, Bazargan, Sanjabi, and Yazdi, who preferred the term "positive neutralism"—were all Iran firsters. And as such, they were all opposed by the revolutionary idealists, who claimed to follow "the Imam Khomeini line" (*Khatti Imam*) rather than "the Mosaddegh path" (*rah-e Mossadegh*).

These idealists were the architects of the other major foreign-policy orientation. They interpreted Khomeini's policy statements to suit their own predispositions and interests. Their interpretation involved, above all else, two major foreign-policy issues: Iran's relations with the East and the West and Iran's export of the "Islamic Revolution." In his overriding concern with establishing a *faqih*-ruled Islamic republic, Khomeini said on December 9, 1979, "A nation that cries in unison that it wants the Islamic Republic, it wants neither East nor West, but an Islamic republic—this being so, we have no right to say that the nation that engaged in an uprising did so in order to have democracy."[14] This statement was made at the height of the Azerbaijan crisis over the adoption of the new constitution. Within this context, Khomeini was emphasizing that in engineering the new republic, Iran should not blindly imitate Eastern socialist or Western capitalist models, claiming that "Islamic democracy" was superior to both Eastern and Western democracies. The idealist interpretation has left out the key phrase "but only an Islamic republic" and has used the slogan "neither East nor West" to advocate that Iran should not have relations with either the Soviet or the U.S. government, nor with governments closely associated with the superpowers.

Regarding the other issue, Khomeini believes in the universal validity of Islam and its export to the rest of the world. In his words, Islam "is not peculiar to a country . . . even the Muslims. Islam comes for humanity. . . . Islam wishes to bring all humanity under the umbrella of justice."[15] *"We hope this will gradually come about."*[16] As a corollary to this concept of an ideal Islamic world order, Iran, as the only *faqih*-ruled Islamic republic, "should try hard to export [its] Revolution to the world."[17] But, he adds emphatically, "It does not take swords to export this ideology. *The export of ideas by force is not export."*[18] In the same speech he added that the way to export revolution was by setting an example of Islamic ethical behavior. The idealists' interpretation overlooks the fact that the call to establish an Islamic world order is what Khomeini called an expression of hope. It prohibits the use of force and requires the export of the revolution through Islamic good behavior.

Two examples of the conflict between these contending foreign-policy orientations during the hostage crisis would suffice. Banisadr worked hard to transfer control of the hostages from their captors to the government so as to obtain their eventual release. He and Qotbzadeh supported the visit of a U.N. commission of inquiry to Iran for that purpose, but the students opposed it. Finally, when the commission was allowed to visit, even before its arrival in Tehran, Khomeini decreed that the hostage dispute would be settled by the Majlis, which was yet to be elected. At Banisadr's urging, the Revolutionary Council recommended (by a vote of eight to three) the transfer of the hostages to government control, only to be rejected by Khomeini. He was supporting the students for the same reasons that he had initially endorsed the seizure of the U.S. Embassy.

The other example relates to the export of the revolution. The students, in pursuing the export of the revolution and in defying the wishes of Foreign Minister Qotbzadeh, sponsored an international conference of some sixteen national liberation movements from across the world. Other revolutionary idealists, such as Muhammad Montazeri, the late son of Ayatollah Hussein-Ali Montazeri, took it upon themselves to try to export revolution by any means, including the use of force. He organized the Iranian Revolutionary Organization of the Masses of the Islamic Republic and wished to dispatch Islamic fighters to Lebanon as early as December 1979, long before the revolutionary guards were sent there in 1982. He was opposed by Banisadr and Qotbzadeh, just as he had been by Bazargan.

The settlement of the hostage dispute ended the students' control of Iran's U.S. policy, a control that could not have been sustained for long without Khomeini's blessing. The stock interpretation that Iran finally decided to take the initiative on September 9, 1980, to settle the hostage dispute—because the hostages were no longer needed as a means of consolidation of power by Khomeini and his followers—requires reconsideration for three reasons. First, although institutionally power had been relatively consolidated—with the adoption of the constitution, the election of the first president, and the election of the First Majlis and its first speaker by September 1980—the ideological and political struggle between Banisadr and his disparate supporters and the triumvirate of Muhammad Beheshti, Mohammad-Ali Rajai, and Hashemi Rafsanjani and their unruly followers became more acute after Khomeini took the initiative to settle the dispute. Second, the U.S. freezing of $12 billion in Iranian assets and varying degrees of economic sanctions by other Western nations exerted significant pressure on Iran. For months Banisadr and the Central Bank believed that the freeze would not affect Iranian assets in U.S. banks in Britain and the rest of Europe and resorted to litigation to try to free the assets, but their efforts were unsuccessful. Third, Iran feared an Iraqi invasion. Border skirmishes had escalated; Iran believed that Iraq's rapprochement with Saudi Arabia included some kind of military coalition. In addition, the Soviet Union rejected all Iranian demands to cut off Soviet arms supplies to Iraq.

Far from ending Iran's confrontational foreign policy, the settlement of the hostage dispute actually intensified it. Believing that the increased activities of the United States in the Persian Gulf, beginning as early as February 1979, aimed at the containment and ultimate destruction of the revolutionary regime, the Iranians saw the United States as the real instigator of the Iraqi invasion of Iran on September 22, 1980. Paranoid or not, this view of the war as having been "imposed" by the U.S. "deputy," Saddam Hussein, to use Montazeri's characterization, was in part responsible for the Iranian decision to carry the war into Iraqi territory in July 1982. The revolutionary idealists, who suspected the United States of supporting Iraqi war efforts and who dreamed of marching to Jerusalem through Karbala, won the debate of the day with the revolutionary realists, who were skeptical. In the six-year interval between July 1982 and July 1988, when Iran accepted the U.N.-brokered cease-fire, the idealists' foreign-policy orientation often prevailed over that of the realists.

Iran's confrontational foreign policy left it with only one major ally in the Middle East, and that was Syria.[19] All the other states of the region felt threatened in varying degrees by Iran's crusade to spread the revolution. In response to this perceived threat, as well as that of the spread of the Iran-Iraq War to their territories, the six Arab Gulf states established the Gulf Cooperation Council in 1981 as a protective mechanism.[20] The export of the revolution by propaganda and annual demonstrations during the Hajj in Saudi Arabia isolated Iran within the region, as did its dispatch of revolutionary guards to Lebanon and its support of the Lebanese Hezbollah and the Islamic Amal. It was further isolated by suspicions of its complicity in the attempted coup in Bahrain in 1981 as well as in the suicide car bombings of U.S. and French forces in Lebanon in October 1983 and acts of violence in Kuwait.[21] In addition, the holding of American, British, French, and German hostages in Lebanon by reputedly pro-Iranian groups was encouraged at least in part by Iran's anti-Western, confrontational foreign policy, which further isolated it.

The crusade to export the revolution, furthermore, aggravated the difficulties in Iran's relations with the Soviet Union. The ethnic and geographic proximity of the two countries fueled the Soviet Union's concern about the possible contagion of the Islamic Revolution among Soviet Muslims. In a real sense, both the United States and the Soviet Union wished to contain Iran's destabilizing export of the Islamic Revolution. To be sure, the Soviet invasion of Afghanistan and especially the resumption of Soviet arms supplies to Iraq in 1982 were the more influential factors in the troubled Soviet-Iranian relations, but Iran's campaign to propagate its revolution was a major factor in Moscow's view of

Iran's "anti-Sovietism." Even the economic relations between the two countries were affected and did not improve until 1986, by which time Iran's idealistic confrontational foreign policy had been significantly tempered.[22]

REALISTIC CONCILIATION

The revolutionary idealists could not then, and do not now, care about Iran's international isolation, to which their confrontational foreign policy has so largely contributed. They repeatedly refer to one of Ayatollah Khomeini's statements to support their foreign-policy orientation: "We must become isolated in order to become independent."[23] But as Majlis Speaker Hashemi Rafsanjani has since complained, such Khomeini statements are often quoted out of context. This statement was made at the time of the hostage crisis, when, in fact, Iran had become internationally isolated partly because of Western diplomatic sanctions and partly because of the international disapprobations voiced by the U.N. Security Council and the International Court of Justice.

Just as Iran has had its revolutionary idealists since the beginning of the revolution, it has also had revolutionary realists. They both believe that Islam is, and should be, the prime unit of people's loyalty in the Iranian polity, but they sharply differ on the relative weight of "Iranianness" and "Islamicness" in the Iranian identity. They also differ in their attitudes toward the existing international system. The idealists are world revolutionaries who want to establish an Islamic world order *now*, despite the fact that Khomeini has said, "We hope this will gradually come about."[24] The realists, on the other hand, who also hope for an Islamic world order, are willing to come to terms with the realities of the existing international system. Hence, unlike the idealists, they are conciliatory in their foreign-policy orientation. Khomeini refers to the differences between the two groups as "two schools of thought," and Hashemi Rafsanjani calls them "factions." Whatever the label, the important cautionary point is that the fluidity of Iranian revolutionary politics is such that today's idealists may be tomorrow's realists, and vice versa, and idealists on one set of issues may be realists on another. This is why the nature of revolutionary Iran's foreign policy is neither linear nor dialectical, but *kaleidoscopic*.

As the supreme arbiter of Iranian affairs, Khomeini himself fits neither the idealist nor the realist category. There are two major reasons for this. First, given the fluidity of Iranian factional politics, he looks after Iran's overall interests by performing the role of the balancer, throwing his weight behind one faction or another, depending on the circumstances. Second, his entire career as the leader of the Islamic opposition to the Shah's regime and as the supreme leader of Iran since 1979 reveals a complex mixture of idealism and realism in his leadership that is difficult for Westerners to comprehend, leading to such pejorative American journalistic labels as "fanatic" and to the constant surprise of the American body politic over the "disarray" of his foreign policy. He endorses the taking of U.S. hostages, and yet he releases them. He decides to continue the war, and yet he finally ends it. Khomeini himself keeps changing the Khomeini line.

Under one set of circumstances Khomeini has contributed to Iran's international isolation, and under another he has led the campaign to break that isolation down. Yet, all these actions have aimed at the fundamental goal of Iran's independence under a *faqih*-ruled Islamic republic. The first requirement of Iran's independence, he said as early as December 1979, was what he called "intellectual independence," which required, among other things, that "we should learn the good things from foreigners and reject the bad things."[25] At the time, he held up the examples of Japan and India for Iran. On October 27, 1982, he said that Iran must end its hermit status in the world, and at his initiative and with his approval, President Ali Khamenei launched Iran's "open-door" foreign policy on July 30 and reiterated it on August 6, 1984—a policy that he said involved "rational, sound and healthy relations with all countries" and aimed at serving Iran's interest and ideology.[26]

Khomeini himself said on October 29, 1984, that it was "inadmissible to common sense and humanity" not to have relations with other governments "since it would mean defeat, annihilation and being buried right to the end."[27] Going even further, he said on November 2, 1985, that "we do not want to live in a country which is isolated from the rest of the world. Today's Iran cannot be that way. Other countries cannot close their borders to others either; it would be irrational. Today the world is like one family, one city. In the present world circumstances we should not be isolated."[28] This is "the new thinking" in Iran; Hashemi Rafsanjani calls it "interdependence."

What, then, does the conciliatory open-door foreign policy mean for the "neither East nor West" principle? It means that in pursuing its overriding goals of Islamic revolution and Iranian independence, Iran must reject both Eastern and Western domination of any kind. In his statement of October 3, 1988, Khomeini categorically announced that a deviation from that principle would be "treachery to Islam and the Muslims," without spelling out what that principle meant.[29] But Hashemi Rafsanjani immediately added that it meant "loyalty to the goals of the Islamic Revolution, independence and negation of foreign domination."[30]

The idealists have rejected this realist interpretation of the principle. When Iran sent a low-ranking delegation to Leonid Brezhnev's funeral, for example, or when Iran's relations with the Soviet Union seemed to be improving, the radicals objected. As a result, the Foreign Ministry sent no one to Konstantin

Chernenko's funeral, but in the latter case Foreign Minister Ali Akbar Velayati said that the "objectives of the slogan ["neither East nor West"] is the negation of alien domination and not snapping of communication. . . . Nowadays, negating political relations with other countries means negating identity of the countries."[31] With respect to Iran's relations with the West, when the radicals objected to the expansion of Iran's relations with West Germany and even with Turkey, Hashemi Rafsanjani said that world realities meant "we do not always have the power to choose. I believe our principles are obeyed, but in some cases we may be limited and we may have to forego some of these principles."[32]

The issue of postwar reconstruction has intensified the debate between the idealists and the realists about the participation of foreign capital and technical know-how in the Iranian economy. While such leaders as Prime Minister Mir-Hossein Mousavi would seem to begrudge such participation, at least by some countries, others welcome it. Hashemi Rafsanjani, for example, said on October 21, 1988, that "we should absorb skilled manpower from abroad and programs should be designed to encourage the return to Iran of skilled Iranians now residing abroad."[33] And Khamenei said on October 7, 1988, that when Iran faces shortages it "should use foreign resources. . . . We cannot prolong the issue of reconstruction for 100 years."[34]

And deeds speak louder than words. Even before the Iran-Iraq cease-fire, more than 70 percent of Iran's total imports came from Canada, Japan, and Western Europe, and more than 50 percent of its total exports went to these same areas.[35] While West Germany and Japan were the main exporters to Iran in 1987, the United States was Iran's main export market until the Reagan administration imposed a total ban on Iranian imports in the fall of that year.[36] Despite the increase in the total value of Iran's trade with the Soviet Union in that same year, it was only about $250 million, as compared with about $2.5 billion with West Germany alone. Iran's economic relations with both the East and the West are expected to expand in the postwar era now that diplomatic relations with Britain, Canada, and France have been resumed.

Iran's principle of the export of the revolution is also undergoing change. The realists insist that the Islamic revolution must start at home, or in what they call the "Islamic citadel." Even Ayatollah Montazeri, reputedly yesterday's archsupporter of the export of the revolution, today says that the way to export the revolution is to "build our country on the basis of Islam" so that it becomes "a model for other deprived countries."[37]

Again, deeds speak louder than words. Mehdi Hashemi, the chief activist exporter of the revolution, was arrested after his faction attempted to smuggle arms to Saudi Arabia during the Hajj in 1986 and before his faction leaked the news of former U.S. national security adviser Robert McFarlane's visit to Iran in conjunction with the U.S.-Iranian arms-deal scandal. He was executed in 1987.[38] Since the acceptance of the cease-fire, the realists have helped with the release of seven French and German hostages in Lebanon, as of this writing, and the release of British hostages may be in the cards as well. Nine American hostages remain in captivity in Lebanon. Iranian leaders have repeatedly offered to help with their release, but it is unlikely that this can actually take place without an improvement in overall U.S.-Iranian relations. Iran may also try to distance itself from the Supreme Assembly of the Islamic Revolution in Iraq (SAIRI), which is linked to the Iraqi underground Al-Dawa dissidents, depending on the degree of progress made in the peace process. The opening of a SAIRI branch in Damascus may be a move in the direction of eventually moving its headquarters out of Iran.

More important to those observers who insist that Iran's continuation of the war after 1982 aimed at the export of the revolution, Khomeini's acceptance of U.N. Resolution 598 must suggest that at least for the Iranian realists the first priority now is the building of the Islamic Revolution at home rather than its export. Despite the reservation, if not outright opposition, of Interior Minister Ali Akbar Mohtashemi to Resolution 598, he at least implied in his statement to the Majlis on September 12, 1988, that after Khomeini's acceptance he was not opposed to the wishes of the "absolute imam." At least for the moment, the differences between the idealists and the realists on the question of war and peace appear to have been resolved in favor of the realists, who are in the political ascendancy.

Iran's decision to accept the cease-fire and to commit itself seriously to the peace process reflects an acute interplay between its battlefield setbacks and its deteriorating socioeconomic conditions. Until February 1987, Iranian leaders had repeatedly promised a "final victory" and once even specified a victory by March 21, 1987, the Iranian New Year. Although the Karbala-5 offensive threatened Basra and sent shockwaves throughout the Gulf and all the way to Washington, its failure despite, or because of, the massive loss of life by the Revolutionary Guard Corps made Iran realize for the first time that the war could not be won. Hashemi Rafsanjani frankly said: "To tell the truth, we cannot see a bright horizon now, so far as ending the war in its present form is concerned."[39] He meant *winning* the war.

It was no coincidence, therefore, that in July 1987, for the first time, Iran did not reject a U.N. resolution out of hand, although admittedly Resolution 598 was more sensitive to Iran's position than the previous ones. Iran had quietly opted for a diplomatic solution to the war, probably sometime after the effects of the disastrous Karbala-5 offensive sank into the consciousness of the Iranian leaders. No matter how important the subsequent battlefield setbacks at

Faw Peninsula, the Majnun Islands, and Shalamjah beginning in April 1988, the fact remains that Iran had already been involved in prolonged discussions with U.N. Secretary General Javier Perez de Cuellar long before the advent of these setbacks.

Even these military setbacks, coupled with the Iraqi *al-Hussein* missile raids on Iranian cities between February 29 and April 18, 1988, however, would probably not have impelled Iran to opt for peace when it did had it not been for mounting economic hardship and the seemingly unbreachable deadlock on socioeconomic reforms. The widespread economic hardship caused by the war intensified in 1986–87 because of a dramatic drop in oil revenues, resulting from an unprecedented fall in oil prices in 1986 and an equally unprecedented increase in Iraq's capability for disrupting Iranian oil exports. The Iraqi attacks on Iranian oil shipments could reach as far south as the Iranian transshipment station on Sirri Island and even the terminal on Larak Island, farther south in the Strait of Hormuz. The U.S. quasi war with Iran made it possible for Iraq to disrupt Iran's oil exports with impunity.

The economic situation became so desperate that on November 13, 1987, the Iranian government called for a "financial jihad," urging those Iranians who could not fight in the war, "such as women, the sick, and those with other excuses," to give financial support instead.[40] But as President Khamenei complained, the rich hung back and were not forthcoming. Khomeini lowered the boom on the rich with his decree of January 6, 1988. He tried to break the long-standing logjam on measures for social justice and economic betterment caused by the veto of government reform bills by conservative members of the Council of Guardians. He created a thirteen-member review council to oversee the decisions of the Guardians in "the interest of the Islamic country."[41] And in accepting the cease-fire in 1988 in a war that he could not win, Khomeini opted for the survival of the "Islamic Revolution," just as he settled the hostage dispute in 1981 for the same overriding purpose.

TWIN IMPLICATIONS

This discussion began with 1978, the year that marked the culminating point in Iran of the rising twofold alienation from the Shah's regime and from the United States. It ends with the central implications of Iran's kaleidoscopic foreign-policy orientations for both countries during the first decade of the revolution. For Iran, there are two: the revolutionary regime needs to come to terms with the realities of the modern world, and it needs to come to terms with itself. The current debate between the revolutionary idealists and the revolutionary realists—like the earlier debate between the revolutionary nationalists and the revolutionary Islamists on the nature of Iran's foreign policy—reveals the still unresolved underlying differences. Yet, the Iranian experience over the decade has produced new ideas that may point the way for Iran to come to terms with the modern world without sacrificing its Islamic ideals. Khomeini has unequivocally stated what Iran's conception of the world should be if it is to come to terms with it: "Today the world is like one family, one city."[42] This is a conception that Hashemi Rafsanjani calls an "interdependent world" and that prompts Khomeini to announce, "We do not want to live in a country which is isolated from the rest of the world."[43] The real challenge facing the revolutionary realists today lies in their persuading the revolutionary idealists to accept this conception as a foundation of Iran's foreign policy.

For most of the decade, the revolutionary idealists have, in effect, rejected this conception of the world, insisting on substituting their view of creating an Islamic world order by pursuing a confrontational foreign policy toward both the East and the West, accompanied by an aggressive crusade to export the Islamic Revolution by propaganda rather than by setting a good example of Islamic behavior as Khomeini has decreed. This policy has isolated Iran internationally to the detriment of its interests and its humane Islamic ideals.

Besides pointing out this lesson, the realists could demonstrate the inescapable reality of the diffusion of world culture, a culture marked by the advancement of science and technology and an insatiable quest for economic betterment, social justice, and political freedom that knows no international boundaries. Both revolutionary Russia and China tried to reject the concept of an interdependent world culture, and both have ended up accepting it. They had no other choice; nor does revolutionary Iran.

The tension between the relative weight of "Islamicness" and "Iranianness" in the Iranian sense of national identity has continued ever since the Arab invasion of Iran in the seventh century. It has been intensified only in the context of an acute encounter between Iranian culture and world culture since the nineteenth century, and especially since the advent of the populist Iranian Revolution a decade ago. The well-known Iranian intellectual Jalal Al-e Ahmad prescribed that Iranians could best resolve this historical tension if the "modernized intellectuals" (raushan-fekran) could unite their political forces with those of the traditional ulama. He did not live to see that in the Iranian Revolution, as in all previous instances of popular uprisings, the coalition between the two would prove to be ephemeral. To date, even the moderate religio-political Liberation Movement of Iran of Bazargan, which is the only "loyal opposition" group in Iran, is not allowed to criticize government policies peacefully and freely. Even such a moderate opposition group charges that it is subjected to acts of intimidation and violence.

For the United States, the implications of the Iranian Revolution suggest a need for America to come to terms with the fact that at least some of Iran's hostile words and deeds are a direct result of Washington's own misguided policies both before and since the revolution. In fact, as seen, the eruption of the revolution itself in part reflected alienation from the United States, most of all because of the popular perception that it was smothering Iran's sense of dignity and independence by its military, economic, and political support of the Shah's regime almost to the very end of his repressive rule.

One would hope that the more conciliatory foreign policy emerging from Iran, combined with the new administration of George H. W. Bush, might occasion a serious reassessment of America's Iran policy. Tehran and Washington might stop their mutual and destructive smear campaigns as a first step in the direction of a constructive and open dialogue. Even an implied approval of such a dialogue by Khomeini would lend it the kind of legitimacy that the realists will need, once he is gone, to cope with the enormous challenge of what may be called the "twofold *perestroika*" of postwar reconstruction and social and economic reforms. To meet this challenge, the realists will need to broaden and deepen their support base among the people. And to help that process along, the United States will need to place its relations with Iran during the second decade of the revolution on a plane of reciprocal interests and mutual respect.

NOTES

1. For the earliest characterization of the revolution in these terms, see R. K. Ramazani, "Iran's Revolution in Perspective," in *The Impact of the Iranian Events upon Persian Gulf and United States Security*, project director Z. Michael Szaz (Washington, DC, 1979), 19–37; Ramazani, "Iran's Foreign Policy: Perspectives and Projections," in *Economic Consequences of the Revolution in Iran: A Compendium of Papers Submitted to the Joint Economic Committee, Congress of the United States* (Washington, DC, 1980), 65–97; and Ramazani, "Iran's Revolution: Patterns, Problems, and Prospects," pp. 33–49 in this volume.

2. See R. K. Ramazani, *The United States and Iran: The Patterns of Influence* (New York, 1982).

3. In reality, however, the Shah often used the United States as its surrogate. See R. K. Ramazani, "Who Lost America? The Case of Iran," pp. 50–67 in this volume.

4. See R. K. Ramazani, *The Foreign Policy of Iran, 1500–1941: A Developing Nation in World Affairs* (Charlottesville, 1966), 63–65.

5. See Akbar Hashemi-Rafsanjani, *Amir Kabir Ya Qahreman-e Mobarezeh Ba Iste'mar* [Amir Kabir or champion of the struggle against colonialism] (Qom, [1967/68]).

6. For the original text of Bazargan's important interview by al-Dustur in Arabic, see the 24–30 December 1979 issue or the translation in Foreign Broadcast Information Service, *Daily Report*, vol. 5, *Middle East and North Africa* (FBIS-MEA), 3 January 1980, 25.

7. FBIS-MEA, 13 March 1979, R-10.

8. See Mohandes Mehdi Bazargan, *Enqelab-e Iran dar Dau Harekat* (The Iranian Revolution in two phases) (Tehran, [1983/84]), esp. 110–11.

9. For details, see R. K. Ramazani, "Treaty Relations: An Iranian-Soviet Case Study," in *The Search for World Order: Studies by Students and Colleagues of Quincy Wright*, edited by Albert Lepawsky, Edward H. Buehrig, and Harold D. Lasswell (New York, 1979), 298–311.

10. FBIS-MEA, 13 March 1979, R-11.

11. Although Washington geared up its muscle-flexing tactics on December 4, 1979, the Iranians had been watching U.S. pressure tactics in the Gulf since February, with increasing concern. Secretary Brown's visit to the Middle East and his statement were fully reported, for example, in *Ettela'at*, [23 July 1979], 12. Iran also put its navy on alert around the Strait of Hormuz. See ibid., [24 July 1979], 12. See also R. K. Ramazani, "The Genesis of the Carter Doctrine," in *Middle East Perspectives*, edited by George S. Wise and Charles Issawi (Princeton, 1981), 165–80.

12. See FBIS-MEA, 21 November 1979, R-9. Banisadr believed that "despite the historical and ideological differences between the West and Iran, the two sides' interests were not so far apart." Ibid., 20 November 1979, R-30.

13. Besides "negative equilibrium," Qotbzadeh listed the other principles of Iran's foreign policy as follows: "non-interference in the affairs of other countries; a policy of an independent Iran; independence in decision-making; and harmonizing ideologies and politics." Ibid., 21 December 1979, 27.

14. Ibid., 10 December 1979, 29.

15. Ibid., 18 December 1979, 10.

16. Foreign Broadcast Information Service, *Daily Report*, vol. 8, *South Asia* (FBIS-SA), 11 February 1987, I-2, emphasis added.

17. *Sourush* (Tehran), March 1981, 4–5. For more details, see R. K. Ramazani, "Khomeini's Islam in Iran's Foreign Policy," pp. 71–93 in this volume.

18. Ramazani, "Khomeini's Islam," p. 81 in this volume, emphasis added.

19. For details, see R. K. Ramazani, *Revolutionary Iran: Challenge and Response in the Middle East* (1986; Baltimore, 1988), 176–78.

20. See R. K. Ramazani, *The Gulf Cooperation Council: Record and Analysis* (Charlottesville, 1988).

21. See R. K. Ramazani, "Iran's Revolution and the Persian Gulf," *Current History* 84 (January 1985): 5–8, 40–41; Ramazani, *Revolutionary Iran*, 42–52, 175–95; and Ramazani, "Sociopolitical Change in the Gulf: A Climate for Terrorism?," pp. 263–84 in this volume.

22. See R. K. Ramazani, "Iran," in *Yearbook on International Communist Affairs*, edited by Richard F. Staar (Stanford, CA, 1987 and 1988), 432–36 and 408–12, respectively.

23. *Gozaresh-e Seminar* (Tehran), no. 2 (1983–84): 36. See also R. K. Ramazani, "Revolutionary Iran's Open Door Policy," *Harvard International Review*, January 1987, 11–15.

24. FBIS-SA, 11 February 1987.

25. FBIS-MEA, 14 December 1979, 12.

26. FBIS-SA, 31 July 1984, I-2, and 7 August 1984, I-2.

27. Ibid., 30 October 1984, I-1.

28. Ibid., 4 November 1985, I-2.

29. For Khomeini's reconstruction guidelines, see Foreign Broadcast Information Service, *Daily Report*, vol. 2, *Near East and South Asia* (FBIS-NES), 4 October 1988, 46–48.

30. Ibid.

31. Ramazani, "Iran," in Staar, *Yearbook* (1988), 408–12.

32. FBIS-SA, 17 April 1987, I-3, emphasis added.

33. FBIS-NES, 21 October 1988, 43.

34. Ibid., 11 October 1988, 59.

35. See R. K. Ramazani, "Iran: Burying the Hatchet," pp. 94–110 in this volume.

36. See the table in *Middle East Economic Digest*, 12 August 1988, 8.

37. FBIS-NES, 31 October 1988, 73.

38. See Ramazani, *Revolutionary Iran*, 253–69.

39. As quoted in the *Economist* (London), 14 February 1987, 30.

40. FBIS-NES, 13 November 1987, 61.

41. Ibid., 7 January 1988, 50.

42. FBIS-SA, 4 November 1985, I-2.

43. Ibid.

IRAN'S EXPORT OF THE REVOLUTION

Its Politics, Ends, and Means

Since its creation following several decades of genuine Islamic and popular struggle the Islamic Republic of Iran has considered it one of its main duties to defend dear Islam, its sacred aspirations, and the oppressed Muslims in every region of the world.
—Iran's Ministry of Foreign Affairs, March 7, 1989

Ayatollah Ruhollah Khomeini's imposition of a death sentence on Salman Rushdie ignited a new global crisis. The move demonstrated that Iran's underlying commitment to "the export of the revolution" (*sodour-e enqelab*) was alive and well. It also demonstrated that an assessment of the relative impact of Iran's export activities compared with the indigenous causes of Islamic resurgence in other societies can have profound implications for not only the Muslim world but also the international system as a whole. Such an assessment is the principal burden of this volume, which seeks to inquire into the global impact of the Iranian Revolution. The main objective of this essay is to explore the politics, ends, and means of exporting the revolution in the overall context of Iran's foreign policy.

The appellation "export of the revolution," unlike such terms as "intervention," "aggression," and "self-defense," is not commonly found in the literature of international relations. Yet the basic idea that underpins the act of exporting revolution is part and parcel of ancient as well as modern international relations when defined broadly and not just Eurocentrically in terms of the post-Westphalia international society.[1] As sacred as the Prophet's Islamic Revolution may be, and as secular as the American, French, and Russian revolutions have been, the concept of exporting revolution is a corollary of the phenomenon of the revolution throughout world history. This proposition also holds true for the more recent example of the Iranian Revolution. By intervention, America wants to make the world safe for democracy; witness the cases of Iran, Guatemala, El Salvador, and Nicaragua. And by invasion, the Soviet Union wants to make the world safe for socialism; witness the cases of Czechoslovakia and Afghanistan. And by the export of its revolution, the Islamic Republic of Iran

"Iran's Export of the Revolution: Its Politics, Ends, and Means" was originally published in *The Iranian Revolution: Its Global Impact*, ed. John Esposito (Miami: Florida International University Press, 1990), 40–62, and is reprinted with permission of the University Press of Florida.

wants to make the world safe for Islam; witness the cases of the Persian Gulf, Lebanon, and Soviet Azerbaijan and Turkmenistan.

THE POLITICS

Like the Iranian Revolution itself, the emergence of the revolution's export as a fundamental foreign-policy principle reflected Iran's domestic political dynamics. The revolt in Iran was a populist opposition to both the Shah's foreign policy and domestic politics.[2] The disparate forces of opposition were as united against the Shah's de facto alliance with the United States as they were against his repressive rule. The revolutionary epithet "the American king" reflected a nationwide resentment of the surrogacy of Iran, especially as the Nixon-anointed "policeman" of the Persian Gulf. Whether one traces the roots of the Iranian Revolution to the CIA-engineered overthrow of Mohammad Mosaddegh's nationalist government in 1953, or to the bloody suppression of the Khomeini-led anti-Shah uprising in 1963, or to earlier developments in Iranian society, politics, and culture, the fact remains that at no time before the 1972–77 period had the alienation from the Shah's regime and the United States reached such explosive levels of populist expression.[3]

In the early days of Khomeini's regime, from Mehdi Bazargan's appointment as prime minister of the provisional government in February 1979 until Iranian students seized the U.S. Embassy in Tehran in November of that year, the principle of "equilibrium" (*tavazon*) dominated the theory and practice of Iranian foreign policy. Historically, the principle of equilibrium had great appeal to modern-educated Iranians. Mirza Taqi Khan, better known as Amir Kabir, first introduced the principle into Iranian foreign policy during his short-lived premiership in 1848–51 as an antidote to the European balance-of-power principle.[4] He believed that Iran might better ensure its independence by maintaining an equilibrium between rival British and Russian influences than by aligning itself with one or the other imperial power. During his equally short-lived premiership in 1951–53, Mosaddegh tried to pursue a policy of "negative equilibrium" (*movazeneh-ye manfi*).[5] Covert CIA intervention, however, destroyed his government, at which point the Shah's regime allied itself with a vengeance to the United States until it too was overthrown.

Although a devout Muslim, Bazargan attempted, as a modern-educated engineer, to pursue the same policy toward the great powers as had his old friend and colleague Mosaddegh. His government terminated Iran's membership in the U.S.-sponsored Central Treaty Organization (CENTO) and the Iranian-U.S. defense act of March 5, 1959, while repudiating the nefarious Articles 5 and 6 of the Soviet-Iranian Treaty of 1921.[6] The Bazargan government sought amicable relations with Iran's Muslim neighbors, as evidenced by its desire to strengthen the Regional Cooperation for Development (RCD) arrangement of 1964 with Pakistan and Turkey. According to the testimony of the Iraqi Ministry of Foreign Affairs, the Bazargan government also sought improved relations with Baghdad.[7] And when Ayatollah Sadeq Ruhani threatened to annex Bahrain unless it adopted an Iranian type of Islamic government, Bazargan denounced the Ayatollah's unauthorized statement and sent envoys to Bahrain and Saudi Arabia to allay their fears.[8]

The seizure of the U.S. Embassy in Tehran did more than precipitate the resignation of the Bazargan government on November 6, 1979. It also split Iranian foreign policy right down the middle. Until January 19, 1981, when the dispute over the American hostages was settled, the self-styled student followers of Khomeini struggled for control of Iranian foreign policy against government ministers such as Abulhassan Banisadr and Sadeq Qotbzadeh. Both Banisadr and Qotbzadeh were in effect inspired by Mosaddegh's foreign-policy orientation, although Banisadr rationalized his policy of "equidistance" in Islamic terms. That is, his conception of Islamic foreign policy accorded first priority to the Iranian national interest rather than to the interests of the Muslim world or the whole Third World.[9] For this reason he considered the seizure of the embassy contrary to the law of nations and sought to settle the dispute with the United States by peaceful means. Qotbzadeh, on the other hand, simply subscribed to Mosaddegh's policy of "negative equilibrium" and did not hesitate to describe his foreign policy in those terms.[10]

The students' hostility toward the United States was paralleled by their friendly attitude toward anti-American and anti-Western liberation movements. According to Bazargan, the students were supported by the leftist elements of the Tudeh (communist) Party and the Mujahadeen-e-Khalq organization, and this may well have been true at the time of the embassy takeover. Subsequently, however, the Islamists on the extreme right dominated the student faction, representing what can best be described as the radical idealist followers of Khomeini.[11] Many such idealists were also to be found among Khomeini's clerical disciples. Whether lay or clerical, these radical idealists interpreted the Ayatollah's call for the export of the revolution to mean that it should be put into practice at any price. In defiance of Iranian policymakers, particularly Banisadr and Qotbzadeh, the students sponsored an international conference in Tehran of some sixteen liberation movements from around the world. Other radical idealists, such as Muhammad Montazeri, the son of Ayatollah Hussein-Ali Montazeri, took it upon themselves to try to export the revolution by any means, including the use of force. Muhammad Montazeri organized the Iranian Revolutionary Organization of the Masses of the Islamic Republic and wished to dispatch Islamic fighters to Lebanon as early as December 1979, long before the revolutionary guards were sent there in 1982. He was opposed by Banisadr and Qotbzadeh, just as he had been by Bazargan.

Although, as we shall see, Khomeini's call for the export of the revolution had deep roots in his ideology and in the Irano-Islamic political culture, I suggest it emerged from the crucible of the hostage crisis. The seizure of the U.S. Embassy on November 4, 1979, and the fall of the Bazargan government two days later were dubbed by the Khomeinists as the "second revolution," an event Khomeini himself considered even more significant than the overthrow of the Shah's regime. From the perspective of Iranian domestic politics, this second revolution represented the first successful move by the Islamists against the centralists or nationalists, who are pejoratively labeled "liberals" by their opponents. The anti-liberal Islamists consisted of lay and clerical, as well as radical idealist and pragmatic realist, factions. They were opposed by other clerical idealists such as Hussein-Ali Montazeri, clerical realists such as Hashemi Rafsanjani, lay idealists such as Mir-Hossein Mousavi, and lay realists such as Ali Akbar Velayati.

This second revolution also marked the transformation of Iran's fundamental foreign-policy principle of equilibrium to one of a struggle between good and evil. Under the equilibrium principle, the government took the international system for granted and tried to protect and promote Iran's national interest by maintaining a balance of power and influence in relation to other states. After the second revolution, the makers of foreign policy questioned the very legitimacy of the existing international system; they sought to protect and promote Iran's Islamic interest by rejecting the dominance of both superpowers in the international system and by exporting the revolution throughout the world. In other words, the second revolution introduced into Iran's foreign policy the twin principles of "neither East nor West, but the Islamic Republic" (nah sharq, nah gharb, faqat jumhuri-i Islami) and "the export of the revolution" (sodour-e enqelab). We shall explore in the following section the foundations of these two principles. Suffice it to say here that they were essentially incorporated into the Republic's new constitution, which was ratified in early December 1979, about a month after the embassy takeover.[12]

Because of the secrecy surrounding many of Iran's activities, it is difficult to state with certainty when the principle of export of the revolution was first implemented. One can, however, make the case that it was not fully put into practice until after the "third revolution," that is, after the fall of President Banisadr in June 1981. More specifically, it is possible to argue that the principle was formally adopted during the tenure of Mir-Hossein Mousavi as foreign minister

(July–December 1981). This claim can be substantiated as follows: First, none of the foreign ministers before Mohammad-Ali Rajai, that is, neither Karim Sanjabi, Ibrahim Yazdi, Abulhassan Banisadr, nor Sadeq Qotbzadeh, believed in the export of the revolution, although Banisadr did talk about the "universal mission" of the revolution. Second, although a lay Islamist and a believer in the export of the revolution, Rajai was preoccupied with settling the hostage dispute with the United States during part of his short tenure. Third, Mousavi was the first foreign minister to envisage the need for creating a committee in the Ministry of Foreign Affairs that would "determine the basis of the foreign policy from an ideological perspective, and the principle of rule of theocracy."[13] Moreover, he decided to draw up a "plan for an Islamic front" worldwide, which he said would be "followed up" by the Iranian Ministry of Foreign Affairs "because the fight against imperialism should take place all over the world."[14]

Of even greater consequence, however, was the establishment of the Islamic Revolutionary Council as an umbrella organization. It included such groups as the Supreme Assembly of the Islamic Revolution in Iraq (SAIRI), the Islamic Revolution Movement of the Arabian Peninsula, the Islamic Front for the Liberation of Bahrain, and a liberation group for Syria and Lebanon. These groups were linked to the Islamic Revolutionary Guard Corps (IRGC) through its Islamic-liberation-movement unit. According to Iran's Constitution, the IRGC itself "will be responsible not only for defending the borders, but also for the mission stated in the Book, of holy war in the way of God and fighting to expand the rule of God's law [Sharia] in the world."

The suppression of the liberal nationalists and leftists as a consequence of the second and third revolutions ensured the political ascendancy of the Islamists. But just as the disparate political forces had all joined hands in opposition to the Shah's regime and had then quickly divided after its fall, the Islamists had at first united their forces against the liberal nationalists and leftists and had then broken up into factions after their triumph against their opponents. In regard to Iran's foreign policy in general, the Islamists divided into what can best be described as "radical idealists" and "pragmatic realists." Khomeini referred to this division in terms of "two schools of thought," while Hashemi Rafsanjani simply speaks of them as "factions." What is meant by "radical idealist" and "pragmatic realist" should become clear in light of the following discussion of the ends and means of the export of the revolution.[15]

THE ENDS

To understand the desired outcome of the export of the revolution, one must examine not only Khomeini's political philosophy but also those aspects of the Irano-Islamic political tradition from which even the Ayatollah could not escape. Space does not permit a detailed exploration of these subjects here, but their relevance to the ends and means of the revolution's export requires at least a brief analysis.

One of the fundamental features of Iranian political culture, which dates back to pre-Islamic Persia, is the incessant quest for the establishment of an ideally virtuous society, defined primarily in terms of universal justice. As noted by Adda B. Bozeman, pre-Islamic Persian statesmen posed "for the first time in historically known terms" the problems of moral principles in international relations in the sixth century BC, when the tyranny of empires plagued the fabric of community everywhere. The Persian Empire attained "universal" peace for some two hundred years in large part as the result of a "policy of tolerance." Bozeman attributes this tolerance to "the statesmanship rather than . . . the religious ethics of the sixth century B.C."[16] In other words, the foreign policy of tolerance in ancient times reflected a kind of prudent realism rather than religious idealism.

It was indeed prudent for these early statesmen to recognize the cultural diversity of the peoples they ruled as a means of maintaining the Persian Empire, an empire vaster than any preceding it west of China. But I suggest that this realism was inseparable from an essentially religiously based idealism that required that Persian statesmen, as well as their subjects, observe the norm of justice in their own conduct. Only the just individual and society, it was believed, were good. The government and the governed were equally bound by Zoroastrian ethics to think "good thoughts" (pendar-e nik), to speak "good words" (goftar-e nik), and to do "good deeds" (kerdar-e nik). All this was commanded by the cosmic "Force of Good," Ahura Mazda, which was expected to triumph over the rival "Force of Evil," Ahriman. The ruler no less than the ruled had to abide by the commandment of Ahura Mazda. "By Ahura Mazda's will," said King Darius, "I am of such nature that I am a friend to the just; I am no friend to the unjust. What is right is my desire. I am not a friend to the man that followeth falsehood."

Neither modern Iran nor Islam itself could escape these pre-Islamic cultural values, particularly the ideal of a just society. The Western observer Malise Ruthven notes the overriding importance of justice in Islam: "Whereas Christianity is primarily the religion of love, Islam is above all the religion of justice."[17] And, I may add, in the Shii cultural tradition in general and in that of Imami Shiism in particular, justice ranks the highest among all values. The violent and bloody martyrdom of Imam Hussein at Karbala symbolizes the historical injustice suffered by the Shia at the hands of such a cruel oppressor (zalem) as Shamr. The heroically oppressed (mazlum) Imam Hussein will only be avenged when the Mahdi, or the Twelfth Imam, reappears (zohur) to establish justice throughout the world.

This essentially chiliastic hope for a just world order among the deprived Shia (mahroomin) was defensive in nature and grew out of the conflict between the Shii minority and the Sunni majority. For Persian Shia this messianic hope was at first a shield against the Arab conquest in the seventh century. Later, in the sixteenth century, when the Safavid dynasty made Shiism a state ideology for the first time in Islamic history, Shiism was still defensive in nature; it was primarily a protective mechanism against the aggression of the powerful Sunni Ottoman Empire.

During the two centuries preceding the Iranian Revolution, the ancient Irano-Islamic quest for justice underpinned Iran's struggle for independence from Russia, both tsarist and communist, and from the Western powers, first Britain and then the United States. Led partly by the Shii ulama, the popular demand for a "house of justice" (adalet khaneh) ignited the Constitutional Revolution of 1905–11, which sought to limit both the tyranny of absolute monarchy and the Anglo-Russian political and economic domination of Iran. Mohammad Mosaddegh viewed his Nationalist Movement of 1951–53 as an essentially "moral" struggle against the age-old British "enslavement" (enqiad) of Iran. Interestingly, the same concept of enslavement was used by Khomeini in characterizing the nature of U.S. domination in 1964, when the Pentagon extracted a humiliating status-of-forces agreement from the Shahs' regime. Thus, as different as Mosaddegh's essentially secular Nationalist Movement and Khomeini's religious Islamic movement are in nature, they share the goal of an overriding quest for justice, a hallmark of the legacy of the Irano-Islamic political culture.

What kind of justice did Khomeini envision, and how does it relate to the export of the revolution? Khomeini wanted a universal justice and believed that only an Islamic world order could bring that about. Furthermore, only a faqih-led Islamic republic such as Iran could pave the way for the establishment of an Islamic world order. This concept of the Velayat-e Faqih (leadership of the jurisprudent) is the innovative contribution of Khomeini's political thought. Traditionally, the leadership of the Shii community belongs to God, to the Prophet Muhammad, and to the infallible imams (ma'sumin), but Khomeini extended that leadership to the faqih, to whom belongs temporal as well as spiritual authority, which he should exercise in the absence of the Hidden Imam, who will appear "at the end of time" (akhar-e zaman) in order to establish a just world order. Khomeini was quite emphatic that the goal of Islam is to bring justice to the entire world, not simply to Iran or even simply to the Muslim world:

"Islam is not peculiar to a country, several countries, a group [of people or countries] or even the Muslims. Islam has come for humanity. Islam addresses the people and only occasionally addresses the believers. Islam wishes to bring all of humanity under the umbrella of its justice."[18]

This concern of Islam with mankind is clearly reflected in the Iranian Constitution. Although Article 11 provides that the Iranian government "should exert continuous efforts in order to realize the political, economic and cultural unity of the Islamic world," Article 154 states that the "Islamic Republic of Iran considers its goal to be the happiness of human beings in all human societies." Thus, the unity of the Muslim world and the happiness of mankind constitute the ultimate goals of the foreign policy of revolutionary Iran, and the unity of the Muslim world is viewed as the first step toward the eventual happiness of humanity at large. But what constitutes the essence of that happiness?

The answer to that question may be explored in the context of Khomeini's view of the nature of the Islamic Revolution in Iran. In contrasting modern revolutions, including the French and Russian, with the Iranian, he contended that those revolutions were inspired primarily by "material" considerations, whereas the Iranian Revolution was motivated mainly by the "divine."[19] Because of this distinctive spirituality of the Iranian Revolution, "Islamic justice for all" can bring happiness to mankind as a whole. This essentially Manichaean dichotomy between the material and spiritual is well known in the intellectual history of the Middle East, but Khomeini was the first in modern times to interject it into the discourse on Iran's international relations.

An example of this effort is found in Khomeini's letter of January 1, 1989, to the Soviet leader Mikhail Gorbachev, in which he stated in no uncertain terms that both the East and the West were ideologically bankrupt because they lacked spiritual values. Khomeini offered to fill this "ideological vacuum" with Islamic values, which alone "can be a means for the well-being and salvation of all nations." Marxism "does not answer any of the real needs of man. It is a materialistic ideology, and it is not possible to save humanity through materialism from the crisis of lack of conviction in spirituality which is the most fundamental ailment of human society in the West and the East." While many in the West have welcomed Gorbachev's *glasnost* and *perestroika*, Khomeini advised him: "I strongly urge you that in breaking down the walls of Marxist fantasies [*khialat*] you do not fall into the prison of the West and the Great Satan." Reiterating that the unhappiness in both the West and the East reflected the lack of spirituality, he told Gorbachev categorically: "One should turn to truth. The main difficulty of your country is not the issue of ownership, economics, or freedom. Your difficulty is the lack of true faith in God, the same difficulty which has also dragged the West toward decadence and a dead end. Your principal problem is a long and futile combat with God, the origin of existence and creation."

In trying to introduce Gorbachev to the alternative path of Islam as contrasted with the Western way of life, Khomeini suggested that the Soviets could conduct research in Islam by referring, "in addition to the books of Western philosophers, to the books written by Farabi and Bu-Ali Sina." He also referred him to the books of Sohrevardi regarding "the philosophy of illumination" (hekmat-e Eshraq) and to the works of mystics, "particularly those of Muhyiddin ibn Arabi." In conclusion he said, "I openly announce the Islamic Republic of Iran, as the greatest and most powerful base of the Islamic world, can easily help fill up the ideological vacuum of your system."[20]

The twin foreign-policy principles of Khomeini's Iran are implicit in the letter to Gorbachev. First, by rejecting both the Eastern and Western ways of life on the ground of lack of religious spirituality, Khomeini was invoking his favorite principle of "neither East nor West." Second, by suggesting that Iran, as the most powerful base of the Islamic world, could easily fill the ideological vacuum everywhere in the world, Khomeini was actually engaging in the export of the revolution, in this instance to the Soviet Union by means of philosophical discussion. With respect to the first principle, he had declared a decade earlier that "a nation that cries in unison that it wants an Islamic Republic, it wants neither East nor West, but only an Islamic republic—this being so, we have no right to say that the nation that engaged in an uprising did so in order to have democracy."[21] In Khomeini's worldview, "Islamic democracy" is superior to both Eastern and Western varieties. With respect to the second principle, about a decade earlier Khomeini had said: "We should try hard to export our revolution to the world. We should set aside the thought that we do not export our revolution, because Islam does not regard various Islamic countries differently and is the supporter of all the oppressed peoples of the world. On the other hand, all the superpowers and all the powers have risen to destroy us. If we remain in an enclosed environment we shall definitely face defeat."[22]

Thus, when the export of the revolution is viewed in light of the Irano-Islamic political culture and Khomeini's political philosophy, three overriding goals become apparent. In the short term, it is a means for defense of the Islamic Republic led by one supreme *faqih* or three to five *fuqaha*. It is also a means for ensuring the security of the Republic internationally, particularly in the Persian Gulf, and in the long run, it is a means for the ultimate establishment of a world order under "the umbrella of Islamic justice." A note of caution is in order, however. While the shorter-term goals are relatively unambiguous, it is not clear whether the long-term objective can indeed be termed a "goal," despite the fact that the Iranian Constitution obligates the government to exert continuous efforts toward realizing the comprehensive unity of the Islamic world and, in fact, uses the very word "goal" in regard to "the happiness of human beings in all human societies" as the ultimate end. One reason for this lack of clarity is the fact that the Irano-Islamic quest for a just world order is, as we have seen, an essentially chiliastic and largely defensive aspiration. The other reason is that in Khomeini's view the attainment of universal Islamic happiness is a matter of hope and gradual occurrence. In his words, "We hope this will gradually come about."[23]

COERCIVE MEANS

Greater ambiguity surrounds the means by which the revolution is to be exported. The first and most important question is whether the use of force is allowed. On numerous occasions, Khomeini and his disciples have consistently declared that "swords" should not be used. Note, for example, the Ayatollah's dictum: "It does not take swords to export this ideology. The export of ideas by force is not export."[24] Or this statement: "When we say we want to export our revolution, we do not want to do it with swords."[25] But does this mean that the use of armed force is prohibited? At first glance, Khomeini's view that the use of force is permissible only in self-defense, a guideline compatible with both Shii legal norms and the principles of modern international law, seems to prohibit the use of military force, presumably in whatever form, for the export of the revolution. But the concept of self-defense in Khomeini's ideology presents the same kind of problem of definition that it does under Article 51 of the Charter of the United Nations: what constitutes self-defense? In fact, Khomeini's idea is even more ambiguous; his worldview accorded the territorial nation-state a lower priority than that granted the abode of Islam, which has no recognizable borders anywhere around the world.

The difficult nature of this theoretical ambiguity is best exemplified by Iran's nearly eight years of bloody war with Iraq. At the outset of the war, Khomeini told the Iranians, "You are fighting to protect Islam and he [Saddam Hussein] is fighting to destroy Islam. At the moment, Islam is completely confronted by blasphemy, and you should protect and support Islam. . . . Every person should defend Islam according to his ability."[26] Since it is generally agreed that Iraq invaded Iran on September 22, 1980, it may be said that Iran was at the time acting in self-defense as the concept is defined territorially, although it did so in the name of Islam. This impression was reinforced by Khomeini himself in March 1982, when the successful Iranian offensive in the Shush-Dezful area foreshadowed the recovery of Khorramshahr in May and the eviction of almost all Iraqi forces from Iranian territory by July: "Today Iran is still bound by what it said at the outset; we have no intention of fighting against any country, Islamic or non-Islamic. To date we have engaged only in self-defense which is a divine duty and human right enjoined upon all. We have never had an intention of committing aggression against other countries."[27]

And yet on July 13, 1982, Iran carried the war into Iraqi territory, and not until July 18, 1988, did Khomeini decide to stop fighting. Why did he not do so six years earlier? Was the war continued in self-defense or in order to export the revolution? Until February 22, 1989, every Iranian leader had denied that Iran's insistence on "final victory" aimed at exporting the revolution, but on that date Khomeini himself said:

> Every day of the war we had blessing, which we utilized in all aspects. *We exported our revolution to the world through the war;* we proved our oppression and the aggressor's tyranny through the war. It was through the war that we unveiled the deceitful face of world-devourers; it was through the war that we recognized our enemies and friends. It was during the war that we concluded that we must stand on our own feet. It was through the war that we broke the back of both Eastern and Western superpowers. It was through the war that we consolidated the roots of our fruitful Islamic revolution.[28]

Short of defensive war, what other coercive means are allowed for exporting the revolution? Considerable ambiguity surrounds this question also. Just as war was denounced, military intervention was also condemned by Khomeini and other Iranian leaders. Ayatollah Hussein-Ali Montazeri stated categorically on October 30, 1988, that "the question of exporting revolution . . . is not a matter of armed intervention." But "the Constitution provides the basis for trying to perpetuate . . . this revolution *both at home and abroad.*" Moreover, in pursuing the goal of universal happiness, "while practicing complete self-restraint from any kind of influence in the internal affairs of other nations, [the Islamic Republic of Iran] will protect the struggle of the weak against the arrogant, in any part of the world."[29] And Khomeini's assurance that Iran had "neither ambition in, [nor] right, to any country, unless it is solely a matter of self-defense"[30] does not help clarify the limits of Iranian intervention because of the thorny ambiguity of the concept of self-defense. Nor does former President Ali Khamenei's unequivocal statement that the Constitution prohibits Iran's interference in the internal affairs of other nations either clarify the ambiguity or stop interventionist actions by radical idealist factions such as that of Mehdi Hashemi, which tried using pilgrims to smuggle arms to Saudi Arabia in the summer of 1986.

In order to point out the theoretical ambiguities surrounding the means of exporting the revolution, I have so far distinguished between the concepts of "defensive war" (*jang-e defai*) and "offensive war" (*jihad*) because in Imami Shii legal thought the latter is the prerogative of the infallible imams rather than of the *faqih*, who can declare only a defensive war. I have also distinguished between "war" (*jang*) in general and "intervention" (*modakheleh*), particularly military intervention. But in the current literature of international relations, all such distinctions may be subsumed under the general concept of intervention, which includes a whole spectrum of activities, from propagandistic broadcasts to armed invasion across international frontiers[31] to, in my view, the export of revolution.

Accordingly, then, this comprehensive view of intervention includes all export activities of revolutionary Iran during the Khomeini era. The Iranian government has been accused of a wide variety of interventionist acts, ranging from inciting propaganda to protracting war. The principal targets of the export of the revolution have been four major geographic areas: the Persian Gulf, the Soviet Caucasus and Central Asia, Afghanistan, and Lebanon. In the Persian Gulf the specific targets were Bahrain, Saudi Arabia, and particularly Kuwait. In the Soviet area they were Azerbaijan and Turkmenistan. In Afghanistan and Lebanon, Shii Muslims were the primary targets, although the eight pro-Iranian factions of the Afghan Mujahadeen are based in Iran, while the pro-Iranian Hezbollah movement is located in Lebanon. Only in Lebanon has Iran maintained a contingent of revolutionary guards, with initial Syrian blessing, since the invasion of Lebanon by Israel in June 1982. And only in Lebanon have pro-Iranian factions continued to hold Western hostages, while Iran claims that its own hostages are held by the Phalangists and are still alive, despite indications to the contrary.

Besides hostage taking by pro-Iranian factions in Lebanon, Iran has been accused of other forcible interventionist acts. These include, for example, the attempted coup in Bahrain in December 1981, the suicidal truck bombing against the Americans and French military contingents in Lebanon in October 1983, and the multiple bombings in Kuwait in December of the same year. The Iranian revolutionary guards aided and abetted the local Shii militants and engaged in armed conflict with the Israeli force in Lebanon.[32] One could also add the accusations against Iran regarding the hijacking and bombing of planes and even the March 1989 pipe-bombing of a van in the United States. The van was driven by the wife of Captain Will C. Rogers III, who had ordered missile firing on an Iranian passenger plane over the Persian Gulf on July 3, 1988, resulting in the death of 290 people. Militant Iranian students in the United States were suspected of complicity in the bombing. But the practice of exporting the revolution by terrorist acts is at times as mysterious as its theory is ambiguous.

Is it any less mysterious and more clear what peaceful means are preferable, in theory and in practice, for exporting the revolution? Generally the answer is yes. During the Khomeini period, three such noncoercive means emerged: the export of the revolution by example, by supporting liberation movements, and by propaganda.

Regarding the export of the revolution by example, two approaches stand out. One approach aims at a thorough Islamization of Iran itself. This approach was described by Ayatollah Montazeri in October 1988:

> The question of exporting revolution . . . is not a matter of armed interven-
> tion. The aim is, rather, that if we build our country on the basis of Islam, if
> we make the customs of the Prophet and the immaculate Imams our model,
> and if we implement the aims, ideals, and values which have been stressed
> by Islam, then by virtue of that fact, our country and our revolution will be-
> come a model for other deprived countries and those countries oppressed by
> and subject to cruelty from superpowers. They will choose our way in order
> to liberate themselves from the yoke of arrogance.[33]

The second approach is that of postwar reconstruction of the Iranian society and economy. Hashemi Rafsanjani believes that the world thinks mistakenly that "we wanted to export our revolution by invading other countries, through war and military action." But, he adds, "if under the present [postwar condi-tions] we manage to create an acceptable type of society and set up a suitable model of development, progress, evolution, and correct Islamic morals for the world, then we will achieve what the world has feared; that is, the export of the Islamic revolution."[34] On another occasion, he expressed a similar thought by saying that the White House "used to think that the Islamic Revolution intended to export itself through conquest." He then added: "This frightened our neigh-bors[, but] now they know that if we claim to export our revolution we intend to present to the world the thought, the idea, and the path of the Koran. After eight years of war we stand more steadfast, more determined, and with more experience concerning our ideals and aspiration pertaining to the revolution."[35]

According to the Constitution, the export of the revolution by supporting liberation movements applies most particularly to "expanding international relations with other Islamic movements." We need not dwell on this subject, because it was discussed previously. Suffice it to add here that the support of liberation movements is the most preferred option of radical idealists. For ex-ample, Montazeri, who advocates the thorough Islamization of Iran itself, also maintains that the Iranian Revolution "has no limits, no frontiers" and adds:

I would say that we must make arrangements so that the world of Islam and all victimized and deprived peoples can in some way be connected to the center of this great movement—a movement which has disrupted the existing world balance. They should be helped with ideology and Islamic thought. Eventually, the revolution and leadership must be separated from the framework of the limited regulations of state and government [keshvar va dolat].[36]

Another radical idealist, Interior Minister Ali Akbar Mohtashemi, also favors this approach: "We are not an isolated revolution, imprisoned within our borders. We support other Islamic movements in other countries. These include the Afghan Mujahidin, Iraqis, Palestinians, and Lebanese. We feel a responsibility to support these movements."[37]

The export of revolution by propaganda includes a great variety of methods, with implementation not necessarily confined to Iranian officials. For example, on one occasion Khomeini encouraged student athletes traveling abroad to export the revolution by the example of their ethical Islamic behavior: "Your deeds, your action, and your behavior should be an example, and through you the Islamic Republic will go to other places, God willing."[38] But export abroad by propaganda is the special responsibility of diplomats, as Khomeini once explained to the Iranian ambassadors and chargés d'affaires: "We shall have exported Islam only when we have helped Islam and Islamic ethics grow in those countries. This is your responsibility and it is a task which you must fulfill . . . this is a must."[39] In the words of Foreign Minister Ali Akbar Velayati: "We will continue to export our revolution, but in cultural terms. The Western countries are doing the same thing. They export their culture, their way of thinking, and their values with the help of the mass media or universities where foreign students are trained."[40]

Iran also uses foreign religious leaders (ulama) to export its revolution. In addition to receiving streams of individual foreign clerics, Iran organizes and hosts international congresses for them. When five hundred foreign ulama gathered in Tehran in May 1983, Khomeini told them: "You should discuss the situation in Iran. You should call on people to rebel like Iran."[41] In addition, both foreign and Iranian scholars are also used for the export of the revolution. For example, more than 1,000 Islamic scholars attended a conference on Islamic propagation in January 1989 to analyze "various methods of communication, ways of countering Western propaganda and spreading the message of Islam." Scholars attending this meeting came from such places as Nigeria, Pakistan, India, the Philippines, Egypt, Turkey, Hong Kong, Britain, France, Switzerland, Senegal, and Guyana.[42]

Salman Rushdie's novel The Satanic Verses was seen by Khomeini as a conspiracy against Islam. In pronouncing a death sentence on Rushdie on February 14, 1989, he said:

> I inform the proud Moslem people of the world that . . . *The Satanic Verses* . . . is against Islam, the Prophet and the Koran. . . . The issue of the book . . . is that it is a calculated move aimed at rooting out religion and religiousness, and above all, Islam and its clergy. . . . The issue for them [the Western powers] is not that of defending an individual—the issue for them is to support an anti-Islamic and anti-value current, which has been masterminded by those institutions belonging to Zionism, Britain and the USA which have placed themselves against the Islamic world, through their ignorance and haste.[43]

From the Iranian perspective, Khomeini's death sentence not only meted out Islamic punishment for blasphemy and apostasy but also aided the export of the revolution. Even though the forty-six-member Islamic Conference Organization (ICO) did not explicitly endorse Khomeini's death sentence in its resolution published on March 16, 1989, the Iranian press tried to reap a propaganda advantage by hailing the conference as a triumph for the Islamic Republic of Iran. "Declaring Salman Rushdie an apostate by the ICO, a big victory for Iran," screamed the headline on the front page of *Ettela'at*. *Kayhan*, *Jomhuri-ye Islami*, the *Tehran Times*, and *Kayhan International* also trumpeted the Iranian victory. The editorial of *Abrar* stated: "Contrary to what the West expected, the ICO . . . in support of the leadership and government of the Islamic republic verified Imam Khomeyni's *fatwa* [religious decree, demanding Rushdie's death] . . . by diplomatic language."[44]

EXPORT OF REVOLUTION REDEFINED?

Axiomatically, Iran's policy of exporting revolution, like any other aspect of its foreign policy, reflects the dynamic interaction between Iran's domestic politics and its external environment. In concluding this essay, it is appropriate to specify that the aspect of Iran's domestic politics that most often shaped the government's export-of-revolution policies during the first decade of the Iranian Revolution was the style of Khomeini's leadership. In order to serve Iran's overall interest in "Islamic unity," he consistently played the role of the supreme balancer among the various political factions, including the radical idealists and the pragmatic realists. On February 22, 1989, he acknowledged such a leadership style in an officially dubbed "very important" address to the instructors and students of religious seminaries and congressional imams: "For the sake of maintaining balance among various factions I have always issued bitter and sweet instructions because I consider all of them as my dear ones and children."[45]

In keeping with this balancing role, Khomeini threw his weight sometimes behind radical idealists and sometimes behind pragmatic realists, depending on the circumstances. In supporting the taking of American hostages by militant students, he in effect went against the moderate government of Mehdi Bazargan. As a consequence, the hostage crisis became the crucible of Iran's confrontational foreign policy in general and its export of the revolution in particular. In effect, Khomeini also supported the radical idealists when, on July 13, 1982, he decided to invade Iraq with the double goal of recovering pockets of Iranian territory and exporting the revolution.

And yet, by accepting the cease-fire on July 18, 1988, Khomeini in effect threw his weight behind the pragmatic realists, who had never rejected out of hand U.N. Resolution 598. For months after the acceptance of this resolution, the power of the pragmatic factions seemed to be on the rise. They began developing diplomatic relations with France, Britain, and Canada, strengthening relations with West Germany, and making postwar reconstruction their first priority. It was then that the idea of exporting the revolution by the example of an economically prosperous, politically progressive, and socially popular Iran gained the support of the realist factions. Hashemi Rafsanjani acknowledged candidly that "if the meaning of exporting revolution is to bring the message to people's ears, I must say that our aims are not yet sufficiently clear in the mind of the people of the world."[46] This apparent rush to open up to the West, however, seemed to have alarmed the radical idealists. The Rushdie affair came to their aid.

Between his pronouncement of Rushdie's death sentence on February 14, 1989, and Khomeini's own death on June 3, 1989, the pendulum once again swung in favor of the radical idealists. In his address of February 22, 1989, mentioned above, Khomeini not only blasted as usual at the "liberals" and the "hypocrites" (Mujahadeen-e-Khalq) but also for the first time admonished the pragmatic realists. The imposition of a death sentence on a British subject residing outside Iran's borders was Khomeini's last effort to export the revolution. In criticizing the seeming haste of pragmatic realists to mend fences with Western nations, he said:

> It is not necessary for us to go seeking to establish extensive ties because the enemy may think that we have become so dependent and attach so much importance to their existence that we quietly condone insults to beliefs and religious sanctities. Those who still continue to believe that and warn that we must embark on a revision of our policies, principles and diplomacy and

that we have blundered and must not repeat previous mistakes; those who still believe that extremist slogans or war will cause the West and the East to be pessimistic about us, and that ultimately all this has led to the isolation of the country; *those who believe that if we act in a pragmatic way* they will reciprocate humanely and will mutually respect nations, Islam and Muslims—to them this [Rushdie's novel] is an example.[47]

This criticism of the pragmatic realists, coupled with Khomeini's reception of Soviet Foreign Minister Eduard A. Shevardnadze during his visit to Tehran in February 1989, appeared to Washington as a tilt toward the East in Iran's foreign policy. The U.S. government saw the Soviet Union poised to exploit the strain between Iran and Western European nations over the Rushdie affair. It also resented Soviet chumminess with Iran while nine American hostages were still held captive by reputedly pro-Iranian factions in Lebanon. The June 1989 visit of the influential speaker of the Iranian Parliament, Hashemi Rafsanjani, to the Soviet Union, his reception by Mikhail Gorbachev as a head of state, and the signing of long-term economic and military agreements all aroused Western, particularly American, suspicion of an Iranian tilt toward the Soviet Union.

And yet, paradoxically for revolutionary Iran, the road to Washington may well turn out to be through Moscow. In following the fundamental tenets of its own foreign policy, Iran will have to balance its cooperation with the East by cooperating with the West to avoid dominant influence by or dependence on either bloc.[48] This is the real meaning of Iran's "neither East nor West" principle as interpreted by every major Iranian leader over the past decade. Even Khomeini admitted in his will that Iran's need for foreign aid was an "undisputed fact," despite his vigorous warning against dependency on either the East or the West.

More critically, the unprecedented opening to the Soviet Union may well signify the beginning of Iran's reentry into the international community, including normalization of relations with the United States. If so, Iran's doctrine of the export of revolution may well be redefined to allow for normal relations with other nations. And that, above all else, will require Iran's renunciation, both in words and in deeds, of the use of direct or indirect force as a means of exporting revolution. The prospects for Iran's successful export of the revolution through setting an example of its own "Islamic ethical behavior," to borrow the late Ayatollah Khomeini's words, may be brighter in the near future than they were during the entire first decade of the Islamic Republic. It is likely that the political ascendancy of Ayatollah Sayyid Ali Khamenei as Khomeini's successor and of Hashemi Rafsanjani as the strongest president since the establishment of the Republic may result in a non-interventionist definition of the principle of the export of the revolution. Both these leaders have demonstrated a sense of political realism and a determination to base Iran's relations with other nations, including the United States, on the concept of equilibrium rather than on the idea of a struggle between good and evil. To the extent that such a fundamental change may occur, future efforts at exporting the Iranian Revolution will be relatively tame during the second decade of the life of the Islamic Republic of Iran.

NOTES

1. The modern international system dates back to the Peace of Westphalia, signed on 24 October 1648. The treaty marked the end of negotiations between France and Sweden and their opponents, Spain and the Holy Roman Empire, which took place in two Westphalian cities in Germany. By its terms the sovereignty and independence of the different states of the Holy Roman Empire were fully recognized, rendering the Holy Roman emperor virtually powerless and hence signaling the demise of religion in politics after the Thirty Years' War. No comparable event has occurred in Islamic history.

2. For details, see R. K. Ramazani, *The United States and Iran: The Patterns of Influence* (New York, 1982).

3. Three important events in 1972–77 ignited this populist explosion: President Nixon's decision in 1972 to sell the Shah all the conventional military weapons he wanted; the boom of rising oil prices in 1973 followed by the sudden bust, which transformed the Iranians' rising expectations to increasing alienation from both the Shah's regime and the United States; and the Shah's creation of the Rastakhiz Party in 1975, which symbolized the height of political repression and compounded the psychological and financial dislocations that the economic boom and bust had already produced. For the earliest characterization of the Iranian Revolution as a "twin revolution," see R. K. Ramazani, "Iran's Revolution in Perspective," in *The Impact of the Events upon Persian Gulf and United States Security*, project director Z. Michael Szaz (Washington, DC, 1979), 19–37; Ramazani, "Iran's Foreign Policy: Perspectives and Projections," in *Economic Consequences of the Revolution in Iran: A Compendium of Papers Submitted to the Joint Economic Committee, Congress of the United States* (Washington, DC, 1980), 65–97; and Ramazani, "Iran's Revolution: Patterns, Problems and Prospects," pp. 33–49 in this volume.

4. See R. K. Ramazani, *The Foreign Policy of Iran, 1500–1941: A Developing Nation in World Affairs* (Charlottesville, 1966), 63–65.

5. See R. K. Ramazani, *Iran's Foreign Policy, 1941–1973: A Study of Foreign Policy in Modernizing Nations* (Charlottesville, 1975), 181–250.

6. The Soviet Union claims that these articles give it the unilateral right to intervene militarily in Iran whenever it judges that its security is threatened from Iranian territory. For decades Iran has vehemently opposed this Soviet interpretation. Reza Shah secretly tried to cancel the articles in 1935, and his son made a similar effort in 1958–59. The Bazargan government's cancellation of these articles was affirmed on November 10, 1979, by the Revolutionary Council. For details, see R. K. Ramazani, "Treaty Relations: An Iranian-Soviet Case Study," in *The Search for World Order: Studies by Students and Colleagues of Quincy Wright*, edited by Albert Lepawsky, Edward H. Buehrig, and Harold D. Lasswell (New York, 1979), 298–311.

7. Iraqi Foreign Minister Saadoun Hammadi stated: "I should say for the record that Mr. Bazargan was also cooperative and tried to strengthen relations between the two countries." See Ministry of Foreign Affairs, Republic of Iraq, *The Iraqi-Iranian Dispute: Facts v. Allegations* (New York, 1980), 65.

8. For details, see R. K. Ramazani, *Revolutionary Iran: Challenge and Response in the Middle East* (Baltimore, 1986), 49.

9. Banisadr believed "that despite the historical and ideological differences between the West and Iran, the two sides' interests were not so far apart." See Foreign Broadcast Information Service, *Daily Report*, vol. 5, *Middle East and North Africa* (FBIS-MEA), 20 November 1979.

10. Ibid., 21 December 1979.

11. See Mohandes Mehdi Bazargan, *Enqelab-e Iran dar Dau Harekat* [The Iranian Revolution in two phases] (Tehran, [1983/84]), 94–95.

12. Neither of these principles is explicitly mentioned in the Constitution, but their meanings are incorporated in various provisions. For example, Article 152 in effect relates to the "neither East nor West" principle in the original sense that Iran rejects Eastern and Western domination but not relations with the United States and the Soviet Union, whose rupture the extremists demand. This article states: "The foreign policy of Iran is founded on the basis of ending any type of domination, safeguarding the complete independence and integrity of the territory, defending the rights of all Muslims, practicing nonalignment with respect to the dominating [U.S. and U.S.S.R.] powers and maintaining mutual peaceful relationships with non-belligerent nations." The principle of the export of the revolution is implied not only in the phrase "defending the rights of all Muslims" but also under other headings in the constitution, such as "Style of Government in Islam," "Army of the Book," "Public Relations and Media," and Article 154. For the text of the Constitution, with R. K. Ramazani's introductory note, see *Middle East Journal* 34 (Spring 1980): 181–204.

13. See Foreign Broadcast Information Service, *Daily Report*, vol. 8, *South Asia* (FBIS-SA), 8 July 1981.

14. Ibid., 28 October 1981.

15. See R. K. Ramazani, "Iran's Foreign Policy: Contending Orientations," pp. 111–27 in this volume.

16. Adda B. Bozeman, *Politics and Culture in International History* (Princeton, 1960), 49. The reason for the disagreement with Bozeman in the following paragraph is that while she recognizes the influence of Zoroastrianism on Iran's worldview, she fails to realize that Zoroaster's call to fight against infidels, Turks, and nomads in order to convert the whole world into the domain of good was an injunction subordinated to the higher norm of a just world order commanded by Ahura Mazda.

17. See Malise Ruthven, *Islam in the World* (New York, 1984), 227.

18. FBIS-MEA, 18 December 1979.

19. FBIS-SA, 11 February 1987.

20. Foreign Broadcast Information Service, *Daily Report*, vol. 3, *Near East and South Asia* (FBIS-NES), 9 January 1989.

21. FBIS-MEA, 10 December 1979.

22. Ibid., 24 March 1980.

23. FBIS-SA, 11 February 1987.

24. *Soroush*, March 1981.

25. FBIS-SA, 25 August 1983.

26. *New York Times*, 19 October 1980.

27. FBIS-SA, 1 April 1982.

28. FBIS-NES, 24 February 1989, emphasis added.

29. Ibid., 31 October 1988, emphasis added.

30. *Kayhan*, 26 July 1982 [in Persian].

31. See Michael Joseph Smith's excellent article "Ethics and Intervention" in *Ethics and International Affairs* 3 (1989): 1-26.

32. See Ramazani, *Revolutionary Iran*; Ramazani, "Iran's Islamic Revolution and the Persian Gulf," *Current History* 84 (January 1985): 5–8, 40–41; Ramazani, "Sociopolitical Change in the Gulf: A Climate for Terrorism?," pp. 263–84 in this volume; and Ramazani, *The Gulf Cooperation Council: Record and Analysis* (Charlottesville, 1988), 33–59.

33. FBIS-NES, 31 October 1988.

34. Ibid., 17 and 14 October 1988.

35. Ibid., 26 September 1988.

36. Ibid., 28 February 1989.

37. Ibid., 8 February 1989.

38. FBIS-SA, 9 March 1982.

39. *Soroush*, March 1981.

40. FBIS-NES, 21 September 1988.

41. *Kayhan Hava'i*, 23 May 1984.

42. FBIS-NES, 2 February 1989.

43. *BBC Summary of World Broadcasts*, 24 February 1989.

44. FBIS-NES, 20 March 1989.

45. For the full text, see *BBC Summary of World Broadcasts*, 24 February 1989.

46. FBIS-NES, 14 February 1989.

47. See *BBC Summary of World Broadcasts*, 24 February 1989, emphasis added.

48. For details, see R. K. Ramazani's analysis in the *Washington Post*, 2 July 1989, C2.

THE SHIFTING PREMISE

OF IRAN'S FOREIGN POLICY

Toward a Democratic Peace?

The all-important foreign-policy component of Iranian president Mohammad Khatami's election has been universally overlooked, partly because of the reformist rhetoric of his election campaign. This essay argues that the pivotal synergy in President Khatami's worldview between reforms at home and peace abroad was the principal reason why his overall message resonated so dramatically with young Iranians. More self-reliant, and also more exposed to worldwide influences of the democratic movement than their parents, these young men and women voted for Khatami significantly because they aspired to greater freedom at home and more cooperation with the rest of the world.

Does the election of Seyyed Mohammad Khatami as president of the Islamic Republic of Iran represent a silent revolution of young Iranians?[1] Twenty million voters, largely women and the young, or 69 percent of the eligible voters, cast their ballots for him in May 1997 in a universally acknowledged free and fair election. Two decades ago the previous generation of Iranians destroyed the Pahlavi regime, sending shock waves around the world. That generation supported Ayatollah Ruhollah Khomeini's slogan: "We must become isolated in order to become independent."[2] Now the children of that revolution are saying they must become democratic in order to become part of the "new world order." This essay argues that this new premise is the real meaning of Khatami's presidency. Were this premise ever to be realized, centuries of Iranian autocracy would be reversed.

Yet, President Khatami's election was a surprise; his effective leadership of the most successful summit meeting in the history of the Organization of the Islamic Conference (OIC), held in Tehran in December 1997, was a surprise; and his courageous overtures to the American people for reconciliation a few weeks later were the mother of all surprises! Why? Because Iran critics cannot believe that a clerically dominated theocracy can cry out for democracy; the self-styled "political realists" see nothing but another changing of the guard in Iranian politics and the continuing struggle for power between two leaders (today

"The Shifting Premise of Iran's Foreign Policy: Towards a Democratic Peace?" was originally published in *Middle East Journal* 52, no. 2 (April 1998): 177–87.

between President Khatami and Iran's spiritual leader, Ayatollah Ali Khamenei, and yesterday between former president Ali Akbar Hashemi Rafsanjani and Khamenei); and the "fatalist" theorists of revolution continue to deny the possibility of any real evolutionary process of change in any revolution.

DEMOCRACY AT HOME AND PEACE ABROAD
Yet, the landslide election of President Khatami had its roots in the fertile soil of just such an evolutionary process of change. It was marked by the heavy social, economic, and political toll of revolutionary fervor; of terror and counterterror, especially in the early phases of the Iranian Revolution; of the calamitous eight-year war (1980–88) with Iraq, at enormous cost in terms of casualties and material destruction; and of the postwar consequences of eight years of massive economic reconstruction that resulted in unprecedented social and economic betterment and equally unprecedented economic and social hardship.

The quest of young Iranians for an open society at home and a peaceful state abroad[3] has two immediate sets of causes; one springs from the depth of internal changes that have taken place in Iran since Khomeini's death in 1989, and the other reflects exposure to global realities. Internally, their aspirations stem from a paradoxical combination of psycho-cultural sufferings and hopeful expectations for a better life. Young Iranians' expectations reflect, in part, the economic development of the previous eight years, during the two-term (1989–97) administration of former president Rafsanjani. Although the young people began then to enjoy a better standard of living than their parents, they also wanted a freer social and political life. Materially, millions of rural people, for example, started to enjoy the comforts of electric power and running water as economic improvement spread to 85 percent of some 60,000 villages; the nation's rate of literacy soared from 45 percent in 1978, before the revolution, to about 80 percent of the population; the life expectancy of the average Iranian reached 65; women joined the workforce in large numbers, contributing increasingly to household incomes; about 40 percent of students in higher education were women; and last, but by no means least, Iranian society began to witness a renaissance of social and political thought that engulfed secular and religious intellectuals alike.[4]

While all these positive developments contributed to the young Iranians' movement for an open society, for a larger public space, and for a say in Iran's active participation in world affairs, the concomitant sufferings have also stoked the fire of discontent, resentment, and frustration. A majority of Iranians find it hard to make ends meet; half of the people are poor even by Iranian standards of living; men try to hold several jobs simultaneously to meet the ever-increasing demands of their families; only a fraction of high school graduates can aspire to be admitted to colleges and universities, largely because of rigid doctrinal entrance tests; and, above all, young men and women feel that their private lives have been invaded by self-appointed, lawless gangs called Ansar-e Hezbollah (the Supporters of the Party of God), who have arrogated to themselves the right to uphold public and private morality in the streets, at schools and universities, and even in the privacy of people's homes.

The aspirations for an open society at home and integration into the international community stem from a combined sense of national pride and a growing consciousness of the need to be part of the democratic movement sweeping across the world. In the aftermath of the revolution, Iranians became less paranoic about foreign powers and their Iranian agents affecting every decision the Iranian government made. Unlike their parents, young Iranians have no memories of Iran's tortured past, marked by foreign interference, intervention, invasion, and occupation mainly by imperial powers. They do not remember the events that impelled even Ayatollah Khomeini, the founder of the Islamic Republic of Iran, to accord the notion of national independence first place in his favorite motto, "Independence, freedom, and the Islamic Republic."

Yet, this younger generation, which has no memory of the CIA-engineered 1953 coup against the popular government of Mohammad Mosaddegh, feels the humiliating effects of the U.S. policy of containment of Iran, especially President Bill Clinton's imposition of a trade ban on Iran in 1995 and the economic sanctions imposed by the 1996 bill sponsored by U.S. Senator Alphonse D'Amato of New York. The fact that the economic effects of the sanctions are more a matter of inconvenience than of hardship does not help to assuage the sense of injury that the Iranian people feel. Added to this injury is the perceived insult by an old Iranian friend, Germany, when a Berlin court implicated Iranian leaders in the assassination of Iranian Kurdish dissidents.[5]

The diffusion of democratic values and the creation of democratic institutions around the world have raised the expectations of the Iranian youth for a freer society. No banning of satellite dishes, video tapes, culturally incorrect movies, and no amount of press censorship and book burning have been able to create a wall around Iran and its intensely curious younger generation. The corollary of the Iranian sense of freedom *from* foreign domination has become, in the past few years, freedom *for* some kind of political participation. Globally, democracy has been spreading across civilizational and national boundaries; at the time of the 1997 Iranian presidential elections about half of the world's countries were considered to be democratic, twice as many as twenty years earlier, when the Iranian Revolution erupted.

No wonder, then, that candidate Khatami's ideas resonated so dramatically with the young. He campaigned inspiringly, unpretentiously, and independently across the country. The conciliatory message of peace coming out of Iran during the campaign was missed by almost all government and academic Iran watchers in the West, who claimed that foreign policy was barely an issue. Khatami's democratic peace refers to social justice, the rule of law, a civil society, individual freedoms, participatory democracy, and government accountability.[6] His concept of social justice calls for a more equitable distribution of wealth, and his view of the rule of law means that no type of autocracy should be tolerated. He demands the elimination of the "immemorial" abuse of law by chauvinistic men against women, and that dogmatic "agitators" who take the law into their own hands and harass the people in the name of Islamic morality be themselves subjected to the due process of law.[7]

Khatami also distinguishes what he calls an "Islamic civil society" from its Western counterpart. To him the latter is rooted in the Greek notion of the city-state, while the former springs from the concept of *Madinat al-Nabi* (the City of the Prophet).[8] This distinction is intended to highlight the moral and spiritual emphasis of the Islamic civil society as contrasted to the Western one. Yet, the difference between the historical and cultural roots of these two concepts of civil society does not necessarily make them incompatible today. Khatami's concept of individual freedoms encompasses social, economic, cultural, and political liberty. He takes pains to differentiate liberty from "liberalism," not so much because the latter is used even more pejoratively in Iran than it is in the United States but because he associates liberalism with "secularism," and as such "liberalism and Islamic doctrine oppose one another. There really is no room for this school of thought in our society," he maintains.[9]

The twin concepts of participatory democracy and government accountability are also relevant to the central concern of this essay. According to Khatami, there are two major political concepts enshrined in the Iranian Constitution: One resembles the principle of sovereignty of the people, who elect their leaders and make them accountable. The other is the concept of *rahbar*, or *faqih* (spiritual guide). Whoever holds the office of *faqih* not only has the power to control the actions of the president but also is responsible for the moral conduct of society. What is important, however, is Khatami's view that the Constitution tries "to weigh both factors equally."[10] This liberal interpretation of the Constitution means that while Khatami accepts the supremacy of the *faqih*'s authority, he does not consider the leader immune from criticism, presumably because he does not believe that anyone should be above the law. Hence, Khatami's interpretation of the Constitution amounts to what this author refers to as a kind of "faqih-guided democracy." This central concept of his administration requires the inculcation of democratic values and the establishment of democratic institutions.

The conjunction of Khatami's concept of democracy at home and peace abroad can best be seen in his worldview and his concept of Iranian foreign policy. He rejects the notion of the clash of civilizations; embraces the principle of dialogue among religions, cultures, and nations; believes in the interdependence of societies, cultures, and economies; and advocates a "proactive and firm foreign policy."[11] This policy, he believes, should be based on nonviolence and friendly relations with all countries as long as they recognize Iran's "independence" and do not pursue "an aggressive policy" toward it.[12] Khatami's essentially peaceful worldview and his commitment to democracy indicate that he will try to pursue a foreign policy that is marked by the concept of "faqih-guided democratic peace," based on the general proposition that democracies behave more cooperatively and peacefully than autocracies in the international system.

A BID TO LEAD THE MUSLIM WORLD

President Khatami's novel view of Iranian foreign policy was very well received at the OIC meeting in Tehran in December 1997, which brought together representatives of all the Muslim states of the world. A combination of planning and fortuity accounted for the success of the summit. The decision to hold the eighth summit meeting of the OIC in Iran was taken at the sixth Islamic summit, held in Dakar in 1991, when some of the ideas of Khatami were foreshadowed in Rafsanjani's address to the summit. Rafsanjani called for a dialogue between North and South in the wake of the collapse of communism, for the elimination of weapons of mass destruction, and for the participation of women in the realms of science and culture, as well as in international economic, social, and political affairs. By all accounts, his address contributed to the decision to hold the eighth summit in Tehran.

The unprecedented number of leaders and high-level officials attending the eighth summit of the fifty-five-member OIC in Tehran also reflected the Khatami administration's own planning efforts. Khatami's campaign messages attracted a great deal of attention from the international community, and especially from Iran's neighbors. Those messages were the principal and earliest signs of Iran's conciliatory offensive. Foreign Minister Kamal Kharrazi also spared no effort to prepare for the extraordinary participation in the OIC meetings of Arab leaders from across the breadth of the Middle East.

Fortuity, however, contributed at least as much to the success of the summit as did the Iranian efforts before and after President Khatami took power. The unique turnout of the Arab states at this particular summit was in part a reflection of the disillusionment Arabs felt at the stalled peace process. Yet, Israeli Prime Minister Binyamin Netanyahu dismissed any suggestion of even partial responsibility on the part of his government for the flocking to Iran of leaders of moderate Arab states. The apparent U.S. failure to revive the Arab-Israeli peace process led to Arab alienation from Washington, a fact that the Khatami administration seized upon with alacrity.

The perceived pro-Israel approach of the Clinton administration to the peace process contributed as much to the success of the Islamic summit in Tehran in December 1997 as it did to the failure of the poorly attended gathering at the U.S.-sponsored Middle East and North Africa economic conference in Doha the previous month. Some Arab newspapers reported that the Palestinian planning minister, Nabil Sha'th, had disclosed that his government had been pressured by the United States to boycott the Tehran meeting.[13] Whether or not that is true, Yasir 'Arafat, the president of the Palestinian National Authority (PNA), claimed, in an interview with a leading Iranian newspaper, that in a forty-minute conversation U.S. Secretary of State Madeleine Albright had talked to him in such a way as to suggest that he "should not go to Iran and engage in discussions."[14] But 'Arafat added that he did go because he expected the Palestinian question to be the major issue discussed at the summit.

Be that as it may, a country accused by Washington of being the world's leading sponsor of international terrorism showed the world that 69 percent of its electorate had freely voted and accorded democratic legitimacy to its new president. Then a fifty-five-member summit conference boosted Iran's international prestige and bestowed on its president the leadership of the OIC for the next three years, conferring on Iran an aura of international legitimacy that is bound to help consolidate President Khatami's domestic authority. Nearly twenty years of efforts by Washington to isolate Iran boomeranged; at least during those three days at the summit the representatives of over 1 billion Muslims, in possession of 70 percent of the world's energy resources, appeared to isolate the United States and Israel in the international system.

PRESIDENT KHATAMI'S SPEECH
AND THE TEHRAN DECLARATION

President Khatami expounded on all the major elements of his foreign policy of democratic peace at the global Islamic summit forum on 9 December 1997. In a striking departure from apologist Islamic thinking, he introduced his address by acknowledging candidly that in recent centuries the Islamic umma (nation) had lapsed into "weakness and backwardness."[15] No possible or desirable solution could be found for this condition by trying to replicate the old Islamic civilization. The solution could be found in a proper and in-depth understanding of the present time, an era dominated by Western culture and civilization. It was imperative that this understanding also include "its [the Western civilization's] theoretical basis and the fundamentals of its values."[16]

Khatami spelled out the implications of the essentially democratic nature of his idea of an Islamic civil society, Madinat al-Nabi, for both domestic politics and foreign policy. Domestically, "the government in such a society is the servant of the people and not their master, and in every eventuality, is accountable to the people whom God has entitled to determine their own destiny."[17] Internationally, he said, "our civil society neither seeks to dominate others nor to submit to domination. It recognizes the right of other nations to self-determination and access to the necessary means for an honourable living."[18] As applied to the Middle East, these principles mean that "peace can be established only through the realization of all the legitimate rights of the Palestinian people, including the inalienable right to self-determination, return of refugees, [and] liberation of the occupied territories, in particular Al-Quds Al-Sharif [Jerusalem]."[19]

An ancient sense of cultural identity underpins Iran's fierce sense of independence in modern times. A corollary to this principle of independence in Iranian foreign policy is the rejection of any global Goliath, such as the United States, which, according to Khatami, is bent on imposing its will on the world. A new and just world order, he maintains, must be pluralistic, as must be the new Iranian society, culture, and polity. In such a new world order there is no room for any regional Goliath either. Because the nature of the "Zionist regime" in Israel, he asserts, is "hegemonic, racist, aggressive and violent"[20] and manifests itself in "gross violation of international law, pursuit of state terrorism and development of weapons of mass destruction,"[21] it is seriously threatening peace and security in the Middle East.

Ayatollah Khamenei's unscheduled inaugural address at the OIC summit sounded even harsher than Khatami's on the peace process and on the West. But Iran watchers and journalists in the United States failed to see that the major elements of Khatami's foreign policy of democratic peace were also embedded in Khamenei's address. In a chorus, the Western media latched almost exclusively onto two blunt statements made by Khamenei. He was repeatedly quoted as saying that the peace process was "unjust, arrogant, contemptuous and finally illogical";[22] and that the West was directing everyone toward materialism "while money, gluttony and carnal desires are made the greatest aspirations."[23] A careful reading of the two addresses, however, reveals that as a matter of fact Khatami's words on Israel and the peace process were even harsher than those of Khamenei.

There were important but unnoticed parallels between the addresses of the two Iranian leaders with respect to Iran's foreign policy of democratic peace. For example, Khamenei declared emphatically that "Iran poses no threat to any Islamic country,"[24] a statement that was warmly received by the Arab states, especially those of the Persian Gulf. He spoke of the need to create an Islamic civil society, to eradicate poverty and ignorance, to create an interparliamentary union of Islamic countries, to realize the idea of an Islamic common market, and, in effect, to "democratize" the United Nations Security Council by establishing a permanent seat on the Council for a representative of the Muslim world.

The Tehran Declaration, adopted at the end of the summit meeting on December 11, 1997, highlighted the principal elements of Iran's newly launched foreign policy of democratic peace. The participants declared solemnly that they wished to "stress the need for cooperation, dialogue and positive understanding among cultures and religions while rejecting the ideology of confrontation which creates mistrust and diminishes the grounds for cooperation among nations."[25] Most significantly, Iran compromised on the statement on the peace process, a process it had earlier denounced. Together with other Muslim states, Iran condemned the continuation of the Israeli occupation of Arab lands and called for "the establishment of an independent Palestinian state with Qods as its capital city."[26] As a seeming quid pro quo for this Iranian compromise, the participants condemned unilateralism and encouraged "all countries to declare the D'Amato Law as null and void."[27]

Probably the most important aspect of the summit for the promotion of Iran's democratic-peace foreign-policy initiative was the unprecedented opportunity for bilateral discussions with Arab leaders and officials, including those of Bahrain, Egypt, Iraq, Saudi Arabia, the United Arab Emirates (UAE), and others. President Khatami, Ayatollah Khamenei, and the influential former president, Rafsanjani, all participated separately and in varying degrees in those bilateral discussions. Despite the great secrecy surrounding these private conversations, it is easy to speculate that a great many issues, including the Iran-UAE dispute regarding the islands of Abu Musa and the two Tunbs, Iran's differences with all the Gulf Cooperation Council (GCC) countries regarding the peace process and the presence of U.S. forces in the Persian Gulf, the differences between Iran and Iraq over the exchange of prisoners of war, and other unresolved issues, must have been discussed. But one of the principal objectives of Iran at the summit was the creation of an atmosphere of trust and confidence with all its neighbors in the Gulf region.

As a means of building mutual trust with the UAE, for example, President Khatami expressed his readiness to meet with the UAE president, Sheikh Zayid al-Nuhayyan, who welcomed the invitation. Even though the "Final Statement" of the eighteenth GCC summit meeting later in December 1997 repeated that the three islands "belong[ed]" to the UAE and called on Iran "to end its occupation policy,"[28] it also mentioned "the need to establish good relations with the Islamic Republic of Iran upon the basis of good neighborliness, mutual respect, and noninterference in internal affairs."[29] The GCC Final Statement also took note of "the Iranian Government's intention to open a new page in its relations with the GCC member states" and hoped for a "positive and practical development"[30] of these relations. In a real sense, the democratic-peace foreign policy of President Khatami will meet its first acid test in the Persian Gulf in the dispute with the UAE, a difficult problem to solve, as this author warned as early as 1972.[31]

AN OLIVE BRANCH FOR THE AMERICAN PEOPLE

There is no more compelling evidence of President Khatami's firm commitment to a foreign policy of democratic peace than his telling the world on December 14, 1997, that "I, first of all, pay my respect to the great people and nation of America."[32] No matter how his statements are interpreted, Khomeini himself always left open the option of resuming relations with the United States sometime in the future provided that "agar adam beshavad" (it behaves itself). President Khatami's conciliatory overture seems all the more magnanimous considering the ever-hardening U.S. containment policy. Washington froze Iranian funds on November 14, 1979,[33] at the time of the hostage crisis at the U.S. Embassy in Tehran during the Carter administration, and broke diplomatic relations with Iran on April 7, 1980. The U.S. presidents Ronald Reagan and George H. W. Bush sided with Iraq during its war with Iran in the 1980s; and the Clinton administration and Congress stiffened the sanctions against Iran in the 1990s. The D'Amato Act, which threatens to punish foreign companies investing $20 million or more a year in Iranian oil and gas development projects, is coupled with House Speaker Newt Gingrich's initiative to allocate $20 million for overthrowing the Iranian government.

Despite all this, President Khatami followed up on his promise to talk to the American people. In a televised statement on January 7, 1998 broadcast on Cable News Network (CNN) International, he told them that the principles of liberty and religion that underpinned the founding of the American republic also underlay the creation of the Islamic Republic of Iran. The fact that controversies over the separation of church and state have raged for centuries in the West, and continue to this day in the United States when Americans keep asking why and how far the government should be separated from religion, did not seem to concern President Khatami. The Iranian Constitution combines the principle of sovereignty of the people and that of God, and institutionally, it sets the authority of the people's elected president side by side with the authority of the *rahbar*, or spiritual guide. Debate over the coupling of religious and political authority has taken place from the birth of the Islamic Republic to the present time.

Despite this extraordinary shift in Iran's approach to international relations in general, and to relations with the American people in particular, the U.S. official response was initially very cautious, and as such, in direct contradiction with the very principles of the Clinton administration's own foreign policy. Clinton made the enlargement of the world's roster of democracies one of the top U.S. foreign-policy priorities. He created new positions in the Department of State for the express purpose of spreading democracy and proposed a 60 percent increase in the funding for the National Endowment for Democracy's programs to encourage elections overseas. Yet, in responding to Khatami's courageous overtures, Clinton and U.S. administration officials confined themselves for a month and a half to saying that they were "intrigued" by Khatami's televised speech and that they found his remarks "interesting." It was not until January 29, 1998 that Clinton responded positively to some of Khatami's proposals, namely, to the idea of an "exchange of professors, writers, scholars, artists, journalists, and tourists."[34] Instead of repeating the hackneyed U.S. formula that focused on "authoritative" government-to-government negotiations or regurgitating three elements of the discredited "dual containment" policy (issues regarding international terrorism, the peace process, and weapons of mass destruction), Clinton endorsed Khatami's recommendation for cultural exchange. "The United States regrets the estrangement of our two nations," the President said in his videotaped greetings on the occasion of 'Id al-Fitr, marking the end of the holy month of Ramadan.[35] Clinton called Iran "an important country with a rich and ancient cultural heritage of which Iranians are justifiably proud."[36] The U.S. president did say that "we have real differences with some Iranian policies, but I believe these are not insurmountable," adding, "I hope that we have more exchanges between our two people and that the day will soon come when we can enjoy again good relations with Iran."[37]

AN ENLIGHTENED CONCEPTION
OF NATIONAL INTEREST

There is an urgent need for policymakers as well as scholars in the United States to begin to conceive of the U.S. national interest in a new and more enlightened way. To be sure, the conventional thinking considers Iran to be of strategic importance to the United States because of its rich oil and natural gas resources, its dominant position on the Strait of Hormuz—the global oil chokepoint—its usefulness as the cheapest and shortest transit route for the transport of energy resources from the Caspian Sea basin to world markets through the Persian Gulf, and its huge potential market for trade and investment for U.S. companies. But as part of a new conception of vital U.S. interests in Iran, we should also realize that an ancient autocracy now has a popularly elected leader who is, for the first time in Iran's long history, firmly committed to engineering an open society in the hope that it will eventually lead to democracy at home and peace abroad.

Khatami's agenda is evidently an ambitious and visionary one that will inevitably be challenged by the constraints of both domestic and international power politics. But it is an unprecedented and popularly mandated mission that has evolved out of Iran's own nearly two decades of revolutionary experience. Even before Khatami's assumption of the presidency, according to the United Nations Special Representative of the Commission on Human Rights, there were "islands of liberty" in the Islamic Republic of Iran. The most difficult and complex question is whether these islands can be transformed, in the future, into an area of liberty at home and of peace abroad in a region marked historically by internal upheaval and interstate war. As the world's leading torchbearer of democracy, the United States should encourage such a process of change in its own enlightened national interest.

NOTES

1. As used in this essay, the concept of young Iranians encompasses those 20 million young men and women voters who came largely from urban communities, who were predominantly literate, and who aspired to a better social and political as well as material way of life.

2. *Gozaresh-e-Seminar* (Tehran), no. 2 (1983–84): 36.

3. A multitude of Iranian and foreign reports before and after the presidential campaign reveal these to be among the aspirations of young Iranians. See, for example, "Children of the Islamic Revolution," *Economist* (London), 18 January 1997, 3–16; and Eric Hooglund, "Mythology Versus Reality: Iran's Political Economy and the Clinton Administration," *Critique* 6, no. 11 (Fall 1997): 37–51.

4. See n. 3.

5. As reported on 10 April 1997, a Berlin court found four persons guilty of the assassination on 17 September 1992 of a group of four leaders of the Democratic Party of Kurdistan-Iran in Berlin's Mykonos Restaurant. According to the court, evidence revealed that decision-making procedures within the Iranian leadership had led to the liquidation of opposition politicians abroad.

6. The closest parallel to Khatami's central thesis in international relations theory is what is known as the "democratic peace" thesis, which holds that democracies are intrinsically peaceful. Most scholars agree that democracies are at peace with each other (dyadic version), while many proponents of the theory suggest that democratic states are less prone to use force even if the regime type of their enemies is nondemocratic

(the monadic variant). Well versed in Kantian philosophy, President Khatami is probably familiar with the origins of this idea.

7. See Milton P. Buffington, ed., *Meet Mr. Khatami: The Fifth President of the Islamic Republic*, translated by Minoo R. Buffington (Washington, DC, 1997), 17.

8. See "Statement by H. E. Seyyed Mohammed Khatami, President of the Islamic Republic of Iran and Chairman of the Eighth Session of the Islamic Summit Conference," Tehran, 9 December 1997, courtesy of Islamic Republic of Iran, Permanent Mission to the United Nations.

9. See Buffington, *Meet Mr. Khatami*, 17.

10. Ibid., 33–34.

11. Ibid., 44–45.

12. Ibid.

13. The allegation regarding U.S. pressure was reported by Fahmi Huweidi, guest contributor, *Asharq Al-Awsat* (London), 15 December 1997.

14. For the text of the interview, see *Ettela'at*, 16 December 1979, 9.

15. See "Statement by H. E. Seyyed Mohammad Khatami," 2.

16. Ibid.

17. Ibid., 4.

18. Ibid.

19. Ibid., 7.

20. Ibid.

21. Ibid.

22. See, for example, *Washington Post*, 10 December 1997. For the full text of Ayatollah Khamenei's address to the summit, see *Ettela'at*, 10 December 1997, 2–3.

23. See n. 22.

24. See n. 22.

25. For the text of the Tehran Declaration, see *BBC Summary of World Broadcasts*, pt. 4, *The Middle East*, 14 December 1997.

26. Ibid.

27. Ibid.

28. For the text of the Final Statement of the eighteenth Gulf Cooperation Council summit, see Foreign Broadcast Information Service, *Daily Report*, vol. 11, *Near East and South Asia* (FBIS-NES), 22 December 1997.

29. Ibid.

30. Ibid.

31. See R. K. Ramazani, *The Persian Gulf: Iran's Role* (Charlottesville, 1972), 56–68.

32. Quoted from Khatami's news conference of 14 December 1997 in Tehran, reported in FBIS-NES, 14 December 1997.

33. Executive Order 12170, in *Public Papers of the Presidents of the United States, Jimmy Carter, June 23–December 31, 1979*, bk. 2 (Washington, DC, 1980), 2118.

34. For the text, see transcript of interview with Iranian President Mohammad Khatami, CNN Interactive, 7 January 1998.

35. *Washington Post*, 30 January 1998.

36. Ibid.

37. Ibid.

REFLECTIONS ON IRAN'S

FOREIGN POLICY

Defining the "National Interest"

One of the most crucial intellectual challenges facing Iran as it enters the third decade of its revolution, I would argue, is how it will define its "national interests" (*manafa-e melli*). Five years before the eruption of the Iranian Revolution, I asked a similar question at the conclusion of a two-volume study of Iran's foreign policy from 1500–1973, when Iran had been ruled by monarchical dynasties from the Safavids to the Pahlavis in modern history.[1] Since the revolution destroyed the ancient monarchical polity, one might inquire why I am still asking such a question. My study of the foreign policy of revolutionary Iran reveals that this question still requires an answer.[2] More important, the need to seek an answer has become more acute since the revolution for reasons that will become clear as I proceed.

This essay is not intended to answer the question I continue to ask. In fact, I do not believe an answer is in sight in the near future. Profound cultural, social, political, and psychological challenges that beset Iran as a Third World society in transition all have bearing on how Iran will ultimately settle on a coherent conception and definition of its national interest. And such a goal will come within the reach of Iran only when its triple-hybricivilization (Iranian, Islamic, and modern) is able to cope more effectively with the drama of its century-plus encounter with the realities of the modern world on its own terms.[3]

Instead, through this essay, I propose to explore this conundrum. Doing so requires that I set forth, up front, the following basic assumptions that lie behind my exploration of the subject:

1. In order to pour meaning into the abstract concept of *national interest*, it is necessary to identify the character of *polity*.
2. More than two decades of discourse about the Islamic Revolution have obscured the deeper reality: that the Iranian state and society are both in a state of *transition*, as are so many Third World nations.
3. Definition of national interest is affected by the nature of the polity's

"Reflections on Iran's Foreign Policy: Defining the 'National Interests'" was originally published in *Iran at the Crossroads*, ed. John Esposito and R. K. Ramazani (New York: Palgrave Macmillan, 2001), 211–37, and is reproduced with permission of Palgrave Macmillan.

interaction with the domestic situation, including politics, but not limited to it, and with the external situation, including international politics, but not limited to it. In other words, the concept of "situation" as used here extends beyond the political realm to cultural, social, economic, intellectual, psychological, and philosophical arenas, whether internal or external.[4]

4. Definition of the national interest requires taking into account worldviews of leaders as well as their foreign policy in action.

Various combinations of the above assumptions constitute the underpinnings of my approach, on the basis of which I shall proceed to explore the meaning of Iran's national interests in terms of four ideal types of interest as guides to foreign policy in Iran's modern history. These are *Sultanic, Ideological-Islamic, Pragmatic-Islamic,* and *Democratic-Islamic.* The inclusion of the prerevolutionary Sultanic type in the discussion is necessary. The revolution destroyed the ancient political institution of monarchy, but I submit that it has not done away with Sultanic sociocultural tendencies, which shaped the behavior of individuals and groups even during the revolutionary period.[5] It is also necessary to note that the revolutionary types are not mirror images of historical reality. They are analytical devices. As such, they overlap in historical reality. For example, the Ideological-Islamic type of interest corresponds generally with the first decade of revolutionary developments, but it by no means implies that Pragmatic-National considerations did not figure in the definition of interest during the Khomeini era. In other words, the ideal types are constructed on the basis of the relative balance between any two components in each type.

SULTANIC INTEREST

In Weberian terms "sultanism" arises whenever traditional society develops "an administration and military force which are purely personal instruments of the master."[6] Within sultanism, the master makes decisions and chooses courses of action on the basis of "nonrational discretion." The Iranian historical experience includes two types of sultanism: traditional and modernizing or transitional. The ruler's mastery of the bureaucracy and the military obtains in both types. But the bureaucracy and the military in the traditional type are more informal than formal, and the opposite holds true in the transitional type.

The best example of the traditional Sultanic type of interest prevailed during the Safavid dynasty. Shah Abbas I (1587–1629) represents sultanism in the exteme. There was perhaps not in the whole world, says a keen observer, "a king that is more Master of the lives and fortunes of his subjects, than is Shah Abbas and his successors."[7] The interest that guided Iran's foreign policy was his self-interest. He and other Safavid shahs modeled their rule after the ancient traditions of Sassanian kings. The Safavid wars with the Ottoman Empire were primarily irredentist and imperial in nature, although they were cast in terms of conflict between the Twelver Shii and Sunni state creeds.[8]

Shah Abbas I's ties with European powers aimed primarily at using them as a counterweight against the Ottoman Empire. Neither he nor other Safavid kings had any genuine interest in understanding the underpinnings of European civilization and power. The great age of European religious revolution passed by Islamic Iran. The extant religious writings (*shariat-namehs*) and secular writings (*siyasat-namehs*) reflected and endorsed both the kings' mastery over the people at home and imperial belligerency abroad. The influential *siyasat-nameh* of Khajeh Nizam al-Mulk, for example, advised rulers on the basis of the traditions of pre-Islamic kings that "people are chattel" (*rameh*) and the king is a "shepherd" (*shaban*). To the shah belonged "all the country and the people."[9] Religious writings, by contrast, viewed the Christian West in terms of Islam's conflict with *dar al-harb*, the un-Islamic abode of war. Recent research concludes that the "Safavid society did little to explore the underlying dynamics of European society and culture."[10]

The rule of Mohammad Reza Shah represents modernizing sultanism. Iran's interest was defined largely in terms of his self-interest. He and his father as Safavid kings modeled their rule after the Sassanians. Social scientists rightly list Muhammad Reza Shah side by side with, for example, Duvalier in Haiti, Trujillo in the Dominican Republic, Marcos in the Philippines, Ceausescu in Romania, and others as an example of sultanism.[11] His absolutism matched Shah Abbas I's, especially after his return to the throne as a result of the CIA-engineered coup. According to a 1965 State Department intelligence report, the Shah personally made all important military, political, economic, educational, social, and other decisions, because "he is convinced that his personal rule is the only way Iran can be governed at the present time."[12] Foreign-policy decisions were his special preserve. He wooed the United States as early as 1941 and won the policemanship of the Persian Gulf by 1968. His foreign-policy blunders over a quarter-century contributed to losing America in the end.[13] The revolutionary epithet "American king" reflected the people's alienation from him and from America for supporting him. My own research as early as 1979 led me to characterize this phenomenon as the "twin revolution."[14] In his last will and testament Ayatollah Ruhollah Khomeini labeled the Shah's Sultanic polity as satanic (*shaitanic*) rule.[15]

The interest that guided Iran's foreign policy during the Khomeini era reflected on balance more the influence of his interpretation of Twelver Shii Islam than the interest of Iran as a *nation-state*. As a historical member of the League of Nations and as one of the fifty founding members of the United Nations, Iran had defined its interest ever since the late nineteenth century and particularly after the Constitutional Revolution (1905–11) in terms of its "political independence and territorial integrity." Modern ideas entered Iranian diplomatic thought—including the very concept of "foreign policy"—side by side with the concept of "national interest." Khomeini rejected this idea, as it derived from his dislike of the idea of "nationalism" (*melli-garai*), and instead interjected a historically unprecedented notion of Islamic governance, derived from his novel interpretation of Twelver Shii jurisprudence, into Iran's political and diplomatic discourse. His favorite motto was "Independence, freedom, and the Islamic Republic." The Islamic Republic idea stemmed from his conception of *Velayat-e Faqih*, the rule of the jurisprudent.[16] This rule emanated from the belief that sovereignty belonged to God, to the Prophet, and to the "infallible imams" (*ma'sumin*) and by extension to the *faqih*. In the absence of the Twelfth Imam and until his appearance at the end of time to create a just and equitable world order, the *faqih* will rule the Islamic Republic of Iran supremely.

In anticipation of this millennarian world order, Khomeini believed that the existing world order should emulate his version of the Islamic state paradigm. Since man's weak mind created the modern international system of nation-states subsequent to the Treaty of Westphalia, Khomeini believed, an "Islamic world order" (my appellation) capable of engulfing all humanity should take its place. "Islam is not peculiar to a country," he said, "to several countries, a group [of people or countries] or even the Muslims. Islam has come for humanity. . . . Islam wishes to bring all of humanity under the *umbrella of its justice*."[17] The most vivid example of the interjection of this worldview into Iranian foreign policy concerned the Soviet Union. In Khomeini's letter of January 1, 1989, to the Soviet leader Mikhail Gorbachev, he castigated the bankrupt materialist ideologies of both the East and the West and offered to fill this "ideological vacuum" with Islamic values that alone, he wrote, "can be a means for the well-being and salvation of all nations," including, of course, the Soviet Union.[18]

The interest that guided Iran's foreign policy on the basis of this tenet of Khomeinist ideology was twofold: negation of both superpowers' domination of the international system as evidenced by his well-known slogan "Neither East nor West but the Islamic Republic," and the export of the Islamic Revolution across the world. No wonder, then, that Iran's interest defined in terms of these doctrines put it at odds with much of the rest of the world in practice.[19]

Consider these examples: The revolutionary government headquartered numerous foreign "liberation movements" in Tehran and was suspected of acts of international subversion and terrorism, especially in the Persian Gulf region. Khomeini wished to see Gulf Arab monarchies adopt governments similar, not identical, to that of the Islamic Republic of Iran, cut their "subservient ties" with the superpowers, and all find safety under the Iranian security umbrella (chatr-i amniyyat).

The reasons for Iran's prolongation of the war against Iraq in pursuit of a "final victory" are still controversial, but the ideological factor cannot be entirely ruled out.[20] To understand this problem it is necessary to remember that U.N. Secretary General Javier Perez de Cuellar, in his report to the Security Council, characterized Iraq's invasion of Iran on September 22, 1980, as "aggression against Iran."[21] But the question persists to date about the Iranian prolongation of forays into Iraqi territory on and after July 13, 1982, by which time Iran had liberated most of its territory from the Iraqi occupation forces.[22] Why, then, did it carry the war into Iraqi lands? In 1989 Khomeini himself said, "We exported our revolution to the world through the war."[23] The explanation of former president Hashemi Rafsanjani in 1999 still did not seem to rule out the possible influence of ideology. He said that Khomeini "decreed that our forces should not enter [Iraqi] populated regions and the armed forces carried out the decree."[24] That directive seems to have left the uninhabited areas of Iraq as open targets.

Two even clearer examples of the influence of ideology on the definition of interest as a guide to Iran's foreign policy should also be mentioned. Khomeini's life-threatening fatwa (religious opinion) on Salman Rushdie for "blasphemy," which marred Iran's relations with the West for years, was heavily marked by ideological preoccupation. It is likely, though, that he used the fatwa as a means of balancing domestic political factions so as to keep order.[25] Perhaps the most clear indication of Iran's national interest defined primarily in terms of ideology is the annual dispute between Iran and Saudi Arabia over political demonstrations of the Iranian pilgrims in Mecca.[26] The worst happened in the 1987 Hajj season, when some 400 pilgrims, including 275 Iranians, died in the clash between the pilgrims and the Saudi police force.

Yet, the definition of Iran's interest even during the Khomeini decade was not completely devoid of practical and national considerations. As a nation-state, Iran had to live in the real world of the international system. In fact, no one changed the Khomeini line in light of world realities more than Khomeini himself, both in terms of declaratory and of practical policies. Just one landmark example of each should suffice. After the hostage crisis, when Western powers in general and the United States in particular imposed sanctions on Iran in order to isolate it, Khomeini declared, "We must become isolated in order to become independent."[27] Yet, after the consolidation of power by his supporters, the settlement of the hostage dispute, and the liberation of Khorramshahr from Iraqi occupation forces, he blamed his zealous followers for Iran's "hermit" status in world affairs, cited the example of the Prophet Muhammad in sending ambassadors to all parts of the world to establish proper relations, criticized his hard-line supporters for demanding that Iran have no relations with the outside world, and declared that such a demand would make no sense because for Iran "it would mean defeat, annihilation and being buried right to the end."[28]

The best example of the consideration of pragmatic interests in Iran's foreign policy during the Khomeini era is the secret purchase of arms from the United States and Israel.[29] Iran's defensive war against Iraq required such a bold move. A deal was struck through intermediaries—American and Israeli arms in return for Iran's help with the release of Western hostages in Lebanon. Six shipments of arms went to Iran, and several American hostages were released, each after Iran received a shipment of arms. Embarrassed by the disclosure of the secret deal by Mehdi Hashemi, a militant Islamist, all Iranian leaders in chorus tried to cover up the transactions by denouncing the Great Satan and ridiculing the American mission arriving in Tehran with a Bible and a cake![30] In the end, Khomeini himself intervened to quash a demand for parliamentary investigation of the scandal, known in the United States as the Iran-Contra Affair.

PRAGMATIC-ISLAMIC INTEREST

The end of the Khomeini era witnessed the beginning of a significant shift in the balance between the influence of ideological and pragmatic aims in Iran's foreign policy in favor of the latter. The shift was subtle and gradual and lasted a good eight years. The notion of an Islamic world order began to wane. The idea of Islam in one country began to gain momentum. Iran was still viewed as the "Islamic citadel" (umm-al qora), but it was viewed so as a model to emulate, not as one to export through incitement of political opposition in other Muslim states. The doctrine of "Neither East nor West, but the Islamic Republic" was also turned on its head when the Soviet Union disintegrated.[31]

More specifically, the confluence of three sets of events, domestic, regional, and global, underpinned the shift of emphasis in definition of Iran's interests and its foreign-policy orientation. Domestically, two factors figured prominently. First, the chaos of the early years of the Khomeini era had been checked for years before Khomeini's death in 1989. In the three years after the outbreak of the revolution, for example, Iran had had three presidents, four prime ministers, and seven foreign ministers. Both the hostage crisis and the Iraqi invasion of Iran played into the hands of militant forces following "the Khomeini line"

(*Khatti Imam*). They suppressed both secular and religious opposition forces, tightened the clerical grip on the social and political organs of the nation, and consolidated and monopolized power.

Second, the problem of succession to Khomeini was resolved speedily. A new president was also elected. Even before Khomeini's death the expected successor, Ayatollah Hussein-Ali Montazeri, had been passed over. Khomeini's choice of Sayyid Ali Khamenei as successor was facilitated by amending the Constitution. The requirement that the *faqih* be a "source of emulation" (*marja-i taqlid*) was dropped, and Khamenei was elevated politically to the rank of Ayatollah. Also, Hashemi Rafsanjani, the influential speaker of the Majlis, was elected president. The American media persistently viewed the two leaders simply as rivals. That was true only in part. Despite stylistic differences, the two leaders' larger interest in the survival of the revolution prevailed. Their dual leadership structure resembled a political tandem bicycle (*daw charkheh-ye daw nafareh*).[32]

Both leaders had shown pragmatic Islamic tendencies. For example, in 1987, when militant Islamists objected to Iran's ties with Soviet-bloc or Western countries, and even Turkey on ideological grounds, Rafsanjani said, "I believe our principles are obeyed, but in some cases we may be limited and we may have to forego some of these principles."[33] Rafsanjani also constructed the foundations of close military, economic, and political relations with the Soviet Union, which endured after its disintegration. To cite an example about Khamenei's pragmatic tendencies, as president he initiated the idea of Iran's "open-door foreign policy" after a visit to China. He said that "Iran seeks to have rational, sound, and healthy relations with all countries" so as to serve both its national interest and Islam.[34]

Regionally, the most important factor underlying the shift of balance of influence between ideology and pragmatic considerations in favor of the latter was the end of the eight-year Iran-Iraq War. The bitter consequences of the war helped Iran to focus attention on its interests as a nation-state in two ways, rather than to behave as a redeemer of the Muslim states and the world beyond. First, Iranian leaders accorded priority to Iran's political independence and territorial integrity as a nation-state. Second, they decided to reconstruct Iran's military capability and increase its economic productivity, which had been devastated by the Iraqi invasion and occupation. The blatant U.S. intervention in the war on the side of Saddam Hussein against Iran deepened the latter's military and economic plight. While the Iraqi forces rained missiles on Iranian people and used chemical weapons on Iranian soldiers, the United States attacked the Iranian Navy, dismantled a couple of Iranian offshore oil fields in the Persian Gulf, and created and supported Iraq's tanker war against Iran.[35] This in part explains the dogged determination of the new Iranian leaders to reconstruct the Iranian military and economy, despite all domestic and international difficulties. In a candid admission, Rafsanjani said that although Iran had great potential for economic growth, "since we came to power, we have not done so much to [achieve it]."[36] In his inaugural address to the Majlis, he was equally candid about Iran's failure to clarify its national interest when he said, "We have not come forward with clear theses [definition of the national interest] in our foreign policy."[37]

Globally, the end of the Cold War and the disintegration of the Soviet Union had far-reaching effects on Iranian thinking about national interest. For the first time in seventy years, Iran's stable international frontiers with the Soviet Union seemed threatened as a consequence of the emergence of a congeries of weak and unstable new republics in Transcaucasia and Central Asia on both sides of the Caspian Sea ("Northwest Asia," my appellation).[38] As we shall see below, Iran's political independence and territorial integrity in the North became a major source of concern just shortly after it seemed that the end of the Iran-Iraq War had put to rest, at least momentarily, the threat from Saddam Hussein's Iraq.

This rise in Iranian consciousness about the critical importance of national interest in the making and execution of foreign policy found many practical expressions in Iran's relations with other nations across the world. But priority was accorded to the protection and promotion of the country's security interest in the South, the Persian Gulf region, and the country's stability in Northwest Asia.

Historically, Iran has viewed the security of the Persian Gulf region to be indispensable to maintaining its political independence and territorial integrity. But in the Khomeini era, as seen, the ideological crusade and the provocative behavior of Iranian rogue elements in and out of government caused animosity with the Gulf Arab monarchies, who established the Gulf Cooperation Council (GCC) as an antidote to the contagion of the Iranian Revolution. Iranian support of anti-Iraqi forces also contributed to the outbreak of the Iran-Iraq War. By contrast, the Rafsanjani administration pursued a national policy of reconciliation with the Arab monarchies. He said categorically that "we do not want to become the policeman [of the Persian Gulf and] humiliate or intimidate our neighbors or make them feel insecure." He pursued consistently a conciliatory policy toward the GCC member states, contained the annual conflict with Saudi Arabia over the Hajj issue, and sought earnestly to improve Iran's relations with the GCC as a whole, despite the old dispute with the United Arab Emirates (UAE) over three Persian Gulf islands. In recognition of this conciliatory stance, the GCC, for example, expressed eagerness in its twelfth summit meeting (December 25, 1991) to "lend momentum to bilateral relations with" Iran "in the service of common interests."[39]

Two examples in particular indicate that the Rafsanjani administration's courses of action were in keeping with his rhetoric. First was Iran's stance in the Persian Gulf War. To the chagrin of Islamic extremists at home, the Rafsanjani government condemned the Iraqi invasion of Kuwait; maintained amicable relations with the Kuwaiti government-in-exile; made common diplomatic cause with Algeria, France, the Soviet Union, and others to find a peaceful solution before Desert Storm; observed U.N. resolutions imposed on Iraq; and made no real attempt to exploit the Shii and Kurdish rebellions in Iraq, against all expectations of the rebels to the contrary. In recognition of Iran's realistic stance, Secretary of State James Baker III believed after the war that "Iran as a major power in the Gulf"[40] should not be excluded from postwar security arrangements in the region, although Washington did exactly the opposite. To the great dismay of Iranian leaders, President George H. W. Bush increased unprecedentedly the U.S. military presence in the Persian Gulf.[41] It also concluded bilateral strategic agreements with most individual GCC states, without the slightest understanding of Iran's ancient self-perception about its important role in the security of the Persian Gulf.

Second, despite President George Bush's exclusionary policy, Rafsanjani displayed unusual understanding of the U.S. military presence in the Persian Gulf by saying that Iran was "not afraid of them [foreign military forces]" and that "they do not constitute a threat."[42] He also said that the United States had "always had bases in Bahrain and Qatar. We have never liked that and always criticized it, and will continue to do so in the future." And Foreign Minister Ali Akbar Velayati said, "It is not reasonable to say that the foreigners must not be present in the region in circumstances in which there is no solution for ensuring the security of the region."[43] This shrewd observation meant that if Saddam Hussein were to try to unleash another invasion against Iran or Kuwait, or for that matter against any other state in the region, the U.S. military presence could act as an effective deterrent after all.

In the North as in the South, Iran's national interest was accorded a higher priority than ideology. While in the South the security of the Persian Gulf was its main concern, in Northwest Asia the region's stability was at stake. Four sets of factors underpinned Iran's interest in the stability of Northwest Asia.

First, given its bitter historical experiences with imperial Russia dating back to the eighteenth century, Iran did not wish to see a new Russian empire rise on its border lands on the ashes of the disintegrated Soviet Union. At the same time, Rafsanjani wanted to make sure that the multifaceted agreements he had made with the Soviets prior to his presidency would be honored by Moscow subsequently. This required tightrope walking between the divergent and convergent interests of Tehran with Moscow.

Second, Iran needed to contain the contagion of the ethnic revivalist movement in former Soviet Azerbaijan, across the border from its own eastern and western provinces of Azerbaijan. As early as 1990, illegal border crossing had concerned Iran, and the call for the creation of "Greater Azerbaijan" by non-Iranian Azeri nationalists could pose a potential threat to Iran's northern borders.[44]

Third, Iran was deeply concerned that the bloody armed conflict between Armenia and Azerbaijan might spill over into the Iranian northern border areas.

Fourth and finally, Iran's increased geostrategic significance as a result of the disintegration of the Soviet Union required a stable Northwest Asia for the promotion of Iran's interests in the region. The newly independent states could provide a vast market for Iranian exports. Iran could become the cheapest and shortest transit trade route for the transport of oil and gas supplies of the Caspian Sea basin across Iran to world markets through the Persian Gulf. Such opportunities could benefit not only Iran but also Western oil companies and Western democracies, as well as, of course, the Northwest Asian republics.

Given these interests, Iran pursued an active and pragmatic policy toward Northwest Asia. To cite a few examples, it forged ties with every single new republic; it took the initiative to include them in an expanded Economic Cooperation Organization (ECO); it created a five-member Caspian Sea organization for better handling of the geopolitical situation and serving the interests of all the littoral states in shipping, fisheries, and the desperately needed protection of the environment; and above all, it mediated effectively between the warring republics of Armenia and Azerbaijan, brokering a cease-fire agreement that facilitated the fact-finding mission of U.N. special envoy Cyrus Vance, an accomplishment that earned Iran the praise of U.N. Secretary-General Boutros Boutros-Ghali. Eight years later, on March 17, 2000, Secretary of State Madeleine K. Albright acknowledged that it was in the common interest of Iran and the United States to encourage "stable relations between Armenia and Azerbaijan."[45]

Enough has been said to show how ideological influences of the first decade of the revolution in the conduct of Iran's foreign policy had begun to be replaced by pragmatic considerations by the end of Rafsanjani's presidency. Embedded in this important shift of emphasis was the resurgence of the concept of Iran as a nation-state in the international community. Despite all the American media propaganda about the threat of Islamic fundamentalism to Northwest Asia through Iran, objective research has made such a claim empirically indefensible. The Islamic component of Iran's national interest became a cultural basis for friendly ties with neighbors rather than a militant ideology for export.

The new pragmatic "Islamic-Iranian" (my appellation) paradigm had a special appeal to Northwest Asian republics for various reasons. The Azerbaijanis share Imami Shii Islam with the majority of the Iranian population and ethnic and linguistic ties with the minority Iranian Azerbaijanis. The Tajiks, by contrast, share ethnic and linguistic bonds with Iranian culture and society, and they, as well as Uzbeks, celebrate the Iranian New Year, Nowruz.

DEMOCRATIC-ISLAMIC INTEREST

The balance between the Ideological-Islamic and Pragmatic-Islamic influences in the thinking and the conduct of Iran's foreign policy, as seen above, had begun to tilt in favor of the latter during the Rafsanjani era. This tilt reflected a degree of domestication of the Islamic Revolution, or in Kenneth N. Waltz's comment on revolutions in general, it reflected the process of "socialization" of revolution to the international system.[46] This process in the redefinition of Iran's national interest occurred despite the fact that both constitutionally and institutionally the concept of *Velayat-e Faqih* continued to dominate Iran's thinking in its domestic and foreign policies. Lucian W. Pye noted decades ago that it is a characteristic of transitional societies for leaders to have a greater freedom of action in the international arena as opposed to the domestic situation.[47]

Yet, the Iranian Constitution provided the foundation not only for socializing the Islamic Revolution to the international system but also for democratizing the Iranian polity as well as foreign policy. Not until the resounding presidential victory of Seyyed Mohammad Khatami on May 23, 1997 (*Dovom-e Khordad*), was any serious discussion of this democratic aspect of the Constitution in vogue. And ever since his accession to the presidency, he has invoked the Constitution repeatedly as the framework within which both Iran's domestic and foreign policies can and should be democratized.

The legal basis for this view rests on constitutional provisions that amount to something like the principle of popular sovereignty.[48] Articles 56 and 6 acknowledge the "sovereign right of the nation" and command that "no one shall take away this God-given right." Numerous other provisions provide for a whole variety of individual and other freedoms, including, for example, freedom and equality of individuals before the law; security and protection of reputation, life, property, dwelling, and vocation; immunity from search and seizure; presumption of innocence; prohibition of torture; and inviolability of dignity and honor of any person who has been apprehended, detained, arrested, or exiled under any circumstances. They also include freedom of the press and publications; freedom of forming parties, groups, and associations; freedom of thought and prohibition of interrogation of people's beliefs; and judicial security and the government's obligation to secure "the rights of the people on an all-out basis, men and women alike."

Yet, paradoxically, the Constitution also embodies the sovereign right of the *faqih* based on the incorporation in Article 110 of Khomeini's interpretation of governance in Twelver Shii Islam. At the very inception of the Constitution, religious as well as secular individuals and groups objected to this dual sovereignty.[49] For example, Grand Ayatollah Shariatmadari believed that Article 110 contravened Articles 56 and 6, mentioned above, but such critical voices were suppressed and were not revived until after the presidency of Khatami.

The significance of this fundamental constitutional argument for the definition of Iran's national interest should not be overlooked, for the all-important reason that Article 9 of the Constitution makes Iran's independence "inseparable" from freedom. And Article 152 provides in part, "The foreign policy of the Islamic Republic of Iran is founded on the basis of . . . safeguarding the complete independence and integrity of the territory" of Iran. In other words, democratization of the Iranian society and state is indispensable to the protection of Iran's complete political independence and territorial integrity as a modern nation-state.

The profound demographic, social, economic, intellectual, and global changes of nearly two decades that underpin the democratic movement led by President Khatami; the unprecedentedly popular elections held for the first time since the revolution of village, town, and city councils; and the domestic struggle and sometimes violent clashes between the "conservatives" (*muhafezeh-karan*) and the "reformers" (*eslah-talaban*) are beyond the scope of this study. Shortly after President Khatami's election, I suggested elsewhere that the synergy between his agenda for reforms at home and for peace abroad had been overlooked.[50] I also suggested that President Khatami's worldview resembles the concept of "democratic peace" in the theory of international relations.[51] The analogy, however, is not intended to be complete. The sovereign right of the *faqih* in the case of Iran transforms that essentially secular democratic theory into a peculiar hybrid concept of "*faqih*-guided democratic peace." Despite this fundamental limitation of the concept of democratic peace in the case of Iran, it is nevertheless useful to point out briefly the intellectual underpinnings of Khatami's worldview, its practical effects on Iran's foreign policy in action, and its potential for redefinition of Iran's national interest in terms of Democratic-Islamic interest.

Some of the more basic tenets of Khatami's worldview may be listed as follows:

1. Religion and liberty are compatible and so are Islam and freedom.
2. Freedom requires the creation of a civil society based on the paradigm of "The City of the Prophet" (*Madinat al-Nabi*), as opposed to the Western concept of civil society that is founded on the model of the Greek city-state.[52] The reason for this distinction is to emphasize the spiritual and moral dimensions of his concept of civil society. At the international level the concept of civil society becomes "global civil society," in the words of Foreign Minister Kamal Kharrazi.
3. The rule of law at home is projected to the international system by emphasizing the role of international law, at least in declaratory policies.
4. Since liberalism is associated, in his view, with secularism, it is regarded as incompatible with Islam, although he insists that Iranians must learn the positive achievements of liberal democracy, such as freedom, limiting and supervising raw power, and "constitutionalizing governance on the basis of the people's will and demands."[53]
5. Although he acknowledges that Western civilization is the preeminent civilization in today's world, Khatami believes that neither it nor its political offspring, secular liberalism, will be triumphant for all time. Yet, this conviction should not be a stumbling block in the way of dialogue among civilizations. Khatami's interpretation of the Renaissance, it seems to me, aims, at least in part, at providing a basis for dialogue between the Islamic and Western civilizations. The "Renaissance's real aim was not to revive classical Greek Culture," he argues; rather its aim was "to revitalize religion by giving it a new language and fresh ideas."[54] This meant that man would not negate, but embrace, religion by "reforming and propagating" it instead of opposing it. Yet, he thinks that over time modernity lost touch with this spiritual origin of the Renaissance and, hence, led to the sociopolitical phenomenon of Western colonization, which failed to adopt "a humanitarian and ethical approach" to man and the universe. At President Khatami's initiative, the United Nations designated the year 2001 as the year of dialogue among civilizations.[55] He hopes that through such dialogue the East can teach the West the vital importance of spirituality in human life and the East can learn the positive achievements of Western civilization.
6. Despite these and other ideas, Khatami does not claim to have an answer for the future of his fellow Iranians. He believes that a future

different from secular liberalism is awaiting humanity. But the important question, he asks, will be whether "we will be able to play a role in human destiny or at least in our own destiny. If the answer is positive, then with what light should we illuminate our path and what should be our journey's provisions?"[56]

The path of dialogue and detente that President Khatami has pursued in international relations within a few short years clearly has led to an unprecedented degree of reconciliation with the rest of the world. This is an unambiguous departure from the first decade of the revolution. Iran's proactive and peaceful foreign policy since 1997 has encompassed the globe. At the most general level it consists of three general components: "decontainment," deterrence, and detente. Decontainment aims at circumventing the American policy of isolating Iran economically, diplomatically, and militarily across the world. Deterrence aims at sufficient military capability to deter any other act of aggression such as Iraq's against Iran, especially in its now even more "dangerous neighborhood," to use Secretary of State Madeleine K. Albright's words. India, Israel, and Pakistan are three nuclear powers in the vicinity of Iran. And detente aims not only at assisting the other two goals of Iranian foreign policy but also at overcoming the deepening pains of what President Khatami calls Iran's "sick economy." With these general outlines in mind, a few concrete examples of Iran's foreign policy since the presidency of Khatami should suffice.

First and foremost, Iran and Saudi Arabia have achieved a degree of rapprochement that had not existed since the outbreak of the Iranian Revolution.[57] The worldviews of President Khatami and Crown Prince Abdullah happen to converge significantly, as both oppose hegemony of the great powers in world politics, both urge their own and other Muslim societies to engage in self-criticism, and Khatami's concept of dialogue and Abdullah's notion of "call" (*dawah*) aim at providing the world with the paradigm of ethical Islamic behavior. The interests of the two countries also converge considerably, though not completely. Both sympathize with the sufferings of the Iraqi people under the United Nations sanction established in 1991, both consider the Iraqi regime as a potential source of threat to their security, both wish to prevent oil prices from hitting rock bottom in the world market, and both share an interest in the development of the Organization of the Islamic Conference (OIC), which has been bankrolled for decades by Saudi Arabia and is currently chaired by Khatami, so that the Muslim states might play a larger role on the world scene. From the Iranian perspective, rapprochement with Saudi Arabia is key to improving relations with other GCC states, despite the dispute with the UAE and that country's unspoken discomfort over the Irano-Saudi rapprochement, and to convincing the Arab monarchies of the need for the littoral states of the region to maintain the security of the Persian Gulf themselves.

Second, Iran has taken giant steps toward transforming the European past policy of "critical engagement" into a policy of positive engagement with it. The key object of the Iranian policy of friendship within the European Union states has been Britain. Iran took the bold initiative to remove the single greatest stumbling block in its relations with London by distancing itself publicly from the Khomeini *fatwa* against Salman Rushdie. In a news conference on September 22, 1998, in New York, President Khatami suggested that the *fatwa* was the expression of Khomeini's own view as an Islamic jurist, reportedly adding that "we should consider the Salman Rushdie issue as completely finished."[58] Two days later, the seasoned foreign minister, Kamal Kharrazi, reportedly told British Foreign Secretary Robin Cook: "The government of the Islamic Republic of Iran has no intention, nor is it going to take any action whatsoever to threaten the life of the author of *The Satanic Verses* or anybody associated with his work, nor will it encourage or assist anybody to do so."[59] Britain announced immediately afterward that it would upgrade its diplomatic relations with Iran by an exchange of ambassadors.

By January 2000, improved relations had entered a level such that for the first time since the revolution an Iranian minister visited London. Foreign Ministers Cook and Kharrazi committed their nations to resolving common difficulties regarding the Iraqi regime, Iraqi refugees in Iran, terrorism, and weapons of mass destruction.[60] In tandem with improving relations with Britain, Iran also has developed ever-closer relations with Italy, France, Germany, Greece, Austria, and others, especially in the economic field, the single most important incentive for better relations with the European Union. From a strategic perspective, of course, Iranian-European rapprochement fits Iran's policy of decontainment vis-à-vis the United States.

Third, and finally, against the backdrop of mutual satanization between Tehran and Washington since the seizure of American diplomats as hostages on November 4, 1979, until the election of President Khatami on May 23, 1997, there seemed to be no real hope for normalization of Iranian-U.S. relations. Yet, President Khatami surprised the world on December 14, 1997, when he said that "I, first of all, pay my respect to the great people and nation of America" and that he hoped that in the near future he would have "a dialogue and talk with the American people."[61] True to his word, on January 7, 1998, he pointed out the philosophical similarity, if not commonality, between the origins of the American and Iranian republics in combining religion and liberty. He then proposed to Americans the idea of an "exchange of professors, writers, scholars, artists, journalists, and tourists," which has been under way ever since.[62]

Apart from people-to-people exchanges between the United States and Iran and a relative thaw in the hostile rhetoric and symbols that has occurred ever since these two Iranian initiatives, the Clinton administration has taken a few tentative steps toward improving the atmosphere of U.S. relations with Iran. For example, it waived the threat of sanctions against the French Total firm and its Russian and Malaysian partners when, in defiance of the Iran-Libya Sanctions Act (ILSA), Total signed a $2 billion investment contract with Iran for its gas field in the Persian Gulf. It allowed U.S. firms to sell food and medicine to Iran; allowed the Boeing Company to provide Iran's national airline with parts to ensure the safety of its 747 passenger aircraft contract; lifted the U.S. embargo on Iranian export of carpets, caviar, and dried fruits; and promised a "global settlement" of legal claims and counterclaims of Iran and the United States at the Hague Tribunal.

Perhaps Iran was more impressed by certain statements on the part of the United States than by these small symbolic steps. Long after President Khatami had expressed regrets in January 1998 for the sufferings of the American people during the hostage crisis, President Clinton surprised even the officials of his own administration in April 1999 by saying that Iran "has been the subject of quite a lot of abuse from various Western nations" and that sometimes "it's quite important to tell people, look, you have a right to be angry at something my country or my culture or others that are generally allied with us today did to you 50 or 60 or 100 or 150 years ago."[63] It was even more music to Iranian ears when Secretary of State Madeleine K. Albright publicly admitted on March 17, 2000, the American role in the overthrow of the popular government of Dr. Mosaddegh and expressed regret for the United States' having sided with Iraq in its war against Iran.[64]

All these small steps and the improved tone of the Clinton administration, the positive Arab response to Iranian efforts for rapprochement, and the ever-increasing ties between Iran and European nations show that Iran's definition of its national interest has begun to move away from the Ideological emphasis of the first decade of the revolution, although in fairness it must be admitted that Rafsanjani's foreign-policy initiatives over eight years paved the way for further conciliatory moves on the part of the Khatami leadership. Overall, ever since the accession of Rafsanjani to power and the presidency of Khatami, the foreign policy of Iran has played a significant role in the painful process of the as yet incomplete reintegration of Iran into the international system.

THE ENDURING QUESTION

To return to the beginning of this essay, when I asked a quarter-century ago what the meaning of Iran's national interest was, I also tried to illustrate the question for American readers by pointing out the enduring debate between realists and idealists about the American national interest. In the 1950s and 1960s, the dominant thinking in the American academy was what is today called "traditional realism" (Kenneth N. Waltz's appellation),[65] as expounded especially by Hans J. Morgenthau. This influential international-relations thinker defined national interest in terms of power for its own sake.[66] Today, the neorealists, led by Kenneth N. Waltz, define national interest in terms of power as an instrument of security. Conversely, Reinhold Niebuhr, the eminent "theologian realist" (my appellation), said that, to be sure, preservation of self-interest was "tentatively necessary" and the balancing of power could serve self-interest, but it was not sufficient. In other words, that the United States should embrace a scheme of higher values than national interest defined merely in terms of power or security.[67]

The founding fathers of the United States are said to have sought to use foreign policy as a means to such higher ends and purposes as individual rights to life, liberty, and the pursuit of happiness, as embodied in the American Declaration of Independence. In 1974, when the Shah was still in power, I asked, What about Iran? What are those higher ends that Iran's foreign policy is trying to serve? And now that the Islamic Republic of Iran has entered its third decade of existence, I ask the same question again. What are those higher ends beyond self-interest that the Islamic Republic of Iran will try to serve?

This essay has shown that since the revolution Iran has tried to experiment with various kinds of definitions of national interest. In the first decade of the revolution, the Khomeinist ideological crusade, aimed at an Islamic world order, outweighed practical-national considerations in Iranian foreign-policy thinking and action. During the following eight years, practical-national considerations outweighed the ideological ones. And since the presidency of Mohammad Khatami, democratic-national thinking has been introduced into Iranian foreign-policy discourse and practice. The pro-Khatami reformers call Iran's new thinking the "democratic-Islamic paradigm" (olgo-ye mardom salari-e Eslami).

As seen, in trying to point out the similarity between the American and Iranian peoples' revolutionary experiences, President Khatami spoke of the combination of religion and liberty in the founding of the American republic and mentioned de Tocqueville as well. Assuming that his American audience had read de Tocqueville, President Khatami did not elaborate, but my guess is that he had this passage in mind: "I do not know whether all the Americans have sincere faith in their religion; for who can search the human heart? But I am certain that they hold it to be indispensable to the maintenance of republican institutions. This opinion is not peculiar to a class of citizens or to a party, but it belongs to the whole nation, and to every rank of society."[68]

I shall return to this parallelism, but it is worth mentioning here that there is a more fitting parallel in the experience of American and Iranian revolutionaries. Religion played a significant role in mobilizing support for resistance of both revolutionary peoples to foreign domination, Britain in the American and, ironically, the United States in the Iranian experience. Regarding the American case, James H. Hutson says: "The plain fact is that, had American clergymen of all denominations not assured their pious countrymen, from the beginning of the conflict with Britain, that the resistance movement was right in God's sight and had His blessing, it could not have been sustained and independence could not have been achieved. Here is the fundamental, the indispensable, contribution of religion and its spokesmen to the coming of the American Revolution."[69]

There is, however, a fundamental difference between the Iranian and American revolutionary experiences insofar as combining religion and liberty is concerned. The American founding fathers did not institutionalize such a combination in the American Constitution; in fact, they separated them in the First Amendment's Establishment Clause. This separation was never intended to be an antireligious or anticlerical move, a reality that is little understood in Iran. As a matter of fact, it has been argued that the Jeffersonian metaphor of the "Wall of Separation" has never been as absolute as has been commonly assumed.[70] To date, in fact, American courts are trying to draw boundaries, case by case, between church and state in American society to protect both religion and state.

The Iranian Revolution, however, created the world's only quasi-theocratic state, which, as seen, was debated at the very inception of the Republic. The Constitution in effect embodies, it seems to me, two God-given rights, one that belongs to the faqih and the other to the people, but the former enjoys superior powers relative to the latter. President Khatami, who embraces the Constitution and acknowledges, necessarily, the supreme leadership of the faqih, seems to be trying to upgrade people's rights within the existing constitutional framework by reforming the Islamic polity. This is fully in keeping with his rejection of "secular liberalism," as seen above. In American political-science jargon, he is a "transformational" president. But fierce, and often violent, opposition to his reform efforts seems to be forcing him toward some kind of an "incremental" presidency. A more apt characterization, I believe, is that he is transformational in vision and incremental in strategy.

The deceptive nature of the main opposition, it seems to me, lies in the fact that it is expressed all in the name of Islam. For example, the twenty-year-old gunman who shot Saeed Hajjarian, a close adviser to President Khatami, told the court with a smile that he believed his victim was "un-Islamic" and that he attacked Hajjarian because he believed he was performing his "religious duties." In the case of Iran, as opposed to most other Muslim states, the problem is deeper than religious fanaticism. I believe it is compounded by what may be called "sociocultural sultanism," a phenomenon that is observable at every level of society in the behavior of the individual, group, and polity.[71] President Khatami seemed to be putting his finger on this very problem when he said, "Autocracy has become our second nature. We Iranians are all dictators, in a sense."[72]

But the quest for individual freedom and democracy in Iranian society is more than a century old. Twice in the twentieth century, the glimmer of hope for democratic polity was dashed, once by Britain and Russia and once by the United States. The revolution first revived that hope and then scotched it, despite the fact that the Constitution couples inseparably, as seen, political independence with freedom. President Khatami believes that the Khomeini motto "Independence, freedom, and the Islamic Republic" constitutes three "enduring" (javidan) slogans of the revolution. The first two principles are the products of Iran's painful encounter with the modern world since the late nineteenth century. They have survived all the turmoil and tragedy of Iranian history because they are compatible with modern standards of international relations and law. The real question is whether the principle of the Islamic Republic, in its present constitutional and institutional configurations, will become increasingly compatible with the realities of the modern world, including Iran's own disrupted, but enduring, democratic movement.

As long as this question remains largely unanswered, definition of the national interest in Iran's foreign policy in the future will remain problematic. It will largely reflect the effects of muddling through the pressures and counterpressures of domestic and international circumstances, without achieving a coherent core of values as the clearly articulated higher ends and purposes of foreign policy. This is the crucial challenge that faces the Iranian foreign-policy community, including thinkers and practitioners of all stripes.

Yet, as an Iranian American thinker who has watched from the United States for over half a century the painful process of Iran's civilizational maturation and the beginnings of the process of democratic transition, I am more hopeful than fearful that the quest of the Iranian people for freedom will not be extinguished in the twenty-first century as it was twice in the twentieth. If my hopes are realized, perhaps liberty can become the highest end and purpose of Iran's foreign policy at the turn of the new millennium, for I firmly believe that without justice, there can be no durable order, and without liberty, there can be no justice.

NOTES

1. My interest in the foreign policy of Iran dates back to 1952, when I was doing research and writing on the legal and political aspects of the Iranian nationalization of the oil industry for my doctoral dissertation. I then discovered that there were no systematic studies of Iran's foreign policy in any language. That set me on the path of working on the subject over the past half-century. See my book *The Foreign Policy of Iran, 1500–1941: A Developing Nation in World Affairs* (Charlottesville, 1966). The influential *Foreign Affairs* recognized that "R. K. Ramazani's book is the only work in any language which gives an objective and detailed account of Iran's international role during this entire period." The book won the first prize of the American Association for Middle East Studies, subsequently renamed MESA. See also my *Iran's Foreign Policy, 1941–1973: A Study of Foreign Policy in Modernizing Nations* (Charlottesville, 1975). This book was recognized by the *Guide to American Foreign Relations Since 1700* as "the best single volume on Iran's foreign policy in the postwar period."

2. See my *Revolutionary Iran: Challenge and Response in the Middle East* (1986; Baltimore, 1988).

3. I first used this concept of "triple hybridity" in a paper titled "Secularism and Islam," delivered at the fiftieth-anniversary meeting of the Middle East Institute, Washington, DC, 28 September 1996.

4. I developed the concept of interactions between foreign and domestic situations and vice versa, between foreign policy and the external situation and vice versa, and between external and internal situations in 1966 and have used it ever since in all subsequent studies. It is characterized as "dynamic triangular interaction."

5. Weber uses the concept of "sultanism," as will be seen, with reference to a type of polity. For reasons given in n. 71 below, I have extended it to apply to individuals and groups as well.

6. See Max Weber, *Economy and Society: An Outline of Interpretive Sociology*, edited by Guenther Roth and Claus Wittich (Berkeley, 1978), 1:231–32. Historically speaking, I find it suggestive to compare the sultanism of ancient China with that of Iran. See *From Max Weber: Essay in Sociology*, translated and edited by H. H. Gerth and C. Wright Mills (New York, 1958), esp. 442–44.

7. For details, see Ramazani, *Foreign Policy of Iran*, 13–32.

8. Ibid.

9. See Seyyed Javad Tabatabai, *Tarikh-e Andishe-ye Siyasi dar Iran* [A history of political thought in Iran] (Tehran, 1988), 61–62.

10. See the thoughtful article of Rudi Matthee, "Between Aloofness and Fascination: Safavid Views of the West," *Iranian Studies* 31, no. 2 (Spring 1998): 219–46.

11. See Juan J. Linz and Alfred Stepan, *Problems of Democratic Transition and Consolidation: Southern Europe, South America, and Post-Communist Europe* (Baltimore, 1996), 51. It should be noted that the authors' typology of polities does not include theocratic or quasi-theocratic such as that of Iran, which is now facing the problems of transition to democracy. This theoretical gap requires research by social scientists. Also, the success or failure of the democratic experiment in the Islamic Republic of Iran could have a far-reaching impact on the Muslim world.

12. I am indebted to Professor Abbas Milani for bringing this report to my attention.

See U.S. Department of State, Bureau of Intelligence and Research, *Studies in Political Dynamics in Iran*, Secret Report No. 13, NSA No. 603.

13. See my *The United States and Iran: The Patterns of Influence* (New York, 1982). See also my "Who Lost America? The Case of Iran," pp. 50–67 in this volume.

14. See my "Iran's Revolution in Perspective," in *The Impact of the Iranian Events upon Persian Gulf and United States Security*, project director Z. Michael Szaz (Washington, DC, 1979), 19–37; "Iran's Foreign Policy: Perspectives and Projections," in *Economic Consequences of the Revolution in Iran: A Compendium of Papers Submitted to the Joint Economic Committee, Congress of the United States* (Washington, DC, 1980), 65–97; and "Iran's Revolution: Patterns, Problems, and Prospects," pp. 33–49 in this volume.

15. See *Imam Khomeini's Last Will and Testament*, published by the Embassy of the Democratic and Popular Republic of Algeria, Interests Section of the Islamic Republic of Iran (Washington, DC, 1989), 23.

16. See Ayatollah Ruhollah Khomeini's work in Persian, *Hokomat-e Islami Va Velayat-i Faqih* [Islamic government and guardianship of the Islamic jurist] (Tehran, 1977).

17. Foreign Broadcast Information Service, *Daily Report*, vol. 5, *Middle East and North Africa* (FBIS-MEA), 18 December 1979, emphasis added.

18. See Foreign Broadcast Information Service, *Daily Report*, vol. 3, *Near East and South Asia* (FBIS-NES), 9 January 1989.

19. See my "Iran's Export of the Revolution: Politics, Ends, and Means," pp. 128–47 in this volume.

20. See my *Revolutionary Iran*, 50–85, esp. 74–76.

21. See his report, "Further Report of The Secretary-General on The Implementation of Security Council Resolution 598 (1987)," U.N. SCOR, 46th Sess., U.N. Doc. S/23273 (1991). See my commentary on the report, "Who Started the Iran-Iraq War?," pp. 287–306 in this volume.

22. I pondered critically the issue of the prolongation of the war as early as 1986. See my *Revolutionary Iran*.

23. See FBIS-NES, 24 February 1989.

24. See Hashemi Rafsanjani's interview in *Hamshahri*, 22 December 1999.

25. Although Khomeini considered his *fatwa* a means of punishing Rushdie for "blasphemy and apostasy," the edict also had a factional balancing dimension to it. See my "Iran's Export of the Revolution"; and my "Iran's Resistance to U.S. Intervention in the Persian Gulf," in *Neither East Nor West: Iran, The Soviet Union, and the United States*, edited by Nikki R. Keddie and Mark J. Gasiotoswski (New Haven, 1990), 36–60.

26. For details, see my *Revolutionary Iran*. See also my "Iran's Islamic Revolution and the Persian Gulf," *Current History* 84 (January 1985): 5–8 and 40–41.

27. See *Gozaresh-e Seminar* (Tehran), no. 2 (1983–84): 36.

28. See Foreign Broadcast Information Service, *Daily Report*, vol. 8, *South Asia* (FBIS-SA), 30 October 1984.

29. See my *Revolutionary Iran*.

30. See my "Iran and the United States; Islamic Realism?," in *The Middle East from the Iran-Contra Affair to the Intifada*, edited by Robert O. Freedman (Syracuse, 1991), 167–82.

31. See my "Iran's Foreign Policy: Both North and South," *Middle East Journal* 46, no. 3 (Summer 1992): 393–412.

32. The American media in general depicted Khamenei and Rafsanjani as rival leaders without comprehending that despite their differences in style they both upheld the same basic goals of the revolution. The same habit surfaced with respect to Khamenei and Khatami after the latter's presidential election. Again, on the fundamentals of the revolution, they ride a political tandem bicycle as well.

33. See FBIS-SA, 17 April 1987.

34. This landmark call for an open-door foreign policy was first made on 20 July and again on 6 August 1984. See ibid., 31 July and 7 August 1984.

35. For details, see my "Iran's Resistance to U.S. Intervention in the Persian Gulf."

36. See my *Iran's Revolution: The Search for Consensus* (Bloomington, 1990), vii–xi.

37. Ibid.

38. See my "Iran's Foreign Policy: Both North and South."

39. Ibid.

40. Ibid.

41. See my *Future Security in the Persian Gulf: America's Role* (Washington, DC, 1991).

42. See FBIS-NES, 23 September 1991.

43. Ibid., 2 January 1991.

44. As a matter of fact, in January 1990 thousands of Soviet Azeris rioted near the Iranian border, harassed Soviet and Iranian border guards, and illegally crossed into Iran. The Rafsanjani administration wished to see no repetition of the same, especially after Azerbaijan became the first among the former Soviet republics to declare its independence, on 30 August 1991.

45. See U.S. Department of State, Office of the Spokesman, "Secretary of State Madeleine K. Albright: Remarks At Conference On American-Iranian Relations," Washington, DC., 17 March 2000.

46. See Kenneth N. Waltz, *Theory of International Politics* (New York, 1979).

47. See Lucian W. Pye, *Politics, Personality, and Nation Building: Burma's Search for Identity* (New Haven, 1962), esp. 28.

48. For a comprehensive legal analysis of the Iranian Constitution, see the two-volume study by Dr. Seyyed Mohammad Hashemi, *Hoqouq-e Assasi-e Jomhouri-e Islami-e Iran* [The Iranian constitutionalism of the Islamic Republic of Iran] (Tehran, 1995–99).

49. See my earliest commentary on the Constitution, "Document: The Constitution of the Islamic Republic of Iran," *Middle East Journal* 34, no. 2 (Spring 1980): 181–204, esp. 181–83.

50. See my "The Shifting Premise of Iran's Foreign Policy: Toward A Democratic Peace?," pp. 148–59 in this volume.

51. The "democratic peace" thesis holds that democracies are intrinsically peaceful. Most scholars agree that democracies are at peace with each other (dyadic version), while many proponents of the theory suggest that democratic states are less prone to use force even if the regime type of their enemies is nondemocratic (the monadic variant). Recently, Edward D. Mansfield and Jack Snyder have argued that democratization can cause war. See their minority view in the anthology edited by Michael E. Brown, Sean M. Lynn-Jones, and Steven E. Miller, *Debating the Democratic Peace* (Cambridge, MA, 1996).

52. See "Statement by H. E. Seyyed Mohammad Khatami, President of the Islamic Republic of Iran and Chairman of the Eighth Session of the Islamic Conference," Teh-

ran, 9 December 1997, 2, courtesy of Islamic Republic of Iran, Permanent Mission to the United Nations.

53. See Seyyed Mohammad Khatami, *Az Donia-ye Shahr Ta Shahr-e Donia: Sayri dar Andisheh-ye Siyasi-e Gharb* [From the world of the city-state to the city of the world] (Tehran, 1994), 285.

54. See Seyyed Mohammad Khatami, "A Message for Europe," statement at the European University in Florence, Italy, 10 March 1999, courtesy of Islamic Republic of Iran, Permanent Mission to the United Nations.

55. This proclamation, which is entitled "The United Nations Year of Dialogue among Civilizations," was embodied in U.N. Resolution 53/22. See U.N. General Assembly, 54th Sess., Agenda Item 34, 12 November 1999.

56. See Seyyed Mohammad Khatami, *Az Donia-ye Shahr Ta Shahr-e Donia*, 293, my translation.

57. See my "The Emerging Arab-Iranian Rapprochement," *Middle East Policy* 6, no. 1 (June 1998): 45–62.

58. As quoted in the *New York Times*, 23 September 1998.

59. As quoted in the *Washington Post*, 25 September 1998.

60. See *Hamshahri*, 12 January 2000.

61. Quoted at Khatami's news conference in Tehran, reported in FBIS-NES, 14 December 1997.

62. President Khatami's televised statement was broadcast on Cable News Network (CNN) International.

63. Despite this statement by President Clinton, ten days later Assistant Secretary of State Martin Indyk repeated the usual litany of "dual containment." See *Washington Post*, 1 May 1999.

64. See U.S. Department of State, Office of the Spokesman, "Secretary of State Madeleine K. Albright."

65. See Kenneth N. Waltz, "Realist Thought and Neorealist Theory," *Journal of International Affairs* 44, no. 1 (Spring 1990): 21–37.

66. See Hans J. Morgenthau, *Politics among Nations: Struggle for Power and Peace*, 5th ed. (New York, 1972).

67. I am basing my characterization of Reinhold Niebuhr not only on the basis of his own works but also on Michael Joseph Smith, *Realist Thought: From Weber to Kissinger* (Baton Rouge, 1986).

68. Alexis de Tocqueville, *Democracy in America*, translated by Henry Reeve, vol. 2 (London, 1835), 232–33.

69. See James H. Hutson, *Religion and the Founding of the American Republic* (Washington, DC, 1998), 40.

70. Ibid.

71. My extension of Max Weber's concept of "sultanism" from polity to society, including individuals and factions, is based not only on Iran's own historical experience with both rampant factionalism and authoritarianism but also on the basis of demonstrated intolerance and violence of extremist conservatives against moderate reformers in the name of Islam. In this context, they are practicing "religious sultanism." This characterization fits perfectly what the Iranian writers are saying about their fate at the

hands of die-hard conservatives within and outside the regime. I suggest only a number of new sources in Persian in order to illustrate the depth of the problem of religious sultanism that Iranian reformers face today. On the serial political murders, see, for example, Hamid Kaviany, *Dar Jostojouy-e Mahfel-e Jenayatkaran* [In search of the criminal circle] (Tehran, 1999); and Emad ed-Din Baqi, *Trajedy-e Domokracy Dar Iran* [The tragedy of democracy in Iran], 2d ed. (Tehran, 2000). Regarding the special clerical court's trials of Abdullah Nouri and Mohsen Kadivar, see, respectively, *Defa'iyat-e Abdullah Nouri* [The defense by Abdullah Nouri] (Tehran, 1999); and Zahra Rudi Kadivar, ed., *Baha-ye Azadi: Deja'iyat-e Mohsen Kadivar dar Dadgah-e Vizheh-ye Ruhaniyat* [The price of freedom: The defense of Mohsen Kadivar in the special clerical court] (Tehran, 1999). For an informed analysis of the Iranian sociopolitical predicaments, see Ali Akbar Mahdi, *Farhang-e Irani, Jama'-ye Madani va Daghdagheh-ye Domokracy* [Iranian culture, civil society and concern for democracy] (Tehran, 1998).

72. Mohammad Khatami, "On the Virtues of the West," *Time* (electronic version), 19 January 1998.

IDEOLOGY AND PRAGMATISM

IN IRAN'S FOREIGN POLICY

This essay hypothesizes that the tension between religious ideology and pragmatism has persisted throughout Iranian history. The Iranian Revolution simply put it on graphic display in the contemporary period. The essay also suggests that the dynamic processes of cultural maturation seem to be shifting the balance of influence increasingly away from religious ideology toward pragmatic calculation of the national interest in the making and implementation of foreign-policy decisions. The obvious implications of all this for U.S.-Iranian relations are mentioned.

The balance of ideology and pragmatism in the making of Iranian foreign-policy decisions has been one of the most persistent, intricate, and difficult issues in all Iranian history, from the sixth century BC, when the Iranian state was born, to the present time. For example, in assessing the decisions of Cyrus the Great for maintaining peace in the Iranian "world state," Adda B. Bozeman suggests that pragmatism rather than ideology dictated Cyrus's decisions.[1] In my own works over the past half-century I have tried to hypothesize that the conundrum of the relationship between ideology and state interest has challenged Iranian policymakers ever since the establishment of the Safavid dynasty in 1501.

Here, however, I would like to ask questions about the ideology-pragmatism challenge by drawing concrete examples from the pre-Islamic as well as Islamic periods of Iranian foreign policy. Richard N. Frye's seminal works on ancient Iran inspire me to do so.[2] Within the limited scope of an essay, of course, even raising questions in the broadest strokes is quite an intellectual challenge. But the overarching purpose of this essay is only to suggest that the tension between ideology and interests in foreign policy making has persisted throughout Iranian history.

PRE-ISLAMIC EXAMPLES

In her classic *Politics and Culture in International History*, Bozeman suggests that Cyrus succeeded in establishing not only the first world state but also the first "international society" in large part because he was motivated by

"Ideology and Pragmatism in Iran's Foreign Policy" was originally published in *Middle East Journal* 58, no. 4 (October 2004): 549–59.

prudence rather than ideology in making policy decisions. Cyrus established a cosmopolitan state at a time when "the tyranny of empires plagued the fabric of community life everywhere." In such a world, she continues, "the Persian Empire, vaster than any preceding empire west of China, attained universal peace for some two hundred years in a large part as the result of tolerant respect for the cultural diversity of the subjugated peoples."³ Cyrus's political prudence more than religious ideology underpinned his law. Richard Frye notes that Cyrus's law, which predated the Roman law, allowed the religious laws of Egyptians, Babylonians, and Hebrews to stay in force.

The testimonies of ancient commentators seem to attribute Cyrus's observance of the practical circumstances in decision making to his personal character. Herodotus testifies to his "statesmanship and liberality." Xenophon's *Cyropaedia* finds Cyrus "deserving admiration," above all for honoring his people "as if they were his own children."⁴ Of course, the Bible reveres Cyrus for liberating the Jews from Babylonian captivity. Even the temple in Jerusalem was rebuilt in the fifth century BC "with Persian assistance."⁵ To this day, Iraqi Jews trace their origins to his liberation policy. It is significant that in accepting the Nobel Peace Prize, Shirin Ebadi proudly declared to the world on December 10, 2003, "I am an Iranian, a descendant of Cyrus the Great" and "I am a Muslim."⁶ This showed that a quarter of a century of "Islamization" had failed to undermine the strong attachment of the Iranian people to their pre-Islamic cultural heritage, including its concern with human rights. Also, as will be seen, despite the Islamist zeal in the early phase of the Iranian Revolution, the Iranian foreign policy makers never stopped taking into account national interest in making pragmatic decisions.

The role of interests as well as ideology in the foreign policy of Cyrus's successors seems much more difficult to surmise. We know that Darius I (522–486 BC) invoked "the favor of Ahura Mazda" in his statecraft in general. We also know, from what Josef Wiesehofer tells us, that the Magi (*majus*) during the Achaemenid dynasty (558 BC–AD330) performed only religious, administrative, and educational functions and also played a part in royal investiture. The implication seems to be that the Magi had little or no influence on the king's policy decisions. This suggests that Cyrus's successors may have attached greater weight to the imperial interest than to religious ethics, just as Cyrus had done before them. Until more direct evidence becomes available, the question remains whether Xerxes I launched military campaigns against Greece to erase the humiliation of Darius I in the Battle of Marathon or to spread justice, by the favor of Ahura Mazda, to non-Iranians?

One may conjecture that the Sassanid dynasty's (AD 224–651) foreign policy makers might have tilted the balance in favor of ideology more than the Achaemenids after their appearance in AD 226. Richard Frye tells us that the Sassanid Empire was a conscious revival of the Achaemenid state with its pretensions to universality.[7] But the question remains whether their pretensions were motivated by their wish to restore the territories formerly held by the Achaemenids or by their religious ideology. I tend to think that relative to the Achaemenid foreign policy makers the Sassanids in general were perhaps more motivated by Zoroastrian ideology. Two factors in particular may speak to this point. First, we know that at least two Sassanid kings, Ardashir I and Shapur I, claimed divine qualities. Second, and more importantly, the Sassanids made Zoroastrianism the official religion of the state.

That ideologization of the state, however, did not put the Magi in control of the polity. The Zoroastrian priest Tansar in the Sassanid book of council to the kings advised that kingship and good religion were "siblings," not one and the same. This same description was echoed much later by the Muslim writer Mas'udi. Richard Frye notes that the head of the priesthood, Mobadan-Mobad, "became the partner of the Shahinshah." This combination of Zoroastrianization of the state and the partnership between the leading priest and the king does not seem to have tilted the balance in favor of religious ideology in foreign-policy decisions at the expense of state interest. This conjecture seems to be supported by Ardashir I's political testament to his son, Shapur I. In it he said: "Consider the altar and the throne as inseparable; they must always sustain one another. A sovereign without religion is a tyrant."[8]

A couple of examples from Sassanid policy decisions might suffice here. Did Ardashir wage war against the Romans because of his religious zeal to spread Zoroastrian teachings, or in order to regain Syria and the rest of Asia, which had been lost by the Achaemenid dynasty, or for both reasons? Did his son, Shapur I, launch a military campaign against Rome in order to consolidate and legitimate his rule, or did he act to serve simultaneously religious faith and state interest vis-à-vis a foreign power?

ISLAMIC PERIOD EXAMPLES

In some ways the parallels between the Sassanid and Safavid (AD 1502–1736) Empires are striking. Just as the Sassanids had consciously tried to revive the Achaemenid state with claims to universality, the Safavids tried to revive the Sassanid Empire in the sixteenth century AD, also with pretensions to universality. Just as the Sassanids Zoroastrianized the state, the Safavids "Shiitized" the state. Just as the first Sassanid king, Ardashir I (AD 226?–40), claimed divine qualities in founding the Sassanid Empire, Shah Ismail (1501–1524) considered himself "the Agent of God" in founding the Safavid state.

Yet, it is next to impossible to infer from the ideologization of the Safavid state that foreign-policy decisions of the Safavid kings simply reflected some kind of Shii crusading thrust at all times and under all circumstances. To be sure, in Roger M. Savory's words, Shah Tahmasp (1524–1576) "was a religious bigot,"[9] but the complications of his four major campaigns in the Caucasus seem to reveal the extreme difficulty in sorting out the relative influence of ideology and state interest in these campaigns. This complexity arises at least in part from the fact that two "founding races" of the Safavid state, the Iranians and the Turks, had struggled for control of major state posts before these campaigns. Against this backdrop, could one say that Shah Tahmasp waged those campaigns to bring back to Iran Georgians, Circassians, and Armenians as a political means to challenge the privileged position of the qizilbash?[10]

To cite an even more important example, why did Shah Abbas I (1587–1629) sign the ignominious peace with the Ottoman Empire in 1590? In this "treaty" he abandoned the age-old Shii practice of cursing the Sunni "first three caliphs" and also made territorial concessions to the Ottomans. Did he do so because in part he was trying to reform Shii ritualistic practice? Or did he also cede Iranian territories because when he acceded to the throne the Safavid state was too weak to fight on two fronts, against the Ottomans and the Uzbeks? Some forty years ago I suggested that Shah Abbas I might have adopted something like the principle of *cuius regio eius religio* (whoever has the state, his is the religion) for the first time in Iranian history, although this Western concept must have been alien to Iranians at the time.[11]

Some may argue that Shah Abbas I could not have adopted such a secular principle, for two reasons. First, he considered himself to be the spokesman of the Hidden Imam. Second, in practice he was a devout Muslim. He walked, for example, from Isfahan to the Shii holy shrine in Mashhad on a well-recorded pilgrimage. Yet, despite all these indications of his religious piety, his policy decisions were significantly influenced by Iran's perceived state interest. First, Roger Savory tells us that the Shah was a "brilliant strategist and tactician whose chief characteristic was prudence. He preferred to obtain his ends by diplomacy rather than war."[12]

Second, and more important, both Roger Savory and Marshall G. S. Hodgson tell us that the Safavid state by the time of Shah Abbas I had moved away from the dynamic ideology that had motivated the early Safavid movement.[13] In theory the Shah was still *Murshid-i Kamil* for the qizilbash, but in practice he observed Iran's interest earnestly in making foreign-policy decisions of the kind just mentioned. The increasing secularization of the state obviously had a great deal to do with the Shah's foreign-policy orientation.

Against the backdrop of this observation, it should be realized that contrary to conventional interpretations, by the time modern Western ideas, including secularism, arrived in Iran, the Iranians were receptive to these ideas for their own historical and cultural reasons. I tend to see this receptivity to Western ideas not only in the secularizing trend that had been evident in the later Safavid era but in the very origins of the Iranian state during the Achaemenid dynasty. I tend to think Cyrus the Great was probably the first Iranian paradigm of a "secular humanist" political leader when the state itself was in its earliest formative stage. In foreign-policy terms Iranians had over the millennia developed their own secular tendencies by the time of Shah Abbas I. So, the Western modern ideas of nation-state, national interest, and even the concept of modern foreign policy were not entirely alien to Iranians when the Iranian state was exposed to Western modern ideas, especially in the nineteenth and twentieth centuries.

In this light, the whole debate of the past two centuries about the compatibility between Islam and democracy rings especially true. To cite one of the most interesting examples in this debate, as early as the nineteenth century Mirza Yousef Khan, known as Mostashar Dowleh, argued in his important work *Yek Kalameh* (One word) that Islam and secular democracy were compatible.[14] "One word" here was intended to suggest that the rule of law could provide a solution to Iranian backwardness. He compared the seventeen-point French Declaration of Rights of Man and the Citizens and fundamental Islamic tenets and pronounced them compatible.

Enlightened religious and secular intellectuals who led the Constitutional Revolution at the turn of the twentieth century may well have shared the kind of interpretation that Mostashar Dowleh had propounded earlier. The supporters of the Constitutional Revolution aimed not only at the country's independence from foreign control but also at the freedom of the people from the king's tyranny. In other words, the idea of the national interest in foreign-policy decision making was then imbued with the concept of constitutional democracy or representative government. This was true, it may be said, during both the Constitutional regime and the government of Dr. Mohammad Mosaddegh (prime minister, 1951–53). For example, when the First Majlis decided to reject the government's proposal for acquiring foreign loans, to protest against the Anglo-Russian partitioning of Iran, and to hire the American financial adviser Morgan Shuster to help reform Iran's chaotic finances, these decisions all aimed not only at Iran's political independence but also at introducing democratic values into Iranian foreign-policy decisions.

Contrary to conventional interpretations, also, Mosaddegh's decision to nationalize the Iranian oil industry was not simply a matter of nationalistic crusade. To be sure, he depicted his dispute with the British as a choice between "independence" and "enslavement" (*isteqlal ya enqiad*). But his foreign-policy goal of "complete nationalization" of the Iranian oil industry was also inspired significantly by his belief that democratic social and political reforms in Iran would be impossible as long as the oil industry, the backbone of the Iranian economy, was controlled by the British.

By contrast, Iran's foreign-policy decisions can be said to have been devoid of democratic values during the rule of Reza Shah (1925–41) and his son, Muhammad Reza Shah (1941–79). National interest was seen by them as coterminous with the Pahlavis' dynastic interest. Their essentially anticlerical thrust was seen by the masses, who had traditionally close ties to the clergy, as being anti-Islamic. Their harking back to the Sassanid and Achaemenid paradigms was disingenuous. It aimed at legitimation of the Pahlavi rule by dictatorial methods. Muhammad Reza Shah went so far as to crown himself in 1971 by saluting his self-proclaimed ancient predecessor, Cyrus the Great, at the king's gravesite at Pasargadae. Cyrus must have turned in his grave over the pretensions of this modern dictator, who had much more in common with such rulers as Duvalier in Haiti and Marcos in the Philippines than with the humanist Cyrus the Great.

Muhammad Reza Shah's grandiose goal of turning Iran into a "Great Civilization" was animated by dynastic ambitions rather than the national interest of Iran. He tried to achieve this goal by arming Iran to the teeth so that it could become one of the five conventional military powers of the world. In the process he turned Iran into one of America's leading arms purchasers, a surrogate state of the United States, and an American policeman of the Persian Gulf. His popularly opposed status-of-forces agreement with the Pentagon seemed to many Iranians to violate Iranian national interest by reviving the hated foreign capitulatory privileges in Iran. Ayatollah Ruhollah Khomeini called the agreement "a document of the enslavement of Iran." One of the most popular revolutionary slogans said it all: "The American Shah."

REVOLUTIONARY EXAMPLES

To most Iran watchers the Islamic Revolution turned on its head consideration of pragmatic national interest in the making of Iranian foreign-policy decisions. Khomeini's worldview and his supporters' words and actions appeared to support such a conclusion. Khomeini elevated the interest of the Muslim community (*umma*) and denigrated the very idea of a secular national interest by rejecting the concept of "nationalism" (*melli-garai*). He also downgraded the extant international system of nation-states on the grounds that it was the creature of a weak human mind. He advocated an "Islamic world order" (my appellation) for the benefit of humanity. In his words, "Islam is not peculiar to a country, to several countries, a group, or even the Muslims. Islam has come for humanity . . . Islam wishes to bring all of humanity under the umbrella of its justice."[15] Here, again, I see the tenacious hold of the Iranian tradition of pretensions to universality.

The most vivid interjection of this universalist ideal by Khomeini into Iranian foreign policy can be seen in his ideological attitude toward the Soviet Union on the one hand, and toward the Persian Gulf states on the other. In his letter of January 1, 1989, to the Soviet leader Mikhail Gorbachev, he castigated the bankrupt "ideological vacuum" of the East and the West and advocated Islamic values that alone, he wrote, "can be a means for well-being and salvation of all nations," including, of course, the Soviet Union. With respect to the Arab Gulf monarchies, Khomeini wished to see them adopt governments similar, not identical, to that of the Islamic Republic of Iran, cut their "subservient ties" with the superpowers, and find safety under the Iranian security umbrella (chatr-i amniyyat). Khomeini's foreign-policy doctrine of "Neither East nor West, but the Islamic Republic" and his insistence on the export of the Islamic Revolution both stemmed from his overriding aspiration ultimately to create an Islamic-led international order.

The actions of revolutionary Iran no less than its leader's worldview appeared to most Iran watchers to reflect the dominance of ideology to the complete exclusion of the national interest in Iran's foreign-policy behavior. The revolutionary government headquartered numerous foreign "liberation movements" in Tehran and was suspected of acts of international subversion and terrorism, especially in the Persian Gulf region. Perhaps the most telling example of the pervasiveness of ideology in Iranian foreign policy was the explosive dispute in the early phase of the revolution between Iran and Saudi Arabia over political demonstrations of Iranian pilgrims in Mecca. The worst incident happened in the 1987 Hajj season, when some 400 pilgrims, including 275 Iranians, died in the clash between the pilgrims and the Saudi police force. The Hajj, Khomeini believed, was a political as well as religious duty, while Saudi Arabia insisted on its purely religious function.

Yet, the record of Iranian foreign policy since the eruption of the revolution in 1979 reveals that policymakers have seldom disregarded the pragmatic interest of the Iranian state. In *Revolutionary Iran: Challenge and Response in the Middle East*,[16] and in an article entitled "Iran: Burying the Hatchet" in *Foreign Policy*,[17] I argued that a streak of pragmatic national interest existed even in the earliest, most volatile, and most ideological phase of Iranian foreign policy. Given the history of Iranian foreign policy, this argument should come as no great surprise. The foreign policies of the Achaemenid, Sassanid, and Safavid governments showed pragmatic consideration of state interests as well as the presence of religious ideology.

Nevertheless, the conundrum of ideology and national interest in Iranian foreign policy continues to preoccupy Iranian scholars and policymakers alike. In a wide-ranging interview reported on April 5, 2003, for example, Ayatollah Ali Akbar Hashemi Rafsanjani, a former speaker of the Majlis, a former president, and the current chairman of the influential Expediency Discernment Council, insisted that the relative weight of ideology [Islam] and national interest in foreign-policy decision making depends on the circumstances of a particular case at a given point in time.

Perhaps the most striking example of dominance of pragmatic factors over ideological influences in Iran's foreign policy during Khomeini's lifetime was the secret purchase of arms from the United States, "the Great Satan," and Israel, "the lesser Satan." Iran's defensive war against Iraq occasioned such a bold move. A deal was struck through intermediaries. American and Israeli arms were to be shipped to Iran in return for Iran's help with the release of Western hostages in Lebanon. Six shipments of arms went to Iran, and several American hostages were released, each after Iran received a shipment of arms. Embarrassed by the disclosure of the secret deal, some Iranian leaders, particularly Hashemi Rafsanjani, tried to cover up the transactions by denouncing America and ridiculing the American mission, which had arrived in Tehran with a Bible and a cake. In the end, when the internal pressures built up for demanding a parliamentary investigation of the scandal, Khomeini himself intervened to squash the demand. Meanwhile, the Iran-Contra Affair went through a series of hearings in the U.S. Congress.

For me the most vexing question remains the prolongation of the Iran-Iraq War. Did Iran decide to take the war into Iraqi territory on or after July 13, 1982, to export the Islamic Revolution, or did it do so to defend its national-security interests as Iraq continued to occupy Iranian territory? The controversial question persists because by that date Iran had liberated most of its territory from the Iraqi occupation forces. The explanation of Hashemi Rafsanjani in 1999 still did not rule out the possible influence of ideology. He said that Khomeini "decreed that our forces should not enter [Iraqi] populated regions and the armed forces of Iran carried out the decree."[18] That directive seems to have left the uninhabited areas of Iraq as open targets.

In continuing my search for a satisfactory explanation, a year after Hashemi Rafsanjani's explanation, I raised the same question with a major wartime policymaker. I quoted to him Khomeini's own statement to the effect that "we exported our revolution to the world through the war." I was trying to suggest that perhaps Iran's prolongation of the war for another six years was motivated primarily by ideological considerations. The respondent appeared to suggest the opposite. That is, Iran's military forays into Iraqi territory were based mainly on the calculation of Iran's national-security interest. He simply told me that such pronouncements as the one I quoted from Khomeini were nothing but "bragging" (rajaz khaany).[19]

To the pragmatic consideration of the national interest in Iran's foreign-policy calculation President Mohammad Khatami tried to add a democratic dimension. His presidential campaign statements before his first term as president in 1997 emphasized the promise of social and economic reforms. As a result most observers did not seem to realize the important foreign-policy implications of his reformist agenda. His strong advocacy of the need for civil society, the rule of law, freedom of expression, and other requirements of democracy was matched by an unprecedented bid for reintegration of the Iranian society into the modern international system. In other words, he seemed to suggest that democracy at home and peace abroad were two sides of the same coin.[20]

It came as a surprise to many observers that President Khatami's first major foreign-policy statement was addressed to the American people. He drew parallels between the American and Iranian Revolutions by emphasizing the compatibility of religion and liberty. Given the heavy baggage of mutual antagonism between Washington and Tehran on the one hand and the ingenuity of both in missing significant opportunities for reconciliation on the other, U.S.-Iranian relations are still stuck in the mud a quarter of a century after the relations were broken off by President Jimmy Carter.

Yet, during the Clinton administration Iranian hopes for reconciliation seemed to grow. President Clinton surprised his own officials in April 1999 when he said that Iran "has been the subject of quite a lot of abuse from various Western nations" and that sometimes "it is quite important to tell people 'look, others have a right to be angry at something my country or my culture or others that are generally allied with us today did to you 50 or 60 or 100 or 150 years ago.' "[21] It was even more music to Iranian ears when Secretary of State Madeleine K. Albright publicly admitted on March 17, 2000, the American role in the overthrow of the popular government of Mosaddegh and expressed regrets for the United States' having sided with Iraq in its war against Iran. The positive impact of all such conciliatory rhetoric on Iran was drastically negated by the Bush administration's subsequent bellicose approach to the country.[22]

However, Khatami's conciliatory foreign policy in pursuit of Iran's national interest has paid off handsomely elsewhere in the world. For example, the improvement in the relations between Iran and Saudi Arabia was unprecedented. The Iranian-Saudi rapprochement also helped reduce tensions with Iran's other neighbors despite the continuing dispute between Iran and the United Arab Emirates. Beyond the Gulf region, Iran's relations with Lebanon and Jordan took a turn for the better, and the question of restoration of relations with Egypt as well is now under serious consideration.

Perhaps the most important result of Khatami's conciliatory policy, devoid of ideological baggage, has been Iran's expanding ties with Europe. The principal stumbling block in Iranian-European relations had been Khomeini's life-threatening *fatwa* against Salman Rushdie. Iran took a bold step by distancing itself publicly from that ideological decree. In a news conference on September 22, 1998, in New York, President Khatami suggested that the *fatwa* was the expression of Khomeini's own view as an Islamic jurist, reportedly adding, "We should consider the Salman Rushdie issue as completely finished."[23] Two days later Foreign Minister Kamal Kharrazi reportedly told British Foreign Secretary Robin Cook: "The government of the Islamic Republic of Iran has no intention, nor is it going to take any action whatsoever to threaten the life of the author of *The Satanic Verses* or anybody associated with his work, nor will it encourage or assist anybody to do so."[24] The triumph of the national interest over ideology in Iranian foreign policy could not have been more clear.

The Khatami government tried hard to put Iran's national interest above ideology even when the bellicose Bush administration took power. Iran condemned unequivocally the attacks on the Twin Towers and the Pentagon on September 11, 2001, assisted the Bush administration in destroying the Taliban regime, helped with the establishment of Hamid Karzai's interim government, and committed more than $500 million to the reconstruction efforts in Afghanistan. As thanks, President Bush included Iran in his moralistic "axis of evil" phrase, threatened Iran indirectly with a preemptive strike as a "rogue" state that might provide terrorist groups with weapons of mass destruction, and worst of all, abandoned the reformist pro-democracy government of President Khatami by trying to play the Iranian people, on more than one occasion, against the entire regime, including the Khatami government. The Bush administration's visceral rhetoric against Iran paralleled America's unprecedented military presence in states bordering Iran, Afghanistan, Iraq, and the Central Asian states.

No matter what may be said about Khatami's failure in domestic social and political reforms, which he himself frankly admits, his foreign policy has enjoyed relative success. To be sure, serious foreign-policy problems, such as Iran's alleged nuclear-weapons ambitions, its problematic relations with the Lebanese Hezbollah and Hamas, its position on the Palestinian-Israeli conflict, and its stagnant relations with the United States, remain. Yet Khatami's indisputable commitment to democracy in the pursuit of Iran's national interest has been unprecedented. Foreign Minister Kharrazi's strategies and tactics have gone a long way toward advancing Iran's national interest in the world community.

These encouraging developments echo historical antecedents. The success of Cyrus the Great, the founder of the Iranian state, overwhelmingly reflected the dominance of pursuing prudent state interests in foreign policy, as did that of Shah Abbas I. This very tradition of prudence has also been evident in Khatami's overall foreign policy. It took the "Shiitized" Safavid state about eight decades to overcome ideological zeal in foreign policy making. In contrast, the "Islamicized" Republic of Iran has significantly moved away from the intrusion of ideology into foreign policy in only a quarter of a century. I believe that this process of maturation in the making of Iranian foreign policy is unstoppable as the Iranian people's demand for the pragmatization of their government and its foreign policy continues to grow.

A second-term George Bush administration or a John Kerry administration should seriously take into account this demonstrated pattern of pragmatism in the history of Iranian foreign policy making. As seen, in every major period of Iranian history the dictate of circumstances has forced Iranian foreign policy makers to interpret their religious ideology pragmatically in order to advance the state interest. Iran's dire economic circumstances and the drastic geopolitical changes in its neighborhood today impel Iranian reformers and conservatives alike to consider seriously any positive steps America might take toward resuming talks that Washington broke off in May 2003.

NOTES

1. See Adda B. Bozeman, *Politics and Culture in International History* (Princeton, 1960), 43–56. For a detailed comparison of Cyrus's prudent statecraft with the tyranny of other ancient leaders, see Morteza Ravandi, *Tarikh-e Ejtema'ai, Eqtesadi, Siyasi, Honari-e Iran va Bozorgtarin Mellal-e Bastani Az Aghaz ta Zohour-e Nehzat-e Eslami* [The social, economic, political, and cultural history of Iran and the birth of the largest states of the ancient world until the rise of the Islamic movement], vol. 1 (Tehran, 1970), 381–90.

2. Richard N. Frye has authored and edited numerous books and more than 120 articles in English, German, Russian, and Iranian refereed journals. For citations of his works, see Contemporary Authors Online, Gale 2003. My references to his works include his classic *The Heritage of Persia: The Pre-Islamic History of One of the World's Great Civilizations* (Cleveland, 1963); *The Golden Age of Persia: The Arabs in the East* (London, 1975); and personal communications from December 2003 to the autumn of 2004.

3. See Bozeman, *Politics and Culture.*

4. See Josef Wiesehofer, *Ancient Persia: From 550 BC to 650 AD* (1996; London, 2001), 43–44.

5. Old Testament texts ascribe to Cyrus the liberation of the Jews (Judaeans) from their Babylonian captivity. See the words of Deutero-Isaiah as quoted in Wiesehofer, *Ancient Persia,* 44.

6. The full text of Shirin Ebadi's acceptance speech in Oslo has appeared in various languages. For the text in which these specific remarks appear in English, see "The Nobel Lecture given by Nobel Peace Prize Laureate 2003, Shirin Ebadi," http://www

.nobel.no/eng_lect_2003b.html. For easy access to the text in Persian in the United States, see *Iman*, Spring 2004.

7. See, for example, Frye, *Golden Age of Persia*, 1: "The Sasanian Iranians were definitely heirs of Achaemenids."

8. Personal communication with Professor Frye, 2003–4. Ardashir I's political testament to Shapur I is quoted in Sir Percy Sykes, *A History of Persia*, vol. 1 (New York, 1963), 398. The Arab historians Tabari and Mas'udi wrote about the Sassanids. Mas'udi is mentioned here with reference to his most important writing, generally referred to as *Muruj* or *Muruj al-dhahab wa-ma 'din al-jawhar* [Meadows of gold and mines of gems], in four volumes. Iranian scholars attach great importance to this work. For a translation in English, see Paul Lundi and Caroline Stone, trans. and ed., *The Meadows of Gold: The 'Abbasids* (London, 1989).

9. Roger M. Savory also characterizes Shah Abbas I as a "pragmatist" and praises him for his "religious tolerance." See his *Iran Under The Safavids* (Cambridge, 1980), 76–103, esp. 101.

10. Qizilbash (literally "red heads," after their headgear) generally refers to Turkoman tribal forces that had initially been responsible for the rise of the Safavids to power and emerged subsequently as a "military aristocracy." Their religious loyalty to Shah Ismail, the founder of the Safavid dynasty, waned after his defeat in the Battle of Childiran (or Chaldiran) with the Ottoman Empire in 1514. They no longer regarded him as having divine or semi-divine qualities.

11. R. K. Ramazani, *The Foreign Policy of Iran, 1500–1941: A Developing Nation in World Affairs* (Charlottesville, 1966).

12. Savory, *Iran Under the Safavids*, 101.

13. See also Marshall G. S. Hodgson, *The Venture of Islam: Conscience and History in a World Civilization*, vol. 3, *The Gunpowder Empires and Modern Times* (Chicago, 1974), 16–58, esp. 53–58.

14. Published in Tehran in 1912.

15. Khomeini in Foreign Broadcast Information Service, *Daily Report*, vol. 5, *Middle East and North Africa* (FBIS-MEA), 18 December 1979.

16. Published in Baltimore in 1986.

17. Pp. 94–110 in this volume.

18. See Hashemi Rafsanjani's interview in the Persian newspaper *Hamshahri*, 22 December 1999.

19. The conversation took place during a one-month research trip to Iran in 2000.

20. R. K. Ramazani, "The Shifting Premise of Iran's Foreign Policy: Toward a Democratic Peace?," pp. 148–59 in this volume.

21. See "Remarks by President Clinton And First Lady Hillary Rodham Clinton at Millennium Event, White House," in *Federal News Service, Inc.*, 12 April 1999.

22. For the text, see U.S. Department of State, Office of the Spokesman, "Secretary of State Madeleine Albright: Remarks at Conference on American-Iranian Relations," Washington, DC, 17 March 2000.

23. As quoted in the *New York Times*, 23 September 1998.

24. As quoted in the *Washington Post*, 25 September 1998.

REFLECTIONS ON IRAN'S

FOREIGN POLICY

Spiritual Pragmatism

This essay suggests that the evolution of Iran's foreign policy since the revolution in 1979 has incrementally produced an aspirational paradigm for Iran's foreign policy makers that I call "spiritual pragmatic."

Pragmatism is conventionally viewed as the opposite of principle, whether religious, moral, or ideological. The gradual evolution of Iranian foreign policy since the Iranian Revolution, however, demonstrates that foreign policy makers have aspired to create a hybrid of pragmatism and spirituality.

The conundrum of spirituality and pragmatism in history is not limited to Iran, however; it is universal. American foreign policy, for example, shows that this tension is often expressed in terms of realism verses idealism. President Richard Nixon, for example, was regarded as a realist, while President Jimmy Carter was considered an idealist.

Yet American leaders seldom understand this same practicality-spirituality interaction in Iran's foreign policy making. At times, therefore, they candidly acknowledge in private and public that they do not understand Iran's foreign-policy behavior, while at other times they view it as "irrational" or "paranoid." I hope the following reflections will help to create a better understanding of Iran's foreign policy making in the West in general and the United States in particular.

THE IDEAL OF AN ISLAMIC STATE
AND THE REALITY OF WORLD POLITICS

Ayatollah Khomeini. The establishment of the Islamic Republic of Iran reflected the worldview of its founder, Ayatollah Ruhollah Khomeini. He aspired to the ultimate rise of an "Islamic world order" for the benefit of humanity. He said on December 18, 1979, "Islam is not peculiar to a country, to several countries, to a group of [people or countries] or even the Muslims. Islam has come for humanity . . . Islam wishes to bring all of humanity under the umbrella of its justice."

"Reflections on Iran's Foreign Policy: Spiritual Pragmatism" was originally published in *Iranian Review of Foreign Affairs* 1, no. 1 (January 2010): 54–88.

Khomeini showed in action what he meant. On January 1, 1989, for example, in a letter to the Soviet leader Michael Gorbachev he castigated the "bankrupt ideologies of the East and the West" and urged him to adopt "Islamic values for the well-being and salvation of all nations," including the people of the Soviet Union.

Yet, all revolutions mellow, or, in Kenneth N. Waltz's words, "socialize," to the international system. In the case of Iran, for example, the ideal of exporting revolution is not a priority of Iran today as it was in the early years of the revolution. Iran's leaders, like those of other states, have to take serious account of the reality of world politics, as well as their spiritual principles. They encounter what I call an "international constituency."

Since the revolution, Iran's leaders have tried to take account of the reality of this constituency by trying to adapt the *pristine* ideological principles of the early days of the Islamic Republic to the realities of changing world politics. The super idealist Ayatollah Khomeini himself led the way toward an aspirational paradigm of spiritual pragmatism. He sometimes changed what others called "his ideological line" (*Khatti Imam*) and was quite flexible in adjusting his idealistic worldview to the dictates of circumstance. He criticized ideological zealots who were beholden to fossilized ideas at the expense of the national interest.

For example, in facing the realities of domestic political disarray and superpowers' opposition to the revolutionary regime, Khomeini told Iranians, "We must become isolated in order to become independent" (*baayad monzavi shaveem taa mostaqel shaveem*). But when die-hard factions opposed his decision to establish relations between Iran and Turkey and Germany, he admonished them. He cited the example of the Prophet Muhammad, who, Khomeini said, dispatched ambassadors worldwide. Subsequently, after he consolidated power, he rejected a "hermit" status for Iran in foreign affairs and told the hardliners in no uncertain terms on October 30, 1984, that their opposition to foreign relations "would mean defeat, annihilation and being buried right to the end."

Ayatollah Khomeini's pragmatic approach to spiritual ideals is exemplified in the case of Iran's arms deal with the United States. After the exposure of the secret deal, Iranian leaders, especially Ayatollah Akbar Hashemi Rafsanjani, vigorously denied the deal and ridiculed the surprise visit of Americans who came to Iran bearing a cake and a Bible. But the fact remains that Iran needed arms to defend itself against Iraqi aggression. Under the circumstances, Khomeini believed that a deal with even the "Great Satan" was advisable.

To cite another example, Khomeini reluctantly accepted U.N. Resolution 598 of 1988, saying he was drinking poison. He set examples in his lifetime for future leaders of Iran to follow, showing that in foreign affairs to compromise with the enemy is not appeasement. On the contrary, it is a sign of strength. In regard to the United States he said Iran would establish relations with America "if it behaves humanely" (*agar aadam be-shavad*).

Iran's leaders have tried to follow Ayatollah Khomeini's example of spiritual pragmatism. President Sayyid Ali Khamenei, who later became the Supreme Leader, articulated that aspiration in terms of what he called Iran's "Open Door Foreign Policy." He said on July 20 and again on August 6, 1984, "Iran seeks to have rational, sound and healthy relations with all countries" so as to serve not only Islam but also Iran's national interest. That is to say, he aspired to blend pragmatism and Islamic spirituality as he interpreted the term "spirituality."

President Rafsanjani. Rafsanjani was impelled in his two terms in office to emphasize Iran's post–Iran-Iraq War practical needs. He pressed for economic development and military reconstruction. He downplayed ideological doctrines. He said, "We cannot build dams with slogans." In effect, he went beyond adapting Islamic principles to the dictates of national interest. He said on April 17, 1987, "I believe our principles are obeyed, but in some cases we may be limited and we may have to forego some of these principles."

Rafsanjani debunked the slogan "Neither East nor West" after the demise of the Soviet Union. Instead he pursued a realistic "Good Neighbor Policy." He reversed hitherto hostile relations between Iran and Saudi Arabia, where, for years, Iranian pilgrims had fueled agitation with political demonstrations during the pilgrimage season (Hajj). Also, in spite of the dispute with the United Arab Emirates over three islands in the Persian Gulf, he developed good relations with smaller Gulf monarchies. Moreover, he established amicable relations with the new post-Soviet states of Central Asia. With no ideological baggage, he emphasized Iran's common interests in culture, economic development, and trade with these states.

President Khatami. President Seyyed Mohammad Khatami emphasized that practical actions must take place in the context of "spirituality and morality." He called his paradigm "Islamic democracy." He introduced a degree of social and political freedom unprecedented since the revolution.

Khatami reawakened hope that the revolution's promise of freedom would finally be realized. Expatriates like me hoped that the age-old autocracy would ultimately vanish from Iran. In addressing Khatami at the United Nations on September 4, 2000, I concluded my remarks by saying, *"There can be no durable political order without equitable justice under the law and no justice without liberty."*

Khatami's attempts at reforming the political system (*nezam*) from within, however, were blocked by die-hard religious and civilian politicians. His legislative proposals for limiting the extensive powers of the Council of Guardians in vetting presidential and parliamentary candidates were blocked by the ultra-conservative politicians in the name of Islamic purity.

Yet Khatami's detente policy was successful. His proposal for dialogue among civilizations was endorsed by the U.N. General Assembly, giving a mandate to the secretary-general to promote dialogue through dissemination of information, conferences, and seminars. His conciliatory words and actions improved Iran's international image in a manner unprecedented since the revolution.

Despite U.S. animosity, he offered the American people an olive branch. He said boldly on December 14, 1997, "I respect the American people and nation," and on January 7, 1998, he told the American people of Iran's interest in the exchange of professors, writers, scholars, artists, journalists, and tourists with those from the United States.

Khatami creatively tempered Khomeini's ideological *fatwa* on the British writer Salman Rushdi. His foreign minister, Kamal Kharrazi, told British Foreign Secretary Robin Cook on September 24, 1998, that "Iran has no intention, nor is it going to take any action whatsoever to threaten the life of the author of *The Satanic Verses.*"

Iran's response to the terrorist attacks in America on September 11, 2001, during the George W. Bush administration, could not have been a better example of pragmatism. Within hours after the attacks by al-Qaeda extremists, Khatami condemned the "terrorist horrific attacks" perpetrated by "a cult of fanatics." Khamenei was the first cleric in the Muslim world to call for "holy war" (*jihad*) against terrorism as a "global scourge," and many Iranians held candlelight vigils for the American victims of terrorism.

The Khatami government also helped the United States to defeat the anti-Iranian Taliban regime, which had harbored the anti-American al-Qaeda terrorists in Afghanistan. Iran also aided the establishment of the new government of Hamid Karzai and extended $500 million to his government for reconstruction over five years.

Bush's response to all these conciliatory policies outraged Iranians. In his first State of the Union address, on January 29, 2002, he included Iran with North Korea and Iraq in an "axis of evil," a designation that was then, as now, an insult to Iranians of all political stripes.

When in August 2002 a group opposed to the regime outside Iran (Mujahadeen-e-Khalq) divulged a secret nuclear facility at Natanz, the suspicion of the West, especially the United States, about Iran's intentions intensified. Western leaders accused Iran of trying to make nuclear weapons. To contain Western suspicion, Khatami asked the International Atomic Energy Agency (IAEA) to send inspectors to Iran in February 2003. The IAEA reported afterward that there was no evidence of a nuclear-weapons program in Iran. From then on,

Iran negotiated with the IAEA and with Britain, France, and Germany (EU-3), presumably to remove doubts about Iran's nuclear intentions, and went so far as to voluntarily suspend nuclear enrichment for about two years. The Bush administration stayed out of the European discussions with Iran and pressured the Europeans to take a hard stance in negotiating with Iran.

Iran hoped all along that there could be a deal between the two sides to settle the nuclear dispute. The EU-3 offered incentives in return for Iran's continued suspension of nuclear enrichment. Iran considered the incentives to be "pseudo-concessions" (shebh-e emtiazat) and insisted that Iran had the "inalienable right" (haq-e Mosallam) to enrich uranium for peaceful purposes under the Nuclear Non-Proliferation Treaty (NPT). All along, the United States and Israel threatened possible military strikes on Iran's nuclear facility at Natanz, which prompted the soft-spoken Khatami to say Iran would respond to attacks with "hell fire."

President Ahmadinejad. Did Ahmadinejad aspire to the paradigm of pragmatic spirituality as had his predecessors? This question is difficult to answer. His words and demeanor have proved quite controversial. The West in general and the United States in particular have considered his foreign policy to be "confrontational." His harsh statements have differed significantly from the conciliatory remarks of Rafsanjani and Khatami. Ahmadinejad's strident statements about wiping Israel off the map and his denial of the Holocaust, although tempered later during his first term, have been viewed in the United States as a threat to regional peace and security. Israel claimed then, as it does now, that a nuclear Iran poses an "existential threat" to the Jewish state.

Many argue that Ahmadinejad's vitriolic rhetoric has harmed Iran and Iranian interests, embarrassed Iranian expatriates around the world, and even displeased Iran's friends, such as the former U.N. secretary-general Kofi Annan, who said he was "dismayed" to hear certain statements. Domestically he has been even more controversial, especially since the June 12, 2009, elections and the cataclysmic events that have gripped the country and the entire governance structure—to which I will briefly turn in the final section of this essay.

The real question of concern to this essay, however, is whether Ahmadinejad's ultraconservative interpretation of spirituality and his reputation as an ideologue demonstrate that he has not been pragmatic in foreign policy making. To address this question, it is best to examine his nuclear policy in detail, which, contrary to conventional wisdom, shows that he has been somewhat pragmatic.

He resumed uranium enrichment, criticizing the Khatami government for suspension. His action alarmed the IAEA, the West, and Israel. But he insisted, as had Khatami, that Iran's nuclear program aimed at producing nuclear energy for peaceful purposes, especially for electricity. He also continued to negotiate with the IAEA, as had Khatami, but his relatively confrontational stance soured relations with the Agency. The Agency had complained for years that Iran had not been forthcoming with satisfactory answers to its questions about Iran's nuclear program, answers that would enable the Agency to report that there was no military dimension to Iran's nuclear program—that there was no smoking gun.

The IAEA finally decided, under U.S. pressure, to refer Iran's dossier to the U.N. Security Council for the first time. The Khatami government had managed, with the help of Iran's chief negotiator, Hassan Rouhani, to keep Iran's case out of the Security Council. The Council passed three major resolutions demanding that Iran stop enriching uranium. It also imposed sanctions, which Iran viewed as "unwarranted and illegal." Iran's defiance of the Council, however, was partly in reaction to the IAEA reference of its case to the Council.

Nevertheless, Ahmadinejad continued to negotiate with the IAEA and P5+1 (the five permanent members of the Security Council—the United States, Russia, China, France, and Britain) and Germany. He welcomed the Bush administration's belated decision to send Under Secretary of State William J. Burns to participate in the P5+1 discussions with Iran. He said on August 3, 2008, "Iran has always been willing to solve the long-standing crisis over the disputed nuclear program through negotiations." These reassurances notwithstanding, the negotiations went nowhere. The P5+1 offered Iran incentives in 2006 and in 2008 that Iran did not find to be meaningful enough to accept.

To continue Iran's long-standing interest in settling all issues in dispute with the United States, including the nuclear one, through diplomacy, Ahmadinejad sent on November 6, 2008, an unprecedented congratulatory letter to the American president-elect, Barack Obama. He welcomed Obama's determination to engage Iran in negotiations without preconditions.

In pursuing engagement with Iran, President Obama sent a New Year (Nowruz) address on March 21, 2009, to the Iranian people *and government*, the first such address to be made by an American president since the revolution. His remarks about the greatness of Iranian culture were music to the ears of the people of Iran. Khamenei, however, responded with a litany of Iranian grievances against the United States. More specifically, he said he did not wish to prejudge the intentions of the new president, whom, he said, he did not know; but he demanded action to match Obama's "slogan of change."

Nevertheless, conservative Ayatollah Khamenei has supported negotiations with the IAEA and P5+1. On October 1, 2009, the representatives of Iran and the United States sat across the same table in Geneva for the first time since the revolution to discuss the nuclear issue. Other members of the P5+1 also participated in the talks, and the Iranian and American representatives also held sideline talks for forty-five minutes in a reportedly positive atmosphere.

Iran's nuclear negotiations from October 1 to the end of 2009 fell into two broad categories. One concerned Iran's nuclear program, particularly its nuclear facility at Natanz. The other focused on the newly discovered facility under construction at Fordou, a village near the holy city of Qom.

Regarding the first category, an October 1 meeting in Geneva led to a tentative agreement between Iran and the P5+1. Iran accepted it in principle. The agreement provided for Iran to ship 2,600 pounds (1,200 kilograms) of its low-enriched uranium (LEU) to Russia by January 15, 2010, for processing into fuel rods that would then be sent to France for further processing and finally returned to Iran for its nuclear research reactor in Tehran to be used for medical purposes.

To detail the technical and legal terms of the agreement, Iran's ambassador to the IAEA, Ali Asghar Soltanieh, met with his American, Russian, and French counterparts on October 19 and 20 in Vienna to consider a draft proposal prepared by the IAEA. The proposal originated from Iran's request to the IAEA to refuel the small medical reactor, which has long been subject to international inspection and is not considered by the West to be part of a nuclear-weapons program.

The IAEA director, General Mohamed ElBaradei, said the proposal was a "very important confidence-building" measure and that "an agreed arrangement could defuse a long-standing crisis and open space for negotiation." He also expressed cautious optimism that the draft agreement would be approved by the deadline he had specified, October 22.

The draft agreement, however, gave Iran pause. The key concern of Iran was then, as it had been in 2007, when a similar deal was made but rejected by Ayatollah Khamenei, "an infringement of Iran's sovereignty." As a result, Iran did not respond by the October 22 deadline. Voices of opposition to the deal were heard in Iran soon after the deal was made public. For example, on October 25 Ali Larijani, Iran's Speaker of the Parliament and former chief nuclear negotiator, warned that the West was trying to "cheat" Iran and might never return its enriched uranium. Apparently Iran informed ElBaradei on October 29 that it would not send its enriched uranium abroad, a verbal remark that he thought was not a final response from Iran.

On November 18, 2009, Iran's foreign minister, Manoucher Mottaki, in an interview with the Hindu, outlined three options. First, Iran itself would further enrich the fuel. Second, Iran would purchase the fuel from other countries as in the past. Third, Iran would consider further the IAEA-brokered proposal, to which it had already provided an "initial response."

In reacting to the West's continued suspicion that Iran intended to build nuclear weapons in spite of its active negotiations, the chief of Iran's Atomic Energy Organization (AEOI), Ali Akbar Salehi, stated, "It is against our tenets, it is against our religion, to produce, use, hold or have nuclear weapons. We have been saying this for decades."

On December 12, Mottaki announced Iran's counterproposal. He said, "We suggested that the exchange take place over the course of some years." He further informed the P5+1 that Iran "could deliver 400 kilogram uranium enriched to 3.5 percent on Kish Island and receive its equivalent enriched to 20 percent." In return Iran would demand a 100 percent guarantee that it would receive this further enriched fuel.

In explaining the course of the negotiation, Mottaki said, "They [the United States, Russia, and France] told us to provide the 3.5 percent enriched nuclear fuel and receive the 20 percent fuel, and we agreed with the general outlines of the proposal, but we suddenly realized that the Western media reported the 1,200 kilograms of nuclear fuel would be shipped out of Iran so that Iran" would be unable to produce nuclear weapons. "Is this," he asked rhetorically, "a response to confidence building?"

Reportedly, the United States dismissed the Iranian offer, but as of this writing, there has been no official response from the United States. Mottaki said that Iran had not received an official response, and "[we] do not insist that the other side respond to the proposal. We just wanted to open a way for the other side." The deal was said to have required that the nuclear material be exchanged all at once, and be 1,200 kilograms and sent to Russia in one batch.

Iran had suspected all along that the West, especially the United States, hoped that the deal would stop Iran from acquiring a greater ability to enrich uranium, at least for a while. The suspicion was fueled on November 2, 2009, when the U.S. Secretary of State Hillary Rodham Clinton urged Iran to accept the deal and emphasized that it would not be altered.

The next day, Ayatollah Khamenei repeated what he had said in response to Obama's New Year address in March, that he would not prejudge "the slogan of change," but now he said the practice of the United States contradicted its rhetoric. With an eye to Clinton's inflexible statement, he said, "On the one hand Americans talk of negotiations. On the other hand they continue to threaten and say the negotiations must have our desired results."

The United States' apparent dismissal of Iran's proposal was followed by discussions aimed at imposing tougher sanctions on Iran. Obama had set the end of the year as the deadline for Iran to be forthcoming in negotiations, otherwise stiffer sanctions would be imposed, presumably by the U.N. Security Council, assuming that Russia and China would support such a move. Obama had been encouraged by Russia's apparent willingness to go along with further sanctions. China had also been approached by Dennis Ross and others in Beijing, who argued that the United States could not stop a country from military action against Iran if that country believed Iran's nuclear program posed an "existential threat," referring to Israel's repeated threats of military strikes against Iran's nuclear facilities.

Yet, on December 11 the U.S. defense secretary, Robert M. Gates, while foreseeing "some significant sanctions imposed by the international community" on Iran if it did not agree to the Geneva agreement, discounted the idea of a military strike against Iran. He said, "You never take any options off the table [meaning using military force], but the reality is that any military action would only buy some time, maybe two or three years."

Iran, however, viewed its counterproposal as a way of opening, not shutting, the door for negotiation. Mottaki said it was up to the other side to respond. He added, "Today it is not possible to frighten countries through threats or sanctions, and the language of sanctions goes back to the 1960s." On December 21 he added, "We do not insist on our proposal. We aimed to open a door for the other side." He added, "It [the proposal] is one step forward to prove goodwill and a suitable opportunity for them."

To take up the second aspect of the nuclear dispute: at Iran's invitation, the IAEA inspectors visited the Fordou nuclear facility, which had been discovered by the United States and which Iran had announced soon thereafter. The IAEA reported on November 16, 2009, that Iran's belated "declaration of the new facility reduces the level of confidence in the absence of other nuclear facilities under construction, and gives rise to questions about whether there were other nuclear facilities in Iran which had not been declared to the agency."

Iranian officials explained that they had been motivated to build an underground plant because of "the threats of military strikes against Iran," a reference to possible military action against Iran by Israel, the United States, or other Western powers.

The IAEA's concern, however, continued. On November 27 its Board of Governors adopted a resolution censuring Iran. It urged "Iran to comply fully with its obligations under . . . the resolutions of the Security Council and meet the requirements of the Board of Governors, including by suspending immediately construction at Qum" and clarify "the purpose of the enrichment at Qum and the chronology of its design and construction."

Iran was angered, and officially pronounced its rejection of the resolution on

November 29. On the same day that the resolution was announced, Ahmadine-jad said that Iran would study what it would take for Iran to further enrich the existing stockpile of nuclear fuel in a medical reactor rather than rely on Russia or another nation. He also declared that Iran planned to build ten more nuclear plants. The Iranian Parliament also reacted defiantly. More than two hundred members signed a letter urging that the agency's presence in Iran be further restricted, while a few others called for the withdrawal of Iran from the NPT—a measure that I believe has never been seriously considered in the higher eche-lons of the Iranian government.

ROOTS OF SPIRITUAL PRAGMATISM

The salience of the spiritual pragmatic paradigm over the three de-cades since the revolution has deep roots in what I call "Iran's diplomatic cul-ture," defined as those values, norms, mores, modes of thinking, and ways of acting that have developed over centuries as a result of Iran's diplomatic inter-action with other nations. These attributes have survived change and have influ-enced generations of Iran's foreign policy makers and diplomats and their ne-gotiating style. For example, in talking to Iranians directly, Americans should anticipate that Iranian diplomats will come to the table with certain expecta-tions that it would behoove American diplomats to understand at the outset. I will outline below the implications of such expectations for the U.S. Iran policy.

Wisdom and rationality, which are the hallmarks of spiritual pragmatism, were embedded in Iran's diplomatic culture as early as the birth of the Iranian state in the sixth century BC. I choose two Iranian leaders or policymakers in history who are acknowledged as the supreme examples of pragmatic state-craft, Zoroastrian Cyrus of the pre-Islamic period and Shii Shah Abbas I of the Islamic era.

Herodotus praises Cyrus (558–530 BC) for his "statesmanship and liberal-ity," the Bible reveres him for liberating the Jews from Babylonian captivity, and Adda B. Bozeman credits him with establishing the first "international soci-ety," which is to say, a society that respected the human rights of the conquered peoples living in the Persian Empire. Above all else, she says, Iranians were the first people in history who concerned themselves with the relationship between morality and self-interest, a relationship that is, I think, at the foundation of spiritual pragmatism.

Shah Abbas I (1587–1629) was a devout Muslim who believed he was "the spokesman of the Hidden Imam." Yet, according to Roger Savory, a leading Canadian historian of Safavid Iran, the Shah moved away from "strict Shia ide-ology," was a "brilliant strategist and tactician, and preferred to achieve his ends by diplomacy rather than war." In a bold move to restore Iran's territories lost in incessant wars waged by his predecessors, the Shah signed a peace treaty with the Sunni Ottoman Empire in 1590 in which he abandoned the customary cursing of the "first three Caliphs," a unique example of humane tolerance of sectarian difference.

Iranian policymakers, as I said before, have always aspired to create a hybrid of pragmatism and spirituality. That aspiration since the revolution, it seems to me, has been often expressed in terms of the Quranic-based norm of hikmah (wisdom) in Arabic and hekmat in Persian. Hekmat has two dimensions, pragmatic (hekmat-e 'amali) as well as spiritual (hekmat-e nazari or elahi).

I wonder whether the pragmatic dimension (hekmat-e 'amali) is compatible with the Western, particularly American, philosophy of pragmatic instrumentalism as expounded by American philosophers, especially John Dewey and my late friend and colleague Richard Rorty, one of the most influential American philosophers of his time. Rorty asked for my advice before going to Iran for a lecture on "Democracy and Philosophy." He told me after his return that he was surprised to hear that Iranians were reading his philosophy writings. Rorty, like Habermas, who is known to many enlightened Iranians, believed that membership in a religious community would be taken over in time by "constitutional patriotism," which I suggest has been a hallmark of Iranian aspirations since the Constitutional Revolution.

American charges of "irrationality" and "fanaticism" in Iran's foreign policy reflect ignorance of such profound intellectual engagement of Iranians with American thought. Such charges prompted me to publish in 1986 *Revolutionary Iran: Challenge and Response in the Middle East*, which demonstrated that even at the height of religious fervor, in the first five years of the revolution, Iran's foreign-policy decisions included pragmatic strands. My book also argued that the United States should temper its containment policy and engage Iran, which only now is Obama trying to do.

IMPLICATIONS FOR U.S.-IRANIAN RELATIONS

The central implications of these reflections for the United States' Iran policy are intellectual and practical. Westerners, especially Americans, often make unwarranted assumptions about the forces that drive Iran's foreign policy. Here are six examples of such assumptions.

First, it is assumed that factional politics determine Iran's foreign policy; moderate leaders are conciliatory, whereas hardliners are confrontational. Iran's diplomatic culture proves this wrong. Foreign policy makers everywhere, including in Iran, change their stance according to the dictates of circumstances. In other words, decision makers take soft or hard positions depending on the issue at hand. Thus, today's moderates may become tomorrow's radicals.

Second, it is assumed that Iran's contradictory principles determine its foreign policy. The principles of semi-divine *faqih* and popular sovereignty in the Constitution, it is argued, render foreign-policy decisions and actions "incoherent." This is partly true, but this assumption fails to take note of the effects of international politics and of Iran's diplomatic culture, as defined above, on Iran's foreign policy making.

Third, it is assumed that the ideology of Iran's policymakers determines their decisions. Political Islam, it is argued, makes for "irrational" policy decisions (this is essentially the Kissingerian dogma that revolutions never change).

Fourth, and paradoxically, it is assumed that Realpolitik rather than ideology drives Iran's foreign policy, that ideology is simply used to rationalize crass power politics. On the contrary, Iran's diplomatic culture demonstrates that ideology and power politics sometimes coexist, sometimes clash, and other times fuse. Different policymakers accord different weights to ideology relative to practical realities.

Fifth, it is assumed that great powers are the real players in the international system and small, weak, or underdeveloped nations are their pawns. Such an assumption disregards the momentous post–World War II processes of decolonization and the emergence of newly independent nations that control their destinies and make foreign-policy decisions on their own despite great-power intervention. Iran's recent history demonstrates graphically that since the revolution Iran has made independent decisions despite unrelenting Western, especially American, pressures, sanctions, and threats of military force.

Sixth and finally, there is a pervasive biased attitude that prevents Westerners from understanding Iran dispassionately. Nearly a half-century ago Lucian W. Pye, a renowned American social scientist, argued perceptively, "All the illogical reactions of race and class, of paternalism and piety, of pride and prejudice combine in various ways to blur the Westerner's image of transitional peoples."

Western policymakers knowingly or otherwise often fall victim to such untested assumptions and biased attitudes. Having observed U.S. policymaking from the inside for nearly six decades, I think faulty assumptions often underpin U.S. policymakers' mistaken policies toward Iran. Former secretary of state Condoleezza Rice, for example, flatly confessed in public that she did not understand Iran. Presidential candidate Obama, to cite another example, said, "I would engage in negotiations with Iran, with no conditions, because *we don't really understand how Iran works*" (emphasis added).

The sincere intention of President Obama to engage Iran, however, seems to have become saddled by what is called a "dual track" strategy, the brainchild of Dennis Ross, who now serves in the National Security Council. On the one hand, the United States is negotiating with Iran on the nuclear issue. On the other hand, it is threatening tougher sanctions and hinting implicitly at a possible military attack on Iran.

The representatives of any country, especially the United States, need to take into account some core expectations of Iranian negotiators. I extract several of these from the history of Iran's diplomatic culture as follows:

First and most important, Iran expects the United States to understand that Iran's foreign policy is fundamentally driven by a fierce commitment to independence rooted in Iran's steely sense of *national identity*. The invasion of Iran by Alexander of Macedonia and other invasions by such foreign forces as Arabs, Turks, Mongols, Afghans, and Iraqis did not deny that sense. Even the Arab invasion did not rob Iran of its Persian identity. Unlike Egypt, Iran refused Arabization and over time embraced Shiism, whose core tenets were compatible with those of Zoroastrianism, Iran's ancient religion. Above all else, the Persian language helped maintain Iran's sense of national identity. The tenth-century epic poet Ferdowsi wrote in his *Book of Kings*, "I revived the Iranian identity through the Persian language" (*'ajam zendeh kardam be-din Parsi*). Iranians often cite Ferdowsi from memory today.

In this context the United States should understand that when it imposes sanctions on Iran unilaterally or through the U.N. Security Council, and when Israel threatens to attack Iran, Iran's national pride is offended. Iran will resist any coercive foreign action in the future as it has in the past.

Second, Iran expects the United States to recognize its strategic importance and its status as a major player in the Middle East. In the Persian Gulf, Iran straddles the Strait of Hormuz, the global oil chokepoint; it connects the Middle East to Central Asia and South Asia; it is the largest Shii state in the Muslim world; it is endowed with rich oil and gas resources; it has the largest industrial base of all countries in the Middle East; and it has greater influence in Afghanistan and Iraq than any other regional state.

Given all this, the United States should anticipate that Iran will retaliate against any attack. If attacked, it will likely target the American presence in the Middle East, especially in the nearby Persian Gulf, where the oil fields of the United States' friends and allies are within Iran's easy reach. Iran could also mine the Strait of Hormuz, which will endanger the world economy, including Iran's as well. Such possible acts of retaliation will likely open a third war front for the United States in the Middle East with catastrophic consequences for both countries.

Third, Iran expects the United States to respect it as an equal partner in negotiations. Iran's long memory of condescending Western attitudes does not help negotiations. Obama's respectful attitude is appreciated in Iran, but Iran also expects actions to match words about change. If the United States should indeed dismiss Iran's nuclear counterproposal out of hand, it could jeopardize an unprecedented opportunity for the two nations to settle all disputes of the past thirty years through negotiations.

Fourth, Iran expects empathy. In realizing this, former president Bill Clinton said in April 1999, Iran "has been the subject of quite a lot of abuse from various Western nations," and sometimes "it is quite important to tell people, look, you have a right to be angry at something that my country or my culture or others that are generally allied with us today did to you 50 or 60 or 100 or 150 years ago."

And fifth, Iran expects the United States to explore creatively the areas of potential common interest with Iran. Here are some common goals that it behooves both countries' decision makers to consider constructively:

- Stability in Afghanistan and Iraq under representative governments.
- Security of uninterrupted flow of Persian Gulf oil supplies to world markets.
- Non-proliferation of nuclear weapons worldwide.
- Prevention of a nuclear arms race in the Middle East.
- Regional security and economic cooperation in the Persian Gulf and beyond.
- Cooperation against Taliban insurgents and al-Qaeda terrorists.
- Modernization of Iran's oil industry so as to increase global oil supplies.
- Exchange of scholars, students, parliamentarians, and athletes, among others.

LOOKING AHEAD

As Winston Churchill once said, "The further backward you look, the further forward you can see." Having looked backward, what can one say about the future of the aspirational paradigm of pragmatic spirituality in Iran's foreign policy making?

It bears repeating that Iranian leaders were the first in international history to concern themselves with the conundrum of moral imperatives and pragmatic necessity. All Iranian leaders, from Ayatollah Khomeini to Ahmadinejad, have aspired to create a hybrid of the two, but they have given different weight to practical and spiritual considerations. Rafsanjani did not hesitate to forego Islamic doctrines if it was practically necessary, Khatami struck relative balance between the two, and although Ahmadinejad has produced an image of recalcitrance, he has not been able to disregard the imperative of practical necessity, or, in other words, to ignore the institutional imperatives of complex domestic politics or the demands of the international constituency.

Will future Iranian policymakers also aspire to create a hybrid of practicality and spirituality? The answer will partly depend on the outcome of a complex combination of the emerging political trends within Iranian society and the global community, while the ancient quest for spirituality will continue.

Domestically, younger-generation Iranians will demand freedom as Iranians have done ever since the Tobacco Protest of 1891–92. Khomeini had promised not only independence but also freedom, which appears to lie at the heart of the current protest movement. By the end of 2009, there were clear signs of creeping radicalization of university students, who have always been central to social movements and popular demands for a wide range of rights recognized in the Constitution of the Islamic Republic of Iran.

Even the older-generation revolutionaries such as Mir-Hossein Mousavi and Mehdi Karroubi, the perceived leaders of the opposition, and Rafsanjani and Khatami called for internal reform of the Islamic system. They all emphasized the centrality of the role of the people in Iranian society and politics.

Globally, unstoppable changes will interact with domestic transformations in Iranian society to advance universal values of freedom and democracy. Global trends will continue toward greater rates of literacy, accelerated urbanization, greater accountability of government to the people, deeper economic interdependence, broader cooperation against the scourge of terrorism, tighter control of infectious diseases, higher standards of health, more efforts to reduce global warming, and less of a gap between the rich and the poor.

What lies behind the dilemma of spirituality/pragmatism is essentially the relationship between state and religion, which is as old as Iran's history. This relationship is the single most fundamental challenge Iran faces today and into the foreseeable future. The unprecedented criticism of the Islamic system as it exists today demonstrates that Iran will have to *redefine* the system.

Although the future cannot be predicted, one thing is predictable. The Iranian demand for freedom, democracy, justice, and higher human-rights standards will persist. Human-rights aspirations are universal, not simply Western. Iran must observe human-rights standards because they are compatible with its own values—as stipulated in clear terms in the provisions of the Constitution, which still seems to be the main rallying point of the mainstream protest movement. The roots of these standards are essentially the same values in Iran and America. In America as in the West in general they spring from the Christian belief in the oneness of humanity. In Iran they are embedded in the hybrid Perso-Islamic heritage. Ancient Iran is said to have made the world's first human-rights declaration, while in Islam all humanity is one in the sight of God. Ayatollah Khomeini was speaking to this fundamental Islamic value when he said, "Islam has come for humanity."

No one has articulated this ideal better than has one of the greatest poets of Iran, Sa'di (1184–1283/91), a traveler for decades in the Islamic world of his time. I memorized his beautiful and profound lines about seven decades ago, when I was a schoolboy in the land of my birth: "The sons of men are members in a body whole related, / For of a single essence are they and all created / When Fortune persecutes with pain one member sorely, surely / The other members of the body cannot stand securely. / O you who from another's trouble turn aside your view / It is not fitting they bestow the name of 'Man' on you."

III

SECURITY IN THE

PERSIAN GULF

SECURITY IN THE PERSIAN GULF

Who should maintain the future security of the Persian Gulf? This question looms large in the minds of policymakers in the United States, Western Europe, Japan, and, of course, the Persian Gulf states. The fact that this question is raised with a deep sense of urgency in numerous capitals of the world indicates the extent to which Iran was perceived as having ensured Gulf security before the outbreak of its recent revolution. Although American rhetoric spoke of pursuing a "twin-pillar policy," the United States itself actually relied primarily on Iran to perform the role of the "policeman" for the Gulf region.

Prior to the Arab-Israeli War of 1973, the perception of Iran as the main protector of Gulf security was reinforced by the American reluctance to fill the power vacuum left by Britain as a result of its historic decision to withdraw forces in 1971 from the area "east of Suez," including the Persian Gulf. As the most populous and the strongest military power in the area and as the main country straddling the strategic Strait of Hormuz, through which some 57 percent of world oil trade must pass to world markets, Iran was willing to undertake the burden of responsibility for Gulf security—the immediate problem then being the creation of a federation of the Trucial and other small states near the entrance to the Gulf.

When Saudi Arabia emerged as a world financial power after the 1973 war, it seemed for a time to be regarded as the "linchpin" of American policy in the Persian Gulf. The Carter administration in particular seemed to have some preference for the financial power of Saudi Arabia as contrasted with the military power of Iran. In fact, however, the idea died on the vine. Saudi Arabia lacked the population and military power necessary for playing a major security role in the Gulf region, and in any case Riyadh was unwilling to undertake such a role.

But Saudi Arabia was willing, especially after the assassination of King Faisal in 1975, to use its monetary prowess in support of a more active diplomacy, as a means of neutralizing the influence of such "radical" states as South Yemen and Iraq and bolstering the governments of such "moderate" states as Oman, North Yemen, and Egypt. Although Saudi dollar diplomacy was extended to states located outside as well as within the Persian Gulf, it complemented the

"Security in the Persian Gulf" was originally published in Foreign Affairs 57, no. 4 (Spring 1979): 821–35, and is reprinted by permission of Foreign Affairs, copyright 1979 by the Council on Foreign Relations, Inc., www.foreignaffairs.com.

Iranian security role in the Gulf area. Saudi Arabia's increasingly active diplomacy, added to Iran's security policy, poured concrete meaning into the hitherto empty rhetoric of an American "twin-pillar policy."

Plainly, Iran will no longer act in any sense as a pillar of American policy in the Persian Gulf. Even before the short-lived government of Dr. Bakhtiar was formed, he told the United States that a future government in Iran would abandon Iran's "policeman" role and would confine its security concerns to the defense of the country's national boundaries. Now, with the Khomeini forces precariously allied with the Bazargan government, this policy seems nailed down. In response, Washington circles appeared to be weighing two possible alternatives. One was to search for a new "second pillar," on the assumption that Saudi Arabia would now be willing to play some Gulf-wide security role, but could not do so alone even if it were willing, because of its small population and still low levels of military and underlying economic strength. On this view, despite its geographic distance from the Persian Gulf proper, Egypt loomed as a desirable candidate partly because it shares the Saudi concerns with the perceived Soviet and communist threats to the region around the Red Sea.

The other initial idea about Gulf security was a spin-off from a larger conception of American security that called for reliance on "regional influentials," to borrow the phrase of National Security Adviser Zbigniew Brzezinski. India would presumably qualify as such a regional power center in the Indian Ocean with its twin arms of the Persian Gulf and the Red Sea.

Most recently, however, Secretary of Defense Harold Brown's visit to the Middle East in February 1979 has suggested a new American security formula in the Middle East that may be broader than either of these. Clearly, it is a formula for a more forward American policy, overturning the previous, more distant approach of the Carter as well as the Nixon and Ford administrations toward the Persian Gulf. His pronouncements were intended particularly to assuage Saudi anxieties, which had been intensified largely by the perceived American failure to support the Shah's regime, in the context of a background of perceived Soviet and communist gains in Afghanistan and especially in the Horn of Africa. But they also went further than ever before in warning the Soviet Union that the United States would not tolerate any future threat to vital American interests in the region as a result of either overt Soviet incursions or Soviet-supported communist coups in the Gulf states and in signaling to Moscow that the United States is committed to a growing military and economic relationship with "pro-Western" governments of the Middle East toward the same end.

Apparently, what is now envisaged would include a sharp increase of American military supplies and economic aid to "pro-Western" governments outside the Gulf as well as within it, including Saudi Arabia, North Yemen, the Sudan,

Egypt, Jordan, and Israel. Saudi Arabia would be expected under the new formula to play a more prominent military and economic role in the small states of the lower Persian Gulf. Significantly, the new formula would also include the expansion of a "quick-strike force" of American paratroopers and marines (an idea first broached by Secretary Brown a year earlier) to be used in case of a request for help by Saudi Arabia or other oil-producing Gulf states threatened with the turmoil of a Soviet-supported coup. Moreover, it would possibly involve the construction of more port facilities for major American ships in the Indian Ocean naval base of Diego Garcia. However, President Carter stated at the end of February that American bases in the Middle East itself are not envisioned.

This new American commitment to the future security of the Persian Gulf has clear advantages and disadvantages. If in fact it clarifies the intention and resolve to defend vital American interests in the Persian Gulf, it may well reduce the chances of Soviet miscalculation and simultaneously assure American friends and allies of the U.S. commitment to their independence.

One need not be a doctrinaire student of geopolitics to realize, in light of actual Soviet behavior, that ever since the end of World War II Moscow has sought to expand its power and influence—at the expense of the West in general and the United States in particular—in a widening circle of regional states lying south of Soviet borders. The Soviet thrust, first into the Northern Tier and then into the Eastern Mediterranean, has since 1968 been extended into the Indian Ocean–Persian Gulf area. Its principal instruments have included the encouragement of nationalization of Western oil companies and the acquisition of oil and gas privileges for the Soviet Union, propaganda attacks on the CENTO alliance and American military sales, transfer of Soviet arms, support for national liberation movements, massive infusion of Soviet and Cuban arms supplies and military personnel, encouragement of communist participation in national-front governments, and support for communist coups. Now the potential for Soviet and communist pressure on the states located in and around the Persian Gulf has increased substantially as a consequence of the Iranian Revolution. Anti-American sentiments have been fomented by Soviet propaganda, and there are emerging signs of Soviet influence on militant leftist elements in Iran.

The other great advantage of the emerging American security posture is the apparent reversal of the decade-old reliance of the United States on one or two local powers to maintain regional security. The indiscriminate sale of billions of dollars' worth of arms to the Shah's regime had been justified as a way to avoid the commitment of American troops to the defense of the strategic Persian Gulf. To be sure, the Shah's own preoccupation with military strength underpinned his enormous purchases of sophisticated military equipment, but U.S. eagerness to comply with Iranian requests during the Nixon administration paved the way for the massive transfer of arms once the explosion of oil revenues made this financially possible for Iran and economically profitable for the United States. However one evaluates the diverse causes of the Iranian Revolution, there is little doubt that these unrestrained arms transactions contributed to its outbreak. They not only diverted badly needed funds from social and economic projects but also placed unprecedented burdens on Iranian skilled manpower resources and economic and communication infrastructures.

And the new American commitment to the economic and military strength of half a dozen states (Saudi Arabia, Egypt, Jordan, Israel, and secondarily North Yemen and the Sudan) seems a healthy corrective to the previous temptation to treat Saudi Arabia as the "linchpin" of American policy in the whole Gulf area.

There are, however, several disadvantages to the nascent American security posture. One is the potential polarization of the Middle East into camps of "pro-Western" and other nations. Secretary Brown's new prescription would seem to suffer potentially from all the previous shortcomings of American security policy in the Middle East, especially since the creation of the Baghdad Pact (subsequently the Central Treaty Organization, or CENTO). His commitment to the security of the "pro-Western" regimes in the Middle East, like Secretary Dulles's commitment to the Northern Tier states in the 1950s, may be portrayed as a new American effort for the "enslavement" of Middle Eastern governments. And his planned American "quick-strike force," which would come, on request, to the aid of any government threatened by a Soviet-supported coup, smacks of the ill-fated Eisenhower Doctrine, which allowed the United States to go to the aid, also on request, of any pro-Western government threatened by "international communism." That doctrine was invoked by a Middle Eastern government only in one instance, the Lebanese crisis of 1958, and in hindsight the cost of its invocation far exceeded the actual benefit. Neither the Eisenhower administration nor the Chamoun government gained in the long or even the medium term from American intervention in that earlier Lebanese civil war. It simultaneously increased popular resentment against the United States and deepened ancient communal divisions within Lebanese society.

A second potential disadvantage is the intensification of arms transfers to the Middle East. No aspect of past American security policy in the Middle East has been subjected to greater criticism. Whatever the short-term financial benefits of unrestrained arms sales, on balance indiscriminate arms supplies can contribute more to destabilization than to stabilization of the region. This apparent new American commitment to a sharp increase in arms supplies also raises serious questions about President Carter's often repeated, but still unfulfilled, goal of limiting the sale of arms worldwide.

A third shortcoming of the new American security formula is the possibility that it may hobble efforts to achieve security in the Persian Gulf by linking them to the extremely difficult Arab-Israeli peacemaking process. These efforts aim at two quite different objectives: to align the "pro-Western" Gulf regimes with the United States and to break the deadlock on peace negotiations. The increased American security commitment to Israel as well as Egypt, Jordan, and Saudi Arabia is intended to attain both objectives. However, as a result of this coupling, the more easily attainable objective of future security in the Persian Gulf will almost certainly be obstructed by the intractable Arab-Israeli conflict.

However, the greatest shortcoming of the new American security scheme is that it addresses threats to Gulf security that may be more hypothetical than potential. The United States has made it emphatically clear, and rightly so, that the American commitment is intended for defense against "external threats." This appears to exclude threats emanating from within the region as well as internal coups—unless either is supported by the Soviet Union. As a consequence, two of the more likely sources of instability and conflict in the Persian Gulf are not covered.

First, let us take domestic crises. If the Iranian Revolution has taught us nothing else, it should have made clear that the sources of domestic conflict and upheaval in the Persian Gulf societies are more pressing than hitherto anticipated. Unlike the Dhofari rebellion in Oman, which received ample Soviet and communist support both directly and indirectly, the Iranian opposition was transformed into a full-scale and bloody revolution within a year primarily as a result of misguided and disastrously executed economic, social, and political decisions of the indigenous elite. As early as 1972, and repeatedly thereafter, I warned that international capability was no true substitute for internal political stability in Iran no matter how actively it tried to project its power abroad in the pursuit of its national objectives.[1] Without any significant outside aid, thousands of strikers and millions of street demonstrators finally brought down with their bare hands one of the world's best-equipped military forces. It is not likely that Saudi Arabia, for example, will face the challenge of internal communism; it hardly has a native proletariat. But there is ample reason to envisage the outbreak of a genuine indigenous internal convulsion to which the present American security scheme would be irrelevant.

Second, this scheme would not bear directly on the containment of regional conflicts. The Persian Gulf region is as rich in potential conflicts as in oil, although, as we shall see, the Gulf states have had a remarkable record of peaceful settlement of their disputes. The spillover of conflicts from the more conflict-prone adjacent areas into the Gulf region proper is also a major problem. The Arab-Israeli War of October 1973, the Arab oil embargo, and the explosion of oil prices have been followed by the growth of unprecedented social and economic ties between the Gulf states proper and other Middle East societies on the one hand and South Asian nations on the other. It is difficult to envisage a future Arab-Israeli war that would not quickly spread to the Gulf area as a result of Saudi Arabian arms transfers to the Arab confrontation states or an Israeli preventive or preemptive attack on Saudi Arabia. It would also seem more likely today than, for example, in 1971 that a conflict in South Asia would swiftly spread to the Gulf area—probably not as a result of another Indo-Pakistani war but of an armed conflict between Afghanistan and Pakistan or Afghanistan and Iran. Again, a political upheaval in Afghanistan or Pakistan, or a separatist movement in Baluchistan or Pushtunistan, would be likely to spill over into the Gulf.

On balance, therefore, the new American security formula could at best aid the objective of security in the Persian Gulf only indirectly, peripherally, and partially. The American commitment to the security of Saudi Arabia against "external threat" and internal Soviet-supported coups seems to address, in the last analysis, two hypothetical threats emanating from the Soviet Union, and the increased U.S. security commitment to Egypt, Israel, and Jordan can hardly contribute to the solution of the urgent problem of security in the Persian Gulf proper.

The uninterrupted flow of oil supplies to the world is the pivotal problem, and the bulk of the Gulf oil, including Saudi oil, must pass through the strategic Strait of Hormuz, whose security must be our paramount concern. Furthermore, the Iranian Revolution has shown for the first time that the disruption of oil supplies can be used as an instrument of domestic political coercion by a noncommunist opposition and that it can have as adverse an effect on oil exports as an oil embargo. Without necessarily implying that oil workers in other Gulf states are susceptible to the same kind of call for strikes as in Iran, the main point is that Secretary Brown's emerging security formula would be clearly inadequate as a deterrent against potential threats to oil supplies arising from both domestic crises and regional conflicts in the heart of the oil fields and in the main artery of oil transportation.

The most effective way to cope with domestically and regionally based threats would be for the Persian Gulf states themselves to continue their own search for indigenous security arrangements. This search is all the more appropriate at this particular time, when the sense of a common security concern has heightened to an unprecedented degree in the wake of the Iranian Revolution. Any in-

digenous security arrangements made at the initiative of the Gulf states themselves could have the full support of the United States if the local states should
so desire. Such arrangements could prove more effective not only against domestic and regional threats but also against Soviet threats if the local states
should choose to seek American and other Western support.

The problem with Secretary Brown's security formula for the Persian Gulf is
not merely the shortcomings discussed above. Equally important, its existence
might cause the United States to overlook the great potential for indigenous regional security arrangements in the area. A wide variety of considerations now
seem conducive to the definition of common security problems in the Gulf, the
adoption of common security strategies, and ultimately the creation of common
procedures and institutions for the collective attainment of common objectives.

First of all, the Persian Gulf is a distinct and compact region. Geographically
it is an "arm" of the Indian Ocean and a "finger" of the Middle East. These two
larger regions are relatively undefinable, but the Gulf area is physically set apart
as a shallow and narrow semi-enclosed sea. It is connected to the high seas only
by the strategic Strait of Hormuz, squeezed between the Iranian shore and the
Omani tip of the Musandam Peninsula.

Second, all Persian Gulf states have a vital stake in freedom of navigation
and the control of pollution. The Gulf's special geographic features have been
acknowledged repeatedly at international conferences on the law of the sea as
a justification for the adoption of special regional regulations. Because of its
limited access to the Gulf waters, Iraq has been the greatest advocate of the concept of "transit passage" through the Strait of Hormuz, while Iran, as one of the
Strait states, has favored a kind of "regulated transit passage," and Oman, as
the other Strait state, has insisted on the application of the traditional concept
of "innocent passage" to the Strait. Despite such divergencies regarding the details, however, all eight Gulf states share a deep sense of obligation with respect
to the maintenance of secure and unimpeded navigation. The Gulf waters constitute not only their main trade artery and the vital route for their oil exports
but also an increasingly important source of their food supplies. Because they
share the shallow and narrow waters and navigable channels of the Gulf, the
littoral states also share a deep sense of common concern with the problem of
pollution.

Third, all the Gulf states have a heightened interest in social- and economic-
development projects. The revolutionary rise in oil revenues has financed ambitious economic-development projects, particularly in the large oil-producing
states of Saudi Arabia, Iran, Kuwait, and Iraq. The Iranian revenues increased
from $194 million in 1972 to $22 billion in 1974, and their massive infusion
into the economy lay at the heart of the social and economic dislocations that

in combination with political repression and unprecedented corruption led to revolution. Saudi Arabia has also launched an extremely ambitious economic-development plan (1976–80) that calls for a spectacular $140 billion expenditure. Saudi society is now having to grapple with the side effects of swift modernization. The signs of rapid inflation, corruption, and waste are already visible, and their adverse political consequences cannot be ruled out. The Gulf states in general have in common the blight as well as the blessing of sudden wealth.

Fourth, all the Gulf states are prone to internal political upheaval, but the larger oil producers, particularly Saudi Arabia, are more susceptible to political convulsion.

It would, however, be a mistake to predict the rise of a religious opposition against the Saudi royal family on the model of that in Iran. The danger of this kind of analogy is increased by talk about the phenomenon of the so-called resurgence of Islam. To be sure, the signs of religiously based political opposition are everywhere to be seen in the Muslim world, from Mauritania to Malaysia, but two points should be borne in mind in order to avoid drawing false analogies. First, the relationship of the religious leaders (the ulama) and the wielders of political power has been generally different in the Sunni, as contrasted with the Shii, communities. For example, the ulama in Egypt and Saudi Arabia have not been so completely kept out of the political process as they were in Iran. Second, the Iranian Revolution probably owes much of its fervor and zeal to the character of Shiism as a historically revolutionary, messianic, and legitimistic movement. The anti-establishmentarian thrust of Shii Islam is also marked by a perpetual drive for social justice and equality hallowed by an ethos of martyrdom that is unparalleled in the larger world of Sunni Islam.

The doctrinal-political differences between Shii and Sunni Islam do not of course preclude the rise of religiously based opposition in the Sunni communities, whether secularized as in Turkey or traditional as in Saudi Arabia. What will make the real difference, however, is the basic human conditions, as one learns from the Iranian experience. All Gulf regimes would face potential internal political explosions if their peoples felt dissatisfied, hopeless, and resentful of great disparities in wealth and power.

Fifth, the Gulf states share not only a common aspiration for economic modernization and an uncertain political future but also an urge for the control of their own destiny in world politics. Political awakening is the hallmark of every Gulf society at a crucial time when the outside world increasingly covets their oil, their most precious and finite natural resource. Many of them have enjoyed the status of independent states for less than a decade, and all of them share the desire to maintain their territorial integrity and political independence in the future. The West in general, they know, is committed to the maintenance of their political independence. For this fundamental reason none of them is likely to become permanently "anti-Western." Just as the Iranians have risen to challenge their excessive dependence on the West in general and the United States in particular, Iraq has begun to question its heavy dependence on the Soviet Union. On balance, suspicion of the Soviet Union is prevalent in the Gulf societies, and the perception of a common threat from Moscow is yet another potential element of commonality among them.

Despite all these factors of commonality, would it be realistically possible for the Gulf rulers and governments to develop a sense of common security responsibility? Since all the peoples of the Gulf are Muslim, would it be possible to develop such a sense out of their common faith? The commonality of faith in general is counterbalanced by the division between the Sunni and the Shii communities in the Gulf area. Most Iranians and more than half of the Arab population of Iraq are the followers of Shii Islam. Given the fact that these are the two most populous nations of the Gulf, the Shii believers numerically predominate in the Gulf.

However, Saudi Arabia, though with a much smaller population, is the site of two of the most holy places in Islam (Mecca and Medina), the birthplace of Islam and the home of a distinctively puritanical branch of Islam (Wahhabism). Furthermore, this sectarian division is compounded by the cultural disparity between Arabs and Iranians. For these reasons, therefore, Islam is unlikely to play a unifying role in the Gulf and might at times exacerbate regional differences.

Yet, as noted in the previous section, there are cohesive factors that do counterbalance these ancient sectarian and cultural divisions. Those elements of cohesion are more "modern," in the sense that they largely represent the ethos of the "world culture," one that knows no boundaries of religion, culture, and race. It is a culture in the process of worldwide diffusion and is based on "advanced technology, and the spirit of science, on a rational view of life, a secular approach to social relations, a feeling for justice in public affairs, and, above all else, on the acceptance in the political realm of the belief that the prime unit of the polity should be the nation-state."[2] Will these states that are in the process of becoming modern nations in this age of rampant nationalism be able to develop in practice extensive ties translatable over time into an obligation to maintain their security collectively?

This important question should be addressed on the basis of the experience of the Persian Gulf states themselves. Most of these have attained the status of independent and sovereign political entities only recently. Nevertheless, their past interrelationships contain an important clue to their future ability to cooperate with each other.

Fortunately, the Gulf states, as contrasted with the Arab confrontation states and Israel, have not been plagued with the kind of intractable conflict that has plunged those countries into four wars in thirty years. The most remarkable fact about the experience of the Gulf states, on the contrary, is their demonstrated ability to settle peacefully numerous multifaceted, overlapping, and interlocking disputes in a short span of time. These include the Bahrain settlement (1970), the historic Iran-Iraq conflict resolution (1975), and a series of other agreements between Iran and every Arab state of the Gulf and between the Arab states themselves, like the important agreement between Iraq and Saudi Arabia over the land boundary in the Neutral Zone and the agreement between Saudi Arabia and Abu Dhabi over the Buraimi oasis.

Why should there be this predilection for peaceful settlement of disputes in the Persian Gulf? My own examination of the record suggests that the impressive web of agreements that the Gulf states have developed over the years has been rooted in the imperative of practical necessity. Given the universal urge for social and economic development in the area, on the basis of uninterrupted income from oil and in the face of the nightmare of oil depletion, the Gulf states have accorded regional security the highest priority because they are, in the last analysis, hostages of each other.

Armed conflict diverts scarce resources from economic development in any society, but in the Gulf area it would destroy the very foundation of economic betterment and political survival. The dramatic settlement of the conflict between Iraq and Iran is the best illustration of the influence of this all-important mutual vulnerability on the security behavior of the Gulf states. After decades of smoldering hostility, Iran and Iraq decided to resolve their ancient and festering conflict as soon as it became clear that armed skirmishes might finally lead to an all-out war that would result in the mutual destruction of their oil facilities and the disruption of their oil exports.

The experience of the Gulf states also reveals that they have in fact gone beyond the avoidance of armed conflict and the peaceful settlement of disputes in their search for regional security. Ever since the settlement of the Shatt al-Arab dispute between Iraq and Iran in 1975, the Gulf leaders have pressed forward for mutual-defense cooperation despite a number of setbacks. In that year their foreign ministers first discussed in Jiddah the possibility of plans for mutual defense against external threats, and also, significantly, mutual aid in case of internal coups. Subsequent developments in the Horn of Africa and the coup in Afghanistan intensified their common concern with the advance of Soviet power and influence around the Persian Gulf. This concern reached a new peak by the middle of 1978, when Iraq began to share the Saudi and Iranian perceptions of the threat to their security. The Shah and the Iraqi leader, Saddam Hussein, even held "security consultations."

Has the Iranian Revolution increased or decreased the chances for further development of a security consensus in the Persian Gulf area? The answer will, of course, partly depend on the outcome of the revolution, but, assuming that an Islamic republic in some form is established, a best-case and a worst-case scenario may be envisaged.

The best case would be an Iran turned inward but still clearly anticommunist that confined its security perimeter to the defense of Iranian national boundaries, pursued a hands-off policy in the Gulf, and concentrated its energies on badly needed domestic economic reconstruction and political consolidation. Such a regime would presumably pull the remaining Iranian troops out of Oman (if it has not already done so). It would perhaps try to settle the Iranian disputes with the Sheikh of Sharjah over the Gulf island of Abu Musa and with the Sheikh of Ra's al-Khaymeh over the two Tunbs.

If so, the atmosphere for regional cooperation in the Gulf area would certainly improve. The Shah's overbearing manner often alienated Iran's neighbors, and the decline in Iranian assertiveness (as well as military power) could contribute to better relations and a fully shared perception of the external threat. The dramatic change already evident in Iran's policy toward the Arab-Israeli conflict would also ease past tensions between the Arab states of the Gulf and Iran over the Shah's favorable policy toward Israel. The new regime's embrace of the Palestine Liberation Organization (PLO), however, would not necessarily endear it to all Arab states, including some in the Gulf area. In fact, if the new regime should push its association with the PLO too far, it might indeed alienate several leading Arab states, including Egypt and Saudi Arabia, as long as they have "moderate" regimes.

At worst, the new regime could turn outward virulently. If the Shah's Gulf policy was inspired by the glories of ancient Persia, the new regime's might be influenced by the golden age of Islam. Pan-Shiism would embitter Iran's relations with not only the anti-Shii Wahhabis of Saudi Arabia but also the Sunni Ba'athist minority of Iraq, who dominate the Iraqi Shii majority. Any outward thrust by a new Iranian regime would surely sour Iran's relations with its major Gulf neighbors.

In either case the importance of Iran for the future security of the Persian Gulf would continue. Under the best-case scenario, the Gulf states and Iran might finally be able to develop a sense of common obligation to maintain their security against external threats and internal subversion and coups, and Iran's cooperation would be of critical importance. However, should Iran prefer to stay out of any collective security arrangement, there would be no reason for the Arab states of the Gulf to abandon past efforts toward the adoption of common security arrangements that would stand them in good stead even if Iran's security concerns were confined to the defense of its own territory and maritime interests.

The United States should not only encourage local initiatives toward security arrangements and be prepared to assist the regional states to achieve their own common security goals, but it should also try to persuade other advanced industrial countries in the OECD to join in common efforts to develop both economic and security ties with a prospective group of Gulf states if they choose to invite Western support. The United States, as contrasted with its NATO allies, is much less dependent on Persian Gulf oil. The Strait of Hormuz is potentially a global chokepoint largely because of the great dependence of Western Europe and Japan on Persian Gulf oil. (The socialist world's dependence on Gulf oil is relatively minimal at the present time, although it may well increase in the near future.) There is no convincing reason why the United States should try to go it alone in forging economic and security ties with a prospective group of regional states in the Persian Gulf. But there are all sorts of good reasons for doing so in cooperation with some other oil-consuming nations of the Western world.

Existing economic and military ties with the Gulf states, of course, already involve the OECD governments and corporations. This is partly due to the common interest of the Gulf states in diversifying the sources of their technology imports despite a general preference for American know-how. The European Community as a whole is a significant market for the Gulf states because of geographic proximity and the lesser cost of transportation, as well as traditional patterns of trade. As has been revealed in Euro-Arab and European-Iranian dialogues, this market would be of the greatest interest to Iran and Saudi Arabia for the future export of their petrochemicals. Western Europe has also been an important source of military equipment for the Gulf states. This is again the result of their determination to diversify their sources of arms, despite a general preference for American military equipment, especially sophisticated weapons.

Second, although an American near monopoly of arms supplies to the Gulf states would help our balance-of-payments deficit, the long-term cost is too great. Our excessive military sales to Iran became a major target of religious and political opposition to the Shah's regime not only because of the perceived economic and social harm involved but also because they symbolized the military and political commitment of the United States to the survival of an unpopular regime. A prudent future arms-sales policy would have a better chance of success if the Gulf states understood that despite their preference for American arms, the United States and its allies were committed to spreading the sale of military equipment among themselves. Such a common Western arms policy might reduce the pressure on Washington from the Gulf states for excessive amounts of American arms.

Third, and finally, increased bilateral partnerships between the United States and individual Gulf states that seem bound to result under Secretary Brown's new security formula would tend to entail even greater American omnipresence in the Gulf region, whereas the Iranian Revolution has shown that this should be all the more avoided. The excessive presence of nationals from any one nation would inevitably become unpalatable to indigenous populations, not only as a perceived infringement on their political independence but also as an imagined affront to their cultural and religious values.

In sum, a comprehensive economic and security partnership between a group of Gulf and OECD countries along the lines suggested in this essay would in the long run better contribute to the processes of regional order as well as peacemaking in the Middle East than would the security formula of Secretary Brown. Since the chances of regional cooperation are far greater in the Persian Gulf sub-area than in the Arab-Israeli zone of the Middle East, the Persian Gulf model of indigenous security arrangements could be expanded subsequently to include the other interested states, including Israel, when the Arab-Israeli conflict is satisfactorily resolved.[3]

Moreover, comprehensive security cooperation among a group of Gulf and OECD states would place the United States in a better position to pursue the larger long-term goal of establishing "rules of the game" between the superpowers in the Middle East. Without the threat of the Soviet hand on the economic throat of the Western industrial democracies and Japan at the Strait of Hormuz, the United States would eventually be able to enter into negotiations with Moscow from a position of strength. These would be aimed at the threefold objective of mutual reduction of arms supplies to the Middle East, mutual limitations on naval deployment and use of base facilities in areas adjacent to the Gulf, and mutual acceptance of restraints on direct and indirect intervention in local conflicts in and around the Persian Gulf.

In the foreseeable future, however, the vital interests of the industrial democracies and those of the Gulf states, which are basically compatible, must be protected by means of any combination of skillful multilateral and alliance diplomacy that the realities of the situation permit. The challenge to American leadership is unmistakably clear. The courage and resourcefulness with which it is met today will make a significant difference to world peace and prosperity to the end of the century.

NOTES

1. See R. K. Ramazani, *The Persian Gulf: Iran's Role* (Charlottesville, 1972), 96–102.

2. See Lucian W. Pye, *Aspects of Political Development* (Boston, 1966), 8. I have called attention to the utility of Professor Pye's concept of "world culture" with respect to the study of modernization and Islam. See R. K. Ramazani, "Islamic Studies: A Concept and Approach," guest editorial in *Muslim World*, October 1968, 279–83.

3. I argued before the Iranian Revolution that American policymakers should not compartmentalize the Middle Eastern problems into those of the Arab-Israeli and Persian Gulf sub-areas as if they were separable, since the problem of order-building is universal in the entire Middle East. See R. K. Ramazani, *Beyond the Arab-Israeli Settlement: New Directions for U.S. Policy in the Middle East* (Cambridge, MA, 1977).

THE STRAIT OF HORMUZ

The Global Chokepoint

Ensuring the uninterrupted flow of Persian Gulf oil to world markets through the Strait of Hormuz is an economic, a political, and a strategic imperative. Yet fears and suspicions as to how this basic goal might be achieved tend to complicate both the identification of the problems involved and the proposals for overcoming them. Shah Mohammed Reza Pahlavi used to exaggerate the vulnerability of the strait in order to demonstrate the indispensability of his regime to the maintenance of the strait's security with the assistance of the United States. The Iranian revolutionary regime seems to exaggerate the invulnerability of the strait in order to show that regime's independence from the United States. Within the Western world there are those who overestimate the vulnerability of the strait as a means of pushing military contingency plans for quick reaction to Persian Gulf crises, and others underestimate its vulnerability in order to discourage plans for U.S. military intervention.

This essay attempts to steer away from these preconceived notions. There must be room for a rational and objective discussion of this admittedly important subject. It argues that the Strait of Hormuz is potentially the world's most important economic chokepoint and that it can be transformed into an active chokepoint by a variety of conflict situations. It also seeks to propose that the uninterrupted flow of Gulf oil to world markets through the strait might be aided by cooperative efforts such as the creation of a common patrol authority as well as unilateral and bilateral arrangements aimed at minimizing threats of disruption. Finally, it speculates that the establishment of such an authority might, in the long run, aid further efforts toward regional cooperation and, it is to be hoped, ease superpower tensions in and around the strategic Strait of Hormuz.

THE IMPORTANCE OF THE STRAIT

A complex of geographic, economic, and legal factors combine to characterize the Strait of Hormuz as a potential global chokepoint. To begin with, the strait is wider than the other major Indian Ocean straits that are traversed by oil tankers. Nowhere in its 104-mile length is it narrower than the

"The Strait of Hormuz: The Global Chokepoint" was originally published in *The Indian Ocean and Global Politics*, ed. Larry W. Bowman and Ian Clark (Boulder: Westview Press, 1981), 7–20.

Strait of Bab el Mandeb at the entrance to the Red Sea, the Strait of Tiran at the entrance to the Gulf of Aqaba, the Strait of Malacca, or the Strait of Singapore. This should be no cause for comfort, however, because (a) none of those other straits carries as much tanker traffic as the Strait of Hormuz; (b) the more favorable width of the strait does not necessarily mean that all of its waters are navigable; and (c) the strait itself and its northern terminus, which forms the entrance to the Persian Gulf, are studded with numerous islands. Although the strait's entrance to the Gulf of Oman is more than fifty nautical miles wide, it narrows to slightly over twenty miles at its northeastern end between Larak Island on the Iranian side and the Quoins on the Omani side. The oil tanker traffic is, in fact, heavily concentrated in Omani territorial waters, where the deeper navigational channels exist.

The economic stakes in the Strait of Hormuz are global in nature. Although it connects the high seas through the Gulf of Oman to only a semi-enclosed sea, rather than to other high seas, it is the world's most important international oil highway, because the Persian Gulf happens to be the world's largest known site of oil reserves and production. Concern about oil prices tends to focus world attention on the OPEC countries as a cartel at the expense of an adequate appreciation of the overriding importance of the Gulf states as the main suppliers of the world's oil. The six Gulf states of OPEC (Saudi Arabia, Iran, Iraq, Kuwait, the United Arab Emirates, and Qatar) produce roughly 30 million barrels of oil daily, and the seven non-Gulf states of OPEC (Libya, Venezuela, Algeria, Nigeria, Indonesia, Gabon, and Ecuador) produce only 3 million barrels a day. This means that 57 percent of the world oil trade must pass in oil tankers through the Strait of Hormuz to world markets at the rate of one every eleven minutes.

Given this overwhelming share of the Gulf states in the total OPEC supplies, the vital importance of the Strait of Hormuz to the major oil-consuming nations becomes obvious. Japan receives almost 90 percent of its oil imports from OPEC; Western Europe, about 80 percent; and the United States, approximately 70 percent. Although the United States is the world's single largest producer of oil (about 10.3 million barrels a day), it is simultaneously the world's largest single consumer of it—about 19 million barrels a day in 1979. The Tokyo-agreement ceiling for the United States of 8.5 million barrels of oil imports a day through 1985 would hardly begin to dent the pressure of the U.S. demand on the world oil supply. President Carter's ambitious goal of cutting U.S. imports in half over a decade still leaves open the immediate and continuing problem of U.S. dependence on foreign oil, even assuming total success for U.S. projected efforts at conservation and its search for alternative sources of energy, as well as stepped-up U.S. exploration for oil in the United States.

The Strait of Hormuz is even more vitally important to the Gulf states themselves. Given the fact that oil revenues constitute the backbone of the Gulf economy, oil exports through the strait must be maintained. Even Iraq, which exports a higher percentage of its oil through pipelines than any other Gulf state, is heavily dependent on the uninterrupted flow of oil exports through the strait. Furthermore, all Gulf states are vitally dependent on non-oil seaborne trade. The flow of capital goods for economic development, food supplies, and arms from the outside world is on the rise, despite the drop in Iran's arms imports since the fall of the Shah's regime.

At the moment the Strait of Hormuz is less significant to the Soviet Union and the states belonging to COMECON (Council for Mutual Economic Assistance). The trade of socialist states with Iraq is important, but it is by no means as significant as the overall trade of the West with Iraq. The trade of prerevolutionary Iran was important to Moscow, but the bulk of the Iranian trade with the Soviet Union takes place overland rather than through the strait. However, there are strong indications that the Soviet Union is already feeling the energy squeeze because of shortfalls in its planned oil production, and it may well become a competitor of the major noncommunist oil customers of the Gulf states in the near future.

In contrast to the socialist states, the less developed countries (LDCs) are significantly dependent on oil tanker traffic through the Strait of Hormuz. Between fifty and sixty LDCs import Gulf oil, and in 1977 it was estimated that LDCs would receive over 5 million barrels a day from the Persian Gulf area. Although the OPEC nations dislike hearing about the so-called South-South dichotomy between the oil-rich and the oil-poor nations of the underdeveloped world, a disruption of the oil flow from the Gulf would adversely affect many Brazils and Thailands of the Third World, as every oil price rise does. The World Bank program of technically aiding the LDCs to produce their own oil might make them self-sufficient in a decade, although at the moment that is more a matter of hope than of prediction. In the meantime they—like the Gulf states, Japan, and the Western industrialized world—will be dependent on an uninterrupted flow of oil through the Strait of Hormuz.

The uncertainty of international legal norms compounds the problems of such an uninterrupted flow of oil through the strait. If most coastal states of the world extended their territorial sea limit from the traditional three to the current twelve miles, some 116 international straits would be brought under sovereign jurisdiction of coastal states. The Strait of Hormuz is no exception. Both Iran and Oman, the two Persian Gulf states bordering the strait, claim twelve miles of territorial sea. As a result, the narrow section of the strait that falls roughly between latitude 30°–50° north and longitude 30°–20° east would lie completely within their claimed sovereign jurisdiction, and therefore there would be no high sea in that area of the strait and no free airspace above it. Even if this were not the case, there would still be the problem that the vessels entering the strait customarily proceeded within Omani waters, where the main channels of navigation exist.

The uncertainty about general international legal norms and the unilateral extension of the Iranian and Omani territorial sea limits parallel the absence of any particular agreement governing the Strait of Hormuz. Prior to the Iranian Revolution, Oman and Iran agreed (March 7, 1974) to ensure the safety of navigation by joint patrol. Although legally Oman was a participant in patrolling the strait, in actual practice only Iran had the requisite naval capacity to maintain the safety of navigation. The revolutionary situation in Iran has raised questions about the status of the Omani-Iranian agreement.

Unlike the Turkish straits, which are governed by the Montreux Convention, no legal regime as yet has been determined for the Strait of Hormuz. In light of the vital, global economic significance of this international waterway, the absence of any governing legal norms in general or agreement among the Gulf states in particular adds to the uncertainty of freedom and safety of navigation.

POTENTIAL THREATS TO THE STRAIT

Conflict situations might transform the Strait of Hormuz from a potential to an active global chokepoint. These situations generally fall into three broad categories: interstate conflicts, domestic crises, and acts of non-state entities. Interstate conflicts fall into three subcategories: conflict between the superpowers, between the Gulf states and major oil-consuming nations, and among regional states.

In a general nuclear or conventional war between the United States and the Soviet Union, the blockage of the Strait of Hormuz must be assumed. Given its vital economic significance to the industrialized democracies and its close geographic proximity to the Soviet Union, the strait would probably be mined by the Soviet Union in order to cripple the West. In peacetime it is unlikely that the Soviet Union would bluntly cut the flow of oil supplies through the strait unless the Soviet Union was prepared to risk a nuclear war with the NATO countries.

The second type of interstate conflict that might make oil tanker traffic hazardous through the Strait of Hormuz would be hostile military intervention by the United States in the Persian Gulf oil fields. It is often suggested that such intervention would be countered by retaliatory destruction of oil installations. But such a drastic course of self-inflicting action would probably be less acceptable to the Gulf states than the closure of the strait, which in the short term would hurt the United States more than the Gulf states. A retaliatory course of action, however, would hurt not only the interventionist power but every country in the world that is dependent on Gulf oil supplies and all Gulf states that are dependent on imports. Quite apart from the risks of such retaliatory measures, possibly unacceptable military risks, such as Soviet military intervention, or the infeasibility of successful operations have been cited as arguments against U.S. military intervention in the Gulf oil fields. In any event, the creation of a quick-reaction military strike force was still in the planning stage in late 1979, despite the fact that the idea of such a force had been discussed at the Pentagon as early as the late 1960s.

The third type of interstate conflict that might render the oil tanker traffic through the Strait of Hormuz hazardous would be armed conflict in the regions adjacent to the Persian Gulf area. Until the conclusion of the Egyptian-Israeli peace treaty, the most obvious such conflict was the Arab-Israeli one. Even if no oil embargo were to be imposed in any new Arab-Israeli war, the strait would be blocked as a consequence of a rapid spread of hostilities to the Gulf area. The Arab states of the Gulf would participate in a new war against Israel, partly because both opportunities and capabilities for arms transfer from the Gulf states to the "confrontation states" of the Middle East increased after the 1973 Arab-Israeli war. But the peace treaty between Egypt and Israel may well have decreased the chances of disruption of oil tanker traffic through the strait to the extent that the treaty has reduced the threat of an outbreak of a new war.

Besides interstate conflicts, internal wars might disrupt the oil flow through the Strait of Hormuz. At the moment the only case in point is the possible revival of the civil war in Oman. The insurgency in the Omani province of Dhofar was declared crushed by Sultan Qabus bin Said in December 1975, largely as a result of successful Iranian-Omani joint military operations. Subsequently Iran's military presence in Oman was actually terminated in the course of Iran's revolution. As early as 1971 the Popular Front for the Liberation of Oman and the Arabian Gulf (PFLOAG) guerrillas attempted to occupy the Omani enclave at the tip of Musandam Peninsula, overlooking the Strait of Hormuz. With the Iranian military withdrawal from Oman and the abandonment of air and naval outposts in the region, the Dhofari rebellion was expected to revive. However, as late as September 1979, when I visited Oman, there was no major sign of concern about the revival of the Dhofari rebels. Sultan Qabus lost his major Gulf ally when the Shah fell, and the Sultan has become all the more aware of the threat that the rebels could pose to the strait as well as to his regime. Clearly, the fall of Oman to forces hostile to Western interests could pose a serious threat to the safety of navigation through the strait. During my visit to the Musandam Peninsula, I was told of two plans undertaken by Oman for the better protection of the safety of navigation through the strait. One plan, which reportedly went into effect on November 1, 1979, was to move the inbound and outbound shipping channels to safer and deeper waters north of the traditional channels by establishing a new separation zone. The other plan was to improve navigational safety by completing facilities on the island of Ghanam, near the village of Khassab, at the tip of the peninsula. Presumably these efforts would reduce the chances of terrorist attacks on oil tankers.

The prospect of successful terrorist attacks on oil tankers, however, is hotly debated for two reasons. First, it is argued that many bypasses in the strait are beyond the effective range of most weapons on the shore. Second, it is pointed out that armed guerrillas would find it difficult, if not impossible, to attack oil tankers without a base from which the guerrillas could operate. Nevertheless, the U.S. Department of State warned about the possibility of terrorist attacks on oil tankers in July 1979, and Sheikh Ahmad Zaki Yamani, the Saudi Arabian oil minister, stated the problem as follows: "The Palestinians are growing ever more desperate, and I wouldn't be surprised if one day they sank one or two supertankers in the Strait of Hormuz, to force the world to do something about their plight and Israel's obstinacy. This would block the channel through which pass 19 million barrels daily. This would make the present crisis seem like child's play."[1]

Assuming that terrorist attacks could take place, which I doubt, it is unlikely that the sinking of "one or two" tankers could actually block the strait. Nevertheless, it could produce great fears about the vulnerability of the strait's channels.

A more hazardous situation could arise, however, if instead of an attack on oil tankers by tactical rockets from the shore, the navigable channels of the strait were seeded with mines. This kind of action is apparently more within the realm of possibility. Both Iran and Saudi Arabia are equipped with minesweepers; thus the Gulf states themselves have some capacity for such action should the need arise. The revolution in Iran has by no means lessened Iran's interest in the safety of navigation through the strait, although the Iranian naval authorities today, as contrasted with the period before the fall of the Shah's regime, are far more skeptical about the prospects of terrorist attacks on oil tankers.

PROTECTING THE STRAIT

What could reasonably be done to minimize the potential threats to the uninterrupted flow of oil to world markets through the Strait of Hormuz? As noted, such threats would most likely arise from regional wars, internal wars, or terrorist acts rather than from U.S. military intervention in Gulf oil fields or from a direct, deliberate interdiction of oil tankers by the Soviet Union. Apparently for the purposes of assuring Saudi Arabia and other friendly Arab states of U.S. support in the aftermath of the Shah's downfall, of putting the Soviet

Union on notice that the United States is determined to defend its vital interests in the region, and of preparing for swift military action in the event of a real and clear threat to U.S. vital interests, the Carter administration agreed on June 21–22, 1979, to undertake a modest increase in the U.S. military presence in the Indian Ocean–Middle East area. This was believed to mean that one or two destroyers would be added to a small flagship and two destroyers. It also meant that (1) the number of regular U.S. task force deployments in the Indian Ocean would increase from three to four a year; (2) U.S. air force combat aircraft would stage more routine "demonstration" visits into Arab countries; and (3) a new emphasis would be placed on military sales and high-level contacts with Oman and the smaller sheikhdoms of the Persian Gulf.[2]

These recommendations formed part of a continuous review of U.S. options in the area, particularly in light of the ripple effects of the Iranian Revolution on the security of the Persian Gulf. The recommendations were the early results of the process set in motion in February 1979, when U.S. Defense Secretary Harold Brown visited the Middle East. In an appraisal of Secretary Brown's proposals to the Middle East leaders at the time, I evaluated the advantages and disadvantages of his formula and suggested alternatively the necessity and the feasibility of security cooperation between the countries of the Organization for Economic Cooperation and Development (OECD) and the Persian Gulf states.[3] My principal concern was that the United States might be inclined to proceed alone, without appropriate consultation with other OECD countries and particularly without taking adequate note of the sensibilities of the local states and the lessons of the Iranian Revolution. I argued that "the vital interests of the industrialized democracies and those of the Gulf states, which are basically compatible, must be protected by means of any combination of skillful multilateral and alliance diplomacy."[4] If the modest and symbolic increase in the U.S. military presence is not intended to exclude U.S. security cooperation with regional and OECD states, it may well aid such cooperation in the foreseeable future for the security of the Persian Gulf area in general.

In the context of this essay, however, there is the more specific need to protect the international oil tanker traffic through the Strait of Hormuz. The security of this strategic waterway, as a global chokepoint, must be accorded the highest priority. For the bulk of the Persian Gulf oil to reach world markets without interruption, the security of the oil tanker traffic through the strait must be assured. Even when all other major chokepoints of the Indian Ocean—such as the Strait of Bab el Mandeb, the Mozambique Channel, the Strait of Malacca, and others—are secure, that security will be no cause for comfort as long as there are still potential threats to the safety of navigation through the Strait of Hormuz.

The protection of oil tanker traffic must be the business of the local states as well as of the interested and capable external powers. There is not a single local state that would benefit from the interruption of the oil flow through the strait, and more importantly, all the Gulf states have shown that they are vitally interested in maintaining the freedom of navigation through the strait as a matter of principle. The immediate need for the protection of oil tanker traffic through the strait, however, cannot wait for the universal adoption of that principle through the extremely slow process of the Law of the Sea Conference. The littoral states have repeatedly stated that because of the particular characteristics of the Persian Gulf and the Strait of Hormuz, they would prefer bilateral or regional arrangements (not necessarily to the exclusion of a universal agreement) as a means of creating legal norms governing maritime security, safety of navigation, prevention of pollution, fisheries, and the exploration and exploitation of resources. They have already signed an important convention for the prevention of pollution (April 24, 1978) with the help of the United Nations, and there is reason to believe that they can also agree on the maintenance of the freedom of navigation through the Strait of Hormuz. Although the Iranian-Omani bilateral agreement (March 7, 1974) provided for the security of the strait, it failed to enjoy the acceptance of the other Gulf states because, in effect, Iranian power dominated the strait as British power had previously.

A Gulf-wide agreement on the regime of the Strait of Hormuz could aid the safety of international navigation there. Like the Montreux Convention governing the Turkish straits, such an agreement among the Gulf states would ensure a degree of predictability. At the moment not only is the Strait of Hormuz unguarded, but its status is shrouded in ambiguity. The clarification of legal norms governing the status of the strait would obviously not automatically assure security for oil tanker traffic, but it could be a first step toward that goal.

To achieve that goal, however, any agreement on the regime of the Strait of Hormuz must be backed by power. Given the vital interests of the major oil-consuming nations in the freedom of navigation through the strait, it would seem unreasonable to expect them to refrain from unilateral measures, including improvement of their military presence, to protect their vital interests. This is especially true as long as the Gulf states themselves are unwilling or unable to agree either on the governing principles or on the requisite power to support them. This is exactly why the often-stated ideal of "local security by local powers" has had a hollow ring to it to date. In the long run that ideal would have a better chance of realization if the regional states could first cooperate among themselves and later combine their efforts with those of interested external powers as a means of enhancing the prospects of effective protection of the safety of navigation. Given the suspicion of some Gulf–Indian Ocean states about the Western powers' motives, it would be advisable not to prejudice such an effort by planning to involve the oil-consuming nations of the West at the very outset. This might have been the main reason for the rejection of the Omani proposals by Iraq in the summer of 1979, although the foreign minister of Oman denied that his country had suggested Western participation.

Unfortunately, the deterioration of relations among the Gulf states since the Iranian Revolution would seem to reduce the prospects of cooperation among them. The pronouncements and actions of some Iranian clerical leaders have stirred deep concern in Bahrain and Kuwait about the intentions of the revolutionary regime, despite repeated assurances that Iran does not plan to export its revolution, opposes interference in the affairs of other states, and denies the revival of its territorial claim to Bahrain. Iraq's denunciation of its 1975 Shatt al-Arab agreement with Iran has the potential of reversing all the hopeful signs of accommodation among the Gulf states that followed that agreement. Nevertheless, one would hope that enlightened self-interest would make the Gulf states realize that their goal of economic and political self-reliance cannot be aided by the increase in tensions and conflict situations. On the contrary, such circumstances have historically made the Gulf states more vulnerable to foreign manipulation, interference, and intervention.

FUTURE PROSPECTS FOR THE STRAIT

It is to be hoped that eventual cooperation between the regional and interested external powers for the protection of the oil tanker traffic through the Strait of Hormuz will produce significant positive effects on the wider concerns of the Indian Ocean states and the superpowers. The notions of a zone of peace, a nuclear free zone, demilitarization, an Asian collective-security system, an Asian common market, and the like, have been bandied about for a long time. Regardless of their merits or demerits, they have one thing in common. They are too broad, too ambitious, and largely unrealistic. There is nothing wrong with dreaming big dreams, but one must care about their realization.

The idea of common efforts for the protection of oil tanker traffic through the Strait of Hormuz does not have the high-sounding effects of any of those other ideas, but it is more concrete and perhaps more practicable. It should be much easier, for example, to organize a small common patrol authority to supervise the passage of oil tankers through the strait than to provide a universal security arrangement for the entire Persian Gulf–Indian Ocean area.

There is every reason to believe that such a modest and concrete cooperative effort in a matter of vital importance to all concerned could act as a catalyst for larger long-term goals of cooperation among the Indian Ocean states. For example, the idea of a common patrol authority for the Strait of Hormuz could be expanded to a common patrol authority for the Indian Ocean if it proved attainable and effective in practice. Obviously the creation of a larger authority for the Indian Ocean would require the cooperation of states bordering the other major chokepoints in the Indian Ocean, and it would be unrealistic to start with such a grand idea. It is more vital, urgent, and feasible to begin with the idea of an authority for the strait and hope that the idea will catch on as a model for cooperation in the Indian Ocean as a whole. Furthermore, cooperation on one complex set of problems, such as the protection of oil tanker traffic through the Indian Ocean chokepoints, may well have a salutary effect on interested leaders for working together on other common problems. This sectoral approach to the problem of regional cooperation has already been attempted successfully in the Persian Gulf area with respect to prevention of pollution, delimitation of the continental shelf, peaceful settlement of disputes, research on solar energy, reclamation of desert lands, water conservation, and medical care.

High-sounding but unrealistic proposals are not, of course, the monopoly of regional academicians and practitioners. The goal of superpower cooperation in the general area of the Indian Ocean has not been helped in the past by such dramatic pronouncements as President Carter's call for "complete demilitarization" of the Indian Ocean (March 16, 1977). The Soviet Union has no vital economic interest in the Strait of Hormuz at the present time, although it has considerable political and strategic interests in the general Indian Ocean–Persian Gulf area. One need not view these Soviet interests from a doctrinaire geopolitical perspective of a Soviet design for land and naval encirclement of the entire Eurasian landmass to realize their nature. The actual behavior of the Soviet Union reveals that ever since the end of World War II Moscow has sought to expand its power and influence—at the expense of the West in general and the United States in particular—in a widening circle of regional states lying south of the Soviet Union's borders. The Soviet thrust into the Northern Tier, the Eastern Mediterranean, and finally into the Indian Ocean–Persian Gulf area has concentrated in each case on a chokepoint—the Turkish straits, the Suez Canal, and the Strait of Hormuz, respectively. In none of these regions have instruments of Soviet policy been confined to the deployment of naval arms, although Soviet naval power has increased enormously in the Indian Ocean area since 1968. In that area Soviet instruments have included the encouragement of the nationalization of Western oil companies, acquisition of oil and gas privileges for the Soviet Union, propaganda attacks on Western military sales, transfer of Soviet arms, encouragement of communist participation in national-front governments, support of communist coups and national liberation movements, and massive infusion of Soviet and Cuban arms supplies and military personnel.

Soviet-U.S. competition in the Indian Ocean–Persian Gulf area has increased substantially since the Iranian Revolution. President Carter strengthened U.S. naval forces in the area in March 1979, dispatching the 80,000-ton carrier *Constellation* and several escorting warships. The Soviet navy sent the 40,000-ton *Minsk*, two powerful guided-missile cruisers, and the *Ivan Rogov*, the biggest warship ever built by the Soviet Union. This Soviet move brought superpower naval muscle flexing to the northwest quadrant of the Indian Ocean for the first time.

The creation of a common patrol authority for the Strait of Hormuz proposed in this essay may well reduce Soviet-U.S. competition at this vital chokepoint. Any common action that ensures the uninterrupted flow of Gulf oil to world markets would minimize global unease in time of crisis. Furthermore, one would hope that the reduction of tensions between the two superpowers at this potential global chokepoint would eventually enable the United States and the Soviet Union to enter into calm and realistic negotiations aimed at the long-term objectives of the mutual reduction of arms supplies to regional powers, mutual limitations on naval deployment and use of base facilities in areas adjacent to the Strait of Hormuz, and mutual acceptance of restraints on direct and indirect intervention in local conflicts in the Indian Ocean.

NOTES

1. See the text of Yamani's interview with senior editor Arnaud de Borchgrave, in *Newsweek*, 9 July 1979, 21.

2. *Washington Post*, 1 July 1979.

3. R. K. Ramazani, "Security in the Persian Gulf," pp. 215–28 in this volume.

4. Ibid.

SHIISM IN THE PERSIAN GULF

The world's oil heartland also happens to be the Shii heartland. Out of an estimated 750 million Muslims in the world, about 11 percent are Shia. More than half of them are Twelver or Imami Shia who live in the Persian Gulf region, as majorities of the citizen populations in Bahrain, Iran, and Iraq and as minorities in Kuwait, Oman, Qatar, Saudi Arabia, and the United Arab Emirates (UAE). Iran is the single largest Shii Muslim–inhabited country in the world as well as in the Gulf region; 95 percent of its 40 million citizens are Shia. Iran also happens to be the single most populous state, the most strategically located country—abutting at once the Soviet Union and the Strait of Hormuz—and putatively still the most powerful state of the region despite the recent material toll that the revolution and the war with Iraq have exacted.

Shiism in the Persian Gulf region may be viewed from different perspectives. It may be seen from the wider perspective of the resurgence of Islam in general and from Khomeini's perspective of what I call "Islam of the Oppressed" in particular. It may be studied as a Third World phenomenon, since, despite the oil wealth, the Gulf societies are essentially underdeveloped. And finally, it may be examined as a specimen of a worldwide surge of "fundamentalism" that encompasses Judaism and Christianity as well as Islam. Who could fail to notice the intriguing parallel behavior among "fundamentalists" in all three monotheistic religious traditions in the face of the existence of such radical groups as the Egyptian al-Takfir wa al-Hijra, the Shii Hizbollahi, some of the followers of the evangelist Jerry Falwell, and the Jewish Gush Emunim.

Such exercises in speculative thought, however, cannot aid the study of Shiism in the Gulf region. Empirical research, both documentary and in the field, forms the basis of the conception of Shiism in the Gulf in this essay,[1] although the broader relevance of this conception to the Middle East area as a whole will also be considered at the end. As conceived here, Shiism is both an ideological and a sociopolitical movement. It is the official creed of the Iranian state, a major determinant of its policies, and a major force that influences the behavior of Shii groups and individuals outside as well as within Iranian society, whether a given Shii group constitutes a minority or the majority of the population of a given Gulf society. The ideology involved in this definition is based primar-

"Shi'ism in the Persian Gulf" was originally published in Shi'ism and Social Protest, ed. Juan R. I. Cole and Nikki R. Keddie (New Haven: Yale University Press, 1986), 30–54.

ily on the interpretation of Islam by the Shii leader Ayatollah Ruhollah Khomeini, an interpretation that is today the official Iranian creed, embodied in the Constitution of the Islamic Republic of Iran, and the primary ideological force among his followers. Among the Shii populations in the other Gulf states, Khomeinism is to be sure an influential force for certain, but not all, groups, just as it is not for all Iranian Shii Muslims either.

As a sociopolitical movement, Shiism today is simultaneously both a negative and a positive force. It was more quietist than activist in the historical past. Negatively, it is a widespread movement of social and political protest against perceived domestic "tyranny" (zulm) and foreign domination (tahmil), a movement supported yesterday by a wide variety of groups as well as the followers of Khomeini against the Shah's regime and supported today primarily by diverse Shii groups within the other Gulf societies, although not exclusively by them. Positively, it is a widely shared social and political aspiration for a better life, especially for justice and equity, an aspiration that was shared yesterday by various lay and religious forces in Iran and is shared today primarily by the Sunni-dominated Shii groups in the other Gulf societies.

Most important of all, the conception of Shiism as both an ideological and a sociopolitical movement in this study is informed by a complex legacy of emotional and spiritual frustration and hope, a mix of sentiments that is deeply rooted in the experience and eschatology of the Shii cultural tradition. The frustration stems largely from the repeated failure of Shii leaders in actual historical circumstances over the centuries to realize an ideally just society for their community. And the hope springs from an abiding chiliastic faith that ultimately the just society will be established by the messianic Mahdi, who will appear (zuhur) before the Day of Resurrection (qiyamah, or ruz-i qiyamat, as the Iranians popularly call it). Neither Khomeini's ideology—especially as it relates to his conceptions of government and international politics—nor the social and political protest and aspirations of the Shii people can be fully comprehended without bearing in mind this profound ethos of the Shii cultural tradition.

Essential for an understanding of Shiism as an ideological movement in the Persian Gulf today is first an analysis of Khomeini's conception of security in the Gulf within the context of his basic ideas about government and international politics. Then Shiism as a sociopolitical movement will be analyzed by selecting three case studies of the Shia in Iraq, Saudi Arabia, and Bahrain. At the end, the broader relevance of this study to the question of Shiism in the Middle East as a whole is considered with a view to its policy implications.

KHOMEINI'S CONCEPTION OF
SECURITY IN THE PERSIAN GULF

Khomeini's conception of security in the Persian Gulf requires three conditions. First, all states of the area should establish for themselves "true Islamic governments." What should these governments be like? The answer partly lies in understanding the centrality of the idea of the guardianship of the jurisprudent—*Velayat-e Faqih*, "rule of the leading cleric"—in Khomeini's political thought. Regardless of the scholarly controversy about the compatibility of that idea with the Shii tradition, Khomeini's interpretation requires that all spiritual and temporal authority be vested in a supreme jurisprudent (*faqih*) or, in the absence of consensus on one person, in a group of supreme jurisprudents (*fuqaha*). Does this mean that all Gulf states should establish governments that are identical with the Iranian government? In Khomeini's view the answer is no; it would suffice for their new governments to be similar to, if not identical with, the Iranian model. What does that similarity imply? The answer is not wholly clear, but it is evident that besides clerical rule—instead of "shameful and reactionary" monarchies—true Islamic government must also be supported by all strata of the people, especially by the disinherited (*mustaz'afeen*).

The second prerequisite for Gulf security is "true independence." This condition requires complete severance of all "links and associations" between the littoral states of the Gulf and the superpowers. This requirement should be examined in light of Khomeini's view of the international system as a whole. His conception of that system rejects the primacy of the territorial state as the basis of the modern international system because the ephemeral idea of the territorial state is the creation of mortal man. In place of such a system, he desires what I call an "Islamic world order."[2] He believes that such an order will be eventually established as a result of the formation of an "Islamic world government," and that such a government in turn will be realized ultimately with the appearance (*zuhur*) of the absent Twelfth Imam as the messianic Mahdi, or Master of the Age (*Sahib-i Zaman*). In his absence (*ghaibah*), however, the ground should be prepared for the coming of the Mahdi by creating the rule of the *faqih*, to whom all legitimate temporal and spiritual authority belongs during the waiting period.

The policies of the state of the *faqih*, aiming as they do at the eventual creation of such an Islamic world order, will inevitably entail confrontation between that state and the superpowers. Such a conflict is inevitable because the superpowers have arrogated all power (*qudrat*) to themselves. In Khomeini's own words, "We must settle our accounts with great and superpowers, and show them that we can take on the whole world ideologically, despite all the painful problems that face us."[3] It is in the context of these basic ideas that the

Iranian slogan "Neither East nor West, only the Islamic republic" (*nah sharq, nah gharb, faqat jumhuri-i Islami*) should be understood, not the irrelevant notions of equidistance or nonalignment as these terms are ordinarily understood. Khomeini's view differs from Mosaddegh's idea of negative equilibrium (*movazeneh-ye manfi*), and especially from the Shah's so-called positive nationalism. These ideas in effect accept the Western notion of power politics, whereas Khomeini's religious, millenarian, and idealistic view rejects the global role of both superpowers; they are both considered to be illegitimate players in the international system they dominate.

Any country, including the Gulf states, that has close and necessarily dependent relations with the superpowers is also considered to be an illegitimate player in the world arena, simply by association. The United States is the Great Satan (*shaitan-i buzurg*), and its Gulf associates are mini-Satans (*shaitanha-yi kuchik*). The Soviet Union is regarded as a lesser Satan, but it is satanic nevertheless. Both superpowers belong to the camp of the oppressors (*mustakbarin*), which dominates the camp of the oppressed peoples (*mustaz'afeen*). In Khomeini's Quranic-inspired sentence, "The oppressed or the meek must triumph over the dominant powers" (*bayad mustaz'afeen bar mustakbarin ghalabih kunand*).

The key notion that underlies the denunciation of the current role of the superpowers and their associates is domination (*tahmil*). It is a notion closely related to the historical Shii concern with tyranny (*zulm*). Not only the "capitalist imperialists" and "socialist imperialists" but also their "Zionist, Fascist, Phalangist, and Communist instruments" as well belong to the oppressors' camp, whereas the economically poor, the socially disadvantaged, and the culturally deprived individuals, groups, and masses of people belong to the camp of the meek. In such a context, no state can claim true independence so long as it establishes and maintains intimate relations with super or lesser powers within the oppressors' camp.

The third ideological prerequisite for Gulf security is Arab acknowledgment of Iran's spiritual propriety and political primacy. To understand this requirement in its wider context, once again we have to relate it to Khomeini's more general ideas about government and international politics in the context of Shii cultural tradition. The key Shii notion here is salvation (*najah*). The ultimate establishment of the Islamic world order by means of the creation of the world government of the *faqih* has already been advanced one major step by the establishment of the first and only government of God on earth in Iran. In Khomeini's own words, "Islam is a sacred trust from God to ourselves, and the Iranian nation must grow in power and resolution until it has vouchsafed Islam to the entire world." In such a context, the liberation of mankind is a divine obligation of the Iranian people, an obligation that makes Iran in Khomeini's view what

I call the Redeemer Nation. In pointing out this notion of special leadership qualification of Iran for the creation of the virtuous political order everywhere, one of Khomeini's disciples states, for example, that if the Muslims want the establishment of Muhammad's Islam, they should entrust the political leadership of their countries to a religious leader, and "this magnificent fact has only come to the Islamic country of Iran, and Imam Khomeini . . . has accepted the responsibility for the political leadership, formation of the Islamic Government as well as the Commander-in-Chief of the Armed Forces."[4]

For the sake of Gulf security, other Gulf states should acknowledge not only Iran's spiritual propriety but also its political primacy. In Khomeini's view, all power is a divine gift. But from a historical perspective his perception of Iran's political primacy in the Gulf region resembles significantly the view of all past Iranian secular rulers as well. The Shah used to talk about Iran's security perimeter (harim-i amniyyat), and Iranian leaders today speak of its security umbrella (chatr-i amniyyat). In the words of Hojatoleslam Hashemi Rafsanjani, Speaker of the Majlis, "We declare once again that the security of the Persian Gulf is more important to us than to any other party, and we will strive to maintain the Gulf's [security] as much as we can. If one day we should despair as a result of the enemy's [Iraqi] madness and recklessness and are compelled to make the Gulf unsafe, then no one will be able to prevent us."[5] This means that although the revolutionary regime has rejected the Shah's notion of Iran as the policeman of the Gulf on behalf of the United States, it has by no means abandoned the idea of Iran's political primacy in the entire Gulf region. This also means that although revolutionary Iran, like prerevolutionary Iran, accepts the general notion of Gulf security by Gulf states, it continues to consider itself as primus inter pares.

It ought to be obvious from the foregoing analysis that Khomeini's views about government and international politics in general and his conception of the requirements of security in the Persian Gulf in particular make it mandatory for Iran to export its Islamic Revolution. But the significance of the subject makes it necessary to examine it in greater detail. Does Khomeini's ideology specifically require such an export? If it does, what means are considered permissible? Can force be used as a legitimate means? And what kind of peaceful means are considered to be most desirable?

Clearly, in Khomeini's view export of the Islamic Revolution is obligatory. In his own words, for example, "We should export our revolution to the world," and "today we need to strengthen and export Islam everywhere. You need to export Islam to other places, and the same version of Islam which is currently in power in our country." The source of this obligation is the view that only in Iran has the government of God been established, and as the Redeemer Nation, Iran must aim at the liberation of mankind from the yoke of the superpowers and their allies, who dominate the structure of the international system.

What is not so clear in Khomeini's ideology, however, is the kind of means that he considers legitimate for exporting the revolution. On numerous occasions, he has declared categorically that "swords" should not be used. For example, on one occasion he said, "It does not take swords to export this ideology. The export of ideas by force is not export"; on another occasion he said, "When we say we want to export our revolution, we do not want to do it with swords." But what does this mean? Does it mean that the use of force is prohibited? No clear answer has been given so far on the specific meaning of such a prohibition, and hence I shall explore this question further within the context of Khomeini's view of war rather than export of revolution.

His idea of war follows the traditional Shii legal theory. He considers resorting to holy war (*jihad*) as the prerogative of only the infallible imam, and in his absence the *faqih* is stopped from waging an offensive war. But defensive war (*jang-e defai*) is another matter since it is in self-defense, and hence the *faqih* is duty-bound to resort to it by all means. Generally, this conception of use of force appears to be compatible with the modern principles of international law. Article 51 of the Charter of the United Nations embodies such a principle, although it is well known how troublesome this Charter principle has always been. Given the primacy of states in the existing international system, governments do not ordinarily submit to an impartial forum the question of what constitutes self-defense; they usually act as judges in their own cause, especially if they expect an impartial judgment to go against them.

The problem of what constitutes self-defense, however, raises even more difficult questions in the case of Khomeini's international legal thought. The fundamental reason for this is his rejection of the primacy of the territorial state, as explained before. In his view the defense of what he calls "the homeland" appears time and again after "the defense of Islam." If this implies that defending Islam rather than Iran is a higher value in theory, then the problem arises seriously in practice since the abode of Islam transcends the boundaries of the Iranian state. To cite an important example, when Iran carried the war into Iraqi territory on July 13, 1982, it justified its action largely in terms of the defense of Islam. My view that the defense of Islam rather than Iran is the primary principle in Khomeini's theory of self-defense is evidenced also by his statement to the representatives of the Islamic Conference Organization. He told them categorically that their mediation efforts were contrary to the Quranic precept that requires that "if one tribe invades the other then all others are obliged to defend the latter in war, until they obey God. Once they obey God, then make peace with them." This sounds like what I call an Islamic conception of collective security. It shows that the value of Islamic faith is accorded a higher priority than that of the territorial state in Khomeini's theory of individual and collective self-defense.

Assuming that only defensive war is permissible, what about the use of force short of war? For example, does Khomeini's ideology allow acts of terrorism and subversion in exporting revolution? The question has obviously far-reaching practical implications in the light of the charges leveled against Iran for its alleged involvement in all kinds of terrorist acts in the Middle East, including the Gulf region. Again since no answer can be constructed on the basis of statements specifically on the subject of export of revolution, we should look elsewhere. The Iranian Constitution as well as Khomeini's own statements indicate that revolutionary Iran should observe the principle of noninterference ('adam-i dikhalat) in the affairs of other states. In admonishing the Gulf Arab leaders for supporting Iraq, for example, he declares, "We have neither ambition in, nor right to, any country, and God Almighty has granted us no permission to interfere in any country, unless it is solely a matter of self-defense." But what constitutes self-defense is as ambiguous here with respect to interference as in the case of war.

Is it any more clear what peaceful means are preferable in Khomeini's ideology? Without attempting to enumerate all kinds of acts short of use of military force, two major instruments in particular are highly valued for export of revolution. One is the example of Iranian Islamic behavior, and the other is publicity or propaganda. Khomeini urges Iranian diplomatic and consular as well as other officials, individuals, and groups of private citizens to observe Islamic ethics in their behavior as the best means of exporting revolution. He also places a great deal of emphasis on the value of propaganda by private as well as official individuals and institutions for export of revolution. Given the great importance of the sermon in the Shii cultural tradition, it is considered to be one of the most powerful instruments for promoting Islamic revolution at home and abroad.

The prominent role of the Iranian clerics in this respect is widely known, but the importance that Khomeini and his disciples attach to the role that foreign Muslim clerics should play in importing revolution into their own societies has been little noticed. Quite apart from receiving streams of individual clerics (ulama) from other Muslim countries since the revolution, the Iranian clerics, most particularly Khomeini and Montazeri, have been very keen in gathering together foreign ulama in Iran for the purpose of export of revolution. For example, Khomeini told some five hundred clerics during the final session of "the second global congress of the world Friday prayers leaders" on May 13, 1984: "You should discuss the situation in Iran. You should call on people to rebel like

Iran" (da'vat kunid mardum-ra bih-inkih nazir-i Iran qiyam kunand). He also said, "Friday imams, congregational imams, ulama of Islam all over the world, you should note that all the powers today have risen against Islam, and not against Iran. You should note that we all have great duties at this time. If they find the opportunity and if you do not pay attention, Islam will be uprooted."[6] They surely did pay attention. In closing their meeting, the congress members declared that they "accept Ayatullah al-'Uzma [the great sign of god] Imam Khomeini as having the necessary qualifications for the [I]mamat [leadership] of Muslims, and we will invite Muslims to follow his call." That, of course, includes Khomeini's most repeated call of all, the export of revolution.

Khomeini's call on the ulama to incite rebellion parallels his own repeated direct and indirect sermonizing to Gulf leaders; sometimes he has even condemned them for their alleged servility to foreign powers. For example, on one occasion he said: "It is hoped that the heads of these governments, some of whom are indulged in sensuality, some preoccupied with their debaucheries, some embroiled in clashes with their brethren, and some emasculated by their fear of the United States, will be awakened [by my warnings] into an Islamic humanitarian consciousness, thus putting an end to their sordid governments and rejecting all superpowers, just as our heroic nation has done."[7]

SHIISM: CONTAINMENT AND CONTAGION

As seen by the Gulf Arab leaders, revolutionary Iran presents a far more formidable threat than did the Shah's Iran. The degree of threat perceived differs from state to state, but what frightens them all is this addition of Khomeini's Shiism to Iran's putative political power. To be sure, the Gulf Arab leaders regarded the Shah's Iran as a hegemonic state, but this perception never concerned them the way Khomeini's Shiism does today. Paradoxically, at a time when the raw military power of the state in Iran, as opposed to the Shah's days, has declined and that of the Gulf Arab states relative to revolutionary Iran's has increased, the Gulf Arab leaders feel all the more threatened. The fundamental reason for this is the Arab fear of Shiism on two closely related levels.

On one level, Gulf Arab leaders fear Khomeini's hostile ideology backed by the power of the Iranian state. From the perspective of that ideology, their governmental systems are seen as basically illegitimate and their states as completely subservient to alien powers, and both conditions must be changed by the revolutionary establishment of truly Islamic government and truly independent states. As also seen in this perspective, there can be no true security and stability in the Persian Gulf until such revolutionary changes are accompanied by the Arab acknowledgment of Iran's spiritual propriety and political primacy.

On the other level, the Gulf Arab leaders fear Khomeini's Shiism for its potentially adverse effects on the Shii communities in their own countries. To be sure, Khomeini never tires of warning against division between the Sunni and the Shii Muslims, although, contrary to the general view, pan-Islamism is *not* the ultimate goal of his Islam; it is merely a way station to the establishment of the Islamic world order. Yet, the fact that Khomeini's ideology is nonsectarian, or ecumenical, is no real source of comfort to Gulf Arab leaders; the susceptibility of their Shii communities to the Khomeini appeal is considered to be a constant and dangerous source of potential threat to the political stability of their conservative regimes. In other words, to them Khomeini's Shiism poses a twofold external and internal threat, and the urgent question is how to contain simultaneously the threat of the powerful revolutionary state of Iran and the potential contagion of Khomeini-type Shiism within their own societies.

Iraq. In absolute terms, Iraq has the most Shia of any Arab country, numbering over 8 million Shii Muslims; they are 60 percent of Iraq's population. Furthermore, Iraq happens to be the site of the holiest Shii shrines, in Karbala, Najaf, and Kazimain, names that are powerful symbols of faith for millions of Shii Muslims in the world. Finally, the Sunni-dominated, secular, and Ba'athist regime of Saddam Hussein rules the only Arab country in the Persian Gulf that abuts the Shii-dominated and populated state of Iran over a stretch of hundreds of miles of land and river boundaries.

These concrete circumstances influence Saddam Hussein's perceptions of the threat of Shiism and his regime's response to it. As opposed to the historical past, Iranian-Iraqi relations in the few years between 1975 and 1979 were characterized by an unprecedented degree of cooperation; Saddam Hussein and the Shah even consulted each other on the security of the Gulf region as a whole. Even after the revolution, the Bazargan government got along rather well with the Iraqi regime, but its fall on November 6, 1979, reversed all that. The relations have been marked ever since by an unprecedented degree of hostility, epitomized by the Iran-Iraq War, which started in September 1980 and has been the longest, bloodiest, and costliest war in contemporary Middle East history.

The underlying conflict between Iran and Iraq involves both dimensions of Shiism. First, the Khomeini religious Islamic ideology, backed by the power of the Iranian state, clashes with Hussein's secular Ba'athist ideology, which is also backed by state power. Khomeini is perceived to believe in the continuing primacy of Iranian power and the new spiritual priority of Iran in the Gulf region, a belief that no other state has the right to challenge. From this perspective, only Saddam "the infidel" (*kafir*) had the gall to do so by invading Iran. As we have seen, Khomeini also believes that it is the sacred duty of Iran to project and export its power and ideology abroad, and yet Saddam Hussein "arrogantly" sets himself up to contain the Islamic Revolution. On the other side, Saddam Hussein believes that the Iranian Revolution simultaneously presents an opportunity and a threat. It was seen as an opportunity for him to project the long-desired Iraqi power into the Gulf region at a time when internal and external problems besetting the revolutionary regime appeared to weaken the Iranian power position; it was seen as a threat because the new Iranian ideology is intrinsically opposed to that of his regime. Saddam Hussein believes that Khomeini's religiously based ideology is antithetical to the Ba'athist secular ideology, in which Arabism, not Islam, is the core value. Long before the outbreak of the war, when Khomeini was characterizing the Ba'athist ideology as an imported amalgam of such alien ideas as socialism and nationalism as opposed to the "authentic" Islamic ideology of Iran, Hussein vehemently rejected Khomeini's dogma. Any Islamic ideology of Iran, Hussein argued dogmatically, that contradicts Arabism is "not Islamic at all."

Second, the Iran-Iraq conflict also involves Shiism at the grass-roots level of the people. Saddam Hussein fears the threat of Iraqi Shii dissidents to his regime. The Shii Muslims have always considered themselves the underdogs, or to use their own characterization, the deprived (mahrumin), despite their overwhelming majority in Iraqi society. They have seldom perceived their share of power and prosperity as fair or just, whether ruled by the Ottomans, the British, and the monarchy in the past or by the minority Sunni-Ba'athist regime of the Takriti clan at the present time.

Yet not all the Iraqi Shii Muslims who predominate geographically in the southern parts of Iraq and hail socioeconomically from the rural areas and such poor urban localities as the slums of the township of al-Thaurah, for example, want a Khomeini-type Islamic government. Nor have they all joined the underground Shii movements, which have been ably discussed by Batatu.[8] As he points out, the Islamic Call (Al-Dawa al-Islamiyah) is older than the Muslim Warriors (Mujahadeen-e-Khalq), the other major Iraqi Shii party, but Ayatollah Sayyid Mahdi al-Hakim, son of the founder of the party, the late Muhsin al-Hakim, dates the beginnings of the Al-Dawa to "after the 'revolution' of 1958" rather than "in the late 1960's" as Batatu first suggested.[9] Batatu himself now favors an earlier date. "The main objective of this party," according to Mahdi al-Hakim, "is to establish an Islamic state. . . ." "The leaders of the Da'wah party," he continues, "had also consulted the leaders of al-Ikhwan al-Muslimun who broadly agreed that the objective of establishing an Islamic state constituted the best program of cooperation between the Shii and Sunni Muslims."[10] As Batatu points out, the Mujahadeen-e-Khalq Party, which was established in 1979, was "strongly affected by Iran's popular upheaval," but as the Iranian

Revolution has in fact developed over the years, especially under the impact of the Iran-Iraq War, it has been, I should add, the Ikhwan-inspired Al-Dawa rather than the Khomeini-inspired Mujahadeen-e-Khalq that has cooperated most closely with the revolutionary regime in Iran. The leading figure in this cooperation has been Hojatoleslam (Khomeini uses this title for him; Batatu calls him Ayatollah) Muhammad Baqir al-Hakim, another son of the founder of the Al-Dawa, mentioned above.

Although the late Ayatollah Sayyid Muhammad Baqir al-Sadr—the most respected Iraqi *'alim* (learned religious leader), who was executed by the Ba'athist regime in April 1980—had not been associated with the Al-Dawa, his martyrdom to date inspires all Shii dissidents in the Gulf region, including particularly the Iraqis living in Iran. There are over 350,000 Shia from Iraq in Iran today, including those Iranian residents of Iraq who were expelled by the Iraqi regime at the outset of the war, Iraqi refugees from various countries, and Iraqi prisoners of war. The organization of the Iraqi activist Shii Muslims in Iran is called the Supreme Assembly of the Islamic Revolution in Iraq (SAIRI) and is led by Hojatoleslam Muhammad Baqir al-Hakim. The Hakim family has paid dearly for its embrace by the Iranian government. On June 17, 1983, al-Hakim made public that the Ba'athist regime had executed six members of his family, and other sources indicated that three of them might have been his brothers. The assembly publishes a bulletin reporting on the activities of the Shii dissidents in Iraq. It also has training camps in Iran and dispatches Iraqi warriors (*mujahadeen*) to the war front to fight on the side of Iran against Iraq, as evidenced, for example, by their large-scale participation in the Iranian advance to Hajj 'Umran, on the northern front. Should Iran's war of attrition against Iraq succeed, in all probability the Iraqi Shii dissidents will be aided by the Iranian government to advance into Iraq for the establishment of an Islamic republic, perhaps headed by al-Hakim.

It is well known that Iran's stickiest peace condition is the removal and punishment of Saddam Hussein for his "war crime." But it is seldom noted that the Iraqi Shii dissidents in Iran are in fact being groomed for the postwar establishment of an Islamic republic in Iraq. In addressing the SAIRI on September 20, 1983, for example, Khomeini told the Iraqi Shii dissidents in Iran: "You should aim to form an Islamic government and to implement God's commands." "God willing," he said, in concluding his address, "you will be successful in your efforts to be a mujahid along the path of God. God willing, you will return to Iraq, *where we too will join you in the shrine of Imam Husain*, peace upon him. God bless you all."[11]

The Iraqi underground Al-Dawa Party clearly supports the Iranian-based SAIRI. For example, when in March 1984 Ayatollah Khomeini called on all Iraqi militant forces to rally around the SAIRI in its efforts to overthrow the Iraqi regime, the party responded immediately. It regarded "its religious duty" to uphold and further activate the assembly so that the party's members could take "pride in defending Islam and in liberating suppressed masses who are denied their civil rights under the Baathists' rule [sic] in that country." Although both the SAIRI and the Al-Dawa represent Shii dissidents, Iranian leaders constantly encourage cooperation and unity between them and Sunni dissidents. In practice, the Iraqi underground opposition to the regime has at times involved collaboration between Shii and Sunni dissidents, and this is no mere Iranian wishful thinking. For example, the bombing of the Iraqi government–controlled television stations and the air force headquarters in the spring of 1983 was done by the Sunni as well as pro-Khomeini Shii Muslims in Baghdad.

Saudi Arabia. Only superficially would it appear that the rise of an Islamic state should have improved rather than aggravated the relations of Saudi Arabia and Iran, considering that Saudi Arabia is a renowned Islamic country. But, in fact, the conflict between Khomeini's Shiism and Saudi Islam underpins what I call a cold war between the two largest states of the Persian Gulf today. The Shah's relations with King Faisal and with Crown Prince Fahd did not always fare well, but the potential power rivalry between Saudi Arabia and prerevolutionary Iran was muted by the common interests of the two basically conservative regimes in opposition to communism, in a special relationship with the United States, in opposition to Iraqi Ba'athist-sponsored subversion, especially in smaller Gulf states, and in resistance to the potential threat of the Soviet Union. The House of Saud tolerated the overbearing posture of the Shah so long as this unpalatable attitude seemed to be balanced by his welcome efforts to preserve the status quo in the region, particularly at a time when the Saudis themselves seemed to prefer an insular, indirect, and limited kind of diplomacy to a more comprehensive, active, and forward policy before the Camp David Accords and the Egyptian-Israeli peace treaty, which subsequently isolated Egypt and propelled the Saudis into the forefront of Arab diplomacy.

For these reasons in particular, when the Iranian Revolution erupted, Saudi leaders firmly stood by the beleaguered Shah. In 1978–79, Prince Sultan and Prince Fahd urged the other Arab governments to support the Shah, and even after the seizure of power by the Iranian revolutionary forces (February 11, 1979), the devout King Khalid prayed, in his personal message to Khomeini, for God to guide him "to the forefront of those who strive for upholding Islam and Muslims." The King's prayer was answered, but Khomeini did not emerge in the forefront of the kind of Islam that the King would have preferred. The Saudis, like the Iraqis, hoped to maintain a semblance of correct relations with the Bazargan government. But once the Khomeini followers snatched the reins of power from the less doctrinaire elements after the fall of Bazargan, the conflict between Tehran and Riyadh became almost inevitable. Until then the Saudi leaders had feared, above all, the potential seizure of power by the communist elements within the chaotic revolutionary politics in Iran. To their surprise, the Khomeini disciples monopolized power step by step to the exclusion of all other forces, including the communists. The ensuing domination of Iranian politics by the followers of the Khomeini line spelled unexpected trouble for the House of Saud. Shiism of any kind had always been antithetical to Wahhabism, let alone the kind that Khomeini now adopted as the official creed of the revolutionary state. For the Saudis, as for the Iraqis, the challenge of Shiism has been twofold.

On the diplomatic level, Saudi Arabia and Iran clash both ideologically and politically. For the sake of clarity, on the basis of Khomeini's ideology, I characterize this overall conflict as one between Iran's official Islam of the Oppressed (mustaz'afeen) and Saudi Arabia's official Islam of the Oppressors (mustakbarin). The former denotes Khomeini's revolutionary, populist, and millenarian Islam, and the latter describes the official Saudi conservative, unitarian, and elitist Islam. This basic conflict may be broken down into its four principal ingredients as follows: republicanism versus monarchism, populism versus elitism, universalism versus insularism, and anti-Westernism versus pro-Westernism.

Saudi Arabia's originally popular, not populist, Islam has over time become a conservative legitimizing force for the House of Saud. The eighteenth-century coalition between the religious reformer Muhammad ibn 'Abd al-Wahhab and the local ruler Muhammad ibn Sa'ud formed the basis of not only an Islamic state but also an essentially royal political system. In other words, Islam was transformed from an initially revivalist force to a conservative formula for legitimacy in Saudi Arabia. On the other side, Khomeini's Islam, which initially accepted the concept of a limited monarchy, has been transformed into an anti-monarchical revolutionary force.[12] Second, Saudi official Islam is endorsed by the conservative religious establishment as well as the House of Saud, whereas Khomeini's Islam presumably embraces all strata of the society in which the uplifting of the underdog, or the oppressed (mustaz'afeen) is the hallmark of its revolutionary mission. Third, although Saudi official Islam is the traditional guardian of Islam's holiest sites, at Mecca and Medina, on behalf of the Muslim world, it is still comparatively insular as opposed to Khomeini's Islam, which aims ultimately to establish Islamic world order everywhere. Fourth, Saudi official Islam enjoys a special relationship with the United States and the West in general, whereas Khomeini's Islam is irreconcilably opposed to both superpowers and their allies as a matter of ideological as well as political preference. In this context, the Saudi government becomes the agent of the Great Satan, and the Saudi allies in the Gulf become mini-Satans, and all of them, like Israel, belong to the "oppressors' camp." If Iraqi Ba'athist ideology is regarded as atheistic, Saudi Muwahhid Islam is considered blasphemous.

On the sociopolitical level, Saudi Shii Muslims, as contrasted with the Iraqi, constitute a minority. Some estimates put them at 115,000 and others at 200,000 to 300,000. In any event, they probably number about 5 percent of the citizen population. Their relatively insignificant number is far outweighed by their demographic concentration, strategic location, and crucial profession. They are concentrated in the oil-rich Hasa Province, where they constitute between 40 and 60 percent of the workforce in the oil industry. In Saudi Arabia not only are such statistics considered highly sensitive, and hence not always reliable, but also the conditions and activities of the Shii community are shrouded in great secrecy. Not a single Saudi official I have talked to during my visits to the kingdom has ever denied past mistreatment of the Shii minority and the persistence of anti-Shii attitudes among the Saudi Sunni Muslims. But in all fairness, the Saudi Shia have also been prejudiced against what they pejoratively call the "Wahhabi" faithful (they prefer to be called unitarians or Muwahhidun). In any event, the Shia of the Eastern Province continue to resent especially the perceived discriminatory acts of the Juluwis, the provincial governors. One of my Shii respondents, for example, told me that the Wahhabis believe that "you must keep the dog hungry so that it will follow you," and another told me that the "Shia suffers not so much from an empty stomach as from a sense of injured dignity."

It is no wonder that the cry for justice ('adl) symbolized the two major recent Shii uprisings in Saudi Arabia as it had so many throughout Islamic history. The first Shii disturbance in the Eastern Province, in late November 1979, was, no doubt, inspired by the Iranian revolutionary upheaval. Some 90,000 demonstrators carrying portraits of Khomeini defied the government ban on the religious commemoration of the martyrdom of Imam Hussein on Ashura, the tenth of the month of Muharram. During the riots a number of people were killed, and the National Guard soldiers, who are perceived symbolically as the agents of Saudi repression, were among them. The second Shii unrest took place also in the Eastern Province, in February 1980, when the demonstrators demanded, among other things, that oil should remain in the ground since the revenues from its sale did not help alleviate the sufferings of the oil workers.

One of my most reliable Saudi Sunni respondents recounted the two Shii disturbances as follows:

The revolution in Iran which was led by a religious leader stirred up emotions and struck a responsive chord in Qatif. The religious factor, however, was not the only reason for the disturbances. Until ten years ago, all villages in the Kingdom suffered from a lack of basic services. Basic services were not getting to them. The situation in the cities and urban centers was far better than it was in the villages. This created a climate—a fertile soil for disgruntlement, contributing to the response in Qatif to the events in Iran. Note that no disturbances occurred in al-Hasa, because it is more of an urban area. But in the villages, the situation was different. Villagers felt they were deprived of benefits [mahrumin].

Regardless of the accuracy of the details, one can hardly find better evidence for the proposition that the perceived threat of Shiism to the House of Saud is not simply an external matter of the Shii ideology as expounded by Khomeini and backed by the power of the Iranian state; more important, it is one of susceptibility of alienated elements within the Saudi Shii community to the Iranian appeal. All my official Saudi respondents invariably pointed out the recent expenditure of billions of dollars by the Saudi government for the betterment of the standard of living among Shii Muslims. Even many of my private respondents were keenly aware of government efforts for the betterment of Shii living conditions ever since King Khalid met with Shii leaders in Qatif in the wake of the above-mentioned disturbances. One private respondent optimistically told me in 1984 that the Shia in Qatif were now "immune to the Iranian influence" because of the government extension of social services to them, and also because of the increasingly better attitude of Saudi officials toward the Shii minority. Another respondent pointed out that perhaps the government had overdone a good thing! He said, and I quote him verbatim:

> There are now people [in Saudi Arabia] who believe that attention to Qatif [by the Saudis] far exceeds that given to other villages. Yesterday [March 7, 1984], the cabinet decided to build six hundred villas in Qatif, but only four hundred in al-Hasa, although al-Hasa is bigger and larger. In fact Qatif now ranks fourth in the government's priorities—after Riyadh, Damman, and al-Qasim which is being overlooked despite its half a million people. All this is congruent with the need to eliminate any climate which would be conducive to injustice.

The Saudi Shii problem is potentially susceptible annually to the catalyst of the Iranian pilgrims to Mecca. Ever since the revolution, the pilgrims from Iran have tried to use the ceremonies for the purpose of proselytizing the Khomeini brand of Islam. The Iranian pilgrims constitute the single largest, most cohesive, and most politicized group of Shii pilgrims from any Muslim country in the world. In recent years, they have numbered about 100,000 each year. They have taken posters of Khomeini and revolutionary tracts to Mecca, staged political demonstrations, and shouted slogans against the United States, Israel, and Iraq. These have been reported by the Western press, although the facts of each crisis have been disputed by Tehran and Riyadh.

What is less known, however, is the underlying conflict between Khomeinist and Saudi official Islam as it relates specifically to the opposing conceptions of the Hajj itself. At the height of the dispute between Saudi Arabia and Iran over the behavior of the Iranian pilgrims in 1981, King Khalid wrote Ayatollah Khomeini, complaining that the Iranian pilgrims had in his name acted in ways "contrary to the aims of pilgrimage and the honor of holy places," and their behavior not only "disturbed and disgusted other pilgrims" but no doubt would also "damage Iran's credibility and prestige."[13] Khomeini rejected the King's version of events. More important, he contested his view that the purpose of pilgrimage was religious worship only. He contended categorically that under all prophets, especially the prophet of Islam, pilgrimage had been "completely linked to politics," and their separation was the idea of the superpowers.

What is important from a practical standpoint, however, is that, despite the recurrence of the problem, Saudi authorities do not allow themselves to be provoked; they bend over backwards not to give any offense to Shia. One of the leading Saudi officials dealing with the problem told me that they try to pursue a two-pronged strategy. First, they continue to maintain a dialogue with the Iranian authorities about the logistical problems associated with the travel and stay of such a large group of pilgrims from Iran, regardless of doctrinal differences. Second, they handle the troublemaking pilgrims with utmost care, seeing to it that they leave Saudi Arabia with the least possible disturbance. So far, this cautious and pragmatic policy seems to have paid off rather well.

Bahrain. Our last case study of Shiism in the Persian Gulf focuses on the only archipelago state of the region. Bahraini Shii Muslims constitute 71 to 98 percent of the citizen population of 238,420. This means that, although percentage-wise Bahrain has the largest group of Shii Muslim citizens of any Gulf Arab country, in absolute terms it ranks third after Iraq and Saudi Arabia. But the Bahraini like the Iraqi and Saudi Shii Muslims are found predominantly in the rural areas and Sunni Muslims in the urban centers, and they, like the other Arab Shii Muslims, live under the rule of an indigenous Sunni minority. But, unlike both Iraq and Saudi Arabia, this tiny state carries the burden of an ancient Iranian claim to its territory, which was for all practical purposes settled in 1971, when the Shah relinquished the claim of sovereignty to the island state; his government was the first to recognize its independence.

The Iranian Revolution, however, revived the ancient claim in a new form. Unlike Iraq and Saudi Arabia, Bahrain felt the brunt of the impact of the revolution even before the fall of the Bazargan government. A leading Iranian cleric, Ayatollah Ruhani, announced in 1979 that he would lead a revolutionary movement for the annexation of Bahrain, unless its rulers adopted "an Islamic form of government similar to the one established in Iran." The claim was qualitatively different from the old Iranian claim; previously it had always been a claim based on the "uncontested Iranian sovereignty" over the territory of Bahrain. But the Ruhani claim reflected the earliest clerical bid for export of the Islamic Revolution to other Gulf states, in this case through the threat of physical annexation.

The threat caused the Bazargan government considerable embarrassment. It was trying to maintain equitable relations with all states, most particularly with the neighboring Gulf states. Bazargan in effect tried to blame Ruhani's "unauthorized" claim to Bahrain on the revolutionary chaos in Iran, which, he repeatedly complained, had a "thousand chiefs." Bahraini officials, however, would not let the matter rest at that; they embarked on a feverish diplomatic exchange with other Arab leaders, who joined them in a chorus of sympathetic support. Bazargan's ambassador to Riyadh, Muhammad Javad Rezavi, declared, "We respect other nations' sovereignty and Iran has no claim or ambitions of any sort on any part of the Gulf." Bazargan's envoy, Sadeqh Tabatabai, went to Bahrain to ease the mounting tensions between Tehran and Manama, where he assured Bahrain that Ruhani's statement did not represent the official position of the Iranian government and also told the correspondent of the Kuwaiti newspaper al-Qabas that the whole thing had been a "misunderstanding."

What really shocked the Bahraini and other Gulf Arab leaders was the discovery of an alleged Iranian-supported coup plot two years later, in December 1981. The whole region seemed to be gripped by this essentially quixotic plot, the facts of which are still debated, but the Arab view of it may be related on the basis of documentary research and on-site interviews. Briefly, the Bahraini government announced on December 13 that it had arrested a group of "saboteurs," allegedly trained by Iran. Subsequently, the Bahraini interior minister charged that the group planned to assassinate Bahraini officials; it belonged to the Islamic Front for the Liberation of Bahrain, with headquarters in Tehran; and all its sixty members were Shii Muslim. Actually the group turned out to have had seventy-three members, including sixty Bahraini and eleven Saudi as well as an Omani and a Kuwaiti national; there were no Iranians among them by anyone's account. But at the time five unidentified armed men reportedly presented a written memorandum to the Bahraini Embassy in Tehran in which they claimed responsibility for the group arrested in Bahrain. At the time Bahrain also asked Iran to recall its chargé d'affaires. After a long-drawn-out investigation and trial, the plotters were finally sentenced in May 1982, receiving jail sentences ranging from seven years to life imprisonment.

The results of my interviews on this plot in Bahrain and Saudi Arabia may be summarized as follows: Arab officials seem absolutely convinced that the Shii dissidents arrested had been both trained and equipped by Iran; the Saudi officials seem to have been closely involved in the whole process of investigation through consultation and exchange of intelligence information. Also, every official I talked to in the region seemed to confirm what the secretary-general of the Gulf Cooperation Council (GCC)—Majlis al-Ta'awun li Duwal al-Khalij al-Arabiyah—Abdullah Bisharah, had said in February 1982: "What happened in Bahrain was not directed against one part of this body but against the whole body." This was an enigmatic way of saying what the Arab press had already reported, that is, that besides Bahrain, Saudi Arabia and other Gulf Arab countries had been the targets of the plot. Finally, private Bahraini Shii respondents told me that the plotters had been trained in paramilitary camps in Iran's holy city of Qom by a certain "Hadi Mudarrisi," presumably an Iraqi Shii Muslim who carries a Bahraini passport. Others believe that they were trained by Hojatoleslam Mudarrisi, who had lived in Bahrain in exile from Iran during the Shah's regime. The latter information is corroborated by more reliable private sources. Bahraini respondents also told me that the plotters got such "light sentences" either because Iran threatened revenge if they were executed or because the Liberation Front for Bahrain and the Arabian Peninsula threatened to punish members of the Bahraini royal family if the court handed down death sentences. I suspect these are perhaps more rumors than accurate reports, but that is also part of the Gulf political scene.

No single incident attributed to Shii radicals until December 1981 had threatened the Gulf Arab leaders so much. The Saudis behaved as if they were even more threatened than the Bahrainis themselves. The Saudi interior minister, Prince Nayif, minced no words about the alleged Iranian involvement in the plot to overthrow the Al Khalifa regime. He called on Iran to stop supporting "sabotage activities" in the Gulf, reminded the Iranian leaders that they had said earlier that they would not be "the policeman of the Gulf," and charged that today "they have unfortunately become the terrorists of the Gulf." More important, Saudi Arabia rushed to sign four bilateral security agreements, with Bahrain, Qatar, the United Arab Emirates (UAE), and Oman, but Kuwait has held back ever since resisting also Saudi pressure for a single collective internal-security agreement among all the GCC members. During my visit to Saudi Arabia, I found the Saudi officials still hopeful about the prospects of such an agreement perhaps during the organization's fifth summit meeting, in November 1984. Meanwhile, however, the GCC interior ministers, with an eye to the alleged Iranian support of the Shii coup plot, have agreed in principle that "intervention by any country in the internal affairs of one of the member states is considered to be intervention in the internal affairs of the GCC states."

The panicky reaction of the GCC leaders to the Shii coup plot at the diplomatic level tends to blur the older and deeper sociopolitical problem of Shii dissidence in Bahrain. From such a perspective, the more important facts of the Shii coup plot are almost universally overlooked. To mention just a few, about 30 percent of the members of the coup plot group were disaffected Arab students, about 17 percent were unemployed workers, and the overwhelming majority were young, alienated, indigenous Shii nationals of the Gulf Arab states. To be sure, the catalyst of the Iranian Revolution, with all that it has entailed ideologically and politically, exacerbates the problem of Shii dissidence—as in fact the Sunni dissidence as well—in Bahrain as well as other Gulf Arab states, but the problem long predates the advent of the revolution. Certainly, the Bahraini Shii Muslims seem to believe that their most active organization, the Islamic Guidance Society (IGC), was established, they told me, in 1972 and began activities in earnest in 1976, before the revolution in Iran. Today the IGC is considered by the Bahraini authorities to be "an illegal political organization," the Central and Ideological Committee (CIC) of which receives its orders from "foreign quarters."

The president of the IGC, Ibrahim Mansur Ibrahim, who is better known as Ibrahim al-Jufairi, was arrested in February 1984, eleven days after the arrest of another member of the IGC, Muhammad Abdullah Muhammad Hussein. He reportedly "confessed to possessing pistols, ammunition and a rocket-propelled grenade." I was told in Bahrain that Muhammad Hussein was arrested at the nearby village of al-Markh, where he had hidden arms and ammunitions, perhaps left over from the coup plot of December 1981. The coup plot has certainly made for tighter security measures against suspected Shii dissidents, particularly those of Iranian origin or with Iranian connections.

To go back to earlier years, the first major Shii unrest in Bahrain occurred in the wake of the Iranian Revolution in 1979, when a Shii leader by the name of Muhammad 'Ali al-'Akri was arrested and incarcerated. But the second major Shii unrest was triggered by the arrest of Ayatollah Sayyid Muhammad Baqir al-Sadr in Iraq in January 1980, before he and his sister, Bint al-Huda, were executed in April. I was also told that the Shii demonstrations at the time had been directed against the Iraqi embassy and bank in Manama and not the regime, but a Shii leader named Jamil 'Ali, better known among the Bahrainis as al-Thaur, was arrested and "beaten to death" subsequently; the Bahraini police, however, claimed that he had "died in custody." In November of 1980, when I happened to be in Bahrain during Ashura, I learned that the Shii mourners commemorating the martyrdom of Imam Hussein carried the picture of "the mutilated Body" of al-Thaur with the inscription "Martyred by the Pharaonic Regime."

In answer to my questions about Iran, one of my Bahraini Shii respondents enthusiastically offered the following observations without ever suggesting that Bahrain should have an Iranian-type Islamic government:

1. The only Muslim country in the world that dares to successfully defy both the East and the West and maintain its independence is Iran.
2. The Iranian government is the only oil-rich government in the "Arabian Gulf" that distributes wealth among the people equitably.
3. It is only the wealthy, the privileged, and the upper-class individual in Iran who does not like Ayatollah Khomeini.
4. Who says freedom is squashed in Iran? Even Sunnis and Christians can talk and act freely!
5. Should Iran win the war against the Aflaqite regime in Iraq, the Bahraini Shii Muslims, like all others, will be delighted.

When I asked another Shii respondent if he could list the views of the Shii Bahrainis about their own government, he replied as follows:

1. We don't say the ruler of Bahrain should be a Shia because the majority of the people are, but we want to have more say in our government; the present Shii membership in the cabinet does not include important ministries; it is a kind of tokenism.
2. We want freedom of the newspapers. We also want a parliament; you know we used to have one, but we don't have one now. On the whole, we want more participation.
3. An Islamic government could help all this. It could give our children more Islamic education.

Only a gullible analyst would jump to the conclusion that the Shia are really asking for "democracy"—far from it. When I pressed the same respondent about what he meant by "freedom," "participation," or "parliament," and how an "Islamic government" could help all that, he simply replied that such a government would follow "the right path" (sirat al-mustaqim). We should remember, I might add, that in Iran "the right path" has become the "Khomeini line" (Khatti Imam), and that any deviation from it cannot be tolerated. Instead of reading our own wishes into such terms, they should be understood in the context of the Shii cultural tradition. In this context, such terms as "participation" most often turn out to be an inchoate way of expressing the Shii sense of having been unjustly treated in the historical past, and the belief that justice will prevail if only the "right government" is established by "the right people."

PROPOSITIONS

Given the underdeveloped state of the study of Shiism in the Persian Gulf region, there can be no firm conclusions here. Rather, I will present two major propositions intended (1) to integrate the main findings of the foregoing empirical analysis based on documentary and field research, (2) to point out their central policy implications.

1. Shiism is a major force in both the foreign policy and the domestic political process of all the states of the Persian Gulf in varying degrees as an international ideological and sociopolitical movement that cuts across state boundaries. In Iran, it is the official ideology of the state, a major determinant of its foreign and domestic policies, and a particular interpretation of Islam by Ayatollah Ruhollah Khomeini (Khatti Imam) that is supported by various groups. Khomeini's basically revolutionary, millenarian, and populist Islam clashes with the ideological orientation of all other Gulf states, particularly with the conservative Saudi Islam and the revolutionary Iraqi Ba'athism. In war, however, as with Iraq, and in cold war, as with Saudi Arabia—which briefly warmed up on June 5, 1984, when the Saudis shot down an Iranian F-4 aircraft— Khomeini's Islam is perceived by the Gulf Arab leaders as not just an external ideological threat backed by the power of the Iranian state. Rather, it is seen as an internal revolutionary force, either potentially, as evidenced by Shii dissident groups in Bahrain and Saudi Arabia, or actively, as shown by the underground existence of the Al-Dawa, which is supported by the Iranian-based Iraqi SAIRI, led by Hojatoleslam Muhammad Baqir al-Hakim.

2. The policy implications of Shiism in the Middle East as an ideological and sociopolitical movement involve both regional and external powers. The United States, for example, poorly estimated the situation in Lebanon, largely because of misperceiving Shiism, and paid dearly as a result in both human life and credibility by subjecting hundreds of American Marines to the terrorist acts of angry Shii activists, who are by no means representative of the Shii Muslims today, as the extremists (ghulat) were not in the historical past. The United States would suffer even more in the Persian Gulf region—the world heartland of Shiism as well as its oil heartland—should it intervene militarily in the area by deploying ground forces. Sociopolitical and ideological Shii movements do not call for military solutions, and Henry Kissinger, who simplistically advocates the containment of Shiism as well as communism in the region, has yet to say how he

proposes to do that. The external powers, the United States or any country, have failed to understand that despite sociopolitical and ideological fragmentation, Shiism today is emotionally and spiritually united, as in the historical past, in opposing foreign and domestic tyranny (*zulm*) and in demanding justice (*'adl*).

Regional, no less than external, powers have difficulty in understanding Shiism. On the Mediterranean side of the Middle East, the Israelis do not seem to appreciate that all their persistent efforts for cooptation, manipulation, and recruitment of Shia cannot possibly provide any real solution for their dilemma in southern Lebanon. Despite all factional divisions and incessant jockeying for power, the Shia—moderate and radical, armed and unarmed—are united in their opposition to the perceived tyranny of Israeli occupation. Those Israelis who view their own destiny in terms of foreign persecution and the suffering of the Jews throughout history and also in terms of religious hope for the Promised Land do not seem to appreciate the Shii sense of historical suffering (*masa'ib*) and the emotional and spiritual hope for the establishment of justice by the promised Mahdi.

Fellow Muslims do not seem to show much better understanding of their Shii brethren either. The Iraqi, the Bahraini, the Saudi, and other regimes have yet to realize that neither resort to war, as by Iraq, nor diplomacy, nor a mix of military deterrence and diplomacy by all other Gulf Arab states alone can contain the perceived threat to their security. Nor do they seem to realize that no degree of religious pretense, socioeconomic cooptation, and political manipulation will resolve their Shii majority or minority problem whether or not their Shii citizens are susceptible to the appeal of Khomeini's Islamic ideology. The Shia perceive their accumulated grievances in terms of their historical experience as the most deprived group (*mahrumin*), and also in terms of the emotional and spiritual promise of salvation (*najah*) and the establishment of justice by the Mahdi before the Day of Resurrection (*qiyamah*). This is, in my view, the fundamental force that underlies Shiism, and no regional leader can afford to ignore it. Khomeini himself is no exception. His Islamic Revolution will no doubt suffer grievously from a failure to heed in practice this ancient and inexorable Shii quest for justice. The "government of the oppressed," as he characterizes the Iranian government, will help the masses "to inherit the earth," he repeatedly promises. But that government will, instead, look increasingly more like the government of the oppressors if the Iranian leaders continue to fail to bring their millenarian revolutionary goals within mundane, realistic means.

NOTES

1. The research materials on which I have drawn for this essay have been collected since 1979 from documentary sources and extensive interviews during repeated visits to

the Middle East in connection with a book project on the foreign policy of revolutionary Iran. Nevertheless, I have provided a number of references here pending the publication of the book (i.e., Juan R. I. Cole and Nikki R. Keddie, eds., *Shi'ism and Social Protest* [New Haven, 1986]). I would like to acknowledge the support of the University of Virginia's Energy Policy Studies Center and the Center for Advanced Studies for their generous support of my research.

2. For details, see R. K. Ramazani, "Khomeini's Islam in Iran's Foreign Policy," pp. 71–93 in this volume.

3. *Sukhan-raniha-yi Imam Khumaini Dar Shish Mahi-yi Avval-i 1359* [The lectures of Imam Khumaini during the first six months of 1980] (Tehran, 1980), 8.

4. *Tehran Journal*, 4 November 1981.

5. Foreign Broadcast Information Service, *Daily Report*, vol. 8, South Asia (FBIS-SA), 24 October 1983.

6. For the text in Persian, see *Kayhan Hava'i*, 23 May 1984. In English, see FBIS-SA, 14 May 1984.

7. FBIS-SA, 23 September 1983.

8. See H. Batatu, "Iraq's Underground Shi'a Movements: Characteristics, Causes and Prospects," *Middle East Journal* 35, no. 4 (Autumn 1981): 578–94, and his chapter in Cole and Keddie, *Shi'ism and Social Protest*.

9. For the text of his interview in English, see *Impact International*, 25 April–8 May 1980. In Batatu's chapter in Cole and Keddie, *Shi'ism and Social Protest*, although not in his article in the *Middle East Journal*, he summarizes al-Hakim's and other recently available accounts and concludes that Al-Dawa was founded in 1960 or soon thereafter.

10. *Impact International*, 25 April–8 May 1980.

11. See FBIS-SA, 21 September 1983.

12. Ramazani, "Khomeini's Islam."

13. Ibid., 27.

SOCIOPOLITICAL CHANGE IN THE GULF

A Climate for Terrorism?

In no other region of the world has the onslaught on American life, liberty, and property taken a greater toll in recent years than in the Middle East.[1] The region as a whole has become the global hotbed of terrorism. By the end of 1985, the Middle East accounted for 45 percent of the world's terrorist attacks, some of which originated in the area but were completed in Europe.[2] The bulk of terrorist activities within the Middle East have been concentrated in Lebanon and the Gulf region. This essay focuses on the Gulf region, starting with a review of the most serious terrorist incidents since 1983, the majority of which have taken place in Kuwait.

As of 1986, four major incidents had shaken up the tiny sheikhdom and its five partners in the Gulf Cooperation Council (GCC). This regional grouping has viewed the terrorist attacks in Kuwait as attacks on the security and stability of all its member states. Iraq, on the other hand, has made every effort to implicate the Khomeini regime in all these incidents as part and parcel of its war strategy against Iran. I shall outline briefly the principal facts of each incident as a point of departure for the analysis that follows.

The first major terrorist incident in Kuwait took place on December 12, 1983, when simultaneous bombings at the U.S. Embassy, the French Embassy, and other targets killed five and wounded eighty-six persons. As in the truck bombings of the American Marines and the French paratroopers in Lebanon (October 23, 1983), the "Islamic Jihad Organization" claimed responsibility. Quietly, all the GCC regimes blamed Iran, as did Western sources.[3] The seventeen Iraqis, out of twenty-five convicted for the crime, all belonged to the Iraqi underground Shii party known as Al-Dawa. The demand for the release of these imprisoned terrorists has triggered other acts of terrorism not only in Kuwait but also in Lebanon, where Shii activists captured both American and French nationals. They have been bargaining chips in efforts to obtain the freedom of fellow Shii detainees and, in some cases, relatives.

The second attack verified the dangers confronting a nation choosing to imprison terrorists. On December 4, 1984, a Kuwaiti airliner bound for Karachi (with 155 passengers and 11 crew members) was hijacked by Shii terrorists,

"Sociopolitical Change in the Gulf: A Climate for Terrorism?" was originally published in *Crosscurrents in the Gulf: Arab Regional and Global Interests*, ed. H. Richard Sindelar III and J. E. Peterson (New York: Routledge, 1988), 110–26.

taken to Tehran, and held there for six days. Two Americans were killed and several Kuwaitis wounded before the surviving passengers were freed.[4] Within a year after the sentencing of the terrorists in the embassy bombings by a Kuwaiti court, other Shii terrorists had abducted six Americans in Lebanon and the Islamic Jihad had made calls to the effect that if their fellow Shia were not released they would execute their captives.

Kuwait was again the target of terrorism when an explosives-laden car rammed into the motorcade of the Amir, Sheikh Jabir al-Ahmad Al Sabah on May 25, 1985. Two members of the Amiri Guard and a passerby were killed and eleven others wounded. The Islamic Jihad's spokesman congratulated the Amir on his escape and expressed the hope that the message had been clearly understood. Contacting a foreign news agency in Beirut, the spokesman also warned that a new blow would soon be directed against the "reactionary Arab regimes."[5]

The assassination attempt, like the hijacking of the Kuwaiti airliner, seemingly was motivated by the desire to force the release of the seventeen prisoners convicted in Kuwait in exchange for American and French hostages held in Beirut. Apparently this was inferred from two facts: the shadowy Islamic Jihad's demand, ten days before the attempted assassination, for the release of the prisoners, and Prime Minister Sheikh Sa'd al-'Abdullah Al Sabah's rejection of the demand immediately after the attack. According to the Kuwaiti daily *al-Anba'*, however, the car bomber was a member of the Al-Dawa Party, as had been those convicted for the multiple bombings mentioned above. Generally, "Islamic Jihad" has been considered a cover name for a variety of terrorist groups.[6]

More importantly, there was a real fear at the time for the welfare of the embryonic Kuwaiti parliamentary democracy as a result of the sheikhdom's mounting security concerns. Heir apparent and prime minister Sheikh Sa'd warned that the attack on the Amir might force Kuwaitis to sacrifice the liberal ways they had become used to in secure times. A tough antiterrorism bill was approved by the Cabinet on June 9, 1985, providing the death penalty for terrorist acts resulting in loss of life. Other penalties were envisaged by the bill for membership in antigovernment underground groups—obviously referring to Al-Dawa—and for writing and publishing seditious material.[7] Details of the bills are difficult to learn, but as late as nearly a year later there was evidence of some concern among Kuwaiti intellectuals regarding the potential erosion of Kuwaiti democracy. Some expressed concern over the possible suspension of parliamentary life as a result of pressure from the Prime Minister, while others seemed to believe that the Amir was fully committed to the continuation of the assembly and was happy with the outpouring of affection for him by so many Kuwaiti people after the attempt against his life.

A fourth terrorist incident in Kuwait took place on July 11, 1985, when bombs exploded at two popular cafes in the al-Sharq and al-Salmiya areas and killed eleven people and wounded eighty-nine.[8] Responsibility for the bomb blasts was claimed by the "Arab Revolutionary Brigades Organization," which had in the past claimed credit for attacks on diplomats from Jordan and the UAE in Europe, India, and the rest of the Gulf region. The Kuwaiti newspaper al-Ra'i al-'Aam once again tried to blame Iran for the incident, but lacking reliable information it simply commented on accounts of the forces opposed to the Khomeini regime.[9]

Although these four major terrorist incidents in Kuwait since 1983 constitute the most serious terrorist activities in the Gulf region in recent years, the problem of terrorism in the area has not been confined to Kuwait. A real turning point was the year 1979, when the triple crises of the Iranian seizure of American hostages, the capture of the Grand Mosque in Mecca, and the burning of the American Embassy in Islamabad took place. In 1981, the discovery of an abortive coup plot in Bahrain sent shock waves around the Gulf. Other terrorist plots in Qatar, Saudi Arabia, and elsewhere in the Gulf have been attempted. Some have succeeded and some have failed.

This brief sketch of some recent terrorist activities in the Gulf area should be viewed within the context of three broad points.

First, the focus on the Gulf region by no means implies that terrorism is an exclusively Shii phenomenon. To be sure, the Gulf region is the world's Shii heartland. Most Shii Muslims of the world live in the region. Also, to be sure, the largest number of terrorist acts in recent years have been committed by Shii inhabitants of Lebanon. Nevertheless, terrorist acts have been committed by Sunnis as well, such as those who killed President Sadat in Egypt. Furthermore, Islamic terrorist factions are active in other parts of the Muslim world, as evidenced by the Moro National Liberation Front in the Philippines and the al-Zulfiqar group in Pakistan.

Second, terrorism is not an exclusively religious phenomenon in the Middle East. The resurgence of terrorism among purportedly religious groups in recent years has overshadowed the terrorist activities of other radical groups that are secular both in ideology and in political orientation, such as the Libyan-backed Abu Nidal group (200–300 members), the Popular Front for the Liberation of Palestine (PFLP), the PFLP–General Command, the Palestinian dissidents led by Abu Musa, and the Syrian-backed al-Sa'iqa group, not to mention such non-Muslim groups as Armenian terrorists, the Jewish Defense League, and the Maronite extremists who massacred innocent refugees in the Palestinian camps of Sabra and Shatila in Lebanon in September 1982.

Third, the large percentage of terrorist incidents in the Middle East in recent years should not obscure the fact that terrorism is a worldwide phenomenon. To cite a few examples, narco-terrorism in Latin America is a new phenomenon, adding to the already mounting terrorist activities by a variety of groups with or without the support of Cuba and Nicaragua, just as Sikh terrorism has surfaced in India in the past couple of years. Besides these examples from the Third World, outside the Middle East and the Muslim world, it is well to remember the notorious Western European terrorist groups such as the Red Army Faction, which has attacked American and NATO-related installations in Germany, the Italian Red Brigades, and the Basque separatists in Spain.

EXPLAINING TERRORISM

So much for the "what" of terrorism in the Gulf region. But what can be said about the "why" of it? There are, of course, general theories about international terrorism, ranging from the principle of self-determination and "wars of national liberation" at one extreme to international crime at the other. But here we are concerned more specifically with theories about Middle Eastern terrorism. There are several current explanations of terrorism in the Middle East.

First, there is a historical explanation, which discovers the roots of today's terrorism in the "character" of Islamic history, particularly in the fact that there existed in the twelfth century an Islamic terrorist sect known as the "Assassins" (Hashshashin). Second, there is a school of thought that considers all terrorist acts as intrinsically criminal and hence all terrorists as "thugs" whose frustration and fanaticism are exploited for selfish political ends by such unscrupulous leaders as the "mad dog" of Libya, or by such notorious factional bosses as Abu Nidal, Abu 'Abbas, and others. Third, there is the explanation that views terrorism in the Middle East "as a reflection of the age-old frustration born out of the failure to achieve a Palestinian state." Finally, there is a school of thought according to which radical Islamic fundamentalists, who hate Americans more than Russians, simply use terrorist acts to get their way.

The problem with these and similar explanations of terrorism is that they are largely based on speculation about motivation. Furthermore, explanations about Middle Eastern terrorism also share with general theories about international terrorism one other important feature: they are all simplistic because they are monistic. A single motivation is used as a basis for explanation, be it the right of self-determination in general or Palestinian self-determination in particular.

Yet in reality, it is impossible to get at a diagnosis of terrorism simply in terms of motivation of an individual or a group. The principal difficulty is twofold. First, without too much exaggeration, it may be said that there are perhaps as many motivations as there are terrorists. There are terrorists who kill for a cause, for revenge, and even for kicks. Second, it is often impossible to distinguish between a motivation and an excuse for a given terrorist action. The cynics would have us believe that terrorists simply use ideological slogans—for example, Islam, Arabism, or Zionism—to cover their greed for power and fame. But, in reality, an ideology may well be both a cause and an excuse for action, although methodologically it is not always easy to distinguish between the two.

One way of avoiding the pitfalls of monistic, or single-causal, explanations is to try to relate terrorism to its environment. I propose to do this not as an excuse for, nor as a justification of, terrorism, but in order to understand it. As conceived here, environment is the aggregate of geographical as well as ideological, social, economic, cultural, psychological, and political conditions that influence the life of an individual or community.

An environmental approach to the study of terrorism is based on five major assumptions. First, terrorism is partly a dependent phenomenon because it cannot be totally separated for study from its environmental base. An individual or a group may kill for any motivation, but the act of violence cannot be isolated from its context. Second, terrorism is locational. The phenomenon is said to be "international" either in the ordinary sense that acts of terrorism take place in every region or country of the world or in the more technical sense that individuals and groups who commit terrorist acts are controlled by sovereign states, commonly called state-sponsored terrorism. In this latter sense "international terrorism" is distinguished from "transnational terrorism," which refers to acts carried out "by basically *autonomous non-state actors*," whether or not they enjoy some degree of support from sympathetic states.[10] In either case, we still assume that terrorism is locational, and thus its study must be placed in the context of a given country, region, or other location if it is to be adequately understood. Third, terrorism is situational. That is, besides asking where it takes place, it is necessary to ask *when* it happens. Fourth, being partly a dependent variable, terrorism should be regarded as multicausal because the environment that influences the behavior of an individual or a group contains many different factors. Fifth, and last, terrorism is dynamic because environmental factors, being interconnected, constantly interact.

One would hope that as applied to the Gulf region as a whole, this broader environmental approach to the study of terrorism will aid in understanding the ideological, social, economic, cultural, psychological, and political complexities that underlie the problem. It leads to six major clusters of factors, analytically separable but interacting with one another over time and space to influence individual and group behavior, including the behavior of extremists on the fringes of Gulf societies. The radicals resort to the threat or use of force as their only recourse, regardless of whether their motivation is religious or secular, personal or communal, rational or emotional.

IRAN'S REVOLUTIONARY PARADIGM

Although the impact of the Iranian Revolution on the Muslim world has yet to be studied systematically, there is a consensus among scholars based partly on first-hand observations that its effects have been felt in Muslim communities all the way from Marawi in the Philippines to Manama in Bahrain, and beyond.[11] What is the nature of that impact? Does it diminish or intensify in relationship to the distance of various Muslim or Muslim-inhabited countries from Iran? Whatever the answer to these questions, there is little doubt that in no other region of the world have the effects of the revolution been as pervasive and persistent as in the Gulf. To be sure, Iran is the single largest Shii Muslim–inhabited country in the world. It is also the most populous state in the region and the most strategically located country—abutting both the Soviet Union and the Strait of Hormuz—and putatively still the most powerful state despite the material toll that the revolution and the war with Iraq have exacted. But none of these factors by itself can account for the regional effects of the Iranian Revolution. Rather, it is the combination of these factors with what may be called the Iranian revolutionary paradigm that has over the past eight years simultaneously appealed to and repelled other societies in the Gulf region. In essence, this paradigm consists of both Iranian ideology and practice.

On the "appealing" side of the ledger, four major elements stand out. First, there are those groups and individuals in the Gulf region to whom Khomeini's claim to an all-Islamic and nonsectarian message has a special appeal. For such people, the fact that Shii particularism cannot be isolated from his overall ideology does not seem to matter. Nor does the fact that Khomeinism is the official creed of the Iranian state. Second, the uncompromising insistence of both Khomeini's ideology and Iranian practice on the absolute goal of political independence is widely believed to contain more than mere rhetoric. The overthrow of the perceived pro-American Shah, the taking of American hostages, the defiance of the Soviet Union, and the destruction of the pro-Moscow communist Tudeh Party seem to many Gulf citizens to accord credibility to the Khomeini claim. Equally, the bitterly anti-American and anti-Israeli crusade of the Khomeini regime and its alliance with Libya and Syria have sympathizers among the Gulf Arabs. The Iranian crusade for Jerusalem, and for creating a Palestinian state by destroying Israel, coupled with Arab hatred of Israel, contributes to radical ideological trends in the Gulf region.

The other two aspects of the appeal of the Iranian revolutionary paradigm concern the perceived social and cultural emancipation of Iran. Khomeini's emphasis on the first concern of the "Islamic Revolution" with the economically poor and socially deprived classes, or the *mustaz'afeen*, has a populist ring that appeals to Shii and Sunni lower classes alike.

In the view of one Bahraini citizen, for example, in no country in the region has the oil wealth been so equitably distributed as it has been in Khomeini's Iran. On the cultural side, the anti-Western, especially anti-American, thrust of Khomeinism combines with an incessant call for "Islamic self-reliance," a call that stirs the hearts and minds of those who believe that Western cultural penetration has created a crisis of identity and a sense of Islamic inferiority. In this context, the widely known Iranian slogan "Neither East nor West" means total emancipation—not simply political nonalignment and economic self-sufficiency—from subservience to the superpowers as a means to the lofty goal of restoring Islamic self-respect.

On the "repellent" side of the ledger, there are also four major ingredients. First, no matter how insistent militant Iranians may be on the all-Islamic character of their ideology, many Arabs believe, probably rightly, that the Khomeini ideology embraces Shii particularism. This perception is repugnant to some Islamic groups such as the Kuwaiti Jami'at al-Islah, although this group's negative attitude toward the Iranian paradigm is balanced by the pro-Iranian stance of the Jami'at al-Saqafa. The second ingredient, closely related to the first one just mentioned, is the conception and practice of the rule of the clerics in the Iranian political system. Many Gulf Arabs, who admire the Khomeini regime for its sustained defiance of the superpowers, reject the model of Iranian governance for their own societies. To be sure, the role of the Arab ulama in the political process of some Gulf Arab countries, such as Saudi Arabia, has increased in recent years; but this development does not place them on a par with the Iranian clerics, who had always played a major role in society and even in politics long before they seized the reins of power from the Shah. Even Arab Shia are not necessarily impressed by the idea of the guardianship of the jurisprudent, *Velayat-e Faqih*, as it is being practiced in Iran.

A third dimension of the Iranian revolutionary paradigm that seems to repel segments of the Gulf Arab citizens, especially the liberal elements, is the perceived souring of the revolution. The magnetic influence of the Iranian revolutionary drama was everywhere to be sensed during 1979–81, but the disappointment with the Iranian experience has increased since then for two major reasons. Given the support of the masses for the revolution at inception, many Arab intellectuals, like most Iranians, believed that the fruits of the revolution belonged to all strata of the society, including the middle classes. But the suppression of a wide variety of middle-class-based political groups and the ever-increasing dominance of the clerics and their lower-class supporters, such as the Hizbollahis, has diminished the appeal that the revolution enjoyed during its first few years. Furthermore, the large-scale purges, summary executions, involvement of teenagers in the war through the Basij (Mobilization Force) and the Pasdaran (Revolutionary Guards), the deterioration of the status of women, and the like, have dampened the earlier appeal of the revolution.

Fourth, as these negative impressions of the revolutionary paradigm began to spread, the ancient cultural differences between Arabs and Persians and between Sunnis and Shia started to surface. The Saddam Hussein regime has tried to exploit the old Arab-Iranian cultural differences in his reference to the battle of al-Qadisiya, when the Arab Muslims defeated the Persian Sassanids in AD 637, in the war with Iran. Unlike the Arab-Persian conflict, however, the Shii-Sunni differences are not exploitable by Arab leaders, because they could boomerang, given the presence of large Shii populations in their societies. Nevertheless, on-site observation suggests clear intensification of sectarian feelings.

Despite the repellent side of the ledger, the appeal of Khomeinism on the whole continues. Even those Gulf Arabs who are repelled by certain perceived negative aspects of the Iranian example have not been able to avoid an intensified atmosphere of political consciousness. This can play into the hands of demagogues and radical politicians, especially in combination with the other factors discussed below.

SOCIETAL "REJUVENATION"

One of the most important of these factors is what the United Nations calls the problem of "rejuvenation," that is, an increasing percentage of young people among the population. Without this problem, the Gulf Arab communities would probably have been less susceptible to Iranian revolutionary agitation, notwithstanding an intensified sense of political consciousness. The problem of rejuvenation in the Gulf area is more acute than in most other Third World regions because of the additional problem of the large percentage of foreigners in Gulf societies and hence the relatively small size of the citizen populations.

We may recall the 1960s, when the effects of the "baby boom" of the earlier decades began to be felt in our own Western European societies. The "rebellious young" became the watchword of those days in explaining the social upheaval that accompanied the arrival of a new generation. The Third World now faces this problem acutely. U.N. statistics show that some 60 percent of the populations in the underdeveloped regions of the world are less than 20 years of age as compared with about 40 percent in the "more developed regions." Taking the politically most active age group in the Gulf, that is, the group between 10 and 34 years of age, about 46 percent of the population of all Gulf countries was between 10 and 34 years old in 1980. Projecting this figure into the year 2000, it will increase to about 48 percent. In the United States, by comparison, Americans of the same age group accounted for about 43 percent of the population in 1980 and will *decrease* to about 35 percent in the year 2000. Among all the Gulf countries, Bahrain had the highest percentage of this age group (51.11 percent) in 1980, while Oman had the lowest (44.10 percent) in the same year.[12]

One of the most striking features of the profile of terrorism in the Gulf region is the involvement of the younger people in acts of political violence. In the Kuwaiti terrorist incident, except for three out of twenty-one terrorists, whose ages are unknown, all were under thirty years of age. More important, out of twenty-one convicted, sixteen were in their twenties.[13] If indeed rejuvenation of the population and social and political extremism go hand in hand, then the trend in the Gulf region is likely to contribute further to an environment of political violence.

Second, to take up the problem of the large numbers of expatriates in the Gulf societies, the problem of rejuvenation is compounded by what may be called the problem of societal perforation because of the large number of expatriates. The intensity of this problem is different from country to country. The UAE ranks the highest among the GCC states. Its foreign population forms more than 80 percent of the total population of a quarter of a million people, and hence its citizen population is less than one-third of the total. Qatar and Kuwait rank after the UAE in terms of the percentage of their foreign population, at 73 percent and 61 percent, respectively.[14]

The correlation between large numbers of foreign expatriates and an environment favoring terrorism may be inferred from two developments. First, every major terrorist act has involved expatriates of one kind or another.[15] Ever since the Iranian Revolution, a number of Gulf Arab countries have been expelling expatriates. Many of them have been sent home in recent years because of drastically declining oil revenues. Saudi Arabia, for example, plans to have 600,000 fewer by the end of its five-year plan in 1990, and Kuwait also plans to change the ratio of foreign to local population from the current 60–40 percent to 50–50 percent. But many expatriates are also being expelled because of a heightened sense of insecurity. Since the multiple bombings, terrorist-plagued Kuwait has deported many thousands of Iranians and also other nationalities. At least 50,000 expatriates have been deported since the assassination attempt against the life of the Amir took place in May 1985.

SOCIETAL ALIENATION

A third cluster of factors that seems to contribute to an environment of radicalism in the Gulf region is societal alienation. There is a general consensus that alienation of individuals and groups can contribute to social and political violence in both underdeveloped and developed societies. When it comes to considering a particular country or situation, however, there seems to be disagreement about the sources of alienation. For example, many observers have identified "modernization" as the key in the resurgence of Islam and the eruption of the Iranian Revolution. Some emphasize rapid economic change, some the slow pace of economic development, and others the maldistribution of wealth.

The Iranian Revolution, as I have suggested elsewhere, was *at inception* a "revolution of rising alienation," stemming from no single economic, political, moral, or ideological source.[16] Rather, it reflected the cumulative effects of a complex of domestic and foreign policies of the Shah's regime over the decades, perceived to be detrimental to the interests and values of a variety of groups and individuals. To many, modernized intellectuals, political oppression, and lack of political freedom under the Shah's rule mattered most of all. But the uprooted masses of peasantry, who were not able to recognize rapid urbanization as the source of their misery, bewilderment, "anonymity," or "crisis of identity," became increasingly estranged from the Shah's regime because of the wretched conditions of their lives. Examples may be easily multiplied to show how different individuals and groups perceived the policies of the Shah as harmful to their values and interests, especially the clerics and their bazaari supporters.

It has been argued elsewhere that Iranian-type revolutions are not likely for other Gulf states, and I suggested above that, on balance, the main effect of the Iranian revolutionary paradigm has been an intensified political awakening in the Gulf region.[17] Yet, societal alienation is also taking place in varying degrees in the Arab Gulf countries, and as in the case of prerevolutionary Iran, its causes are multifaceted. There are various groups and individuals who seem to believe that their values and interests have been adversely affected by the domestic and foreign policies of the incumbent regimes. It is beyond the scope of this study to consider this important subject in detail. But it is necessary to make two additional points that bear on the process of societal alienation.

First, the effects of rapid expansion of mass communications and education have begun to combine with the impact of the processes of rejuvenation and intensified political consciousness. The net result has been the rise of a highly politicized younger generation, particularly among the middle classes. Contrary to the current impression, this expanding political awakening is not expressed exclusively in Islamic terms. Secular nationalism, liberal and conservative, co-exists and competes with Islamic fundamentalism, radical and conservative.

In the open society of Kuwait, it is easier to observe that Islamic fundamentalism, both Shii and Sunni, is challenged today by secular nationalism. In the 1985 parliamentary elections, nationalist candidates gained unexpectedly, while Muslim fundamentalists lost seats they had won in 1981. In less open societies, this same phenomenon is more difficult to observe, but the reassertion of secular nationalism is unmistakable today. One major indicator is the rising demand for a modern type of political participation. Except for those who have been coopted by existing regimes, most of the modern members of the middle classes complain about their closed political systems. Politically aware Bahrainis demand the reopening of their suspended parliament, while their Saudi counterparts complain that they have never had more than the ever-suspended promise of a consultative assembly.

Second, if it was feared a few years ago that rapid modernization, fueled by a massive rise in oil revenues, could trigger societal dislocation, income mal-distribution, and lifestyle disruption, today it is feared that economic recession as a result of the drastic fall in oil prices may cause whole new sources of societal alienation and hence an environment of political radicalism. The alarmists may exaggerate the odds, but the new problems caused by an unprecedented recession are here already. Today's oil bust can be as disruptive as yesterday's oil boom. The oil revenues of the Arab Gulf states have dropped by about 50 percent since 1981, and the landmark decisions of OPEC in 1982 and 1983 with respect to prices and production, like all other subsequent OPEC efforts to avert greater losses of oil revenues, have failed so far. Given their varying levels of development and their different needs and lifestyles, the Gulf societies may be affected unevenly, but all are suffering. The Saudis now have the world's second largest deficit after the United States and were forced for the first time in March 1986 to defer announcement of their 1986/87 budget until the end of the year.

The scrambling by governments to head off the crisis by cutting back on spending, by abandoning dispensable projects, by withdrawing subsidies—especially of water and electricity—and by other economizing measures is leading already to disgruntlement among various groups and individuals. Some Saudi academics complained in 1986 that they had lost about 30 percent of their income because of paying for things for which they never used to pay. But professors are not the only ones who are hurting; bureaucrats, technocrats, businessmen, bankers, and others also complain about the financial squeeze and worry about the overall side effects of the economic slump. Thus, the potential for widespread societal alienation can be serious. This may be particularly true in the case of already disenchanted elements within the various Shii communities in the Gulf.

SHII VICTIMIZATION

The Gulf is the Shii heartland of the world. Out of an estimated 750 million Muslims, about 11 percent are Shia. More than half of these are Twelver, or Imami, Shia who live in the Gulf region, forming majorities of the citizen populations in Bahrain, Iran, and Iraq, as well as minorities in Kuwait, Oman, Qatar, Saudi Arabia, and the UAE. Shii rule only in Iran, not even in Bahrain and Iraq, where they constitute the majority of the citizen populations. This does not mean necessarily that most Bahraini and Iraqi Shia demand Shii rule, but they do want a greater share of power in the Sunni-dominated political process. There are radical Shii activists on the fringes of various societies, most particularly in Iraq, who seek to overthrow Sunni rule by violence.

The Shia of Iraq have regional influence partly because they have the largest demographic base. Iraq has the most Shia of any Arab country, who number over 8 million, 60 percent of the population. More importantly, the Shia of Iraq are the architects of the oldest and largest network of any underground Arab Shii revolutionary movement and organization in the Gulf region. Underground cells or sympathizers of Al-Dawa may be found as far south in the Gulf as the UAE. According to Ayatollah Sayyid Mahdi al-Hakim, son of the late founder, Muhsin al-Hakim, Al-Dawa's beginnings date back to "after the [Iraqi] 'revolution' of 1958. Its aims: establishing an Islamic state."[18]

After the Iranian Revolution and the ascendancy of the Shii clerics in the polity, the relationship between Al-Dawa and the Iranians developed further. The government of Saddam Hussein claims that before the outbreak of the Iran-Iraq War the Iranian leadership pushed party members and sympathizers to acts of political violence in Iraq and cites this provocation as the chief reason for the Iraqi invasion of Iran. Whether true or not, the Khomeini regime has fully aided and abetted Al-Dawa since the outbreak of the war. In addition, the regime hosts the Supreme Assembly of the Islamic Revolution in Iraq (SAIRI), an organization of Iraqi Shii dissidents in Iran. There are over 350,000 Shia from Iraq in Iran today, including those Iranian residents of Iraq who were expelled by the Iraqi regime at the outset of the war. The Iranian government openly uses the Iraqi dissidents in its war against Iraq, one example being the military offensive at Hajj 'Umran, on the northern front, in which many Iraqi "warriors" (*mujahadeen*) actually participated. But the government of Iran defiantly denies that it uses Al-Dawa Iraqi revolutionaries to perpetrate acts of terrorism in other Arab countries. As seen above, however, most of the suspected terrorists in Kuwait have been identified as Iraqi nationals belonging to this underground party.

None of the facts cited so far—the large number of Iraqi Shia, the organization of Al-Dawa, and the Iranian support for it—accounts, however, for Shii-sponsored acts of terrorism in the Gulf region. Rather, these stem from a deep-felt sense of victimization that poisons the social and political atmosphere in Iraq, as it does in varying degrees in other Gulf Arab countries. Among the Gulf Shia the watchword everywhere is "the deprived" (mahrumin), a characterization of the conditions of the Shii population that even some Saudi Sunnis use in talking about Saudi Shia. The Shia in the Arab states consider themselves as the underdogs. For example, while Saudi Shia believe they have been historically mistreated, the Iraqi Shia believe they have never shared the power and prosperity of the Sunnis, whether under the Ottomans, the British, the monarchy in the past, or the minority Sunni-Ba'athist regime of the Takriti clan at the present time.

The widespread sense of victimization among the Shia has been treated in greater detail elsewhere,[19] but it is important to note here the potential for its deepening under the present deteriorating conditions. Every Gulf Arab regime has made genuine efforts in recent years to upgrade standards of living, especially of poorer classes among the Shia. Those who are well off seldom wish to rock the boat and are easily coopted by the Sunni governments. The material betterment of the poor Shia in recent years has not reduced their doctrinal differences with the Sunnis. Nor has it dimmed their bitter memories of historical mistreatment at the hands of Sunni rulers. It has, however, helped somewhat to alleviate past grievances. Present governments must cut corners in order to cope with the consequences of falling oil revenues, but it would be unwise to cut spending on housing, water, electricity, and other amenities enjoyed by the Shii population.

This discussion of the Shii people as a separate group has been intended to emphasize that the process of alienation, for historical, social, political, and doctrinal reasons, has gone much further among the Shia as compared with other disaffected groups, both religious and secular. Hence as a factor influencing the climate of radicalism, Shii alienation should receive more empathetic attention. Such attention may help dissipate the myths that have been spun around the very word "Shia." Especially in the United States, mass ignorance about the Shii people has been replaced by mass prejudice rather than knowledge, as evidenced by the automatic equation of "Shii" with "terrorist," "fanatic," and other pejorative appellations. These new stereotypes have effectively reinforced the already heightened anti-American feeling in the region and contribute materially to the fertile environment for radicalism.

Anti-American sentiment in the Gulf region arose as part of the anti-imperialist movement sweeping across much of the Third World. But it cannot be adequately understood without considering four particular factors. First, unlike the rest of the Third World, the Middle East in general and the Gulf region in particular have been the object of fierce rivalries between the old and the new, and between the great powers and the superpowers ever since Alexander roamed this strategic bridge between Europe and Africa. During the final stages of the fall of the Persian and Islamic Empires, Russian and British imperial rivalries dominated the scene until the French and British chopped up the Arab lands for themselves during and after World War I. The discovery of the world's single largest pool of petroleum only increased the Gulf's ancient strategic value to the rest of the world. Foreign political interference, economic domination, and military intervention have often accompanied great-power and superpower rivalries and contributed to anti-imperialist feelings, mistrust of foreign powers, and spurts of xenophobic nationalism and Islamic radicalism.

Second, unlike the rest of the Third World, where the process of decolonization has been followed by the realization of the principle of self-determination of peoples, that principle has been realized in the Middle East by only one of the two peoples claiming Palestine as their homeland, that is, the American-supported people of Israel. Palestinian nationalists continue to demand the fulfillment of that principle. But the United States opposes the establishment of any full-fledged Palestinian state, even in the small area of the Israeli-controlled West Bank and Gaza. As a result, some Palestinians and other Arabs and Palestinians—and, since the revolution, some Iranians as well—have set for themselves the goal of setting things right by destroying Israel. These groups claim that the Jewish state is the imperialist obstacle to their goals of Arab unity and Islamic solidarity. The historical anti-imperialist sentiment of the Arabs and Palestinians against the British has thus been transferred to the Americans since 1948, as was that of most Iranians after 1953, when the CIA supported the overthrow of the nationalist government of Dr. Mohammad Mosaddegh.

Third, unlike other parts of the Third World, the United States is committed under the Carter Doctrine to intervene in the Gulf by military means, if necessary, to preserve the uninterrupted flow of Gulf oil supplies to world markets, and it has spent billions of dollars on the U.S. Central Command (CENTCOM) since January 1983 in pursuit of this objective. This U.S. policy is repugnant to the politically aware citizens of the Gulf, who perceive CENTCOM as an "interventionist force." This widespread popular perception partly accounts for the insistence by most Gulf Arab regimes on restricting the American military presence to "over the horizon," on having no foreign bases in the region, and on denying the pre-positioning of American military equipment on their soil, despite their dependence on the United States for military buildup and defense.

Fourth, unlike in most other parts of the Third World, the United States today is perceived by various segments of the politicized groups in the Gulf region to be too closely identified with conservative and authoritarian Gulf Arab regimes, as it was in the past with the Shah's dictatorial regime. From such a perspective, forty years of the U.S. security relationship with Saudi Arabia, coupled with President Ronald Reagan's so-called corollary, which seems to promise American defense of the House of Saud so that it will not suffer a fate similar to that of the Pahlavi dynasty in Iran, offers sufficient proof of the subservience of Saudi Arabia and its GCC partners to the United States.

The astronomical expenditure of these regimes on arms purchases—still largely from the United States despite the rhetoric of diversification and "Saudization"—seems to irritate even those elements of the modernized intelligentsia who may be considered "pro-Western." It may not be widely known in the region that on a per capita basis the arms expenditure of Gulf Arab states is the world's highest, but it does not make much difference insofar as the perception of American dominance in the area is concerned. The United States is perceived to be dominant, and this perception contributes to an environment for radicalism.

Khomeini's perception of the "Great Satan" as the source of the "twin evils" of Zionism and imperialism complicates the problem of anti-American sentiment for the pro-American moderate regimes. It would be a mistake to continue to believe that the public efforts of these regimes to distance themselves from the United States merely reflect popular resentment over the close American identification with Israel. No matter how true this impression might have been before the Iranian Revolution, it is true no longer. Today the Iranian anti-American stance has a significant bearing on the attitudes of these regimes. The establishment of diplomatic relations with the Soviet Union by Oman and the UAE to a considerable extent reflects the desire of these regimes to put their nonalignment rhetoric into practice. They wish simultaneously to neutralize the effects of the anti-American crusade of the Khomeini regime and to respond to anti-American sentiment of the politically aware Arab Gulf citizens in order to assure the survival of their regimes.

THE EFFECTS OF THE IRAN-IRAQ WAR

Has the Iran-Iraq War contributed to the environment of radicalism in the Gulf region? It would be easy to assume that since the war largely reflects the effects of ideological and political radicalism, it has no place in a discussion of the causes of radicalism in the Gulf region.[20] But that would be unwarranted.

Having gone on for seven long and bloody years, the war has acquired a life of its own regardless of its causes, and many continue to fear that it might spread to other Gulf states.

The war has contributed to the radicalization of the Gulf political environment in three principal ways. First, it has helped to entrench the extremist faction of the revolutionary movement in power in Iran. The Iraqi invasion played into the hands of the militant Iranians, helping them to consolidate their political control. They had already used the hostage crisis to that end, but the diplomatic and economic sanctions that it entailed had begun to hurt. In seeking a settlement of the dispute with the United States, an Iranian minister conceded that the hostage crisis had been squeezed dry of its usefulness "like an orange." The Ba'athist Iraq, one may add, handed a fresh orange to the Iranian extremists.

The war issue, like the hostage issue, was used in the struggle for power between President Banisadr and his opponents, and in the end his dismissal by Ayatollah Khomeini confirmed the dominance of the radical religious faction. It was no coincidence that the Iranian military successes followed the fall of Banisadr from power and the consolidation of domestic power by his opponents. The hope for moderate politics in Iran had received its first major blow as a result of the fall of the Bazargan government two days after the militant students took over the American Embassy in Tehran. The fall of Banisadr dealt that hope a final blow. By invading Iran, the Iraqi secular radicals hoped to prevent the Iranian religious radicals from consolidating power, but instead they ensured their success. It is anybody's guess whether the Iranian militants would have been as successful in gathering power to them without the help of the war, but the war did strengthen their hand and thus has contributed to the overall environment of radicalism in the Gulf region.

Second, the war has aided the process of radicalization of politics in the Gulf region by giving the militant Al-Dawa Party a new lease on life. The Ba'athist killing of Ayatollah Sayyid Muhammad Baqir al-Sadr—the most respected Iraqi Shii 'alim (learned religious leader)—in April 1980 played into the hands of Al-Dawa, the Ba'athists falsely charging that he had been associated with the party.[21] The twin murder of the Iraqi Ayatollah and his sister stirred anger, resentment, and frustration among many Shii communities in the Gulf region. Yet, Al-Dawa's ability to use this tragic incident to stir up terrorist acts against the Ba'ath Party within Iraq was limited, especially in the face of the ruthless suppression of the Shii dissidents within Iraq.

The start of the war increased Al-Dawa's capability, making it the single most radical and the best organized underground political group in the Arab Gulf countries. On the one hand, the deportation of thousands of Iraqi Shia to

Iran and other Gulf countries expanded the social base from which Al-Dawa could recruit anti-Ba'athist dissidents for its secret cells in the region. On the other hand, the war made it possible for revolutionary Iranians to support Al-Dawa and its terrorist activities within Iraq in the same way that revolutionary Ba'athists have supported the Iranian anti-Khomeini Mujahadeen-e-Khalq faction, led by Massoud Rajavi, in terrorist acts within Iran. As said before, there is little doubt that most of those who have been convicted of participating in terrorist acts in Kuwait have been Iraqi nationals and members of Al-Dawa.

Third, the overreaction of the conservative Arab governments to the nightmare of the spillover effects of the war in their territories is threatening what little chance for liberal politics may exist in the Gulf region. Every major sign of the escalation of the war, like every terrorist incident, has resulted in greater tightening of internal security. Despite the denials of government officials, restrictions on travel, on publications, on information, and on other avenues of freedom of expression and movement have been imposed in the name of security. The fears of Kuwaiti liberals were realized when the Al Sabah family suspended the Kuwaiti National Assembly in July 1986. Their counterparts in Bahrain believe that the Al Khalifa family may well find security a perfect excuse for not considering seriously the idea of reopening that country's suspended parliament, and Saudi liberals see the prospects of establishing a long-promised consultative assembly growing ever dimmer.

The obsession of the conservative Arab regimes individually, or collectively in the GCC, with containing the spread of the war by building up a military deterrence is also of concern to the Gulf liberals. They view the ever-growing arsenals of their countries as a serious threat to their chances for political freedom. They do not deny the need for individual and collective self-defense. But they are skeptical about the usefulness of such a vast military buildup. They point out the small size of their populations, the perforated nature of their societies, and the sectarian divisions in the Arab Gulf states on the one hand, and on the other their excessive dependence on the West, particularly the United States, the inadequacy of trained indigenous manpower, and the diversity of military equipment, as arguments against such a buildup. They also express the fear that, to borrow George Washington's words, "overgrown military establishments [are] inauspicious to liberty."

POLICY IMPLICATIONS

To suggest, as I have, that an analysis of terrorism must take into account the environment regardless of motivation in no way implies that terrorism is excusable or justifiable. It only means that one way of coping with terrorism may be to manage the problems that are posed by its environment.

Even those who categorically view as criminal all terrorist acts must admit that prevention of crime—no less than punishment of the criminal—is a widely accepted precept in our own society, and that improving the environment of crime is critical to its prevention. In the society of sovereign states—where nations are judges in their own cause and where the day is far off when all acts of terrorism will be considered as criminal and punishable by enforceable international legal norms—we should at least try to limit terrorism by improving its environment. To be sure, the United Nations has finally adopted a resolution that unequivocally condemns as criminal "all acts, methods, and practices of terrorism." But until this resolution, with which I concur, becomes an enforceable world law, realistically, all that we can hope for is damage limitation. To this end, this study advances the following implications for U.S. policy in the Gulf:

1. *The United States should resist the temptation to portray Iran as the Great Satan of the Gulf and Islamic radicalism as the twin of Marxism.* Conflict between Iran and the United States or between Islamic fundamentalism and American values and interests is neither inevitable nor permanent, for three major reasons: First, the early appeal of the Iranian revolutionary paradigm among the Arab Gulf people has been diminishing. We risk making it attractive again by fostering an implacable hostility toward Iran, contrary to George Washington's good advice against "permanent, inveterate antipathies to particular nations." Second, regardless of the Iranian example, the resurgence of Islamic fundamentalism has been increasingly challenged by both liberal and conservative secular nationalism in Arab Gulf societies. Third, Iran's new "open door" policy has begun to show definite signs of pragmatic tendencies.

2. *Judging by demographic projections about the rise of an increasingly younger Gulf population by the year 2000, the United States should brace itself for more social and political ferment in the Gulf during the next decade.* The problem of rejuvenation, added to that of expatriates, even though declining in numbers, points to the rise of even more volatile peoples in the GCC countries. A less ubiquitous presence of American expatriates could help the problem of anti-Americanism but not of security, which is posed primarily by Arab expatriates, as evidenced by terrorist incidents. The cutting edge of the rejuvenation problem is the increasing potential for societal alienation.

3. *The current economic recession resulting from the drastic fall of oil revenues may be viewed as either a blessing in disguise or a new cause of further societal alienation.* To the extent that expenditure cutting and belt tightening may put a brake on ostentatious living, waste, and corruption, it may be cause for comfort. However, in my opinion, such an outcome is highly doubtful and we should anticipate increasing disaffection among the young people, who are spoiled and have no stomach for hardship. Most critical is the dissatisfaction of two groups: the

modernized middle classes and the Shii activists. So far the largesse of the regimes has benefited both and kept them relatively satisfied, but the austerity measures currently being considered could trigger widespread alienation if fully implemented. If invited to offer advice on coping with these problems, the United States should emphasize the importance of the equitable distribution of wealth, greater efforts at redressing the grievances of the Shii communities, and opening up the political system according to the promises made to the people by the incumbent leaders themselves.

4. *Although the United States has to learn to live with anti-Americanism, we can avoid intensifying it in various ways.* Diplomacy, rather than the use of force, should become the centerpiece of our Gulf policy. Instead of becoming obsessed with punishing the terrorist, we should find ways of rewarding the moderate majority in Gulf societies. Second, all cultural, educational, and informational programs that can help dissipate the misperceptions of the Gulf people about our intentions and actions should be accorded a higher priority than heretofore. Third, to be sure, the Palestinian problem is not at the root of all causes, but it is an undeniable nationalist movement—despite all its factions and feuds and its exploitation by fellow Arabs. Its legitimate aspirations must be seriously addressed by Washington in the enlightened self-interest of both Israel and the United States.

5. *The United States cannot stop the Iran-Iraq War and thus eliminate its radicalizing effects on the Gulf environment, but it can keep its "tilt" toward Iraq strictly curtailed and thus limit the damage.* Once Iran carried the war into Iraq in July 1982, the American tilt seemed inevitable, but half a decade later this imperative must be weighed against other considerations.[22] Too far a tilt toward Iraq may well discourage Iran's emerging qualms about terrorism, as evidenced by its unequivocal condemnation of the mining of the Suez Canal and the Red Sea, its capture of the hijackers of the Kuwaiti airliner, its help in freeing the TWA American hostages, and its punishment of one of the hijackers of the Saudi Arabian plane. We must retain the option of establishing a dialogue with Iran sooner or later. Iran retained such an option for months after the disclosure of its secret arms purchases from the United States. But it was forced to suspend this option after the Reagan administration increased its military presence in the Gulf.

6. *The United States should continue to aid the GCC states in their efforts to create a credible military deterrence, but it should resist the temptation to embrace the group too closely.* To the Gulf liberals, the deepening dependence on American arms is detrimental not only to the political independence of their countries but also to their personal liberty. Every major escalation in the war and every terrorist incident has been followed by tighter restrictions on the freedoms of movement and expression. To the extent that these restrictions choke off peaceful dissent, they are

believed to increase the attraction of political violence as the only recourse for bringing about political change.

There is no easy or quick way to eliminate terrorism, but implementation of the above suggestions may help contain the environment of radicalism in the Gulf region. The majority of the people of the area are moderate; only a minority is radical. Not all radicals are terrorists—but all terrorists are radical. The real challenge ahead is how to prevent today's moderates from becoming tomorrow's radicals.

NOTES

1. This study is based primarily on observations made and conversations held during the course of numerous visits to the Gulf starting in 1979 and including a last visit in 1986. Otherwise, I have cited documentary sources of information.

2. See U.S. Department of State, Bureau of Public Affairs, *International Terrorism*, Selected Documents, No. 24 (Washington, DC, 1986).

3. The other targets included the headquarters of the American Raytheon Company and the apartment building housing the company's employees, the airport control tower, the Ministry of Electricity and Water building, the Passport Office, and a major petrochemical and refining complex. A Kuwaiti court tried twenty-five defendants on 27 March 1984. Five were acquitted of involvement in the bombings; six were sentenced to death, three of whom were tried in absentia; seven to life imprisonment, four of whom were tried in absentia; four to 15 years; one to 10 years; and two to 5 years. None of the accused was Iranian. Out of the group of twenty-five, seventeen were Iraqis, three were Lebanese, three were Kuwaiti, and two were stateless.

4. Confronted by an Iranian fighter plane upon entering Iranian airspace, the pilot of the Kuwaiti plane claimed that he was running out of fuel, and he was permitted to land at Tehran Imam Khomeini International Airport. Iranian officials condemned the hijacking and the killing of two Americans on board the plane, and eventually Iranian troops stormed the plane, captured the hijackers, and freed the remaining passengers. Iranian judicial authorities promised to put the hijackers on trial and punish them for their crimes.

5. Foreign Broadcast Information Service, *Daily Report*, vol. 5, *Middle East and North Africa* (FBIS-MEA), 28 May 1985. Kuwaiti security authorities said on May 26 that they had identified the Iraqi perpetrator of the attack after "assembling pieces of his fingers and examining his fingerprints." Ibid., 29 May 1985. The Iraqi ambassador to Kuwait, when confronted with the reports that the culprit was a member of the Iraqi Al-Dawa Party, stated flatly that "the party to which the criminal belongs is an Iranian party 100 percent." Ibid. Speaking "frankly," the newspaper *al-Ra'i al-'Aam* hinted that the "criminal act" against the Amir represented the peak of Iranian terror. With some irony, it also reported that the Iranian chargé d'affaires had denounced the incident, sent a bouquet of flowers to the Amir, and extended "congratulations" to him on his escape. It then added that this "stand by Iran and its supporters cannot deceive anybody." Ibid. It was subsequently reported that the Kuwaiti security authorities had arrested twenty persons accused of being connected with the attack and that three of them had admitted their guilt.

6. This consensus refers to the activities of the organization only outside of Egypt, where there is an Islamic faction by the same name. The respected *Middle East Economic Digest*, for example, seems to consider the Islamic Jihad and Al-Dawa two different organizations. It said at the time of the incident that the latter's "aims are broadly similar to those of Islamic Jihad and it is believed there may be some organizational links between the two groups." *Middle East Economic Digest* (MEED), 1 June 1985.

7. Ibid., 15 June, 1985.

8. It was also believed that the victims of the incident were from a variety of nations, including 18 Kuwaitis, 1 citizen from the United Arab Emirates (UAE), 1 Iranian, 2 Egyptians, 2 Iraqis, and others of undetermined national origin. Among the Kuwaiti casualties was a senior Interior Ministry official.

9. The newspaper said in part that "the documents [of the anti-Khomeini Iranian national resistance movement] frankly refer to an Iranian scheme with regard to the GCC countries and frankly provide for the declaration of something resembling war on these countries." FBIS-MEA, 12 July 1985.

10. William Regis Farrell, *The US Government Response to Terrorism: In Search of an Effective Strategy* (Boulder, 1982), 12.

11. See R. K. Ramazani, "Iran's Islamic Revolution and the Persian Gulf," *Current History* 84 (January 1985), 5–8 and 40–41.

12. Computed on the basis of data in United Nations, Department of International Economic and Social Affairs, *Demographic Indicators of Countries: Estimates and Projections as Assessed in 1980,* ST/ESA/SER.A/82 (New York, 1982), 60–61, 250–51, 304–5, 316–17, 320–21, 324–25, and 328–37.

13. FBIS-MEA, 13 February 1984.

14. See table 7 in R. K. Ramazani, *Revolutionary Iran: Challenge and Response in the Middle East* (Baltimore, 1986), 26.

15. The plotters of the aborted coup in Bahrain included four different nationalities. Out of a total of 73 arrested, there were 60 Bahrainis, 11 Saudis, 1 Omani, and 1 Kuwaiti. In the case of the multiple bombings in Kuwait, most of the 25 terrorists convicted were Iraqi nationals. At least 13 were known to be Iraqi, 3 Lebanese, and 3 Kuwaiti, while the nationalities of the suspects at large were not established.

16. See R. K. Ramazani, "Iran's Revolution in Perspective," in *The Impact of the Iranian Events upon Persian Gulf and United States Security,* project director Z. Michael Szaz (Washington, DC, 1979) 19–37; Ramazani, "Iran's Foreign Policy: Perspectives and Projections," in *Economic Consequences of the Revolution in Iran: A Compendium of Papers Submitted to the Joint Economic Committee, Congress of the United States* (Washington, DC, 1980), 65–97; a slightly modified version with the same title in *Revolution in Iran: A Reappraisal,* edited by Enver M. Koury and Charles G. MacDonald (Hyattsville, MD, 1982), 9–41; Ramazani, "Iran's Revolution: Patterns, Problems, and Prospects," pp. 33–49 in this volume; Ramazani, *The United States and Iran: The Patterns of Influence* (New York, 1982); and Ramazani, *Revolutionary Iran.*

17. Over the years I have been struck, during various visits to the Gulf, by the intense interest of the Arabs in the Iranian Revolution. For example, on my last visit to the Gulf, in 1986, I was asked for interviews by two major Kuwaiti publications. For the text of these interviews, see *al-Anba',* 15 February 1986, and *al-Mujtam'a,* 11 March 1986, 29–33.

On the theme of no spread of Iranian-type revolutions in the rest of the Gulf, see also R. K. Ramazani, "America and the Gulf: Beyond Peace and Security," *Middle East Insight*, January/February 1982, 2–9.

18. See R. K. Ramazani, "Shiism in the Persian Gulf," pp. 240–62 in this volume.

19. Ibid.

20. See table 7 in Ramazani, *Revolutionary Iran*, 26.

21. See H. Batatu, "Iraq's Underground Shia Movements: Characteristics, Causes and Prospects," *Middle East Journal* 35, no. 4 (Autumn 1981): 578–94.

22. These other considerations are discussed in detail in "Iran: Burying the Hatchet," pp. 94–110 in this volume.

IV

INTERNATIONAL LAW

AND DIPLOMACY

WHO STARTED THE IRAN-IRAQ WAR?

A Commentary

Since Iraq invaded Kuwait on August 2, 1990, the international legal community has rightly condemned Iraq's aggressive use of military force against its neighboring sovereign state of Kuwait. Considerable discussion has followed about appropriate legal consequences, including sanctions, reparations, and war-crimes trials.[1] By sharp contrast, similar legal attention remains glaringly absent regarding an equally flagrant case of aggressive Iraqi employment of military force, on September 22, 1980, against its neighboring sovereign state of Iran.

International reconsideration of the outbreak of the Iran-Iraq War ought to have been kindled by a highly significant report prepared by Javier Perez de Cuellar, in one of his final acts as U.N. secretary-general. The full text of the report is printed herein[2] for the first time outside the U.N. Secretariat. This essay outlines the reasons for the importance of this report to the international community from the perspectives of international politics and law. Special focus is given to the secretary-general's key finding that Iraq's employment of force against Iran in 1980 deserves the same legal disapprobation as the Iraqi aggression against Kuwait. If this judgment is indeed correct, then the international community cannot in good faith proceed to focus on legal consequences of the Iraqi invasion of Kuwait without serious attention to the legal consequences of Iraqi aggression against Iran in 1980.

Regrettably, political considerations, media distortions, and personal predispositions have long prevented a reasoned pursuit of fact and principle regarding the events of September 1980. The fact that many readers will reflexively shrink from the suggestion that Iran's legal case against Iraq may have merit only emphasizes the need for renewed and dispassionate inquiry into the subject. Those who seek to enhance the moral persuasiveness of international law must be willing to consider whether inconsistencies in the case at hand have undermined the legitimacy of international norms.

"Who Started the Iraq-Iran War? A Commentary" was originally published in *Virginia Journal of International Law* 33, no. 1 (Fall 1992): 69–89.

THE SECRETARY-GENERAL'S REPORT:
THE SILENT RESPONSE

On December 9, 1991, just three weeks before former U.N. secretary-general Perez de Cuellar retired, he delivered to the U.N. Security Council one of the most important reports, if not the most, of his distinguished career. His mandate for preparing the report originates in paragraph 6 of Security Council Resolution 598 of July 20, 1987,[3] which provided the framework that eventually facilitated the arrangement of a lasting cease-fire between Iraq and Iran on August 20, 1988. For reasons explained below, the secretary-general was endeavoring to report on critical responsibilities accorded to him by the U.N. Security Council. Given the tremendous human suffering caused by the Iran-Iraq War, any U.N. attention to the subject deserves intense scrutiny.

Despite the inherent importance of the secretary-general's report, the media in the United States, for the most part, ignored or trivialized the report,[4] and the scholarly community followed suit. British and French coverage of the report was marginally better.[5] Western states have not taken an official position on the secretary-general's report, and American policymakers have not commented about the report on the record.

Among the most telling examples of the American media's disposition to downplay the secretary-general's efforts, the *Washington Post* of December 11, 1991, confined itself to printing a rather jaded Associated Press account of the report without making any attempt at giving it prominent space, let alone providing readers with an appropriate editorial or other commentary.[6] Indeed, no major American paper ran an editorial or opinion article on the report.[7] The Associated Press's gratuitous dubbing of the report as "unusually partisan" revealed its inability to rise above the "hate Iran" propaganda campaign that has plagued Washington far longer than it has any other major Western capital.

When the secretary-general's report has been commented upon at all in the American media, the all-purpose "unnamed diplomats" seem more interested in questioning the secretary-general's motives than in seriously considering the content and merits of his findings. The Associated Press story suggested that the secretary-general's designation of Iraq as the initiator of the war was motivated by his desire to reward Iran for its help in the release of Western hostages held in Lebanon.[8] Such Iraqi-style insinuations[9] are highly speculative. To begin with, it was a coincidence that the secretary-general privately asked Iran and Iraq on August 14, 1991, to write him about their views on the responsibility for starting the war, only six days after a pro-Iranian Shii Muslim group released British hostage John McCarthy with a message for Perez de Cuellar to help free all Western hostages and Arabs detained by Israel. Other speculations about the secretary-general's motives, such as his desire to persuade Iran to be more flexible on the settlement of the remaining prisoner-of-war issues, or to complete his term of office with attention-getting bravado, are equally conjectural.[10] Both long before and after passage of U.N. Resolution 598, the secretary-general had been closely involved in the POW issues.[11] Moreover, by the fall of 1991, when he focused on the issue of responsibility for the war, most of the POWs already had been exchanged. The charge that he was simply motivated by wanting to finish off his term of office with a self-serving resolution of the problem of Western hostages is baseless for yet another reason. It was the Iranian government, and not the secretary-general, that jump-started the freedom of the hostages. He, of course, welcomed the Iranian willingness to cooperate, just as he appreciated the willingness of both Syria and Lebanon to help resolve this agonizing humanitarian problem.[12] The glaring biases evident in such speculations should not be allowed to detract from the universal recognition of the secretary-general's reputation as an impartial leader who played a key role in the resolution of the Iran-Iraq conflict, the most bloody war since the end of World War II.[13]

The Bush administration's official silence on the secretary-general's report, like the U.S. media's neglect, may well reflect the continued hostility of Washington toward Tehran. But feeding this passion helps neither American interests nor the international community's interest in promoting international law. Twelve years after Iraq's invasion of Iran and two years after Iraq's invasion of Kuwait, Washington continues to be obsessed with the trauma of the Iranian hostage-taking of 1979. Washington also continues to be preoccupied with a Manichaean, mechanical, and martial concept of balance of power.[14] This preoccupation is incomprehensible today considering the increasing signs of moderation in Iran's foreign policy since the death of Ayatollah Khomeini, as evidenced not only by Iran's help in the freeing of Western hostages but also by its unflinching cooperation with the United Nations during the Persian Gulf War.[15] The official U.S. silence on the secretary-general's report is all the more difficult to understand in view of Saddam Hussein's increasing defiance of the international community. As is well known, the Iraqi regime has repeatedly created obstacles in the way of the implementation of the U.N. Security Council resolutions, especially in regard to weapons inspection. No less intransigently, the regime has reasserted its old claim to sovereignty over Kuwait, the casus belli of the Persian Gulf War.

UNDERSTANDING THE REPORT

To appreciate the significance of the secretary-general's report, it is necessary to have an understanding of its origins and nature. In paragraph 6 of Security Council Resolution 598, the U.N. Security Council requested "the secretary-general to explore, in consultation with Iran and Iraq, the question of entrusting an impartial body with inquiring into responsibility for the conflict and to report to the Security Council as soon as possible."[16] As shown elsewhere, about six months before the adoption of Resolution 598, Iran had opted for a two-track policy of defense and diplomacy.[17] As a result, paragraph 6 of Resolution 598 was intended to meet partially the long-ignored Iranian demand for the naming of the original aggressor. Hence, when the resolution was finally adopted on July 20, 1987, the Iranian government neither accepted nor rejected it, insisting that "designating the aggressor" (mo'arafy-e motejavez) must precede the cease-fire between Iran and Iraq.[18] Yet by the time Iran finally accepted Resolution 598 on July 18, 1988, it had unequivocally dropped its insistence on the prior establishment of "an impartial body" for the determination of the aggressor.[19] Contrary to conventional wisdom, the Iranian decision did not simply reflect its military setbacks in the war with Iraq, or its unequal skirmishes with the U.S. forces amassed in the Persian Gulf. Rather, it reflected Ayatollah Khomeini's primary concern with the "survival of the revolution" (baqa-e enqelab).[20]

Although the cease-fire did take effect on August 20, 1988, and the peace negotiations did begin under the auspices of the United Nations as early as August 25, a subsequent state of "no war, no peace" developed between Iran and Iraq.[21] Negotiations over the implementation of the provisions of Resolution 598 regarding the withdrawal of forces to international frontiers and the exchange of prisoners of war were for all practical purposes stalemated, in large part due to Iraqi intransigence.[22] Despite persistent efforts by the secretary-general, the Security Council appeared to have lost interest in the festering conflict, and had no desire to pressure Iraq.[23]

Not until after the Iraqi invasion of Kuwait on August 2, 1990, did the regime of Saddam Hussein withdraw Iraqi forces from 2,600 square miles of Iranian territory. Nor had it begun to exchange 100,000 POWs, two-thirds of whom were Iranian nationals. With his back to the wall in the face of the U.S.-led multinational forces, Hussein made an astonishing about-face in his intransigent stance toward Iran. In a letter dated August 14, 1990, he offered Iranian president Hashemi Rafsanjani "everything [he] wanted."[24] Saddam's virtual capitulation had followed a correspondence with the Iranian leader that Saddam Hussein had initiated as early as April 21, 1990, presumably in an effort to neutralize Iran in anticipation of Iraq's invasion of Kuwait.[25]

In requesting Iran and Iraq on August 14, 1991—exactly a year after Saddam Hussein's about-face—to provide him with their views on paragraph 6 of Resolution 598, the secretary-general was in effect discharging his responsibility to explore, in consultation with the parties, the outstanding question of whether an impartial body for determining responsibility for the conflict should then be appointed. The factors that appear to have influenced the timing of the secretary-general's report are as follows:

- For all practical purposes the key paragraphs of Resolution 598 regarding cease-fire, withdrawal of forces to international borders, and exchange of POWs (except for minor issues still to be settled) had been implemented.[26]
- Iraq and Iran had replied—on August 26, 1991, and September 15, 1991, respectively—to the secretary-general's request for their views on paragraph 6.[27]
- The secretary-general was anxious to discharge his duties before the end of his term on December 31, 1991.

In rendering his opinion, the secretary-general said that "it would not seem to serve any useful purpose to pursue paragraph 6 of Resolution 598 (1987)."[28] In other words, he decided not to recommend to the Security Council to set up an impartial body to inquire into the question of who started the war. He based his opinion on the grounds that the events of the Iran-Iraq War "are well known to the international community" and the positions of the parties "are also public knowledge."[29]

He made this recommendation even though throughout the history of Resolution 598 establishment of an impartial body figured rather prominently, particularly insofar as Iran was concerned. For example, immediately after Iran's official acceptance of Resolution 598 on July 18, 1988, the secretary-general suggested, inter alia, that he would announce that he was arranging for the designation of an impartial body to determine responsibility for the hostilities. The impartial body would be drawn from "Justice X of the International Court of Justice" as president and the to-be-named "Mr. Y and Mr. Z."[30] At the time the secretary-general also contemplated that such a body would start its work no later than twenty-one days after the day the cease-fire was to take effect and would complete its work no later than ninety days after that day and report to the secretary general.[31]

"IRAQ'S AGGRESSION AGAINST IRAN"

The secretary-general's announcement of his decision not to recommend designation of an impartial body in the report is preceded by his finding that Iraq is responsible for starting the war. The key cited reason for this finding is Iraq's "illegal use of force" against Iran on September 22, 1980, in "disregard for the territorial integrity of a Member State."[32] In support of this finding, he rejects Iraq's key argument that its invasion of Iran on September

22, 1980, was a matter of preventive self-defense. The report states unambiguously: "Even if before the outbreak of the conflict there had been some encroachment by Iran on Iraqi territory, such encroachment did not justify Iraq's aggression against Iran—which was followed by Iraq's continuous occupation of Iranian territory during the conflict—in violation of the prohibition of the use of force, which is regarded as one of the rules of jus cogens."[33]

In arriving at this conclusion, the secretary-general says he relied on the following sources:

- The letters of Iraq and Iran dated August 26, 1991, and September 15, 1991;
- Consultation with the parties;
- Information from "independent experts"; and
- Official documents of the United Nations since the beginning of the conflict.[34]

The enumeration of these sources does not help clarify exactly what were the principles of international law that were violated. Nor does it clarify what were the specific facts that render the Iraqi actions of September 22, 1980, "the outstanding event."

The main international legal principles and the central facts on which the secretary-general may have relied to arrive at his finding, however, are not too difficult to comprehend. In fact, it is easier to do so today than six years ago, when, on the basis of international law and the facts of the case, this author observed: "Neither President Hussein nor his officials made a convincing case for the abrogation of the treaty or the invasion of Iran."[35] The Iraqis argued that their invasion of Iran was, in Saddam Hussein's words, a matter of "preventive self-defense," and his Foreign Ministry asserted that Iraq's "direct preventive strikes against military targets in Iran" were in accord with the well-known Caroline case,[36] which prescribed "a necessity of self-defense, instant, overwhelming, leaving no choice of means and no moment of deliberations."[37] The Iraqi invasion, however, failed to pass the test of "proportionality" because it "far exceeded the undeniable Iranian provocation."[38] The secretary-general states: "Even if before the outbreak of the conflict there had been some encroachment by Iran on Iraqi territory, such encroachment did not justify Iraq's aggression against Iran."[39]

Additionally, "even if Iraqi actions were in accordance with the Caroline case during the first days of the war, the accordance became highly questionable as time wore on."[40] The secretary-general points to "Iraq's continuous occupation of Iranian territory . . . in violation of the prohibition of the use of force."[41] The prohibition to which he refers is based on the U.N. Charter, which states: "All members shall refrain in their international relations from the threat or use of force against the territorial integrity or political independence of any state, or in any other manner inconsistent with the purposes of the United Nations."[42]

The only well-known exception to this principle is the right of self-defense embodied in Article 51 of the Charter.[43] But far from admitting the Iraqi claim of self-defense as a *preventive* measure either under customary international law or under Article 51 of the Charter, the secretary-general clearly characterizes the Iraqi invasion as an act of "aggression." It is safe to assume that he has in mind both the definition of aggression as set forth in the General Assembly Resolution 3314 of December 14, 1974, and the intensity of the Iraqi military action on September 22, 1980, which, as we have already seen, he considers "the outstanding event."

General Assembly Resolution 3314 provides in article 2 that "the first use of armed force by a state in contravention of the Charter shall constitute *prima facie* evidence of an act of aggression" and then spells out a variety of acts that may constitute aggression, such as invasion or bombardment by the armed forces of a state against the territory of another state and the military occupation that may result from an invasion or attack. The secretary-general's designation of September 22, 1980, as the day the war began clearly rejects the Iraqi contention that the war started on September 4, 1980, when Iran used 175-millimeter cannons against Iraq. It also seems to reject other Iraqi grounds for justifying its invasion, such as alleged Iranian violations of Iraqi airspace 69 times and other Iranian attacks on Iraqi targets 103 times,[44] allegations that were not brought to the attention of the United Nations until after Iraq's massive invasion into Iran.[45] September 22, 1980, has been almost universally recognized as the day the war started. On that day, "Iraq launched air raids on at least 10 major Iranian military installations, thus widening the theater of operations in its conflict with Iran and expanding the border fighting between the two states into an undeclared war."[46]

OTHER INFRACTIONS OF INTERNATIONAL LAW
What other issues does the secretary-general's report treat or omit? In the ancient conflict between Iran and Iraq, the fluvial boundary[47] between the two countries in the Shatt al-Arab—or Arvand Rud, to use the Iranian appellation—has figured prominently, as it did only five days before the war. On September 17, 1980, Saddam Hussein unilaterally abrogated the March 6, 1975, Algiers Agreement,[48] which provides for the *thalweg*[49] as the boundary line in the river and declares "all rights of full sovereignty over [the river]."[50] Yet the secretary-general's report does not take up the Iraqi claim that its abrogation was in response to Iran's noncompliance.[51] Nor does it mention the Iranian

claim that the Iraqi abrogation violates the principles of *pacta sunt servanda*[52] as well as the provisions of the Vienna Convention, especially its article 62, which in effect prohibits a state from invoking the doctrine of *rebus sic stantibus*[53] in regard to boundary agreements.[54] Although this specific dispute does not bear directly on the question of responsibility for the war, the Iraqi abrogation of the 1975 agreement does, insofar as the protocols attached to it require that the parties to a dispute must resort to peaceful means for settlement.[55] Furthermore, as a signatory to the Charter of the United Nations, Iraq, like all other member states, is required to seek peaceful settlement of a dispute before resorting to the use of force.

The secretary-general's report, in paragraph 8, does briefly tackle the violations of humanitarian law in the course of the war, for which he notes that he has "on several occasions dispatched expert missions to the theatre of war to investigate such violations as the use of chemical weapons,[56] attacks on civilian areas,[57] and the bad treatment of prisoners of war."[58] The use of chemical weapons on a civilian population is the special concern of the report. "On one occasion," the secretary-general specifies, "I had to note with deep regret the experts' conclusion that 'chemical weapons ha[d] been used against Iranian civilians in an area adjacent to an urban center lacking any protection against that kind of attack.' "[59]

A necessary consequence of holding Iraq responsible for starting the war is, of course, the obligation under international law to pay reparations. Iranian leaders have frequently claimed as much as $1 trillion for direct and indirect war damage.[60] On December 24, 1991, the secretary-general released a 191-page report that, based on on-site investigations, attempted to specify the direct non-military war damages to Iran at a lower $97.2 billion. Though the 1991 report did not specifically call for Iraq to pay reparations, it did suggest a U.N.-convened "round table" to funnel international reconstruction aid to Iran.[61]

Reactions to the secretary-general's efforts by the former combatants have, not surprisingly, been completely different. Iran naturally felt vindicated by the secretary-general's citation of Iraq as the aggressor,[62] and Ayatollah Ali Khamenei, Iran's spiritual leader, hailed it as their "nation's great victory" in addressing the Iranians in his New Year's message of March 20, 1992.[63] By contrast, official Iraqi organs described the secretary-general's efforts as "a pure personal opinion" with "no legal value" and condemned his reports as originating in "American-Atlantic-Zionist plots against Iraq."[64] Whether Iraq will be able or willing to comply with any impartial assessment of the amount and the method of payment of reparations remains to be seen. If the behavior of the Saddam Hussein regime in the case of Kuwait is any guide, it is unlikely that it will either accept the secretary-general's finding about its guilt in the war against Iran or feel obligated to pay reparations.

Of equal interest, the secretary-general reminds us of another issue by coupling his opinion that designation of an impartial body to inquire into responsibility for war "would not seem to serve any useful purpose" with an urgent plea for "the careful construction" of peace and security in the "whole [Persian Gulf] region."[65] In doing so, he urges the implementation of paragraph 8 of Resolution 598, which "requests the Secretary-General to examine, in consultation with Iran and Iraq and with other states of the region, measures to enhance the security and stability of the region." He also astutely observes that if this provision "had been timely implemented, [it] might have spared the region from the further tragedy that followed."[66] This observation obviously refers to the Iraqi invasion of Kuwait and the Persian Gulf War and is the kind of observation that has also been made repeatedly by others, including this author.[67]

THE UNITED NATIONS AND THE RULE OF LAW

The deeper significance of the secretary-general's report lies in its fundamental and unstated message for the international community in general and the United States in particular. That message concerns the role of the United Nations in promoting the rule of law. Twelve years after Iraq committed an act of aggression against Iran, the secretary-general finally says what the United Nations should have said immediately after the Iraqi invasion of Iran. What did it say then? Why did it fail to call a spade a spade? In the span of the first forty-eight hours, then secretary-general Kurt Waldheim only called for restraint and negotiated settlement.[68] The Security Council did deliberate privately for five hours on September 23, 1980, with the result of a mere information statement by the sitting president of the Security Council expressing the concerns of the Council members and vaguely calling upon Iran and Iraq "to settle their disputes by peaceful means."[69]

The complacency of the Security Council in reaction to the Iraqi invasion of Iran as contrasted with its swift and effective reaction to the Iraqi invasion of Kuwait ten years later is glaring, to say the least. Even a cursory comparison of Security Council Resolution 479,[70] adopted six long days after the Iraqi invasion of Iran in 1980, and its Resolution 660,[71] adopted immediately on August 2, 1990, the very day of the Iraqi invasion of Kuwait, demonstrates the Council's failure in 1980. Resolution 479 characterized the massive Iraqi invasion of Iran as merely "the situation between Iran and Iraq," and callously called upon Iran, the object of blatant aggression, to "refrain immediately from further use of force."[72] Moreover, the Council failed to call upon Iraq to withdraw its forces from Iranian territory. By contrast, Resolution 660 "*Condemns* the Iraqi invasion of Kuwait," and "*Demands* that Iraq withdraw immediately and unconditionally all its forces to the positions in which they were located on 1 August 1990."[73] Clearly acting under chapter VII of the Charter in the case of Kuwait, as opposed to chapter VI in the case of Iran, the Security Council showed its political will from the outset to repel the Iraqi aggression in one case and not the other.

The reasons for this inconsistency are obvious. Iran, as of 1980, was doing wrong under the law of nations. On November 4, 1979, militant students seized the U.S. Embassy in Tehran, took American hostages, and were still holding them in captivity when Iraq invaded Iran. To date many Iranians are inclined to attribute the Security Council's complacency about the 1980 Iraqi invasion merely to American hostility. To be sure, the United States did exercise considerable influence in the Security Council then,[74] and even more influence later in the face of the Iraqi invasion of Kuwait, given the diminished state of the Soviet Union. But the lackadaisical behavior of the Security Council in 1980 reflected more than U.S. displeasure with Iran. The disapprobation of the Iranian behavior was nearly universal, as evidenced, for example, by the unanimous Provisional Order[75] and the judgment of the International Court of Justice;[76] Security Council Resolutions 457[77] and 461;[78] and the resolutions of the Organization of the Islamic Conference in January and May 1980.[79]

Anthony Parsons, then the United Kingdom's ambassador to the United Nations, provides us with a rare glimpse into the Security Council's disposition at the time. Privately, Parsons claimed there was no question in anyone's mind at the Security Council that Iraq was engaged in a major offensive deep into undisputed Iranian territory. But publicly, Parsons sadly reflects that "no one was prepared to champion revolutionary Iran, the disturber of the regional *status quo* and breaker of international law and custom."[80] In response to Iran's legal argument at the time,[81] U.S. Ambassador McHenry revealingly replied by observing the irony that Iran could invoke principles of law, justice, and human dignity regarding the war, while simultaneously defying the Security Council with respect to the diplomatic hostages.[82] Put rather bluntly, the Ambassador, in effect, rationalized that one bad turn deserved another.

None of this justifies the Security Council's obvious failure to act decisively in the face of a blatant act of aggression. Under Article 24 of the Charter, the Security Council has "primary responsibility for the maintenance of international peace and security."[83] It does not have the primary responsibility to exercise international revenge. Had the Security Council been able to resist its instinct for vengeance, it would have found Iraq responsible for the war against Iran and would have been better able to stop a war that raged for nearly eight years[84] and entailed nearly a million casualties and destroyed billions of dollars' worth of property. It would also have spared the world from the scourge of yet another Iraqi act of aggression against another neighboring state.[85] Furthermore, it would have avoided a postwar condition of continuous Iraqi defiance of the Security Council sanctions—on the effective enforcement of which seems to hang the crucial judgment about the viability of the United Nations in the post–Cold War era. Finally, it would have contributed to the development of international law as a means of maintaining international peace and security for the ultimate purpose of fostering the common good of humankind, including especially the noble and suffering Iraqi people.

FURTHER REPORT OF THE SECRETARY-GENERAL
ON THE IMPLEMENTATION OF SECURITY COUNCIL
RESOLUTION 598 (1987)

1. In paragraph 6 of Resolution 598 (1987),[86] adopted on 20 July 1987, the Security Council requested the secretary-general to explore, in consultation with Iran and Iraq, the question of entrusting an impartial body with inquiring into responsibility for the conflict and to report to the Security Council as soon as possible in implementation of that request.

2. In the course of the negotiations during the past three years, I have had several opportunities to consult with the parties on paragraph 6. While those consultations enabled me to get a certain understanding of the divergent views held by both sides, they did not come to a stage where it was felt possible to submit a meaningful report to the Security Council.

3. Following the completion of the implementation of paragraphs 1 and 2 of Resolution 598 (1987), a renewed effort to fulfill the requirements of all other provisions of that resolution was called for in order to ensure the reestablishment of peace between Iran and Iraq in accordance with the comprehensive peace plan provided for by Resolution 598 (1987) and thus to contribute substantially to the current requirements of peace and security in the region. Many of the steps I took in order to intensify all efforts in the implementation of Resolution 598 (1987) have been outlined in my report to the Security Council on that subject (S/23246).

4. For the purpose of paragraph 6, although elements of the positions of the two parties on that paragraph were known to me, I requested the Governments of Iran and Iraq, in identical letters dated 14 August 1991, to provide me in the most comprehensive manner possible with their detailed views on the subject-matter of that paragraph. At the same time, in order to obtain the fullest understanding of the subject-matter, I decided to consult separately some independent experts. On the basis of the replies provided by the parties dated 26 August 1991 for Iraq and 15 September 1991 for Iran, the consultations held with the parties in the past, all relevant information contained in the official

documents of the United Nations since the beginning of the conflict and the information obtained from independent experts, I would now like, in the light of paragraph 6 of Security Council Resolution 598 (1987), to report to the Security Council.

5. It is evident that the war between Iran and Iraq, which was going to be waged for so many years, was started in contravention of international law, and violations of international law give rise to responsibility for the conflict, which question is at the centre of paragraph 6. The area of violation of international law that should be of specific concern to the international community in the context of paragraph 6 is the illegal use of force and the disregard for the territorial integrity of a Member State. There were of course in the course of the conflict massive violations of various rules of international humanitarian law.

6. The Iraqi reply to my letter of 14 August 1991 is not a substantial one; therefore I am bound to rely on explanations given by Iraq earlier. That these explanations do not appear sufficient or acceptable to the international community is a fact. Accordingly, the outstanding event under the violations referred to in paragraph 5 above is the attack of 22 September 1980 against Iran, which cannot be justified under the Charter of the United Nations, any recognized rules and principles of international law or any principles of international morality and entails the responsibility for the conflict.

7. Even if before the outbreak of the conflict there had been some encroachment by Iran on Iraqi territory, such encroachment did not justify Iraq's aggression against Iran—which was followed by Iraq's continuous occupation of Iranian territory during the conflict—in violation of the prohibition of the use of force, which is regarded as one of the rules of *jus cogens*.

8. Of the numerous violations of humanitarian law which were committed during the Iran-Iraq War, many have already been documented by the United Nations and by the International Committee of the Red Cross. At the request of one or both of the parties I have for instance on several occasions dispatched expert missions to the theatre of war to investigate such violations as the use of chemical weapons, attacks on civilian areas, and the bad treatment of prisoners of war. The results of those investigations were all reported to the Security Council and issued as Security Council documents. They referred, sadly enough, to the existence of evidence that serious violations of humanitarian law had indeed taken place. On one occasion I had to note with deep regret the experts' conclusion that "chemical weapons ha[d] been used against Iranian civilians in an area adjacent to an urban centre lacking any protection against that kind of attack" (S/20134, annex). The Council expressed its dismay on the matter and its condemnation in Resolution 620 (1988), adopted on 26 August 1988.

9. The events of the Iran-Iraq War, which for many years provided the news headlines in the world media, are well known to the international community. The positions of the parties, expressed on many occasions in official documents, are also public knowledge. In my opinion it would not seem to serve any useful purpose to pursue paragraph 6 of Resolution 598 (1987). In the interest of peace and in line with the implementation of Resolution 598 (1987) as a comprehensive peace plan, it is now imperative to move on with the settlement process. It is the careful construction of peaceful relations between the parties and of peace and security in the whole region that urgently needs to be tended to. The Security Council, in 1987, already offered the right approach, including in paragraph 8 of that resolution, which, if it had been timely implemented, might have spared the region from the further tragedy that followed. A system of good neighborly relations based on the respect of international law, as was envisaged by the Security Council, is essential in securing peace and stability in the region in the future. It is to be hoped that the Council's call will be heeded.

NOTES

1. Though not the focus of this essay, the subject no doubt will command lengthy bibliographies. For a sampling of diverse initial secondary analysis of key legal issues surrounding the Kuwaiti case, see John Norton Moore, *Crisis in the Gulf: Enforcing the Rule of Law* (New York, 1992); Edward C. Luck and Toby T. Gati, "Whose Collective Security?," *Washington Quarterly* 43 (Spring 1992); Christopher J. Sabec, "The Security Council Comes of Age: An Analysis of the International Legal Response to the Iraqi Invasion of Kuwait," *Georgia Journal of International and Comparative Law* 21 (1991); Burns H. Weston, "Security Council Resolution 678 and Persian Gulf Decision Making: Precarious Legitimacy," *American Journal of International Law* 85 (1991).

2. See end of this essay.

3. S.C. Res. 598, U.N. SCOR, 42d Sess., U.N. Doc. S/RES/598 (1987). The public "debates" attending the passage of Resolution 598 are found in U.N. SCOR, 42d Sess., U.N. Doc. S/PV.2750 (1987). The Security Council, contrary to stubbornly held assumptions, has long since reduced the importance of its public debates in favor of behind-the-scenes consultations and political wrangling in order to avoid public decision-making blocks in the form of vetoes. For examinations of this trend, see G. R. Berridge, *Return to the UN: UN Diplomacy in Regional Conflicts* (New York, 1991); and Lois Feuerle, "Informal Consultation: A Mechanism in Security Council Decision Making," *New York Journal of International Law and Politics* 18 (1985).

4. Evidence of the minor attention to the report in American papers begins with a sampling of the trivial length and location granted to the report: in the *Los Angeles Times*, 85 words on p. A9, and in the *Chicago Tribune*, 101 words on p. 4, both 12 December 1989; in *USA Today*, 91 words on p. A4, and in *Newsday*, 124 words on p. 18, both 11 December 1989. *Newsday* was the only one of these papers to have an independently filed story by its own reporter—and he, Josh Friedman, badly underestimated the significance to

Iran of the secretary-general's report. The *New York Times* and the *Christian Science Monitor* did not even mention the existence of the report during all of December 1991. Search of LexisNexis Library, *New York Times*, and *Christian Science Monitor* files, 1991.

5. Beginning on December 10, 1988, the London-based Reuters wire service and the French News Agency (AFP) carried extensive and daily coverage of the report's release and the extraordinarily diverse reactions to it in both Tehran and Baghdad. Significant nonwire stories on the subject were printed on December 11 in London's *Times* and independent dailies.

Compared with the meager American coverage of the report, even the controlled Arab press better covered the report. For example, the Saudi Arabian daily *Asharq Al-Awsat* captured the importance of the report, while reflecting Arab sensitivity to the matter by noting that Perez de Cuellar had "hurled a parting 'bombshell' at Baghdad." See "Perez de Cuellar Hurls Parting 'bombshell' at Baghdad," *Middle East News Network*, 11 December 1991, available in LexisNexis Library, OMNI file.

6. "Iraq Blamed for Starting War," *Washington Post*, 11 December 1991, A28.

7. Search of LexisNexis Library, MAJPAP file, 1991–92.

8. The secretary-general strenuously denied that his report was hostage-linked. Nevertheless, many U.S. officials believed otherwise. See Don Oberdorfer, "Iran Paid for Release of Hostages," *Washington Post*, 19 January 1992, A1.

9. See Foreign Broadcast Information Service, *Daily Report*, vol. 6, *Near East and South Asia* (FBIS-NES), 20 March 1992, 42.

10. These speculations were repeated to me by an authoritative American official, though without this official's acceptance or denial of their validity.

11. See below, nn. 22 and 58.

12. For an informed review and analysis of the events leading to the release of the hostages, with special attention to the roles of the secretary-general, Iran, and Israel, see Elaine Sciolino, "Tea in Tehran: How the Hostage Deal was Born," *New York Times*, 6 December 1991, A1.

13. Unlike his predecessor, Kurt Waldheim, Javier Perez de Cuellar avoided any appearance of sympathy to either side. While careful not to alienate permanent members of the Security Council, he persistently undertook humanitarian interventions during the conflict with great impartiality, good faith, and technical competence. Thus, unlike the Security Council itself, he earned the trust of the Iranians while retaining grudging Iraqi respect. It can be fairly said that the secretary-general was steadfastly unwilling to be the servant of Iraqi or Iranian propaganda.

14. The United States prefers Saddam Hussein in power over a "unified" Iraq to the uncertainties of his demise in order to maintain a "balance" against Iran. The philosophical roots of such thinking suggest that the United States must dominate the military balance-of-power competition in the Persian Gulf. "Enemies" are defined as any states seeking to challenge or redefine the previous "order." Such myopic thinking blinds us to aggressive tendencies, or our own exacerbation of internal fault lines, within so-called friends in these gambits, whether it be monarchist Iraq in the 1950s, the Shah's Iran in the 1970s, Iraq in the 1980s, or even Saudi Arabia today. For further development of this view, see R. K. Ramazani, *Future Security in the Persian Gulf: America's Role* (Washington, DC, 1991).

15. On the general theme of Iran's moderate foreign policy since the death of Ayatollah Ruhollah Khomeini, see W. Scott Harrop, "Iran's Emerging World Order," *Middle East Insight*, September/October 1991, 46; and R. K. Ramazani, "Iran's Foreign Policy: Both North and South," *Middle East Journal* 46, no. 3 (Summer 1992): 393–412.

16. S.C. Res. 598, U.N. SCOR, 42d Sess., U.N. Doc. S/RES/598 (1987). See also U.N. SCOR, 46th Sess., U.N. Doc. S/23273 (1991) (discussing Resolution 598), reprinted at the end of this essay.

17. See R. K. Ramazani, "Iran's Resistance to the U.S. Intervention in the Persian Gulf," in *Neither East Nor West: Iran, the Soviet Union, and the United States*, edited by Nikki R. Keddie and Mark J. Gasiorowski (New Haven, 1990). For a report on this subject at the time, see Claude van England, "Iran Goes on Diplomatic Offensive to Head off Gulf Confrontation," *Christian Science Monitor*, 22 June 1987, 9.

18. See Abbas Hedayati Khomeiny, *Shoray-e Amniyyat va Jang-e Tahmily-e Araq Alaih-e Jomhouri-e Eslami-e Iran* [The U.N. Security Council and the Iraqi-imposed war on the Islamic Republic of Iran] (1991–92). Reflecting Iran's complete distrust of the Security Council, then Iranian Majlis Speaker Ali Akbar Hashemi Rafsanjani proclaimed on 2 October 1987 that "every ignorant person knows that if we lay down our weapons . . . then there would be no one in the world who would bother to go and identify the aggressor." See FBIS-NES, 5 October 1987, 56–57.

19. See Khomeiny, *Shoray-e Amniyyat va Jang-e Tahmily-e Araq Alaih-e Jomhouri-e Eslami-e Iran*, 172.

20. That is, the combination of severe economic and social crises with painful military setbacks and mass psychological shocks threatened the viability of the revolution itself, thus catalyzing a reconsideration of Iranian war objectives. See Ramazani, "Iran's Resistance to the U.S. Intervention in the Persian Gulf." See also James Weinrauch, "Iran's Response to U.N. Resolution 598: The Role of Factionalism in the Negotiation Process," *American-Arab Affairs* 15 (Winter 1989–90).

21. For key reviews of developments, obstacles, and lack of progress, see U.N. SCOR, 44th Sess., U.N. Doc. S/20442 (1989); and UN *Chronicle* 23 (December 1989).

22. These two issues were at times linked by Iran's extraordinary insistence that POW exchanges had to be preceded by, or at least concomitant with, the withdrawal of Iraqi forces from Iranian soil. For detailed tracking of the POW issues, see "Iran Releases 50 Iraqi War Prisoners to Red Cross," *New York Times*, 26 December 1989, A14; Paul Lewis, "Iran and Iraq Still Hold Thousands of P.O.W.'s," ibid., 26 March 1989, 16; and Lewis, "Iran Ends Flooding of Iraqi Truce Lines," ibid., 28 October 1989, 13. Iran had reason to be cautious: Iraq's diplomatic line during the impasse had become quite rigid, reflecting an attitude that Iraq had "won" the war and had therefore "earned" concessions. For an example of Iraq's hardening position, see Marian Houk, "Iraq Hedges Bets in Rebuilding Gulf Ports," *Christian Science Monitor*, 25 April 1989, 4.

23. For a prescient commentary at the time, see Shireen Hunter, "Final Peace in the Gulf War Would Benefit Everyone," *Christian Science Monitor*, 14 November 1989, 19.

24. "Confrontation in the Gulf: Excerpts from Iraqi Leader's Letter to Iran," *New York Times*, 16 August 1990, A15.

25. For details on this point, see Ramazani, "Iran's Foreign Policy: Both North and South," 396–98.

26. See U.N. Doc. S/23273, para. 3, reprinted at the end of the essay.

27. Ibid., para. 4.

28. Ibid., para. 9.

29. Ibid.

30. Abbas Maleki, "Iran, Iraq, and the UN Security Council," *Iranian Journal of International Affairs*, Winter 1989/1990, 371–84. Maleki provides the most authoritative and succinct account on the subject matter from the Iranian perspective in English.

31. For contextual reporting on the secretary-general's actions, see Paul Lewis, "Cease-Fire Plan of U.N. Leader Rejected by Iraq," *New York Times*, 3 August 1988, A1; and Lewis, "U.N. Chief Says He Will Declare a Cease-fire in the Iran-Iraq War," ibid., 2 August 1988, 11. Unfortunately, the secretary-general's proposals were not acted upon at the time.

32. See U.N. Doc. S/23273, para. 5, reprinted at the end of this essay.

33. Ibid., para. 7.

34. Ibid., para. 4. The secretary-general notes that the Iraqi reply to his letter was "not a substantial one," thus necessitating reliance on previous Iraqi explanations. Ibid., para. 6. As a survey of the Security Council documents suggests, Iraq had previously spared little paper in making its case known. Nonetheless, the secretary-general found the Iraqi explanations not "sufficient or acceptable to the international community." Ibid.

35. For details, see R. K. Ramazani, *Revolutionary Iran: Challenge and Response in the Middle East* (1986; Baltimore, 1988), with a new epilogue on the Iranian-American arms deal.

36. John Bassett Moore, *Digest of International Law*, vol. 2 (Washington, DC, 1906), 412. For a classic textbook discussion of the issues involved in "self defense," see Herbert W. Briggs, ed., *The Law of Nations: Cases, Documents, and Notes*, 2d ed. (New York, 1952).

37. Moore, *Digest of International Law*, 412. Early compilations of these Iraqi statements and the Iraqi case are found in Iraq Ministry of Foreign Affairs, Republic of Iraq, *The Iraqi-Iranian Dispute: Facts v. Allegations* (New York, 1980) and "The Iraqi-Iranian Conflict: Documentary Dossier" (Charlottesville, 1981).

38. Ramazani, *Revolutionary Iran*, 62.

39. U.N. Doc. S/23273, para. 7, reprinted at the end of this essay.

40. Ramazani, *Revolutionary Iran*, 62.

41. U.N. Doc. S/23273, para. 7, reprinted at the end of this essay.

42. U.N. Charter, art. 2(4).

43. "Nothing in the present Charter shall impair the inherent right of individual or collective self-defense if an armed attack occurs against a Member of the United Nations." Ibid., art. 51.

44. Ramazani, *Revolutionary Iran*, at 59. For the Iraqi listing of these events, see above, n. 37.

45. Iraq did not publicly begin to document its case at the United Nations against Iranian "nets of plunder" until the Iraqi foreign minister delivered a letter to the secretary-general on the day of the invasion. U.N. SCOR, 35th Sess., Supp. at 113–14, U.N. Doc. S/14191 (1980).

46. Foreign Broadcast Information Service, *Daily Report*, vol. 5, *Middle East and North Africa* (FBIS-MEA), 23 September 1980, i.

47. For contrasting investigations into this subject, see Khalid Yahya al-Izzi, *The Shatt al-Arab Dispute: A Legal Study*, 3d ed. (Baghdad, Iraq, 1981); and Kaiyan Homi Kaikobad, *The Shatt-al-Arab Boundary Question: A Legal Reappraisal* (Oxford, 1988).

48. See Iran-Iraq: Treaty on International Borders and Good Friendly Relations, 13 June 1975 (implementing the Algiers Agreement of March 6, 1975), reprinted in *International Legal Materials* 14 (1975): 1133 (hereinafter Iran-Iraq Treaty). For an analysis disputing theories that Iraq's agreement was made "under duress," see R. K. Ramazani, "Iran's Search for Regional Cooperation," *Middle East Journal* 30 (1976): 173–86.

49. This is a legal term for a river boundary between states along the center of the deepest navigable channel in the river.

50. FBIS-MEA, 18 September 1980, i. Saddam Hussein's explanation speech before the Iraqi National Assembly is reprinted in Iraq Ministry of Foreign Affairs, "Iraqi-Iranian Conflict: Documentary Dossier."

51. Noncompliance charges included the presumed Iranian failure to withdraw from territories along the central sections of the Iran-Iraq border, as provided for in the Algiers Agreement. The issue of territorial noncompliance was not a valid basis for subsequent abrogation of the Algiers Agreement. See Ramazani, *Revolutionary Iran*, 61. A different noncompliance charge refers to the view that Iran was involved in subversive politics inside Iraq, particularly among its Shii Muslim population—a fact mirrored by Iraq's active meddling among Iran's Arab-speaking population in Khuzistan Province.

52. This is an international customary law doctrine stressing the importance of letting a treaty stand until altered by subsequent treaty agreement.

53. This doctrine means that changed circumstances render a previous agreement a dead letter.

54. Vienna Convention On The Law Of Treaties, U.N. GAOR, Conference on the Law of Treaties, 1st and 2d Sess., at 289, U.N. Doc. A/CONF. 39/27 (1968–69). Article 2, clause (a), specifies that *rebus sic stantibus* may not be invoked as grounds for "withdrawing from a treaty . . . if the treaty establishes a boundary." For a fuller discussion of these issues in the historical context of the 1969 Iranian unilateral abrogation of the Treaty of 1937, see Kaikobad, *Shatt-al-Arab Boundary Question*, 85–93.

55. In the Iran-Iraq treaty signed on June 13, 1975, which explicitly intended to formalize the principles embodied in the Algiers Agreement of March 6, 1975, article 6 specifies a sophisticated seven-point plan, including recourse to an international arbitration tribunal and provision for the peaceful resolution of any disputes involving implementation or interpretation of the treaty. See Iran-Iraq Treaty, art. 6. Such provisions do not suggest any intention to allow unilateral abrogation.

56. Though Iraq repeatedly objected to the secretary-general's involvement in "secondary issues," the secretary-general's technical investigations and confirmation reports of chemical weapons use included: U.N. SCOR, 39th Sess., at 108, U.N. Doc. S/16433 (1984); U.N. SCOR, 40th Sess., at 48, U.N. Doc. S/17127 (1985); U.N. SCOR, 41st Sess., at 114, U.N. Doc. S/17911 (1986). Though each of the reports clearly pointed at Iraqi violations, only the third report resulted in a Security Council statement (not a binding resolution) that condemned, by name, Iraq's continued use of chemical weapons. See U.N. SCOR, 41st Sess., Supp. for January–March 1986, U.N. Docs. S/17932 (1986) and S/PV.2667 (1986).

57. The "War of the Cities" was a recurrent and gruesome feature of the war. On June 2, 1982, the secretary-general was able on his own initiative to arrange a moratorium against such attacks. See U.N. SCOR, 39th Sess., at 124, U.N. Doc. S/16609 (1984). Iraq renewed the attacks in March 1985, leading to an ambivalent Security Council call for an end to the conflict, "commencing with the implementation of the moratorium on attacks against purely civilian population centres." U.N. SCOR, 40th Sess., at 6, U.N. Doc. S/17036 (1985). One further effort by the secretary-general in July 1986 achieved little. UN Chronicle 23 (November 1986): 77–78. Afterwards, the bombardment of purely civilian centers became an all too common terror tactic employed by both sides, yet with greatest effect by Iraq toward the end of the war.

58. U.N. Doc. S/23273, para. 8, reprinted at the end of this essay. The secretary-general's primary investigative report on the POW subject, released in January 1985, had fairly mild criticisms for both parties, noting Iraqi physical and Iranian psychological abuses of POWs they held. U.N. SCOR, 40th Sess., at 48, U.N. Doc. S/16962 (1985). The Security Council then convened publicly on 4 March 1985 for the sole apparent purpose of allowing Iraq's Arab allies to repeat charges not supported by the secretary-general's report. U.N. SCOR, 40th Sess., U.N Doc. S/PV.2569 (1985).

59. U.N. Doc. S/23273, para. 8, reprinted at the end of this essay. The secretary-general is referring to the report of 6 May 1987, wherein "the new dimension" of chemical injury to Iranian civilians was noted. U.N. SCOR, 42d Sess., U.N. Doc. S/18852 (1987). That 1987 report did note that Iraqi soldiers had sustained injuries, though it could not conclusively determine how those injuries were caused (in sharp contrast to the report's assertion that Iraqi bombs and missiles had caused the Iranian injuries). Yet the Security Council's statement of 14 May once again only condemned the use of chemical weapons, without naming the user—suggesting to Iran that the Council "was prepared to condone that behavior by Iraq." UN Chronicle 24 (August 1987): 33–34.

60. This figure was reiterated after the secretary-general's report by the Iranian News Agency. FBIS-NES, 12 December 1991, 51–52.

61. Indirect losses, such as damages to social and educational institutions, were specifically excluded. The 191-page report, distributed to Security Council members, was prepared primarily by U.N. Undersecretary-General Abdulrahim Farrah, who visited Iran from 7 November to 1 December.

62. Immediate reactions by key Iranian leaders and ministries are reprinted in FBIS-NES, 11 December 1991, 67–68, and 12 December 1991, 51–53.

63. See ibid., 20 March 1992, 42.

64. Report from Iraqi News Agency, 21 December 1991, in ibid., 23 December 1991. On 13 December, the official Iraqi newspaper Al-Thawra repeatedly carried scathing attacks on the honesty and impartiality of the secretary-general. See FBIS-NES, 13 December 1991, 34 ("the wicked policies and filthy role played by the U.N. chief"), and 18 December 1991, 20 ("conspiratorial scheme inside the U.N. against Iraq").

65. U.N. Doc. S/23273, para. 9, reprinted at the end of this essay.

66. Ibid.

67. See Ramazani, Future Security in the Persian Gulf; and Ramazani, "Peace and Security in the Persian Gulf: A Proposal," in The Persian Gulf War: Lessons for Strategy, Law, and Diplomacy, edited by Christopher C. Joyner (Westport, CT, 1990), 225–40.

68. U.N. SCOR, 35th Sess., U.N. Docs. SG/SM/2967 (1980) and S/14196 (1980).

69. U.N. SCOR, 35th Sess., U.N. Doc. S/14190 (1980).

70. S.C. Res. 479, U.N. SCOR, 35th Sess., at 23, U.N. Doc. S/RES/479 (1980). Public statements by the Council members explaining and rationalizing their votes are found in U.N. SCOR, 35th Sess., at 1, U.N. Doc. S/PV.2248 (1980).

71. S.C. Res. 660, U.N. SCOR, 45th Sess., at 19, U.N. Doc. S/RES/660 (1990). The vote was a unanimous 14–0, with Yemen not voting on account of no instructions.

72. S.C. Res. 479, U.N. SCOR, 35th Sess., U.N. Doc. S/RES/479 (1980), preface and para. 1.

73. S.C. Res. 660, U.N. SCOR, 45th Sess., U.N. Doc. S/RES/660 (1990), articles 1–2.

74. Interestingly, the United States' U.N. ambassador at the time, Donald F. McHenry, publicly expressed his displeasure with the delay in obtaining the initial Security Council resolution to "the situation." McHenry hinted that the delay might be implicitly connected to Iraq's military strategy. See Bernard D. Nossiter, "U.N. Council Delays Appeal on Gulf War: Islamic Nations, Seeking Backing for Zia's Trip to Iran and Iraq, Frustrate Western Effort," New York Times, 28 September 1980, 18.

75. United States Diplomatic and Consular Staff in Tehran (United States v. Iran), 1979 I.C.J. 7, 21 (Unanimous Provisional Order of 15 December): the government of Iran should ensure the premises of the U.S. Embassy, restore the Embassy to the United States, and ensure the immediate release of all U.S. hostages.

76. United States Diplomatic and Consular Staff in Tehran (United States v. Iran), 1980 I.C.J. 3, 44–45 (24 May): Iran has violated international law and must release hostages and pay reparations to the United States.

77. S.C. Res. 457, U.N. SCOR, 34th Sess., at 24, U.N. Doc. S/RES/457 (4 December 1979), calling on Iran to immediately release U.S. Embassy personnel.

78. S.C. Res. 461, U.N. SCOR, 34th Sess., at 24, U.N. Doc. S/RES/461 (31 December 1979), deploring the continued detention of the U.S. hostages and calling for their release.

79. For an overview of this phase in Iranian policy, see R. K. Ramazani, "Khomeini's Islam in Iran's Foreign Policy," pp. 71–93 in this volume.

80. Anthony Parsons, "In War, Resolution. . . . Iran, Iraq and the Security Council," Encounter 4 (November 1988): 52.

81. Unlike a sophisticated Iraqi diplomatic blitz at the Security Council, Iran did not present its case to the Security Council before the adoption of Resolution 479, having deemed the Security Council to be an appendage of the U.S. Department of State. But Iran's legal case subsequently was refined to the point that on October 23, 1980, Iranian delegate Ali Shams Ardakani called upon the Security Council to condemn Iraqi aggression, if for no other reason than to protect the legitimacy of the Security Council: "What is at stake here in the Council is not the territorial integrity of Iran but the moral integrity of the United Nations. There can be no silence or neutrality in the context of aggression and invasion. There is nothing fair or objective in a formula that purports to be even-handed between victim and aggressor, between right and wrong." U.N. SCOR, 35th Sess., at 1, paras. 84, 89, U.N. Doc. S/PV.22S2 (1980). Ardakani then anticipated President George H. W. Bush's appeal for Kuwait by ten years when he asked, "If the Council chooses, whether through omission or commission, not to discharge properly

its responsibilities in the present context, can any State be expected to take it seriously in other contexts?" Ibid.

82. See U.N. SCOR, 35th Sess., at 1, paras. 69–73, U.N. Doc. S/PV.22Sl (1980).

83. U.N. Charter, art. 24.

84. Instead, Iran perceived the U.N. Security Council for most of the war as a dishonest broker that had taken sides on the war in favor of Iraq—feeding into Iranian self-perceptions of itself and its revolution as besieged unjustly by the entire world. The Security Council remained unwilling for most of the war to redress its question of "original sin" on the war's origins. Thus, without a prior designation by the Security Council of Iraq as the original aggressor, Iranian leaders of all stripes remained reluctant to consider the United Nations as a credible potential facilitator of war termination. For an intensive inquiry into this subject, see Hamad A. Al-Kawari, with W. Scott Harrop, *U.N. Security Council Decision-Making and the Iran-Iraq War, 1980–1990* (forthcoming).

85. Given his obvious triumph at the United Nations in 1980 and thereafter, we can fairly ask why Saddam Hussein should have calculated prior to his gambit in Kuwait in 1990 that the Security Council would not let the aggression stand.

86. The text of this and the following paragraphs is from U.N. SCOR, 46th Sess., U.N. Doc. S/23273 (1991).

IRAN'S HOSTAGE CRISIS

International Legitimacy Matters

The further backward you look, the further forward you can see.
—Winston Churchill

A quarter-century ago revolutionary Iran took over the American Embassy in Tehran and held fifty-two Americans hostage for 444 days—a crisis that has cast a long shadow on Iranian foreign-policy behavior. A quarter-century later U.S. hostility toward Iran continues. Whatever else might be said to be fueling this hostility today, there is little doubt that it is rooted in the hostage crisis of 1979–81. For example, America's current suspicion that Iran plans to go nuclear is based, above all else, on U.S. suspicion of Iran's intentions. Iran claims that its nuclear program is for peaceful purposes, whereas the United States alleges it is for making nuclear weapons. The jury is still out, but the objective assessment of the International Atomic Energy Agency (IAEA) so far does not support the Bush administration's allegation.

As important as the study of the hostage crisis is in terms of understanding U.S. relations with Iran, I believe that the crisis constitutes a significant case study of the importance of international legitimacy in international politics. Liberal international relations theorists such as Joseph Nye are not alone in acknowledging the importance of international legitimacy in world politics. No less a theorist than Hans Morgenthau, the leading traditional realist, believes in the relevance of legitimacy to state power. In his words, "Prestige has become particularly important as a political weapon in an age in which the struggle for power is fought not only with the traditional methods of political pressure and military force but in large measure as a struggle for the mind of men."[1]

Because the concept of "legitimacy" in international relations is elusive, I would like to say up front what it means to me. I think legitimacy is an intrinsic aspect of national power, and balance of power alone fails to explain the dynamics of international politics. In other words, a nation may lose legitimacy in international politics when it dismisses the relevance of world public opinion.

By contrast, a nation may win legitimacy when it exercises power according to widely accepted international rules, principles, and norms.

DEFYING THE WORLD ORDER

The hostage taking became the crucible of Iran's largely confrontational foreign policies for most of a decade. The crisis occurred amidst revolutionary political chaos, economic paralysis, acts of terrorism, armed insurrection, ethnic insurgency, summary executions, and generally a basic lack of internal security in 1979–81, reminiscent of the chaos that marked the end of the Constitutional Revolution in 1911. A multitude of political factions vied for power, many with diverse ideological orientations. The Islamist students who took over the American Embassy claimed to follow the Khomeini line (*Khatti Imam*), the supporters of the National Democratic Front followed Mosaddegh's secular path (*rah-e Mossadegh*), followers of the Fedayan-e Khalq espoused a version of Marxist-Leninist ideology, the members of the Tudeh Party pressed for Soviet-style communism, and the Mujahadeen-e-Khalq (People's Fighters) espoused a mix of Islamic and Marxist tenets.[2] The dominant ideology that influenced the students' action is difficult to identify. Massoumeh Ebtekar, the revolutionary students' spokesperson, claims that they were influenced by Ali Shari'ati, who, she says, "persuaded them to accept the leadership of Imam Khomeini with courage and devotion." I have not been able to verify this statement. She also claims that the students excluded the leftist groups from their ranks.[3]

Khomeini's ideology, however, is more relevant than Shari'ati's to the development of the hostage crisis because he incited students against the United States before the takeover of the American Embassy, and he endorsed their action afterward. What follow are his statements on both occasions. Three days before the takeover, Khomeini used the anniversary of the attack by the Shah's regime on the University of Tehran on November 1 to incite the students by saying that "it is . . . up to the dear pupils, students and theological students to expand with all their might their attacks against the United States and Israel, so they may force the United States to return the deposed and criminal shah."[4] Far more consequential, Khomeini endorsed unequivocally the students' takeover of the American Embassy. His endorsement made the takeover of the embassy the responsibility of the Iranian state. "Our young people resorted to this action," he said on November 5, 1979, "because they saw that the shah was allowed in America. . . . Today we cannot simply remain idle and watch things; today we are facing underground treason, treason devised in these same embassies, mainly by the great Satan, America. They must bear in mind that Iran is still in a state of revolution, a revolution greater than the first one. They must be put in their place and return this criminal [the Shah] to us as soon as possible."[5]

Khomeini did not see the takeover of the American Embassy as a violation of international law and an enduring blow to Iran's international legitimacy. In fact, he denounced the extant international system on the grounds that modern states "are the products of man's limited ideas" and that the world is "the home of all the masses of people under the law of God."[6] That is, that divine Islamic law (Sharia) should be followed rather than man-made modern international law and the post-Westphalia international system of nation-states.

Since the international system was dominated at the time by the United States and the Soviet Union, Khomeini rejected both superpowers. His slogan "Neither East nor West, but the Islamic Republic" reflected his confrontational orientation toward the superpowers of the day. It also underpinned his doctrine of the export of the "Islamic Revolution" worldwide.[7] In his words, "We should try hard to export our revolution to the world . . . all the superpowers and all the powers have risen to destroy us. If we remain in an enclosed environment we shall definitely face defeat."[8]

As important as these ideas of Khomeini are in understanding his worldview in general and his hostility toward the United States in particular, they were inseparable from his perception of the American threat to his revolution and Iranian independence. He believed that the success of the revolution guaranteed Iran's freedom from American domination. But the quest for independence in general has been as old as the history of the Iranian state and has been shaped largely by Iran's tragic experience with foreign invasion, occupation, and interference in Iranian affairs over the millennia.

Regardless of the militant students' claim that they were following Khomeini's ideology, they were no less influenced by the perception of the American threat to the revolution. According to the leader of the student movement, Seyyed Mohammad Mousavi Khoeiniha, the students' takeover was an act of "protest against the admission of the shah to the United States."[9] The protest, according to Khoeiniha, sprang from Iran's bitter memory of the American-engineered coup against the popular prime minister Dr. Mohammad Mosaddegh in 1953. I was told by a former American hostage that while in captivity when he admonished a student for hostage taking, the student responded, "Your country took my whole country hostage in 1953 and held it for a quarter century before the Islamic Revolution."[10]

The takeover and the fall of the gradualist and moderate government of Mehdi Bazargan no doubt helped entrench the Islamist faction in power at the time. However, contrary to conventional wisdom, Khomeini's endorsement of the takeover was not merely an effort to consolidate power. It was also a response to the perceived American threat. Specifically he was alarmed by the visit of Secretary of Defense Harold Brown to the Middle East on February 9, 1979, only eight days after Khomeini's return to Iran. Secretary Brown stated unequivocally that the United States would defend its vital interest in the Persian Gulf oil supplies by military force "if appropriate."[11] This unprecedented statement was coupled with U.S. negotiations with Oman, Somalia, and Kenya for military facilities and with the dispatch of the USS *Constellation* and several supporting warships to the Indian Ocean and Arabian Sea, as well as the strengthening of the small U.S. naval force in the Gulf itself.

With Khomeini's support ensured after the fall of the Bazargan government, revolutionary students blocked every effort made by Abulhassan Banisadr, first acting foreign minister and then the first president of revolutionary Iran, and Sadeq Qotbzadeh, Iran's foreign minister, to settle the hostage crisis. The students also in effect rejected every move by outside powers, individuals, and the United Nations to mediate an end to the captivity of the Americans.[12] My own proposal to President Jimmy Carter for the dispatch of leading Muslim scholars to plead with Khomeini for the release of the hostages was aborted, and I received much flak from Iranian quarters for saying in interviews with *Time* magazine and on NBC's *Meet the Press* program that the takeover was incompatible with Islam, with Iran's proverbial culture of hospitality, and with international law.

The eventual settlement of the U.S.-Iranian dispute, however, did little to repair the damage done to Iran's international legitimacy. As said before, to date, the suspicion of Iranian moves on the world stage may be at least in part traced back to America's prolonged anguish over the hostage crisis. Ironically, the unintended consequences of the takeover first gripped the students themselves.[13] Their intention to seize the American Embassy for only 3 days resulted instead in an unforeseen 444 days, an agonizing period that helped develop international distaste for the revolutionary regime.

DAMAGING INTERNATIONAL LEGITIMACY

The takeover of the American Embassy impaired Iran's international legitimacy. Although the damage lingers on, Iran's major players at the time realized the problem. For example, Bazargan condemned the takeover as a violation of international law and civilized norms of diplomacy and called for the immediate release of the hostages. Khoeiniha was reluctant to inform Khomeini in advance of the students' plan to occupy the American Embassy, apparently on the ground that such an action would amount to "the violation of international rules."[14] In contrast, the former revolutionary students, who attempt today to justify their action as having been compatible with international law on the ground that it was taken in self-defense under Article 51 of the U.N. Charter, seem to be clutching at straws because in reality the international community reacted disapprovingly to the takeover both politically and legally.

To mention some of the most obvious examples of international disapprobation, one must start with the United States itself. The hostage crisis lay at the heart of the 1980 American break of diplomatic relations with Iran, which continues to the present time. It triggered the American containment policy toward the revolutionary regime economically, politically, and militarily. It fueled the suspicion that Iran helped the suicide bombings in Beirut in 1983. It led to the American support of Iraq in the war against Iran after the Iranian offensive against Iraq began in 1982. In addition, it enabled the United States to pressure other nations to curtail their dealings with Iran.

The cost of the students' dismissal of the importance of international legitimacy in world politics far exceeds these and many other American moves against Iran. It isolated Iran in the international system in general as evidenced by the world outcry of disapproval through international forums. A few examples of disapprobation include the unanimous Provisional Order (November 29, 1979) and the Judgment (May 15, 1980) of the International Court of Justice, the U.N. Security Council's Resolution 457 (December 4, 1979) and Resolution 461 (December 31, 1979), and the resolutions of the Organization of the Islamic Conference (OIC) in January and May 1980.

Perhaps one of the most telling indications of the depth of international anger against Iran is to be seen in the contrast between the international community's attitudes toward the Iraqi invasion of Iran in 1980 and the Iraqi invasion of Kuwait ten years later, in 1990. In the case of Iran, it took the U.N. Security Council six long days after the Iraqi invasion on September 22, 1980, to adopt Resolution 479, which even then characterized the invasion as merely "the situation between Iran and Iraq." The resolution called on Iran, the object of aggression, to "refrain immediately from further use of force" and failed to call on Iraq to withdraw its forces from Iranian territory. By contrast in the case of Kuwait, the Council adopted its Resolution 660 on the very day of the Iraqi invasion, condemned the invasion, and also demanded that Iraq withdraw "immediately and unconditionally all its forces to the positions in which they were located on 1 August 1990."[15]

No less indicative of the international community's displeasure with Iran was the cool reception given to former U.N. secretary-general Javier Perez de Cuellar's report of December 9, 1991, to the Security Council, in which he named Iraq's invasion of Iran as an act of "aggression."[16] Furthermore, the American media either ignored this important report or questioned the secretary-general's motives, suggesting that he had designated Iraq as the initiator of the war because he desired to reward Iran for its help in the release of the Western hostages held in Lebanon. Such an insinuation, of course, disregarded the fact that the secretary-general at the time was fulfilling his responsibility under paragraph 6 of the Security Council's Resolution 598 of July 20, 1987, which eventually provided the basis of a cease-fire between Iraq and Iran. The timing of his report had more to do with the fact of his imminent retirement than with anything else.

REPAIRING THE DAMAGE TO
INTERNATIONAL LEGITIMACY

In a sense the very settlement of the hostage crisis in 1981 marked the beginning of the long process of gradual reintegration of the Iranian state into the international community and the rehabilitation of Iran's international image. Khomeini himself recognized the importance of diplomatic ties with other nations once he felt that his revolution was secure. He admonished the extremists who rejected Iran's relations with any other country. He told them that isolation in world affairs would amount to "annihilation." He condemned the mining of the Suez Canal in 1984 on the ground that it was, in his words, "against the sentiments of the world, against Islam, and against common sense."[17] During his lifetime Iran sold oil to the United States indirectly, purchased arms from Israel secretly, and resumed economic relations with Western Europe openly, making the Continent one of Iran's main trade partners.

The process of reintegration of Iran into the international community intensified after Khomeini. President Ali Akbar Hashemi Rafsanjani in his eight years in office in effect turned on its head the doctrine of "Neither East nor West" by expanding Iran's relations with both and by reaching out to the pro-Western Persian Gulf monarchies to an unprecedented extent.[18] With respect to the United States, he observed a strict policy of neutrality in the first Persian Gulf War and upheld U.N. resolutions.[19] He also helped in the release of American and other Western hostages in Lebanon.[20] With regard to the Soviet Union, even before he was president, Rafsanjani set a new foundation for Iranian-Soviet economic and military relations. After the disintegration of the Soviet Union, he vigorously pursued diplomatic, cultural, and economic relations with the newly independent republics in Transcaucasia and Central Asia.[21] He also pressed for greater trade relations with Western Europe and Japan and enhanced the role of Iran in the OIC as a major player.[22]

Efforts to reintegrate Iran into the international system have reached an unprecedented height since the presidency of Mohammad Khatami in 1997. It came as a surprise to most observers that his first major foreign-policy statement addressed the American people. He called for people-to-people exchanges between Iran and the United States as a first constructive step toward the goal of breaking down the wall of distrust that has existed between the two countries since the hostage crisis. His overall conciliatory foreign policy underscored the importance of reducing international tensions, with the knowledge of course that such an emphasis could enhance Iran's image, prestige, and legitimacy in the international system.

In keeping with the essentially conciliatory thrust of his foreign policy, Khatami took the initiative of pressing for dialogue among civilizations in the United Nations. The General Assembly took up his initiative in a resolution calling for the designation of 2001 as the year of dialogue among civilizations. Secretary-General Kofi Annan called for international conferences, seminars, and other forums and the dissemination of scholarly studies worldwide for enhancing dialogue among civilizations.[23]

Khatami took the necessary step on September 22, 1998, toward removing the main stumbling block in Iran's relations with Europe. He described Khomeini's life-threatening *fatwa* against Salman Rushdie as the expression of Khomeini's own view as an Islamic jurist and declared, "We should consider the Salman Rushdie issue as completely finished."[24] Two days later Iranian foreign minister Kamal Kharrazi told British foreign secretary Robin Cook, "The government of the Islamic Republic of Iran has no intention, nor is it going to take any action whatsoever to threaten the life of the author of *The Satanic Verses* or anybody associated with his work, nor will it encourage or assist anybody to do so."[25] A good example of Iran's efforts to breach the wall of distrust with the United States is the Khatami government's help to Washington in destroying the Taliban regime through Iran's proxy, the Northern Alliance; its constructive participation in the Bonn Conference, which resulted in the interim government of Hamid Karzai; and its commitment of more than $500 million to the reconstruction efforts in Afghanistan.[26]

RELATIONS WITH AMERICA AND
INTERNATIONAL LEGITIMACY

As important as Iran's efforts to regain international legitimacy may be, repairing relations with the United States could further aid those efforts. At the moment, however, the hostility of the Bush administration toward Iran is, to say the least, discouraging. President Bush included Iran in his moralistic "axis of evil" along with Iraq and North Korea. He also threatened Iran with a preemptive strike as a "rogue" state that might provide terrorist groups with weapons of mass destruction. The bellicose attitude of President Bush toward Iran has not spared even the reformist government of President Khatami, because his denunciation of the whole regime necessarily included Khatami's government. This position was a complete reversal of the Clinton administration's sensitive and responsive approach to Iran after Khatami was elected president.

Maybe, as the saying goes, enemies over time become like each other. The confrontational attitudes of the neoconservatives in the Bush administration today resemble those of the radical conservatives in the Iranian regime. During the hostage crisis, Iranian extremists dismissed the importance of international legitimacy, and today the Bush administration seems to be doing the same, as evidenced, for example, by its internationally unauthorized invasion of Iraq. The Iranian hard-liners supported the takeover of the U.S. Embassy in Tehran, and the American neoconservatives pressed for the invasion of Iraq. However, one of the most significant features of the Iranian political scene today is the remarkable attitudinal transformation among the former hostage takers. They are among the leading advocates of improving relations with the United States. Whether or not this transformation reflects their striving "to expiate" past wrongs, the fact remains that it is useful for the future of Iran's relations with the United States. Massoumeh Ebtekar claims that "the ultimate aim" of her account of the "fateful" takeover of the American Embassy is to alleviate tensions between Iran and the United States and "to engage the two diverse and different cultures in a constructive dialogue."[27]

CONCLUSION

Improving relations with the United States could further help Iran's efforts for regaining greater international legitimacy. It could also enable Iran to resolve at least some of its major economic problems, particularly by removing the longtime American opposition to its entry into the World Trade Organization (WTO).

Yet no degree of international legitimacy could make up for the regime's waning domestic legitimacy. The Shah's regime, as I wrote before the revolution, acquired considerable national power and international legitimacy, while it lost internal legitimacy.[28] Ayatollah Khomeini called for "law" and justice, but the regime has so far failed to fulfill the revolution's promise of a better life for all the people. At the moment, the reversal of the fortunes of the reformists in the Majlis and the prospect of further reformist setbacks as a result of the impending presidential elections would seem to doom the prospects of change for the better.

To stop here, however, would ignore the popular demands for economic, social, and political change. The continued acts of repression will not stop these demands. They will surely further alienate the people from the regime and undermine its legitimacy. In closing, I reiterate what I said in my address of September 4, 2000, to President Khatami at the United Nations: "I believe there can be no durable political order without equitable justice under the law and no justice without liberty."[29]

NOTES

1. Hans J. Morgenthau, *Politics among Nations: Struggle for Power and Peace*, 6th ed. (New York, 1985), 95.

2. See R. K. Ramazani, "Iran's Foreign Policy: Contending Orientations," pp. 111–27 in this volume.

3. Massoumeh Ebtekar, *Takeover in Tehran: The Inside Story of the 1979 U.S. Embassy Capture* (Vancouver, BC, 2000), 45.

4. For the full text, see Foreign Broadcast Information Service, *Daily Report*, vol. 5, *Middle East and North Africa* (FBIS-MEA), 2 November 1979.

5. For the full text, see ibid., 6 November 1979.

6. See R. K. Ramazani, "Khomeini's Islam in Iran's Foreign Policy," pp. 71–93 in this volume.

7. R. K. Ramazani, "Iran's Export of the Revolution: Its Politics, Ends, and Means," pp. 128–47 in this volume.

8. See FBIS-MEA, 6 November 1979.

9. See Khoeiniha's preface to Ebtekar, *Takeover in Tehran*.

10. Bruce L. Laingen, conversation with the author, 11 November 2004.

11. See R. K. Ramazani, "Security in the Persian Gulf," pp. 215–28 in this volume.

12. Ibid.

13. According to Ebtekar, "At the time, no one ever dreamed takeover would last any longer than three days" (*Takeover in Tehran*, 54).

14. Quoted in Mohsen M. Milani, *The Making of Iran's Islamic Revolution: From Monarchy to Islamic Republic*, 2d ed. (Boulder: Westview, 1994), 166.

15. See R. K. Ramazani, "Who Started the Iran-Iraq War? A Commentary," pp. 287–306 in this volume.

16. For the text of the secretary-general's report, see ibid.

17. R. K. Ramazani, "Iran: Burying the Hatchet," pp. 94–110 in this volume. For a study of this tension between religious ideology and pragmatism in Iran's foreign policy since ancient times, see R. K. Ramazani, "Ideology and Pragmatism in Iran's Foreign Policy," pp. 184–95 in this volume.

18. See R. K. Ramazani, "Iran's Foreign Policy: Both North and South," *Middle East Journal* 46, no. 3 (Summer 1992): 393–412.

19. See R. K. Ramazani, *Future Security in the Persian Gulf: America's Role* (Washington, DC, 1991), 1–28.

20. See R. K. Ramazani, *Revolutionary Iran: Challenge and Response in the Middle East* (1986; Baltimore, 1988), with a new epilogue on the Iranian-American arms deal.

21. See Ramazani, "Iran's Foreign Policy."

22. See R. K. Ramazani, "The Emerging Arab-Iranian Rapprochement," *Middle East Policy* 6 (1998): 45–62.

23. See R. K. Ramazani, "Dialogue: The Need for a Theory," *Global Dialogue* 3 (2001): 46–55.

24. As quoted in the *New York Times*, 23 September 1998.

25. As quoted in the *Washington Post*, 25 September 1998.

26. See Ramazani, "Ideology and Pragmatism in Iran's Foreign Policy."

27. See Ebtekar, *Takeover in Tehran*.

28. See R. K. Ramazani, *Iran's Foreign Policy, 1941–1973: A Study of Foreign Policy in Modernizing Nations* (Charlottesville, 1975); Ramazani, *The Persian Gulf: Iran's Role* (Charlottesville, 1972); and Ramazani, *The United States and Iran: The Patterns of Influence* (New York: Praeger, 1982).

29. For the text of the address, see appendix 1, which was originally published as R. K. Ramazani, "The Role of Iran in the New Millennium: A View from the Outside," *Middle East Policy* 7, no. 1 (March 2001): 43–67; for a discussion of the Iranian quest for democracy in history, see R. K. Ramazani, "Iran, Democracy, and the United States," pp. 335–52 in this volume.

V

THE SHAH AND ISRAEL,

KHATAMI AND BUSH

IRAN AND THE ARAB-ISRAELI CONFLICT

How does one try to explain Iran's policy toward the Arab-Israeli conflict? This is not a rhetorical question. The presumption that the "real nature" of Iran's behavior in respect to the Arab-Israeli conflict is enigmatic persists stubbornly. The so-called enigma is partly because of the paucity of information. Iran is hardly anxious to speak up on all the issues of the conflict under any circumstances. The rather cautious and often secretive approach of the Shah's regime to the conflict is basically the result of a conscious and deliberate policy. It stems largely from a general desire to remain aloof from the quagmire of the age-old and intractable conflict between the Arabs and Israelis and to maintain a balancing posture between the two sides while pursuing Iran's larger foreign-policy objectives.

Another reason for the sense of mystery surrounding Iranian behavior is the fact that the few studies published so far bear indirectly or incompletely on the subject matter. They are useful mainly because they concentrate on the bilateral relations between Iran and Israel or on the implications of the Arab-Israeli war of 1973 for Iranian foreign policy.[1] As such they largely nibble at the edges of the fundamental concern of this essay, namely, Iran's policy toward the Arab-Israeli conflict.

The main purpose of this essay is to explore that policy in broad strokes as a means of aiding its understanding rather than evaluating its premises and results or prescribing a different course and direction for it, although one may hope that better understanding of its past and present will provide a clue to its future. The past and present policies that are found useful for the purpose of this analysis are those that stretch from the very birth of the state of Israel to the present time. The notion that the Iranian liberation of the Hebrews from Babylonian captivity by Cyrus the Great in 538 BC explains Irano-Israeli "amity," or that the clash between the Shii and Jewish creeds and communities influences Irano-Israeli "antipathy," today is largely a matter of speculation. Such basically cultural perspectives seem less useful as a means of policy explication by scholars than as a vehicle of policy rationalization by statesmen.

The distinction is of fundamental importance because to confuse the two can steer the analyst away from the task of explication. As seen from the above

"Iran and the Arab-Israeli Conflict" was originally published in *Middle East Journal* 32, no. 4 (Autumn 1978): 413–28.

examples, contemporary Iranian policymakers can avail themselves of the cultural perspective to rationalize favorable and unfavorable policies toward Israel depending on the circumstances. The same serious limitations of the cultural perspective as a means of explication applies to the attitudes and policies of Iran toward the Arab states. The Shii-Sunni doctrinal differences and Arab-Iranian cultural distinctions can be easily enlisted to rationalize a given unfavorable attitude or policy toward the Arab states, just as "Islamic solidarity" may be invoked to rationalize a favorable one. The key consideration for an understanding of Iran's policy toward the Arab-Israeli conflict, this essay argues, is politico-strategic and concerns the improvement, or at least the preservation, of Iran's regional environment within the broader context of world politics, which is perceived to be more conflictual than cooperative in nature.

CALCULATED AMBIVALENCE

Those who would today characterize the Iranian policy toward the Arab-Israeli conflict as "tilting" toward the Arab side might indeed tend to believe that Iran may be returning to a position somewhat similar to its original stance on the dispute within the United Nations in 1947. At that time, Iran favored the minority plan that advocated a federated state of Palestine composed of two autonomous states, one Jewish and one Arab. Iran, as well as the Arab states, endorsed this plan; it would satisfy the Arab demand for a single independent state with an Arab majority and a limited Jewish immigration. Iran also voted against the partition plan side by side with Egypt, Iraq, Lebanon, Saudi Arabia, and Yemen. Iran's attitude toward the Arab-Israeli conflict between 1948, when the state of Israel was born, and 1950, when Iran accorded it de facto recognition, may be characterized as "calculated ambivalence." The important question is why the Iranian attitude seemed ambivalent during this first phase. One observer attributed it to Iran's sensitivity to "Islamic solidarity" on the basis of what the Shah said during his visit to the United States in 1949.[2]

This explanation seems to mistake rationalization for reason. The real reason for Iran's ambivalent attitude at the time was fundamentally the ambiguous nature of Israeli relations with the Soviet Union. Iran's endorsement of the minority plan and its vote against the partition of Palestine before the birth of Israel were both in keeping with the basic tenets and thrust of Iranian nationalism. Gripped by acute anti-British sentiments and a fierce desire for independence, Iran favored Arab nationalism as it was then expressed. Muslim Iran, like non-Muslim India, sympathized with the Arab states in the U.N. debate and decision on Palestine. However, once the state of Israel was born, Iran began to perceive its relationship with Israel primarily within a larger political and strategic context. That context at the time was the emerging antagonism between the Soviet Union and the United States. Had the Soviet Union failed to support the creation of the state of Israel, Iran would probably have accorded Israel de facto recognition earlier than 1950. Before this date the attitude of Israel toward the superpower antagonism had seemed ambiguous. But by then it was becoming clear that Israel was veering toward the United States; it was also experiencing Soviet propaganda attacks. The less "neutral" the new state of Israel began to appear in the emerging East-West conflict the more acceptable it seemed to Tehran. The extension of full de jure recognition to Israel by the United States in 1949, the Israeli acceptance of the Point Four Program in 1950, and the Israeli opposition to the communist invasion of South Korea in the same year acted as a catalyst in favor of an Irano-Israeli rapprochement. While Iran continued to sympathize with Arab nationalism, it began to feel increasingly uncomfortable with its pro-Soviet expressions, particularly after the Egyptian Revolution in 1952. The closing of the Iranian Consulate in Israel in 1952 marked no basic change in Iran's emerging sympathy for Israel. Rather, that decision was prompted primarily by budgetary pressures on the Mosaddegh government. The drying up of the principal Iranian source of revenues as a consequence of the oil-nationalization dispute with Britain lay at the heart of that decision. Contrary to the claim of the Nasser regime many years later, the Mosaddegh government did not withdraw Iran's de facto recognition of Israel in 1952.

ISRAEL AS A BULWARK AGAINST THE SOVIET UNION

Iran's de facto recognition of Israel in 1950 marked the end of its ambivalent attitude toward the Arab-Israeli conflict from 1948 to 1950. Its sympathetic attitude toward Israel began after the downfall of the Mosaddegh government and the ascendancy of the Shah's regime in 1953. The downfall of the Mosaddegh regime, the settlement of the Anglo-Iranian oil-nationalization dispute, the emergence of American oil interests in Iran, and finally the decision of the Shah's regime to cast its lot clearly with the United States in the East-West conflict by joining the Baghdad Pact coincided with the consolidation of power by the Nasser regime, the Soviet break with Israel in 1954, and above all, the Soviet arms sales to Egypt. In essence the Shah's policy of "positive nationalism" and Nasser's policy of "positive neutrality" reflected basically opposite strategies of alignment and nonalignment with the superpowers on the one hand and divergent regional policies on the other. The "Arab Cold War" between the so-called progressive and conservative regimes paralleled the Egyptian-Iranian cold war on the one hand and the expansion of Irano-Israeli ties on the other. The cultivation of ties with Israel was seen from Tehran not so much as a means of forming a "discreet entente" against hostile Arab states, but as a way of creating an effective Irano-Israeli obstacle to the increasing Soviet power and influence in the Arab Middle East. Iran's opposition to the Israeli invasion of the Suez Canal, like the American, was primarily out of fear of an even greater rise in Soviet power and influence in the area rather than because of sympathies with the Nasser regime. Even the fact that the Suez Canal carried 73 percent of Iran's imports and 76 percent of its exports at the time was of lesser importance than the influence of this basic strategic consideration in Iran's position on the Suez War.

The strategic utility of Israel for Iran as a bulwark against the expansion of Soviet influence in the Middle East increased significantly in the late 1950s and early 1960s for two basic reasons. First, the Iraqi Revolution of 1958 and the defection of the Qasim regime from the Baghdad Pact seemed to bring Arab revolution to the Iranian doorstep. While Cairo relished the withdrawal of Iraq from the Pact organization as a blow to the so-called Zionist plot, Iran saw the balance of forces in the area shifting further against itself and Israel. Within the context of a regional environment that was perceived as becoming more anti-Iranian and increasingly pro-Soviet, Israel appeared to be the strongest anti-Soviet state around. Second, the deterioration of the regional environment for Iran coincided with an acrimonious atmosphere in bilateral Soviet-Iranian relations in the wake of the breakdown of the negotiations for a long-term nonaggression pact between Tehran and Moscow. The propaganda warfare between the two capitals was finally crowned by Khrushchev's personal attack on the Shah on two separate occasions in the wake of Iran's conclusion of an executive defense agreement with the United States in 1959.[3]

While the Soviet propaganda attack on the Shah's regime was abruptly abandoned in 1962—after Iran's pledge to the Soviet Union of no missile bases— the revolutionary Arab states stepped up their campaign against Iran in the Persian Gulf. The charges against Iran were framed largely in the context of Tehran's relations with Tel Aviv. The Nasser regime, for example, charged that Iran sold Israeli fresh and dried fruits to the Gulf sheikhdoms, that Iran planted immigrants in the Arab lands of the Gulf for colonization, and that Iran's favorable policies toward Israel were inimical to both Arabism and Islam. The Ba'athist regime in Syria, to cite another example, analogized the fate of the Arabic-speaking inhabitants of Khuzistan, or as it was labeled, "Arabistan," to that of the Palestinians and went so far as to declare in 1965 that this Iranian province was "an integral part of the Arab homeland."[4]

THE EMERGENCE OF AN ARAB OPTION

However one characterizes the Iranian attitude toward the Arab-Israeli conflict during the second phase—between the time that Iran extended de facto recognition to Israel in 1950 and the outbreak of the Arab-Israeli War in 1967—the important point is that the principal factor underlying the Iranian policy was the perceived political and strategic utility of Israel in the context of Iran's primary objective of forestalling the advance of Soviet power and influence and the spread of communism in the Middle East. Iran, therefore, perceived no contradiction between its friendly ties simultaneously with Israel and with such basically pro-Western confrontation states as Jordan and Lebanon. Because of the same overriding strategic and political considerations that underpinned Iran's basic attitude toward Israel and the Arab states, there was always the potential for Iran's friendly relations with even the revolutionary confrontation states. Iran could befriend them, too, as soon as their strategy seemed to turn against the Soviet Union despite their continued hostility with Israel.

This is exactly what the consequences of the 1967 Arab-Israeli War seemed to promise. Had Iran perceived the Israeli strategic utility primarily in terms of the balance of power between Israel and the Arab states as such, then the unprecedented rise of the Israeli preponderance of power after the 1967 war would have been even more welcome. To be sure, Iran must have privately rejoiced in the fact that the spectacular Israeli victory in the June War in effect cut Nasser down to size, and the withdrawal of Egyptian forces from Yemen removed the perceived Egyptian threat to the Arabian Peninsula. But, no matter how important these and similar considerations, the basic fact remains that the decade-long break in diplomatic relations between Cairo and Tehran continued for several years after the war. It may well be, as a couple of observers seem to suggest, that the resumption of Irano-Egyptian diplomatic relations had to await favorable developments in the Arab-Iranian relations in the Persian Gulf area.[5] But in the context of Iran's more fundamental strategic and political concerns a different interpretation must be attempted.

For Iran the really important consequence of the 1967 war was an emerging subtle shift in the Egyptian attitude toward the superpowers. While it is true that as early as June 7, 1967, the Shah personally denounced the Israeli occupation of Arab territories, the fact remains that no serious attempt toward the resumption of diplomatic relations was made by either Tehran or Cairo. The war seemed to Tehran to have entrenched the Soviet power even deeper in Egypt. Furthermore, the so-called War of Attrition of Egypt with Israel appeared to Iran to enhance Soviet power and influence in the Middle East. Yet, Tehran watched with acute interest the emerging suspicion in the Egyptian attitude toward the Soviet Union and the concurrent preparedness of the Nasser regime to accept the American peace initiative.

The emerging signs of relative moderation in Egyptian foreign policy in general and a new preference for resorting to peaceful diplomacy rather than war by the Nasser regime as a means of recovering occupied territories in particular are welcomed in Tehran. It was no coincidence that in the same year that President Nasser accepted the American peace initiative he was also able to resume the diplomatic relations with Iran that he himself had broken ten years earlier. Had Nasser not died shortly after resuming diplomatic relations with the Shah's regime the improvement in the Irano-Egyptian relations that took place subsequently under President Sadat would have probably been slower because of personal antipathy between Nasser and the Shah. But the important point is that personal antagonism was not allowed to stand in the way of normalizing the relations of the two countries once the foreign-policy orientations of Egypt and Iran seemed to begin to draw closer. Two other points must be noted. First, the seeds of the Irano-Egyptian rapprochement that has intensified since the October 1973 war were sown in effect during the few years preceding the war. Second, as the relations between Cairo and Moscow started to deteriorate, the Tehran-Cairo relationship began to improve, while tensions between Tehran and Tel Aviv surfaced, as might have been expected.

IRAN AND THE 1973 WAR

This brings us to the last phase of Iran's policy toward the Arab-Israeli conflict, namely, the period since the October War. As contrasted with the Iranian attitude during the 1967 war, Iran's sympathies with the Arab states during the 1973 October War found more concrete expression. As is well known, it not only extended medical aid to the Arab states (it had done so in the 1967 war too), but it also sent pilots and planes to Saudi Arabia to help with logistical problems, permitted the overflight of Soviet civilian planes carrying military equipment to Arab states, and disallowed the transfer of Jewish volunteers from Australia to Israel via Tehran.[6] The same basic political and strategic considerations that underpinned the Iranian policy toward the Arab-Israeli conflict from the birth of the state of Israel until the October War continued to influence the Iranian policies subsequently. The real question before Iran in 1973 as in 1967 was not merely the shape of the configuration of power between the Arab states and Israel. Rather, it was the implications of that configuration for the more general and fundamental goal of Iranian foreign policy, namely, the obstruction of Soviet power and influence in the Middle East. Iran assessed the regional balance or preponderance of power in 1973 as in 1967 primarily with a view to the achievement of that overriding objective.

To be sure, Iran was pleased in 1973 to see that the friendly Sadat regime initially made a good show in the battlefield just as it must have been happy to note the defeat of the hostile Nasser regime in 1967. But in both instances the basic attitude of Iran toward the armed conflict between the two sides was motivated primarily by the impact of the Soviet Union and its regional clients. Every other consideration was subordinate to this basic politico-strategic calculation.

Yet the primacy and continuity of this long-standing politico-strategic framework of Iranian policy toward the Arab-Israeli conflict has taken on added significance for Iran since 1968. Stripped of all the details, the historic British departure from the Persian Gulf in 1971; the extension of Iran's so-called security perimeter to the Gulf of Oman and the Indian Ocean in 1972; the rise of Indian power in South Asia in the wake of the dismemberment of Pakistan and simultaneously the rise of Iran as the preponderant military power in the Persian Gulf area in 1971; the October War, the Arab oil embargo, and the explosion of oil prices in 1973–74; the rise of Soviet naval power in the Indian Ocean and its special relations with Iraq and South Yemen since 1968; the armed conflict in the Horn of Africa supported by Soviet-Cuban arms and personnel in the face of retarded American response in 1977–78; together with the Soviet-American rhetoric of detente and the reality of widening competition in the face of the increasing dependence of the economy of the industrialized democracies on Persian Gulf oil in recent years, among other factors, have tended to intensify Iran's regional goals and increase its regional capabilities and responsibilities.

The Iranian quest for security and stability traditionally was confined to its own frontiers. During the past decade, however, Iran's efforts have been in part directed toward the creation of an increasingly enlarged and favorable regional environment. Iran has, therefore, been inclined to plot its policies toward the Arab-Israeli conflict with a view to its impact on the environment that engulfs not only the Persian Gulf and the Arab-Israeli zones but also the adjacent lands and sea-lanes of South Asia and the Horn of Africa.

The first important point about the Iranian policy toward the Arab-Israeli conflict since the October War that should be made is that the universal view that in some way Iran has "tilted" toward the Arab position against Israel is basically inaccurate. The notion of "tilt" assumes the existence of a previously balanced position toward the two antagonists. As already noted, during most of the period between 1950—when Iran granted recognition to Israel—and 1970—when Egypt resumed diplomatic relations with Iran—the severe conflict between the basic foreign-policy orientations of Iran and the principal confrontation states of Egypt and Syria precluded the development of any meaningful relationship with these Arab countries. As a result, Iran's bilateral relations with Israel appeared to some observers as a "discreet entente." What in fact has happened since 1970, and most particularly since the October War, has been the emergence of an Arab option. This unprecedented opportunity for the cultivation of Iranian friendship with the leading Arab states has coincided with the rise of Iranian power within the region.

What is the nature of Iran's basic thinking today on the Arab-Israeli conflict? If Iran's position has not tilted toward the Arab side in the sense that was explained above, then what, if any, change might have occurred in Iran's position? The answer to this question lies in a deeper understanding of Iran's current assessment of the conflict situation.

During the October War, the Iranians believed that "the Arabs this time are not talking of throwing Israel into the sea. They are not after the destruction of the Jewish state. What they are fighting for is the recovery of territories they lost to Israel in 1967."[7] The notion of the limited objective of at least Egypt in the 1973 war, which is implicit in this statement, has been accompanied in the Iranian thought by the perceived diminution of the strategic role of Israel relative to the Arab states in the Middle East. The Shah, for example, told the editor of the Beirut weekly al-Hawadis in the wake of the war that the "Arabs had shown that they could fight and that Israel was no longer undefeatable. [The] Israeli role of the policeman [of the area] has come to an end."[8] The Shah also believed that the Israeli concept of security must undergo change. For example, he stated about a month or so before the signing of the Sinai II agreement between Egypt and Israel that "Israel is making a great mistake in relying on the occupied Arab territories for its security." "In these days of long range planes flying at 80,000 feet," he continued, "and ground-to-ground missiles which go over any obstacle there is no such thing as secure borders for Israel. The Egyptians could bomb Tel Aviv, from west of Cairo. The only security for Israel is an international guarantee of its former borders. If the United States and the Soviet Union gave such a guarantee, it would be almost enough, but probably it would be wise to have it done within the framework of the United Nations—by the Security Council. Both sides need such a guarantee." But the Shah emphasized that another war would not be the last war, "because there will be more wars between Israel and its Arab neighbors. In Damascus or in Cairo? . . . perhaps the Israelis could reach there, but there would still be another hundred million Arabs left to fight them. Has Israel enough men to occupy the whole of the Arab world? Can she go to Algeria? Can she fight Saudi Arabia? Furthermore, can Israel sustain such military expenditures for the next 10 years? Who has to pay for it?" He then asked the American correspondent: "You Americans, for what? For supporting a very immoral question—the occupation by force of the land of some countries by another country."[9]

The fundamental point of this quotation is that in the post–October War period Iran would seem to believe that the requirements of Israeli security could no longer be satisfied merely by the maintenance of military preponderance, although this might have been sufficient at one time. In another wide-ranging interview with the Kuwaiti correspondent of *al-Siyasah*, the Shah stated in August 1975 that "time is not on Israel's side." He also said that there were 100 million Arabs who could use their oil wealth to industrialize and arm themselves and in a short-term or longer conflict could inflict tens of thousands of casualties. "Israel cannot," he continued, "bear such a burden. Until when can it devote so much money to arms purchases?"[10]

Clearly, however, even such an assessment of the future power configuration between the Arab states and Israel would not have automatically led to the cultivation of the friendship with the principal Arab confrontation states. The real key to the understanding of the Iranian thinking on the subject matter is that the rise of Arab power has coincided with an informal coalition of relatively moderate forces in the Arab world, and the combination of the two could best assist the realization of the overriding Iranian goal of creating a regional environment favorable to a greater degree of security and stability that can block the advance of Soviet power and influence. For this reason the Shah has repeatedly criticized the Israeli "intransigence" and has praised Sadat's "flexibility" out of the fear that the failure of a Middle East peace settlement could lead to the destruction of the Sadat regime and the emergence of an "extremist" regime.

Despite this, however, Iran has managed to continue its basic ties with Israel and to resist the pressures for too close an identification of its position with that of even the moderate Arab states. For example, the Shah told the Egyptian correspondent of *al-Ahram* during his visit to Egypt in January 1975 that he had been misquoted by several newspapers to the effect that he had said that "the next Middle East war will be our war." He then added that there "is no question, of course, of Iran participating in the fighting. There are geographical and other obstacles. But our sympathies will definitely be with you."[11] To cite another example, at the time of the Shah's visit to Egypt in 1975, President Sadat had reportedly attempted to convince the Shah to stop using Israel's Eilat-Ashkalon pipeline for shipping oil from the Red Sea to the Mediterranean.[12] If this report could be verified, it is interesting to note that so far no stoppage has occurred despite the fact that Iran and Egypt have planned to build an oil pipeline from Port Said to Port Suez, from where the oil would be taken to Europe via the Mediterranean.[13] Iran's interest in this project, as in the Suez Canal and a free Egyptian port offered to it by President Sadat, must be seen in the context of its regional power interest and the inadequacy of the Persian Gulf ports for meeting Iran's export-import needs rather than as a sign of diminished interest in Israel.

Israel itself has astutely seen Iran's rapprochement with the Arab states in exactly that light. For example, during the Shah's visit to Jordan and Egypt late in 1974 and early in 1975, the *Jerusalem Post* soberly assessed these historic visits in the context of the Shah's "apparent determination to build up his country as a major Middle East power wielding a greater influence in the area and the Israeli-Arab conflict through closer cooperation with the Arabs."[14] Even more to the point, the Mapam *Al Hamishmar* commented that if "the Shah's efforts are aimed at establishing a bloc based on Egypt–Iran–Saudi Arabia, this new arrangement of forces should not worry Israel (though there may be a cooling off of relations with Jerusalem). It should have a moderating effect on Soviet influence and strengthen the political option in the region."[15]

IRAN AS THE REGIONAL INTERMEDIARY?

What is Iran's role in the Arab-Israeli conflict today? If indeed it has avoided taking sides in the conflict since the October War, what kind of a role has it tried to play? The journalistic notion that, as a result of President Carter's visit to Tehran on the eve of the 1978 New Year, Iran has become active in the peacemaking process is too simplistic. As a matter of fact, Iran has been active in the process all along, but because much of the Iranian activity has taken place behind the scenes, it has been difficult for observers to take note of it adequately. There is no simple way of characterizing the role of Iran, largely because it has been multifaceted. Depending on the circumstances, it has ranged so far from that of a "moderator" to that of a "peacekeeper" and not a "mediator." As a Middle Eastern power with links to both sides, Iran could presumably play a mediating role in the peacemaking process in the future, but so far it has been reluctant to do so publicly or otherwise. For example, Vice President Hosni Mubarak briefed the Shah on the Egypt-Israel military committee talks and Egypt's withdrawal from negotiations in Jerusalem, but there was no visible sign of Iran's interest in plunging itself between the two sides. It was believed in Tehran that the Iranian intervention at this time, when the United States was still the major mediating force, would only complicate matters.[16]

Iran's role as a moderating force has surfaced at times. The target of Iran's effort has depended on the circumstances. For example, as soon as the peacemaking process began in the wake of the October War the Shah stated unequivocally that the Arab states must suspend the oil embargo until it was possible to see whether the diplomatic activities then under way would lead to a lasting peace. If the peace moves failed, the Arabs could unsheathe the oil weapon again. But having accepted the cease-fire, the Arabs should not suggest that they bore a grudge against the world.[17] While at this time the Arab states were the object of Iran's counsel of moderation, Israel has been repeatedly advised, and at times even admonished, to be more flexible, as evidenced, for example, during the failure of Secretary Kissinger's shuttle diplomacy. The Shah stated at a press conference in May 1975 that he was "really upset" about the failure of the Secretary's shuttle diplomacy and blamed Israel for the lack of sufficient cooperation in the process.[18]

To cite a more recent example, the Shah hailed the Sadat-Begin peace initiative that was launched in November 1977, but after it bogged down during the summit meeting at Ismailia in December, he threw his support dramatically behind President Sadat at a critical time. He visited Sadat at Aswan on January 9, 1978, stating on his arrival, "I think Egypt is doing precisely what we believe is right."[19] Whether or not Foreign Minister Moshe Dayan had actually briefed the Shah in Tehran before the monarch's visit to Aswan,[20] the Shah believed that the ball was then in "Israel's court."[21] As the prospects of peace dimmed daily, Iran began to put pressures on Israel publicly. For example, the Shah, joined by Indian Prime Minister Moraji Desai, decried in early February 1978 in New Delhi the Israeli attitude as "incomprehensible, uncompromising and stubborn."[22]

Although such a statement might have sounded more like a pronouncement of an arbitrator than the counsel of a moderator, the principal intent was to nudge Israel toward a greater degree of flexibility in the extremely crucial negotiating process. With links with both sides, and with monetary leverage with Egypt on the one hand and oil leverage with Israel on the other, Iran is conscious of the fact that it can potentially play a mediating role in the peacemaking process. At the moment, however, it is deferring to the United States. It is satisfied with its role as a peacekeeper, as evidenced by the participation of the 132d Rifle Battalion of the Iranian Army in the U.N. peacekeeping forces since its arrival on the Golan Heights on September 7, 1975,[23] and by the contribution of an Iranian naval unit to the U.N. Emergency Force for coastal patrol duty on the Egyptian-Israeli sector after the signing of the Sinai II agreement between the parties.[24]

IRAN AND THE MAIN ISSUES
OF THE ARAB-ISRAELI CONFLICT

What is Iran's position on the main issues of the Arab-Israeli conflict? To state that U.N. Resolution 242 is the "touchstone" of the Iranian position is to dodge the question. As is well known, the document is ambiguous enough for almost every state to feel comfortable in supporting it. Yet a close examination of the Iranian words and deeds on the subject against the backdrop of the foregoing discussions should, I hope, shed some light on the problem.

With regard to the problem of Israeli forces on the territories occupied in 1967, as early as June 7, 1967, the Shah demanded their withdrawal. That demand has been repeatedly made on the grounds that "the era for the occupation and usurpation," to borrow the Shah's words, "of the lands of others by force was long past."[25] The real reason for Iran's position is that it is convinced that short of a "reasonable guarantee of withdrawal," to borrow the words of the Iranian representative to the United Nations in 1974,[26] the peace negotiations cannot really get under way.

The more crucial question is whether Iran shares the stated Arab demand for the Israeli withdrawal from "all" occupied territories. No hair-splitting content analysis can help here. Iran is not a party to the dispute about spelling things out in the first place. Furthermore, it is impossible to distinguish between the negotiating and actual positions of the parties to the conflict, let alone to identify the relevant attitude of the third parties. Nevertheless, at least on the surface Iran seems to have endorsed the notion of "complete" withdrawal, as evidenced, for example, by the joint Irano-Egyptian communiqué of January 12, 1975, at the end of the Shah's visit to Egypt.[27] It may be safe to state that in fact the Iranian attitude toward the withdrawal might be closer to that of the United States, namely, the withdrawal of the Israeli forces to some extent from "all" fronts, including the West Bank. But basically, like the United States, Iran believes that the actual drawing of boundary lines is ultimately the responsibility of the parties to the conflict and not of bystanders.

With respect to the question of Jerusalem, Iran's attitude has been quite consistent since the 1967 war. Iran has addressed itself mainly to the control of the Muslim holy places. For example, the Shah told Secretary Kissinger in Tehran soon after the October War that "it is not possible that the Muslim holy places be placed in the hands of non-Muslims."[28] The same statement was made at Aswan by the Shah four years later. Furthermore, Iran has criticized the Israeli settlement policies in general and the Israeli measures in Jerusalem that have been taken presumably in disregard of the spiritual and emotional attachments of Muslims and Christians to the holy places, as evidenced by the joint communiqué issued at the end of President Sadat's visit to Iran in June 1976.[29]

Iran's position on the Palestinian question is more difficult to analyze. But several relevant points can be ascertained. Ever since 1948 Iran has endorsed the notion of "the legitimate rights of the Palestinian people," at first meaning "repatriation," then later meaning "self-determination" of the Palestinian people, as evidenced, for example, by Iran's support of U.N. Resolution 2535 B (XXIV), of December 10, 1969,[30] and by the joint Irano-Egyptian communiqué of January 12, 1975. After the Rabat conference Iran also accepted the notion that the Palestine Liberation Organization's participation was essential to the process of peace negotiations. This was the natural outcome of the Shah's conviction on the importance of the Palestinians to peacemaking even before the Rabat conference designated the PLO as "the sole and legitimate" representative of the Palestinian people. He told the editor of the Beirut weekly al-Hawadis that "if the rights of the Palestinian nation are not fulfilled, there will be no peace in the area."[31] At a press conference held at Niavaran Palace in early November 1974, the Shah acknowledged that Israel's refusal to talk to the PLO would make the peace negotiations more difficult.[32] His representative to the United Nations endorsed U.N. Resolution 3210 (XXIX), of October 14, 1974, which invited the PLO to participate in the deliberations of the General Assembly on the Palestinian question. On November 18, 1974, Mr. Huvayda gave the United Nations the fullest account to date of the Iranian position on the Palestinian question. He declared in part: "Today, for the first time, the problem is now being put in its proper perspective; in other words, the legitimate, inalienable rights of the Palestinian people, as a distinct entity—and no longer as a mass of refugees living off international assistance."[33]

It is quite clear from the text of the above statement that the Iranian representative felt comfortable with the concept of "entity," but in referring to the concept of a Palestinian "state," he must have felt differently. He stated, "I must say that, in our opinion, this is a question of concern primarily to the Palestinians themselves, and the Arab states directly concerned; and since those states have taken a decision on this matter, I cannot see how the General Assembly could possibly express a different opinion."[34]

One could perhaps infer reasonably from these words that the notion of a Palestinian "state" was in effect left in abeyance. But the Shah himself stated shortly after President Sadat's visit to Tehran in June 1976, "We have always said, and still say, that the Palestinians are a reality which cannot be neglected. They too must have a place in which to get together to express their statehood after being refugees, and this nation must become an active country in this region."[35] Even if one were to infer from this strong and relatively unequivocal statement that Iran endorsed the notion of a Palestinian state at the time, it would seem difficult to ascertain the kind of state that Iran might have in mind today. On the one hand, Iran previously held the view that the PLO must be represented on an equal footing with all other interested parties in the Geneva Conference. On the other hand, since President Sadat launched his peace initiative, Iran has been extremely cautious in declaring itself on the subject. It is safe to state, however, that Iran might be reexamining its position. There is evidence that the PLO has been concerned about the possibility of a change in the Iranian attitude since it joined the so-called rejectionist front first in Algeria. The more recent charges of the PLO's complicity in the Cypriot attack on the Egyptian rescue squad and the reported withdrawal of privileges from the Palestinians in Egypt will probably add to the PLO's worries about the future Iranian attitude because 'Arafat knows all too well the Shah's distaste for radicalism and his support for the Sadat regime.

One thing, however, is quite clear. Iran's future attitude toward a Palestinian state or entity will ultimately depend on two points. One is its own assessment of the future orientation of the Palestinian entity. Despite its past endorsement of the PLO, Iran has been quite careful to distinguish among the Palestinian factions. It has watched carefully the relationship of George Habash, the leader of the Popular Front for the Liberation of Palestine, and the Iranian terrorists and dissidents. For example, a letter from George Habash, dated February 4, 1976, to Hamid Ashraf, the head of a terrorist group in Iran, was captured in the hideout of the group.[36] Only a few months later a message from George Habash was read to the anti-Shah Iranian dissidents who were meeting in Chicago, Houston, and Berkeley in the United States.[37] The most revealing statement on the Iranian attitude toward the Palestinians, however, was made by the Shah himself in an interview with the correspondent of the Beirut weekly al-Hawadis on December 13, 1974. He stated, and I quote:

> We have stood and we still stand at the side of the Palestinians, despite the fact that some groups of the resistance trained Iranian saboteurs to infiltrate our territory, kill people, and blow up various installations. We know how to discriminate between the justness of the Palestine question and the wrong-doing directed against us by some Palestinians. What I fear is that the Palestinians may allow international circumstances to make their cause a tool of Soviet or some other international strategy. Egypt, Saudi Arabia, Syria, and the other Arab states would do well to help the Palestinians avoid such pitfalls.[38]

The other consideration that will continue to influence the Shah's future attitude toward the Palestinians is the position of King Hussein of Jordan. Quite apart from the fact that the Shah's personal friendship with the King is much older than his relationship with President Sadat, the two monarchs have for long held significantly similar views on the Middle Eastern political and strategic situation. Furthermore, the Shah is well aware of the fact that the King's participation in the peace negotiations is not only essential if the momentum is to be maintained, but also crucial to the eventual determination of the Palestinian problem. The so-called Jordanian solution might have an appeal to Iran at the moment,[39] but whether it will in the future as well will depend on its passing the basic test of Iran's larger political and strategic interests in the Middle East. Those long-standing interests, as we have already seen in this essay, lie at the heart of one of Iran's fundamental foreign-policy goals. That overriding objective is the creation of a regional environment favorable to the promotion of moderate, nonviolent, and relatively independent local power centers resistant to the advance of Soviet and pro-Soviet power and influence.

This same basic objective will be the principal guide to Iran's future attitude toward Israel as well as the Palestinians. As seen, the perceived political and strategic utility of Israel in the Middle East against the advance of Soviet power and influence has been the bedrock of Iran's quiet but close ties with Israel to date. The Shah's increasing concern with the perceived "intransigence" of Israel in the peacemaking process is rooted in the fear that the breakdown of negotiations and the outbreak of another Arab-Israeli war will more than any other single factor radicalize and polarize the Middle East region. His denunciation of Israeli "intransigence" in New Delhi, mentioned before, and his hint at an oil embargo against Israel on March 5, 1978, in Tehran, were intended as a warning in the hope of nudging the Begin government toward a greater degree of flexibility in negotiations with the Sadat regime.[40] The warning may well mark the beginning of Iran's increasing public pressure on Israel if it appears to the Shah that the Israeli foreign policy can lead to a regional environment inimical to the interests of his regime.

NOTES

1. See Robert B. Reppa Sr., *Israel and Iran: Bilateral Relationships and Effect on the Indian Ocean Basin* (New York, 1974); and M. G. Weinbaum, "Iran and Israel: The Discreet Entente," *Orbis* 18, no. 4 (Winter 1975): 1070–87. See also Shahram Chubin and Mohammad Fard-Saidi, *Recent Trends in Middle East Politics and Iran's Foreign Policy Options* (Tehran, 1975).

2. George Lenczowski, *The Middle East in World Affairs* (New York, 1962), 405–6.

3. For details, see R. K. Ramazani, *Iran's Foreign Policy, 1941–1973: A Study of Foreign Policy in Modernizing Nations* (Charlottesville, 1975), 290–328.

4. For details, see R. K. Ramazani, *The Persian Gulf: Iran's Role* (Charlottesville, 1972), 28–68.

5. See Shahram Chubin and Sepehr Zabih, *The Foreign Relations of Iran: A Developing State in a Zone of Great-Power Conflict* (Berkeley, 1974), 156–69.

6. *Kayhan*, 1 December 1973, weekly international edition (hereafter *Kayhan*).

7. Ibid., 13 October 1973.

8. Ibid., 1 December 1973.

9. Ibid., 2 August 1975.

10. Ibid., 16 August 1975.

11. Ibid., 4 January 1975.

12. *Arab Report and Record*, 1–15 January 1975, 38.

13. *Kayhan*, 19 June 1976.

14. *Jerusalem Post*, 9 January 1975.

15. Ibid., 10 January 1975.

16. *An-Nahar: Arab Report and Memo* 2, no. 6 (6 February 1978).

17. *Kayhan*, 1 December 1973.

18. Ibid., 2 May 1975.

19. *Washington Post*, 10 January 1978.

20. Ibid., 29 December 1977.

21. *Kayhan*, 14 January 1978.

22. Ibid., 4 February 1978.

23. Tehran Domestic Service, 7 September 1975, as monitored by Foreign Broadcast Information Service, in FBIS, *Daily Report*, vol. 5, *Middle East and North Africa* (FBIS-MEA), 9 September 1975.

24. *Kayhan*, 13 December 1975.

25. Cairo Domestic Service, 8 January 1975, as monitored by Foreign Broadcast Information Service, in FBIS-MEA, 9 January 1975.

26. See U.N. General Assembly, 29th Sess., *Record*, A/PV 2264, Agenda Item 9, 10 October 1974.

27. The text is in Cairo Domestic Service in Arabic, 12 January 1975, as monitored by Foreign Broadcast Information Service, in FBIS-MEA, 13 January 1975.

28. *Kayhan*, 1 December 1973.

29. Ibid., 26 January 1976.

30. For the text, see U.N. General Assembly, 29th Sess., *Record*, A/PV 2289, 18 November 1974.

31. *Kayhan*, 1 December 1973.

32. Ibid., 9 November 1974.

33. See n. 30 above.

34. Ibid.

35. *Kayhan*, 26 June 1976.

36. Ibid., 3 July 1976.

37. Ibid., 8 August 1976.

38. For the text, see *al-Hawadis* (Beirut), 13 December 1974, as monitored by Foreign Broadcast Information Service, in FBIS-MEA, 13 December 1974.

39. *Washington Post*, 6 January 1978.

40. Ibid., 6 March 1978.

IRAN, DEMOCRACY,

AND THE UNITED STATES

While the Bush administration includes Iran in its "axis of evil," the Iranian people see this designation as a threat to Iran's historical pro-democracy movement. Decades of mutual vilification between Iran and the United States predated President Bush's moralistic identification of Iran as evil. The hostility between the two countries dates back to the Iranian Revolution of 1979.

The revolution destroyed Mohammad Reza Shah's regime, a longtime strategic surrogate of America in the Middle East, particularly in the oil-rich Persian Gulf. Ayatollah Ruhollah Khomeini, the founder of the Islamic Republic of Iran, endorsed the seizure of the American Embassy and the holding of Americans hostage for 444 days. This single event, perhaps more than any other at the time, fueled American antagonism toward Iran and prompted President Jimmy Carter to break diplomatic relations with Tehran. A quarter of a century later there is still no real indication of a resumption of official relations.

The pro-democracy aspirations of the Iranian people are more than a century old. But never before have so many millions of people struggled so gallantly for democratic values as they are doing today. Young women and men, especially students, are the vanguards of this pro-democracy movement. They are under the age of 30 and form two-thirds of the 65 million or more population of the country. Furthermore, while anti-Americanism is sweeping across the Arab Middle East, the non-Arab Iranians demonstrate genuinely pro-American sentiments.

One objective of this essay is to probe the deeper meaning of the Iranian pro-democracy and pro-American movement. This task is made possible by placing the movement squarely within the broad outlines of the Iranian cultural legacy. The other objective is to show why the people of Iran perceive the Bush administration's foreign policy as a threat to their pro-democracy movement.

THE LEGACY OF THE TRIPLE POLITICAL CULTURE

Iran's cultural heritage has become threefold in nature over the millennia at least in part because of its remarkable continuity. Despite momentous

"Iran, Democracy, and the United States" was originally published in *The Future of Liberal Democracy: Thomas Jefferson and the Contemporary World*, ed. R. K. Ramazani and Robert Fatton (New York: Palgrave Macmillan, 2004), 185–201, and is reproduced with permission of Palgrave Macmillan.

changes the past has always been present in Iranian culture. Even in comparison with such old civilizations as those of Egypt and Syria, "which underwent great changes in the course of two millennia of history," Richard Nelson Frye says, "Iran seems to have preserved much more of its ancient heritage."[1]

Iranian culture took shape between the sixth century BC and the seventh century AD, before the coming of Islam. Pre-Islamic and Islamic cultures both underpin the Iranian sense of identity and one cannot trump the other. Emblematic of these two strands of the cultural heritage is the statement of the Nobel Peace Prize winner Shirin Ebadi. In accepting the prize, she proudly declared to the world on December 10, 2003: "I am an Iranian, A descendant of Cyrus the Great" and "I am a Muslim."

To these two older, premodern strands of Iranian cultural legacy must be added a relatively newer one—that of *modernity*. For two hundred years, specifically, since the imperial Russian invasion of Iran in 1804, Western civilization has penetrated the Iranian culture. Modern ideas of nation-state, constitution, temporal law, civil society, and representative and liberal democratic government, among many others, have been imported by Iranian intellectuals, who in essence believe in the principle of the rule of the people and human rights as opposed to the millennial legacy of autocracy. Modernist Iranians, religious as well as secular, believe that Islam is essentially compatible with fundamental Western political principles. Shirin Ebadi told the sitting members of the European Parliament's Committee on Foreign Relations in Brussels on February 25, 2004, "Islam accepts democracy. There is no conflict between human rights and Islam." The renowned philosopher Abdul Karim Soroush and intellectually oriented President Mohammad Khatami essentially claim the same, although their conceptions of "democracy" and "Islam" are quite different.

To appreciate the historical longevity of the theory of compatibility of Islam with democracy, let me cite a nineteenth-century example. Mirza Yousef Khan, known as Mostashar Dowleh, argued in his important work *Yek Kalameh* (One word) that Islam and *liberal democracy* are compatible.[2] He compared the seventeen-point French Declaration of Rights of Man and of Citizens with the fundamental Islamic tenets and concluded that they correspond. This modern dimension of Iranian culture has also been preserved in history, and in my opinion, just as Iranian rulers cannot exclude either pre-Islamic or Islamic strands from their political culture, they cannot expunge modernity either. They can do so only at the expense of legitimacy of their rule.

INTERACTIONS OF STATE AND RELIGION

In all Iran's history no aspect of its political culture has escaped the dynamic interactions between religion and state. A thumbnail sketch of this phenomenon in premodern history can reveal the epic significance of the coming of modern ideas, especially democracy, to Iranian society and state.

Religion-state interplay prevailed in Iran during both the Achaemenid and the Sassanid dynasties. The Achaemenids set the foundation of the Iranian state in the sixth century BC; it lasted for two hundred years before the invasion of Iran by Alexander of Macedonia. At the end of Greek and Parthian rules in Iran, the Sassanid dynasty revived the Iranian Empire and ruled the state for four hundred years before the coming of Islam in the seventh century AD. Zoroastrian religion interacted with both Iranian dynastic states, but its impact on the politics of the two empires was quite different.

Cyrus the Great, the founder of the Achaemenid dynasty, created the first "world state" and organized the first "international society" in history. In her classic work Adda B. Bozeman writes that in the sixth century BC, when the tyranny of empires plagued the fabric of community life everywhere, the Persian Empire, vaster than any preceding empire west of China, attained universal peace for some two hundred years, in large part as the result of tolerant respect for the cultural diversity of the subjugated people.[3] Prudence rather than religious ethics of the sixth century BC, Bozeman says, influenced Cyrus's statecraft.

Richard Frye, the world-renowned historian of ancient Iran, tells me that Cyrus's law, or king's law, predated Roman law. It allowed the religious laws of Egyptians, Babylonians, and Hebrews, for example, to stay in force.[4] Herodotus testifies to Cyrus's "statesmanship and liberality"; Xenophon in his *Cyropaedia* finds Cyrus "deserving admiration," above all, for honoring his people "as if they were his own children"; and the Bible reveres Cyrus for liberating the Jews from Babylonian captivity. To date, Iraqi Jews trace their origins to Cyrus's liberation policy.[5]

In contrast, Zoroastrian faith more than state interest sometimes shaped Sassanid politics. In a nutshell, two factors seem to have contributed to this difference. First, at least two of many Sassanid kings claimed some kind of divine qualities. Second, the Magi (*Majus*), or priests, organized themselves into a priestly hierarchy. During the long life of these two earliest Iranian states, king and Magi performed different functions and religion and state remained separate. Frye says that even during the reign of the Sassanids, who made Zoroastrianism the official state religion, the head of the priesthood, Mobadan-Mobad, "became the partner of the Shahinshah."[6]

This ancient tradition of separation of religion and state appears to have been cast aside at the turn of the sixteenth century. Shah Ismail, the founder of the new empire, fused state and religion in 1501. He declared himself to be the "Agent of God," as had a couple of the Sassanid kings.[7] He and his successors, like the Sassanids before them, aspired to universality. While the Sassanids had tried to fuse the state and religion by Zoroastrianizing the state, Shah Ismail tried to do so by "Shiitizing" it. Yet Shah Ismail's enterprise eventually failed. Roger M. Savory writes that Ismail failed to prevent the separation of secular and religious powers, which in fact occurred under his successors.[8] Marshall G. S. Hodgson says that by the end of the seventeenth century the religious establishment asserted itself as separate from the state.[9]

While being separate, the clergy, with popular support, gained over time an unprecedented degree of power and authority. In contrast, the state institutions weakened, and the tyranny of kings gradually alienated the people. The intermittent wars between the Safavid and the Ottoman Empires contributed much to state weakness. The Shii-Sunni sectarian as well as territorial conflicts at least in part underpinned the outbreak of wars. However, in my opinion, intellectual stagnation and material backwardness were greater causes of state decline.

Western powers had derived their strength from such momentous developments as the Renaissance, the Reformation, the Enlightenment, and the Scientific Revolution. In contrast, fossilized Islamic and pre-Islamic traditions robbed the Iranians of the power of intellectual creativity and material innovation. Historical backwardness exposed state and society to Western imperial encroachments and with them the profound and epic challenge of modernity to the encrustation of millennial traditions.

Two wars with Russia over lost Iranian territories in Transcaucasia and armed confrontation with Britain over Herat in the nineteenth century further weakened Iran. No less consequential, European commercial and imperial expansion sucked the failing state into the whirlwind of European power politics as never before. Rival British and Russian Empires penetrated Iranian state and society at least in part by extracting all kinds of commercial and economic concessions from autocratic rulers, to such a point that by the end of the nineteenth century Iran was independent only in name. One of these concessions became the first landmark catalyst of Iranian national awakening in modern times. It was granted by Nasser al-Din Shah, of the Qajar dynasty, to a British company for a tobacco monopoly. Viewing it as injurious to both religion and the kingdom, a leading cleric called on people to stop smoking. As a result of the people's protest, the Shah was forced to cancel the concession in 1892.

ABORTED DEMOCRATIC EXPERIMENTS

This first popular movement in modern times preceded the first pro-democracy movement in Iran, known as the Constitutional Revolution (1905–11). Throughout Iran's history until this revolution, religion had played a leading role in legitimizing the one-man rule of autocratic monarchs. By this time, however, modern-educated Iranians pressed the idea of the rule of the people, rather than traditional tenets of religion, as the fundamental basis for political legitimacy. Enlightened clergy, secular intellectuals, and bazaar merchants provided the social base of support for the Constitutional Revolution. The tradition of autocracy and monarchical tyranny on the one hand and unprecedented foreign domination on the other were the twin engines of the revolution.

Hence the two most fundamental goals of the revolutionary forces crystallized over time into the two principles of independence and freedom in the Iranian political culture. They were enshrined in the Constitution of 1906–7 as inseparable principles. In this light, the Iranian Constitution, like the American Declaration of Independence, symbolized for all time the highest values of Iranian political culture—*independence and liberty.*

By modern standards, of course, the Constitution was not a perfectly liberal democratic document, but against the backdrop of thousands of years of autocracy this essentially democratic first step was remarkable. The very adoption of the Constitution in 1906–7 and the establishment of the first parliament (Majlis) in 1906 were unprecedented in Iran's millennial history. Actually, the Constitution was modeled after that of Belgium, while at the same time taking into account Iran's own indigenous norms and institutions. The institution of monarchy was retained, although the monarch's power to grant concessions to foreign powers and to conclude international treaties was subject to the approval of the Majlis. For the first time in history people were enfranchised, but the ancient tradition of rigid social stratification limited their freedom to choose their representatives. They could elect their deputies only from among princes, learned clerics (*mujtahids*), nobles, landowners, merchants, and guild members. The representatives of the people in the Majlis could enact secular laws, provided that they were compatible with the criteria of Islamic law (*Sharia*). A committee of learned clerics was to determine such compatibility. But in fact it was never formed.

This first experiment of the Iranian people with democratic government was tragically aborted. The British and Russian Empires, although old-time rival powers in Iran, allied themselves in the face of the perceived German threat to their interests in Iran. They partitioned Iran between themselves in 1907. They also forced the departure of the American Morgan Shuster, whom the Majlis had hired to reform the nation's finances. His classic *The Strangling of Persia* details the machinations of the British and Russian Empires to crush the nascent pro-democracy government of Iran. The unholy alliance of the Royalist supporters of the Russian puppet Muhammad Ali Shah and diehard conservative clergy, who demanded the establishment of Islamic law as the sole source of law, equally contributed to the demise of the pro-democracy government.

The second opportunity for the Iranian people to try to experiment with constitutional democracy and representative government had to wait nearly four decades. During the first decade Iran nearly disintegrated. Tribal revolts, factional conflicts, a divided government, and the ineffective rule of a young absentee monarch, Ahmad Shah, the last monarch of the Qajar dynasty, left Iranian society in utter chaos. The occupation of the country by warring foreign powers during World War I compounded the disastrous situation. During the 1925–41 period Reza Shah ruled as a secular anticlerical modernizing dictator like his European counterparts, Hitler and Mussolini. Reza Shah did much to unite the country. He also reduced foreign domination, especially by abolishing the century-old foreign capitulatory rights in 1928. He pushed for modern education, modern economic infrastructure, and a modern professional army. But his renewal of the injurious Anglo-Persian oil concessionary contract has never been forgiven by politically aware Iranians.

The end of Reza Shah's dictatorship left his son, Mohammad Reza Shah, on the throne in 1941. Being young and inexperienced in politics, he could not immediately continue his father's legacy of dictatorship until after 1953, as will be seen. The Iranians, therefore, call the 1941–53 period the era of "Revival of Constitutionalism" (ehya-ye Mashrutiat), signifying a reminder of the 1905–11 Constitutional Revolution. The new burst of democratic aspirations was reflected in an unprecedented degree of freedom of expression, press, and party politics. Pro-democracy nationalists, communists, and Islamists battled each other competitively. In the end, the nationalist pro-democracy Dr. Mohammad Mosaddegh was popularly elected and reluctantly appointed by the Shah as prime minister.

Mosaddegh strongly believed that democratic government could not be established durably unless Iran could end the British domination of the Anglo-Iranian Oil Company. He made the nationalization of the oil industry the first and foremost goal of his government. He depicted for the people his nationalization dispute with the British as a choice between "independence" and "enslavement" (isteqlal ya enqiad). He argued Iran's case against Britain at the United Nations in terms of moral as well as economic and political aspirations of the Iranian people. His preoccupation with the goal of nationalization and ultimately the goal of an "oilless" economy left little room for pushing for democratic reforms. He denied, for example, that the landed aristocracy contributed to the social and political malaise of the nation as much as the control of the Iranian oil industry by the British.

Depicting the choice of his government in such absolute terms as between independence and servitude seems to have left little room for realistic compromise in the dispute with Britain. As laudable as the goal of "complete nationalization" of the oil industry might have been, it is questionable whether Iran's technical and marketing capabilities at the time made such a goal attainable. To date, it is not clear to what extent his uncompromising conduct reflected his own predisposition or the pressures of various political and religious factions. For example, I was told by Averell Harriman, President Truman's mediator in the Anglo-Iranian dispute, that every time he thought he had reached an agreement with Mosaddegh it fell apart. Harriman believed that Ayatollah Kashani, an activist anti-British cleric, had, behind the scenes, kept vetoing Mosaddegh's agreements with him.

As will be seen below, a foreign-engineered coup overthrew the Mosaddegh government. The coup is often justified in the West in terms of the fear of a communist takeover of his government. In my own research I have found no real evidence that democratically oriented Mosaddegh had any procommunist leanings or that there was any real threat of the capture of his government by the communist Tudeh Party.[10] On the contrary, there is ample evidence to show that the party made every effort to undermine Mosaddegh's government, without success. What might well have contributed to his loss of support by some of his staunchest allies was his increasing role as a solo player. He gathered extensive powers to himself even at the expense of the Majlis, the symbol par excellence of Iranian historical democratic aspirations.

On balance, however, foreign intervention, more than domestic factional strife, destroyed his government just as in the first Iranian attempt to experiment with democratic politics during the Constitutional Revolution. The CIA, with British help, engineered the coup against Mosaddegh's government in 1953, allegedly because of the "contingencies of the Cold War," a euphemism for U.S. competition with the Soviet Union for power and influence in Iran. It took nearly half a century before former secretary of state Madeleine Albright expressed the regrets of the American government for its intervention against the democratically elected prime minister.

After Mosaddegh's fall from power, Mohammad Reza Shah began to flex his dictatorial muscle with full American support. The Weberian concept of sultanism well applies to the Shah's quarter-of-a-century rule after Mosaddegh. His sultanic dictatorship resembled those of Duvalier in Haiti, Trujillo in the Dominican Republic, and Marcos in the Philippines. To be sure, his Westernization policies contributed much to the modern material progress of Iran at the start, but backfired subsequently for their superficiality. His expansion of modern education helped the rise of modern intellectual and professional middle classes and increased political awakening among an ever-growing population.

But his one-man dictatorial rule left no real room for the development of civil society, freedom of the press, or respect for individual and human rights. His "White Revolution of the Shah and the People," implemented under the pressure of President John F. Kennedy, helped land reforms, but it ultimately worsened the conditions of the peasantry.

His grandiose notion of turning Iran into a "Great Civilization" led to his voracious appetite for buying arms, especially from the United States. He aimed at making Iran one of the five conventional military powers of the world. As an American surrogate, the Shah was anointed as the policeman of the oil-rich Persian Gulf by the Nixon administration. His popularly opposed status-of-forces agreement with the Pentagon seemed to many Iranians to be a return of the old capitulatory rights of foreign powers. Ayatollah Ruhollah Khomeini called the agreement "a document of the enslavement of Iran." Emblematic of the people's alienation from the Shah and the United States was the revolutionary label applied to the Shah, "the American king."[11]

In effect, the Shah, like his father, trumped the Islamic aspect of Iranian political culture. They both tried to legitimize their unpopular regimes by claiming the mantle of the sixth-century BC monarch Cyrus the Great. Mohammad Reza Shah put on a pretentious show by crowning himself in 1971 as the successor of the ancient king at his gravesite at Pasargadae and celebrated the event outlandishly at Persepolis.

"ISLAMIC DEMOCRACY"

The Iranian Revolution of 1979 ended a quarter-century of the American economic, political, and cultural domination of Iran, and half a century of the anticlerical stance of the Pahlavi shahs. In establishing the Islamic Republic of Iran, the Islamist factions succeeded in seizing power despite the opposition of moderate religious as well as secular groups, including pro-democracy nationalists. They placed the clergy in control of the state, contrary to the age-old Shii tradition that prohibits the clergy from ruling the state.

I think the clerical rule of the state was also contrary to the pre-Islamic tradition of separation of religion and state, and as such Khomeini's doctrine of "viceregency of the religious jurisprudent" (Velayat-e Faqih) was unprecedented in Iran's political culture. His creation of a "government of God" in Iran, I would argue, was a unique ambition in the political history of Iran.

Yet in retrospect the revolution intensified the time-honored Iranian sense of political independence. The revolution's greatest achievement, in my opinion, has been the emancipation of the Iranian decision-making process from direct or indirect control of foreign powers. For the first time in some two centuries Iranian policymakers make their own decisions, realistic or unrealistic, prudent or ideological, and ultimately beneficial or harmful to Iran's values and interests. Iran's deep sense of cultural identity lies behind its fierce commitment to its political independence.

In contrast to independence, the principle of freedom has gotten short shrift from the very beginning of the revolution. As noted, within the Iranian political culture the principle of independence has been made inseparable from that of freedom. Khomeini himself set the principle of freedom as well as independence in his well-known credo of "Independence, freedom, and the Islamic Republic," and the Islamic Constitution of 1979 makes these two principles inseparable. Khomeini rejected the age-old secular pro-democracy aspirations of the Iranians. He opposed out of hand the demand of pro-democracy nationalists and Islamic modernists for adding the modifier "Democratic" to the name of the "Islamic Republic of Iran" before the issue was put to a referendum. Ever since 1979 the Islamist factions have opposed democratic competitive politics.

Reformist factions have always argued that the Constitution includes the principle of "the sovereign rights of the nation" and makes the Majlis, the presidency, the local councils, and the Assembly of Experts elective institutions. In contrast, hard-line conservatives insist that according to the Constitution sovereignty belongs to the *faqih* as the representative of the Hidden Imam, and it gives the lion's share of power to him. From the time of the adoption of the Constitution in 1979 to the present time, the irreconcilability of the principle of popular sovereignty and the doctrine of the rule of clergy has been debated.[12]

Just as secular autocracy failed to choke off democratic aspirations, Islamist authoritarianism was unable to stop the gathering momentum of the pro-democracy movement. Ironically, the campaign to Islamicize state and society by fusing religion and state has inoculated an ever-growing population against Islamism and the mixing of state and religion. As noted, about half a millennium ago Shah Ismail Safavid ultimately failed to prevent the separation of religion and state that occurred subsequently under his successors. Is there a lesson in this significant Shii development in history for hard-line conservatives today?

The resounding presidential victory of Mohammad Khatami on May 23, 1997 (*Dovom-e Khordad*), was emblematic of the surge of the pro-democracy movement. Twenty million women and men, 69 percent of the eligible voters, voted for him. By this spectacular action the people in effect tried to throw off the coercive shackles of hard-line conservatives' domination of politics after nearly two decades. Student activists had grown in number over time and a major student organization became active on more than fifty university campuses across the country. But while the reformist camps grew in strength, the die-hard conservative factions increased their antidemocratic actions in the name of Islam and the revolution. Jacques Barzun says: "Revolutions paradoxically begin by promising freedom and then turn coercive and "puritanical," to save themselves from both discredit and reaction . . . old shackles are thrown off, tossed high in the air, but come down again as moral duty well enforced."[13]

This is exactly what has been going on in Iran. Morals police have been mercilessly enforcing medieval norms of conduct, especially with respect to the veiling of women; the religious establishment has reduced the marriage age and reinforced a husband's unbridled right to divorce, but with some slight backtracking under reformist pressures. Zealous Islamists such as the Supporters of the Party of God (Ansar-e Hezbollah) have broken into private homes, presumably to enforce the norms of Islamic purity.

Political repression far exceeds social dictation based on petrified religious traditions. Rogue members of the previous intelligence service have murdered a number of outspoken intellectuals. Reformist newspapers have been banned and their editors arrested and jailed. Even the reformist representatives of the Majlis have been intimidated and sentenced to imprisonment. The conservative-dominated judiciary has relentlessly suppressed freedom of expression, and sentenced to prison terms enlightened clerics as well as secular-minded reformists. Recently it sentenced to death a university professor (Hashem Aqa Jari) for advocating the need for some kind of "Islamic Protestantism,"[14] although the final verdict has not been handed down. Among all acts of suppression of freedom, the performance of the unelected powerful and conservative-dominated Council of Guardians stands out. The Council has repeatedly disqualified reformist candidates from running in various elections. In the February 2004 parliamentary elections the Council went wild in its arbitrary abuse of power. It disqualified thousands of pro-democracy candidates from participating in elections.

Throughout his terms of office President Khatami has advocated "Islamic Democracy" as the way to accentuate the rights of the people. He has pointed out the urgent need to meet the mounting demands of the people for civil society, the rule of law, government accountability, and freedom of expression and action. He believes that Iran is at "a sensitive juncture of its history."[15] He rejects the fossilized interpretations of Islam, as he criticizes the mimicking of the paraphernalia of Western civilization.

Since further discussion of Khatami's conception of Islamic democracy is beyond the scope of this essay,[16] I will summarize his statement published in the United Nations *Human Development Report 2002: Deepening Democracy in a Fragmented World*. He writes that he accepts the reality of democracy, which has evolved over the past century as a value, rejects any one form of democracy as "the one and final version," and advocates the formulation of democracy in "the context of spirituality and morality."[17] These concepts are, of course, ambiguous. If "spiritually and morality" mean that they should guide social norms, not run the state, it would then seem that his formulation would approach something like the idea of liberal democracy. But since Khatami has so far accepted the doctrine of the rule of the religious leader, his Islamic democracy is still entangled in the contradictory principles of the rule of the *faqih* and sovereignty of the people, which has been debated since the eruption of the revolution in 1979.

In terms of the three strands of Iran's culture, it seems to me that the formulation "Islamic Democracy" overemphasizes the Islamic strand almost at the expense of the pre-Islamic and modern dimensions of the triple political culture. In contrast, I suggest the concept "Persian Democracy" as a path to durable political order. The two fundamental values of this formulation are justice and liberty. The value of justice is as old as Iranian culture, pre-Islamic as well as Islamic. The value of liberty is not only universal, but it has also been embedded in the pro-democracy struggle of the Iranian people for more than a century. This is why in concluding my address to President Khatami on September 4, 2000, at the United Nations I said, "I believe there can be no durable political order without justice under the law and no justice without liberty."[18]

What is far more consequential in practice, however, is the decline of the appeal of the Islamic-democracy formula to the people. The disenchantment of reformist factions, especially student activists, with Khatami's failure to fulfill his promised social and political reforms within the context of Islamic democracy is mounting. The increasing frustration of the supporters of the pro-democracy movement began to show in the second presidential election, in 2001, when he gathered 70 percent of the votes, but with a lower turnout as compared with his first election, in 1997. Low turnout also showed up in the second local-council election as compared with the first one. It resulted in a dramatic conservative capture of local councils. Above all, the dismal turnout in the February 2004 parliamentary elections showed the deepening apathy and alienation of politically aware Iranians.

These significant setbacks of the reformists no doubt will prolong the grip on levers of power by conservative factions. Their loosening of some restrictions on social behavior in all probability will not have any dampening effects on the growing demand for secular democracy. Once again university students are in the forefront of rejecting Islamic democracy as the solution to the people's grave deprivation of individual freedoms. The debate on the relation between religion and state has never before been as widespread, as sophisticated, and as unremitting as it is today.

This is a profound reality of the Iranian situation today. It is not lost on keen political observers in America. For example, Fareed Zakaria argues, "Iran might well hold out the greatest promise for liberal democracy and secular politics in the Middle East. Having lived under Islamic fundamentalist rule, Iranians are now inoculated against its appeal."[19] To cite another example, Thomas Friedman writes: "If the Iranian thinkers and politicians were ever to blend constitutional democracy with refined Islam that limits itself to inspiring social norms, not running a state, it could have a positive impact on the whole Muslim world from Morocco to Indonesia."[20] Can the Bush administration understand this profound reality of the Iranian pro-democracy and pro-American movement and stop threatening it?

THE BUSH ADMINISTRATION THREATENS
THE PRO-DEMOCRACY MOVEMENT

Iranians perceive the Bush administration's threat to their pro-democracy movement against the background of foreign destruction of two constitutional democratic governments in the twentieth century, as explained earlier. The memory of the CIA-engineered coup that overthrew the popularly elected pro-democracy government of Mosaddegh in 1953 burns deeply into the collective memory of Iranians and affects the Iranian perception of the American threat today.

Furthermore, the administration's threats are seen in contrast to all previous American administrations' Iran policy since the Iranian Revolution. Despite the confrontational stance of them all, none before the Bush administration had threatened to subvert the regime or attack Iran by military force. The Clinton administration pursued a policy of "dual containment" against Iran and Iraq. But it never tired of probing the possibility of engaging Iran. This was particularly the case after the election of Khatami to the presidency in 1997.

Scholars and officials alike failed to understand the important synergy between Khatami's campaign for social and political reforms and his foreign policy. Essentially, his campaign aimed at democracy at home and peace abroad. It seemed to me at the time that his worldview resembled slightly the democratic peace theory in America.[21] To be sure, after Khomeini, President Ali Akbar Hashemi Rafsanjani had pursued a more pragmatic foreign policy in contrast with the Khomeini era, when Iraq attacked Iran. Rafsanjani helped with the release of Western hostages in Lebanon, maintained a policy of strict neutrality in the Persian Gulf War of 1991, and tried to probe openings with the United States. But President Khatami turned on its head Iran's confrontational foreign policy and earnestly tried to engage America in people-to-people dialogue.

Khatami's conciliatory foreign policy first aimed at relations with the United States, the traditional "Great Satan." In landmark remarks to the American people on January 7, 1998, he drew a parallel to the effect that faith and freedom were compatible in the American historical experience as they are in Iran today. He said that "the secret of American civilization lies in the Puritan's vision which in addition to worshipping God, was in harmony with republicanism, democracy and freedom." He also complimented the American people by stating that the "American nation was the harbinger of independence struggles on human dignity and rights."

Khatami's reaction as well as that of the Iranian people to the savage terrorist attacks on the Twin Towers and the Pentagon on September 11, 2001, showed that the Iranian conciliatory approach to the Clinton administration continued early during the Bush administration. Within hours after the attacks Khatami condemned them as assaults on human dignity and rights. Later he told the U.N. General Assembly: "The horrific terrorist attacks of September 11 2001 in the United States were perpetrated by a cult of fanatics who had self-mutilated their ears and tongues, and could only communicate with perceived opponents through carnage and devastation." Even the conservative Supreme Leader, Ayatollah Ali Khamenei, was the first clerical leader in the Muslim world to call for "holy war" (jihad) against terrorism as a "global scourge." Meanwhile, many pro-democracy activists joined 60,000 spectators who observed a minute of silence during a soccer game in Tehran, and many hundreds of young women and men, many weeping, held a candlelight vigil for the American victims of terrorism.

Against this remarkably conciliatory stance of Iran, the Bush administration's abandonment of the Khatami government and repeated threats shocked both the government and the people of Iran, conservatives and pro-democracy reformists alike. Iranians noticed a drastic reversal of the Clinton administration's Iran policy, which had probed repeatedly the possibility of engaging Iran in some kind of official dialogue. The record of the recent past reveals that the Iranian perception of the Bush administration's threat is real.

This is no place to catalogue numerous policy statements that directly or indirectly threaten Iran. The ones that have particularly roiled the Iranians, however, must be mentioned. In his first State of the Union address, on January 29, 2002, President Bush vowed to stop the spread of weapons of mass destruction and singled out North Korea, Iraq, and Iran for special mention, calling them an "axis of evil." In his speech of June 2002 to the West Point graduating class, he said for the first time that the United States would use force preemptively to the acquisition of prohibited weapons because America should not wait until threats fully materialized. Washington has repeatedly accused Iran of seeking weapons of mass destruction.

The United States has also included Iran in the category of "rogue states" who sponsor terrorism. The thirty-three-page National Security Strategy document of September 2002 highlighted the threat of weapons of mass destruction that might fall into the hands of rogue states. The implication for Iran was obvious.

President Bush's threat to Iran especially surfaced on two occasions. First, in his second State of the Union speech, on January 29, 2003, he repeated the old charges of Iran's search for weapons of mass destruction and support of terrorism. More noticeably, he said, "We also see Iranian citizens risking intimidation and death as they speak out for liberty, human rights, and democracy. Iranians like all people, have a right to choose their own government, and determine their own destiny—and the United States supports their aspirations to live in freedom." The ruse was not lost on the Iranian people, pro-democracy or otherwise. They saw that the president was publicly trying to play the Iranian people against their government. Second, in a controversial statement on July 12, 2002, Bush blasted "the unelected people who are the real rulers of Iran," their "uncompromising, destructive policies," and their "families [who] continue to obstruct reform while reaping unfair benefits." The statement reflected, according to the *Washington Post* of July 23, 2002, the triumph of the hawks in the National Security Council and the Pentagon and had taken the State Department by surprise.

The only official praise for the controversial statement, to my knowledge, came from Zalmay Khalilzad, a senior director of the National Security Council at the time and the present ambassador to Afghanistan. He, like his hawkish cohorts in the NSC and the Pentagon, is known as one of the "neoconservatives" in the administration. In a statement on August 2, 2002, addressed to the well-known pro-Israeli Near East Policy Institute in Washington, DC, he praised the president's statement for its "specificity and moral clarity." To the Iranians, specificity was abhorrent for its direct attack on their government, and its moral clarity was seen as a simplistic black-and-white view of Iranian history, culture, and politics and an astonishing intolerance of complexity. Given the fierce Iranian sense of independence, conservatives and reformists alike got their backs up just as much as they had done in reaction to the "axis of evil" phrase, coined by David Frum.

Powerful neocons with universally acknowledged influence on the Bush administration have been even blunter in their threats to Iran. In their well-known book *An End to Evil: How to Win the War on Terror*, David Frum and Richard Perle say that for Iran there can be no reprieve. " 'The regime must go' because Ayatollah Khamenei has no more right to control . . . Iran than any other criminal has to seize control of the persons and property of others. It's not always in our power to do something about such criminals, nor is it always in our interest, but when it is in our power and interest, we should toss dictators aside with no more compunction than a police sharpshooter feels when he downs a hostage-taker."[22]

To cite another example, the American Enterprise Institute's Michael Ledeen says that besides Iraq, "we must also topple terror states in Tehran and Damascus." The Iranian perception of the American threat, however, is not simply shaped by the Bush administration's major policy statements and the wild commentaries of influential hard-line conservatives who support the administration. The reality of an unprecedented American military presence in Afghanistan, Iraq, and Central Asia, with thousands of miles of borders with Iran, is perceived by Iran as encirclement by an enemy that is the world's sole superpower. Some of the major events that lie behind this perception of encirclement have their roots in Iran's "dangerous neighborhood," specifically, in Iraq and Afghanistan.

The Iraqi invasion of Kuwait and the American-led war against Saddam Hussein's regime in 1991 prompted the United States to increase unprecedentedly its projection of military power into the Persian Gulf region. Until this war the United States had projected its military power from "over the horizon." But immediately after the war it began to increase its military presence in the region exponentially by both unilateral means and bilateral security agreements with the Gulf Arab states.

The first indication of this new policy came in President George H. W. Bush's important address to a joint session of Congress on March 6, 1991.[23] He set the stage then for building a new "framework for peace" and a "New World Order." That order was to replace the Cold War, now that the Soviet Union had disintegrated. The 1991 war provided the opportunity to plant the seeds of Pax Americana in the Persian Gulf. Twelve years later, from Prince Sultan Base in Saudi Arabia, the U.S. Air Force paraded its slogan of "Global Reach, Global Power."

The September 11, 2001, attacks on New York and Washington seem to have played into the hands of Dick Cheney, Donald Rumsfeld, and Paul Wolfowitz, as well as others who had dreamed since the end of the 1991 war of destroying the regime of Saddam Hussein.[24] They and their cohorts managed to capture the mind of Bush with the idea of launching a second war against Iraq to project America's global power. A president who had begun his term with an aversion to foreign affairs and nation-building now called for regime change, democratization of the entire Middle East, preemptive war against potential American enemies, and a global war on terrorism. To date, none of the rationales for this second war have seen the light of day. Iraq, we now know, had no hand in 9/11, no ties to al-Qaeda, no weapons of mass destruction, no nuclear program, and no plan to attack the United States.

Just as the Bush administration's global projection of military power had its genesis in Iran's immediate neighborhood, the seeds of terror attacks on the United States also were planted in the anti-Iranian neighboring state of Afghanistan under the fanatical Taliban regime. To be sure, the terrorists of 9/11 hailed from Saudi Arabia, but their godfather, Osama Bin Laden, rooted his network in Afghanistan. Iran and the Bush administration found a common enemy in Taliban-dominated Afghanistan, with which Iran had nearly gone to war over the murder of its diplomats. The Northern Alliance, long supported by Iran, helped the prosecution of the American war in Afghanistan.

Iran's help to the Bush administration in Afghanistan went beyond the prosecution of war. It cooperated earnestly in the discussions in Bonn that eventually led to the establishment of the Afghan Interim Authority under the leadership of Hamid Karzai, not to mention Iran's commitment of more than $500 million in aid for the reconstruction of Afghanistan. Yet the administration hawks did everything to undermine any degree of warming of relations with Iran. Zalmay Khalilzad probably played a major part in that effort.

Iran could play a major role in stabilizing both neighboring Iraq and Afghanistan. But as of this writing there is no indication of even limited American engagement of Iran. The devastating earthquake in the historic city of Bam in 2003 and Iran's acceptance of American relief aid appeared momentarily to provide a new opportunity for dialogue between the two countries, but so far they have both demonstrated rare ingenuity in missing opportunities for reconciliation. In public-opinion polls the Iranians have shown genuine interest in resumption of relations with the United States, but ever since the Bush administration began its threats against Iran, the expression of pro-American sentiments has been restrained.

The Bush administration must borrow a page from the European book if it is genuinely interested in the progress of democracy in Iran. European governments have engaged the Iranian regime in ways to encourage the Iranian people's pro-democracy movement and to improve human-rights conditions in Iran. The Europeans apparently understand better than their American counterparts that in the Iranian political culture the quest for democracy has been for more than a century intertwined with preserving Iran's political independence. They, therefore, refrain assiduously from making threats against Iran. It is ironic that the Bush administration has failed to grasp the inseparability of the twin principles of independence and liberty in Iran, as they are enshrined in the American Declaration of Independence.

The author of the Declaration and the founder of the University of Virginia, Thomas Jefferson, also believed in promoting democracy as the antidote to autocracy, but by means of liberal education, not the threat of coercion. The following are his memorable words: "Enlighten the public generally, tyranny and oppression of mind and body will vanish like the evil spirit at the dawn of day."

NOTES

1. See Richard N. Frye, *The Golden Age of Persia: The Arabs in the East* (London, 1995), 1–2.

2. I am indebted to Professor Mohammad Tavakoli for providing me with a copy of this work published in Tehran by Nashr-e Tarildi-e Iran in 1912.

3. See Adda B. Bozeman, *Politics and Culture in International History: From the Ancient Near East to the Opening of the Modern Age*, 2d ed. (New Brunswick, 1994), 43–56.

4. I am indebted to Professor Richard N. Frye for our exchange of views on ancient Iran. See his classic *The Heritage of Persia: The Pre-Islamic History of One of the World's Great Civilizations* (Cleveland, 1963).

5. See, for example, Josef Wieshofer, *Ancient Persia*, 4 vols. (London, 1996–2001).

6. Personal exchange of ideas with Professor Richard N. Frye.

7. Shah Ismail also demanded *sajdah*—that is, prostration before him as if he were God. See R. K. Ramazani, *The Foreign Policy of Iran, 1500–1941: A Developing Nation in World Affairs* (Charlottesville, 1966).

8. See Roger M. Savory, "Religion in the Timurid and Safavid Periods," in *The Cambridge History of Iran*, vol. 6, edited by Peter Jackson and Laurence Lockhart (Cambridge, 1986), 610–55.

9. See Marshall G. S. Hodgson, *The Venture of Islam: Conscience and History in a World Civilization*, vol. 3, *The Gunpowder Empires and Modern Times* (Chicago, 1974), 16–58.

10. See R. K. Ramazani, *Iran's Foreign Policy, 1941–73: A Study of Foreign Policy in Modernizing Nations* (Charlottesville, 1975), 231–42.

11. See R. K. Ramazani, *The United States and Iran: The Patterns of Influence* (New York, 1982), 72–124.

12. See R. K. Ramazani, "Document: The Constitution of the Islamic Republic of Iran," *Middle East Journal* 34, no. 2 (Spring 1980): 181–204. See also Ramazani, *Revolutionary Iran: Challenge and Response in the Middle East* (1986; Baltimore, 1988).

13. See Jacques Barzun, *From Dawn to Decadence: 500 Years of Western Cultural Life* (New York, 2000), 35.

14. See the text of Hashem Aqa Jari's talk in "Doktor Sharia'ti va Prozhe-ye Protestantizm-e Islami" [Doctor Sharia'ti and the project of Islamic Protestantism], *Iran Emrooz*, 1998.

15. *Jam-e jam*, External TV, Tehran, in Persian, 0600 (GMT), 28 August 2002.

16. Over the years I have pored over Khatami's work in Persian and English, including numerous interviews and speeches published in Iran and the West. For readers in English I suggest as a start only a few sources here. See Mohammad Khatami, *Islam, Liberty and Development* (Binghamton, 1998); Khatami, *Hope and Challenge: The Iranian President Speaks* (Binghamton, 1997); and Milton P. Buffington, ed., *Meet Mr. Khatami: The Fifth President of the Islamic Republic*, translated by Minoa R. Buffington (Washington, DC, 1997).

17. New York, 2002. For the text of Khatami's contribution to this report, see p. 64.

18. See my "The Role of Iran in the New Millennium: A View From the Outside," pp. 359–64 in this volume.

19. See Fareed Zakaria, "How to Save the Arab World," *Newsweek*, 24 December 2001.

20. See Thomas Friedman, "Iran and the War of Ideas," *New York Times*, 19 June 2002.

21. See R. K. Ramazani, "The Shifting Premise of Iran's Foreign Policy: Toward a Democratic Peace?" pp. 148–59 in this volume.

22. Quoted in Patrick J. Buchanan, "No End to War," *American Conservative*, 1 March 2004.

23. See the text in R. K. Ramazani, *Future Security in the Persian Gulf: America's Role* (Washington, DC, 1991), 21–25. This monograph foretold that another Persian Gulf war would be visited upon the area in a decade.

24. The debate rages about the real reasons for the Bush administration's decision to invade Iraq. Did 9/11 cause the war, or did the preoccupation of policymakers such as Dick Cheney, Paul Wolfowitz, and others with toppling Saddam Hussein's regime since the end of the First Gulf War in 1991? This debate does concern the Iranians. They fear that the same policymakers might push for the invasion of Iran after Iraq. I am indebted to Ambassador David Newsom for calling to my attention James Fallows's "Blind Into Baghdad" and Kenneth M. Pollack's "Spies, Lies and Weapons: What Went Wrong," *Atlantic Monthly*, January/February 2004. See also David Ignatius, "A War of Choice and One Who Chose It," *Washington Post*, 2 November 2003; and Mark Hosenhall et al., "Cheney's Long Path to War," *Newsweek*, 17 November 2003.

AFTERWORD

A better American understanding of Iran's foreign-policy behavior is necessary because the United States has to deal with Iran, whether monarchical or revolutionary republic and whether the American administration is Republican or Democratic. The Obama administration has said no to the opponents of talks with Iran, and there is no doubt that any other administration will do the same, because it is in the national interest of the United States to do so. In the ancient wisdom of Sun Tzu, "Know your enemy."

But talking without adequate understanding is like diving without knowing how to swim. Among the many reasons for America's poor understanding of Iran, two can be briefly mentioned. First, for decades the traditional power realists dominated the study of international politics and foreign policy; during that time, in the international scholar Annette Baker Fox's words, a "stereotype of the small states was that of a helpless pawn in world politics." Since no one believes today that Iran, among other small states, is a helpless pawn, this view has clearly proven to be misguided. Second, the lack of a better understanding continues in Washington in particular, partly because, according to William R. Polk, a leading scholar and practitioner of Middle East diplomacy, the United States uses the "fatally flawed" war-game theory and the National Intelligence Estimate to predict Iranian behavior.

I believe, however, that the problem significantly reflects the American inattention to history. About half a century ago I called attention to the fact that in Iranian culture "the past is ever present" and that reality was, and still is, vital to a better understanding of Iran's foreign-policy behavior. In contrast, in our American culture the past is never present. For example, we tend to dismiss a viewpoint opposed to our own by saying, "That is history!" How well former secretary of state Madeleine Albright understood the importance of understanding the history and culture of other nations. In an address in 2000 to U.S. diplomats and other officials she said that "cultural factors are utterly inseparable from foreign policy," and "the more we know and understand about cultures of those with whom we interact, the more successful our policy will be."

Hassan Rouhani's surprise landslide victory in Iran's recent elections astounded Iranians, Americans, and much of the world. In his victory speech, he claimed he would travel the road to "moderation" and pursue a policy of "freedom" for the Iranian people. Ali Akbar Rafsanjani, during his presidency in 1989–97, sought little conflict with the West and offered the people of Iran a degree of economic freedom. Mohammad Khatami, who took the presidency in 1997–2005, made room for detente with the world and promised a modicum of individual liberty and freedom of speech. But neither one succeeded. They both aspired to combine spirituality and pragmatism in their domestic and foreign policy, but this ran against the most fundamental problem of the Iranian Constitution of 1979: Was the right of the people given the highest priority or the right of the *faqih*? Rouhani might aspire to combine spirituality and pragmatism, but like his predecessor, he will be entangled in the endemic and unresolved problem of choosing between the right of the people and the right of the *faqih*.

I have tried, therefore, during my entire career to explain what seems to drive Iranian foreign-policy decisions by trying to place them in the deeper context of what I call Iran's "diplomatic culture," defined as those values, norms, mores, institutions, modes of thinking, and ways of acting that have developed over centuries, have survived change, and continue to shape Iran's foreign policy making. Here are some of them in a nutshell.

Identity. The Iranian sense of national identity is rooted in a millennial heritage of survival through the rise and fall of four empires and the existence of the Iranian nation-state in modern times. Of all foreign invasions of Iran over thousands of years, only the Arab invasion added an enduring new dimension, Islam, to the Iranian people's sense of Persian identity. Nevertheless, since the Iranians were converted to Shii Islam they have maintained their distinction from the Arab and most other Muslims of the world, who adhere to Sunni Islam. By contrast, for example, the Egyptians became both Arab and Sunni Muslim after the Arab invasion.

Independence. The concept of political independence came to Iran from the West, as did other modern ideas such as the nation and nationalism, but at base it reflects a Persian–Shii Islamic sense of national identity. The goal of maintaining independence has been the key driving force of Iranian foreign-policy behavior both long before and since the Iranian Revolution. The revolution emphasized the Islamic element of Iranian identity at the expense of the Persian component and deepened the drive for political independence. Even Ayatollah Ruhollah Khomeini, the founder of the Islamic Republic of Iran, set the ideal of independence above Islam in his credo.

Power. A combination of Iran as the crossroads between Europe and Asia with ample oil production, second after Saudi Arabia's, and enormous gas reserves, second after Russia's, underpins Iran's strategic importance in international politics. More important, the historic weakness of the Iranian state impels

Iranian leaders to try to make up for it. The Shah attempted to make Iran the world's leading conventional military power, just as the revolutionary regime aspires to make Iran a powerful state in the Muslim world. Pretension to universality is a feature of Iranian diplomatic culture. The Iranians believe that they cannot maintain political independence without developing the necessary elements of power, such as nuclear energy, today. The fourteenth-century poet Hafiz warned Iranians against boasting of grandeur without achieving real power.

Authoritarianism. Autocracy is a hallmark of Iranian political culture. Whether monarchical or theocratic, Iranian autocrats claim authority and legitimacy by divine right. In ancient times the kings claimed the blessing of Ahura Mazda, the Zoroastrian deity, and in modern times the kings proclaimed that they ruled "under the shadow of Allah." Even the secular Shah used to claim divine blessing. Today Ayatollah Ali Khamenei, the Supreme Leader, is thought to lead Iran as its divine representative. The Iranian Constitution, however, proclaims the sovereign right of the Iranian people as well. But this contradiction has never been resolved. Khamenei ultimately makes all major foreign- and domestic-policy decisions.

Factionalism. Factional strife is as old as the Iranian state, established in 558–530 BC. It reflects the complex ethnic, sectarian, linguistic, and geographic diversity of Iranian society. But since the coming of modernity to Iran, Iranian society has been divided along a new line as well, between the traditional and modern, or between those who cling to primordial loyalties to family, clan, tribe, religion, and sect and those who accord overriding loyalty to the modern nation-state. The revolutionary regime would substitute loyalty of the Iranian people to the Muslim community, the *umma*, for loyalty to the Iranian nation-state, but such an idealistic goal is completely at odds with the twin nature of Iranian national identity, which is Persian as well as Shii Islamic. In any event, the regime's attempts to Islamicize Iranian society have failed, and factionalism continues. In reality, the Islamists are factionalized, as are the nationalists, and as were the constitutionalists at the turn of the twentieth century. Today an ultraconservative Islamist faction holds state power and pursues a confrontational foreign policy, while the reformist leaders of the opposition Green Movement live under house arrest. For more than three decades, both conservative and reformist governments have failed to fulfill the revolution's promise of freedom.

Environment. Raymond Aron observed that a small power restricts its ambitions to physical survival and the preservation of its legal independence, while a great power acts to create or maintain "a favorable international environment." I would add that a medium power like Iran acts to create a favorable regional environment. The Shah acted to create a favorable environment beyond the Persian Gulf and the Middle East, as far away as South Asia and the Pacific. The revolutionary regime has tried to spread Iran's influence primarily in the Persian Gulf and the Eastern Mediterranean. To the revolutionary regime, the maintenance of Iran's national security interest requires Iranian primacy in the Persian Gulf, just as it did to the Shah's regime.

Democracy. Democratic aspirations have influenced Iran's foreign-policy decisions twice since the turn of the twentieth century, first during the Constitutional Movement (1905–11) and then during the Nationalist Movement (1951–53). In both instances the democratically elected Parliament made foreign-policy decisions aimed at the overriding goal of political independence, and in both instances democratic aspirations were crushed by foreign intervention—Anglo-Russian and American, respectively. These historical setbacks to democratic aspirations have not extinguished the Iranian demand for freedom. Nor has the brutal repression of political dissent since the disputed presidential election of 2009. As long as Iran is governed by an authoritarian regime, it will use the rhetoric of political independence to trump aspirations for democracy.

Instruments. Iran's foreign policy makers use a variety of tools, including the following:

1. Subversion. This time-honored instrument can be traced to the late fifteenth and early sixteenth centuries. In the centuries of conflict between the Shii Persian and Sunni Ottoman Empires, both waged war as their chief policy instrument, but the Persian Empire also appealed to the Shii population within the Ottoman Empire, which persecuted and deported many Shii activists.

As the only semi-theocratic Shii state among an estimated Shii Muslim population of 200 million, Iran maintains close ties with Shii-governed Iraq and appeals to the Shii populations in Bahrain, Kuwait, Saudi Arabia, and other monarchies in the Persian Gulf and the Hazara in Afghanistan. Hezbollah, the key Iranian proxy, is known to have bombed American personnel in Beirut and Saudi Arabia and to have used Iranian arms in the war against Israel in 2006.

2. Soft power. Iran is winning the hearts and minds of the people of the Middle East to counter foreign enemies, especially the United States. It appeals to the Iraqi population by building schools, hospitals, and roads and peddles influence through hundreds of thousands of Iranian pilgrims traveling to the Shii holy shrines in Iraq. Iran also uses trade and money in its relations with Iraq

and Afghanistan, including, for example, $500 million in reconstruction aid to the government in Kabul over a five-year period.

3. Hard power. In the historical past Iran waged many wars, offensive and defensive, but since the Russian invasion of Iran in 1804 it has been primarily the object of war, including two world wars and the war of aggression by Saddam Hussein's Iraq (1980–88). Iran waged skirmishes with the United States during the Tanker War (1984–88), and on July 3, 1988, the USS *Vincennes* accidentally shot down an Iranian passenger plane, killing 290 passengers.

4. Procrastination. Most often Iran opts for diplomacy rather than war, but it has learned from long experience that it can benefit from prolonged negotiations, as evidenced by its intermittent negotiations with the Ottoman Empire for two centuries, lengthy negotiations with the United States over the hostage crisis, and nuclear negotiations for more than a decade.

I hope the foregoing analysis will aid a better American understanding not only of the fundamental driving forces and instruments of Iran's foreign policy in general but also of Iran' s nuclear policy in particular. The United States claims that Iran intends to make nuclear bombs, while Iran insists that it opposes making and stockpiling nuclear weapons because it is "sinful" (*haraam*) in Islam and that it has "the right to enrich uranium" for peaceful purposes as a signatory to the Non-Proliferation Treaty (NPT).

In approaching Iran's real nuclear intention, I situate it in the wider context of Iran's diplomatic culture, which reveals that since the Iranian Revolution the opposition of the West in general and the United States in particular to Iran's nuclear development has created in the psyche of the Iranian people a need to defend their nation's "inalienable right" (*haq-e Mosallam*) to enrich uranium for civilian uses, such as electricity. This sense strikes deep roots in the Iranian ancient loyalty to national identity, the goal of political independence, and the quest for regional primacy, not dominance.

I believe that had the P5+1 nations—the United States, Britain, France, China, Russia, and Germany—understood Iran's nuclear intention in these terms, no such unrealistic goal of halting Iran's enrichment would have been set. Short of stopping enrichment, Iran would be prepared to accept limits on its enrichment level, perhaps even to the extent of forgoing breakout capability. It all depends, of course, on what Iran will get in return. To set the limits is the key challenge that Iran and its negotiating partners face today, and the failure to meet it through patient and persistent diplomacy could result in a catastrophic regional war with far-reaching consequences for the global economy and international politics.

The essays in this volume show that for more than thirty years Iran has resisted any policy that aims to force it to submit to the demands of the West, particularly those of the United States. It will take another thirty years to see how, and whether, a policy of crippling sanctions affects the regime in Iran. Instead of pressuring Iran, we must now use every possible means to persuade Iran. The United States needs to pursue a policy of genuinely engaging Iran. Tehran views all the so-called incentives offered so far by the West as pseudoconcessions, *sheb-he-ishtebah*. Although preventing Iran from becoming a nuclear state will be challenging, the United States must make every effort to meet that challenge. At the very outset of this volume, I reminded Iranians that the Iranian Constitution calls for a combination of independence and freedom. As a scholar who took refuge in America's freedom over six decades ago, I firmly believe that the United States must uphold its principle of human liberty in Iran.

APPENDIX

The Role of Iran in the New Millennium
—A View from the Outside

This address to President Mohammad Khatami was originally
delivered at the United Nations on September 4, 2000, and was
subsequently published in *Middle East Policy* 7, no. 1 (March 2001):
43–47; the author also organized a seminar on democracy for
him on September 11, 2006, at Monticello, the home of Thomas
Jefferson.

President Mohammad Khatami, ladies and gentlemen:

When I was invited to speak about the role of the Islamic Republic of Iran in
the new millennium in fifteen minutes, I said that I am no academic astrologer,
but agreed to think it over for a few days before accepting. I thought because I
have tried for half a century to deepen Western understanding of Iran by teach-
ing and publishing in the United States, I should be able to say something near
the end of my life that would be worthwhile. I would like, therefore, to talk of
three intertwined propositions that might help clarify thinking on Iran's future
role in the world.

Let me start by saying that many observers believe that because Iran is strategically significant it will necessarily play a greater role in the world in the future
than at present. Such thinkers usually list a variety of factors. For example, they
point out that Iran has been coveted by foreign powers from the time of Alexander of Macedonia. It has been the cradle of one of the world's greatest civilizations. It is located at the center of the world's largest pool of energy. It straddles
prominently the global oil and natural gas chokepoint at the Strait of Hormuz.
It provides the cheapest and shortest transit route at the heart of the ancient Silk
Road for the transport of energy resources from the Caspian Sea basin to world
markets through the Persian Gulf. And it is the most populous country with one
of the largest industrial bases in the vast region stretching from the Caspian Sea
to the Eastern Mediterranean.

My first proposition is that none of these factors, in and of themselves, guar-
antees that the Islamic Republic will necessarily play a larger global role in the
future than at present. Let me say why. If all these factors were enough, then

Iran should have played a significant role in the international system. Yet, from the nineteenth century, when Iran was sucked fully for the first time into the whirlwind of world politics, to the eruption of the Iranian Revolution, Iran has played either the role of a weak and backward buffer state between imperial Russia and Britain or the role of a surrogate of Britain and the United States. It is important to learn from this searing historical experience. It can help illuminate Iran's future role in the world. In Cicero's memorable words: "To be ignorant of what happened before you were born is to remain always a child."

My second proposition is that having learned from such a dismal historical experience, the Iranian revolutionaries created an unprecedented opportunity for their leaders to utilize Iran's strategic significance in such a way as to enable the people eventually to control freely their own destiny and play a major role on the world stage. To accomplish such lofty goals, the revolutionaries tried to create an authentic revolution. They drew at least in part on the unfulfilled historical aspirations of the people for freedom at home and an independent role in the world. Unlike such other contemporary revolutions as the Chinese, the Vietnamese, and the Cuban, the Iranian Revolution evaded the lure of Marxism-Leninism and created what Forrest D. Colburn calls "the most original of contemporary revolutions."

The unfulfilled quest for independence and freedom strikes deep roots in the collective memory of the Iranian people. Two historic opportunities to fulfill these principles were quashed by foreign powers. Russia and Britain divided Iran into spheres of influence in 1907 and destroyed any chance for a constitutional government that could realize both independence and freedom. The American Morgan Shuster aptly characterized their imperial interferences in Iran's internal affairs as "the strangling of Persia." Decades later, the struggle for independence and freedom was once again stopped in its tracks. Ironically, the American government, the historical champion of Iran's independence and freedom, used the CIA to destroy the nationalist government of Dr. Mohammad Mosaddegh. For him the central choice facing Iran in the struggle against Britain was "independence or enslavement" (isteqlal ya enqiad).

Yet, the real blame for the loss of these two opportunities in the twentieth century must be placed primarily at the door of Iran's own dynastic rulers. The Safavid and Qajar rulers in particular tried to mimic the Sassanian imperial paradigm and listened to poor political advice. On the one hand, the writers of siyasat-namehs, such as Khajeh Nizam al-Mulk, advised rulers that people were rameh (chattel) and the king was a shabban (shepherd), and that the people and the country belonged to the king, who could do what he pleased both within and outside of Iran. On the other hand, the writers of shariat-namehs advised the rulers to avoid interaction with the *dar-al-harb* for fear that Iranians would be Christianized if they tried to understand the Western world.

None of these dynastic rulers and their contemporary thinkers, therefore, tried seriously to explore the intellectual and practical secrets of Western progress for the benefit of Iranian society and culture. They were all mesmerized by Western material paraphernalia, especially military hardware, as were the later Pahlavi rulers, who also mimicked the Sassanian imperial paradigm.

Aristotle tells us that learning from a poem is as valid as learning from scientific facts. Had all these rulers and the intellectuals of their times heeded Hafiz's poetic advice, perhaps Iran would have played an independent role in the world long before the coming of the revolution. Hafiz, "The Tongue of the Hidden" (*lisan al-ghahib*) and "The Interpreter of Secrets" (*tarjoman al-assrar*), advised rulers: "Weigh not the seat of power with grandeur / Unless by deeds you've made the seat secure" (my translation; Takyeh bar jay-e bozorgan natavan zad egazaf / Ta-keh asbab-e bozorgi hameh amadeh koni).

The Iranian Revolution did more than destroy the ancient institution of dynastic monarchy. In founding the Islamic Republic, Ayatollah Ruhollah Khomeini captured in his best-known motto the principles of independence and freedom side by side with Islam. The Constitution of the Republic also embraced these principles. But more important and yet least noticed is the crucial fact that in its Article 9 these principles are, to use the language of the Constitution, "inseparable from each other," and the "preservation and safeguarding" of these principles are "the duty of the government and the people."

The goal of independence, as perceived at that time, was achieved, at least in part. A quarter-century of American domination was terminated. For the first time in modern history, Iranian leaders achieved an unprecedented degree of control over their country's destiny at home and in world affairs. Even the brutal invasion by Iraq did not make a dent in Iran's determination to preserve its independence. On the contrary, the eight-year war burned deeply into the Iranian psyche the overriding importance of preserving the nation's independence. But the opportunity for achieving political freedom was not at hand even after the war with Iraq. Reconstructing the nation's crippled economy and military capability was accorded the highest priority for another eight years.

The historic opportunity for the nation to try to achieve political freedom, however, finally arrived. Twenty million young men and women elected you president of the Islamic Republic of Iran in a landmark election on May 23, 1997. Soon after your election I criticized, in print, Iran watchers for overlooking the all-important synergy in your worldview between reform plans for realizing Islamic democracy and justice on the one hand and relations with the rest of the world on the other. I conceptualized these ideas of yours as resembling the theory of "democratic peace" in the study of international relations in the West, but pointed out that in Iran's case it amounts to what I call Islamic democratic peace.

The results are there for everyone to see. Despite all odds, the success of the first local elections in Iran's modern history has paralleled an unprecedented degree of improvement in Iran's relations with the rest of the world. Public-opinion polls in the United States show a favorable change in the attitude of the American people toward Iran. Public-opinion polls in Tehran, too, indicate a remarkable approval of and confidence in Iran's proactive foreign policy in world politics, conducted effectively by Foreign Minister Kamal Kharrazi.

Yet, this is not the time to indulge in self-congratulation. The upshot of my two previous propositions is that no matter how strategically important Iran may be in the world, it will not be able to play a major role in the international system unless and until the Iranian government and people agree to strike a reasonable balance in theory, and especially in practice, among independence, freedom, and Islam, on the one hand, and between these constitutionally mandated guiding principles and the necessity of interacting constructively with the changing objective world, on the other. Hence, my third and final proposition is that the most fundamental challenge that Iran will face in the future is how to experiment effectively with this triple paradigm of Islamic democratic peace.

The Constitution has made independence, freedom, and Islam interdependent. The real question, therefore, is how the government and the people of Iran will achieve consensus in both theory and practice about the boundary lines among these fundamental principles in the context of an inexorably shrinking objective world. Let us for a moment take each one of these three principles separately for the purpose of clarity.

Independence is not an absolute. It is a matter of the degree of dependence, especially in these dot.com times, increasing demand for scientific knowledge and technical expertise. How independent, really, are the energy-dependent powerful industrial democracies? How independent are capital- and know-how-dependent Third World countries? It took the West some 400 years of evolution to be where it is today, but the West will make the equivalent of 20,000 years of progress in science and technology in only one century, let alone in the new millennium. This staggering pace of change could be a boon or a bane to humanity. But the key point here is that such a pace of technological and telecommunications development is bound to produce a world with such a degree of interdependence that to fail to think hard about the vital implications for independence of such a pace of development could be tantamount to committing national suicide.

Nor can the enjoyment of any kind of freedom—cultural, political, economic, or social—be absolute. Take cultural freedom, for example. If it means unyielding cultural relativism, then what will happen to the vital concept of the essential oneness of humankind as a manifestation of God's creation? If, as Nelson Mandela says now and Sa'di said centuries ago, the suffering of one person should inflict pain upon the others, then how could one culture close its eyes to the troubles of others? What will happen to the development of international human-rights law as well as humanitarian law? Should the world community ignore, for example, the indictments of people like Pinochet and Milošević? Similar questions can be raised about political freedom.

How could the demand for democracy in Iran overlook the fact that today about half of the world's independent countries are considered to be democratic? That is twice the number when the Iranian Revolution erupted. The Constitution spells out in great detail both individual and collective rights to freedom, as do the constitutions of many other countries where those very rights are grossly violated in practice.

Finally, let me mention the all-important interrelationship between Islam and the principles of independence and freedom. Insofar as independence is concerned, there is no doubt that in the Iranian Revolution, as in the American Revolution, religion played a significant role in mobilizing resistance to foreign domination. In both instances the religious leaders assured the people that their resistance to foreign domination was right in God's sight and had his blessing. But the comparison stops there. The American Constitution's First Amendment Establishment Clause separated religion from liberty, while the Iranian Constitution fuses them.

But the interrelationship between Islam and democracy raises more fundamental questions. In your creative televised message to the American people, Mr. President, you drew parallels between the founding of the American and Islamic republics in order to suggest that in both cases religion was in harmony with "republicanism, democracy, and freedom." Yet, as you well know, the American Constitution separated religion from government, while the Iranian Constitution joined them.

In the spirit of your idea of dialogue among civilizations, therefore, I suggest that Iranians should have a deeper understanding of the separation doctrine in the American experience, for several reasons. First, the founding fathers of America, from Washington, Madison, and Benjamin Franklin to Thomas Jefferson, undoubtedly recognized that religion is necessary for republican government because religion promotes virtue and morality. Second, some drafters of the American Constitution believed that separation was intended to protect religion, some thought it was to protect government, and James Madison considered it necessary for protecting both. Third, if the metaphorical "wall of separation" between religion and liberty had ever been as absolute as some imagine, the American courts would not have tried to draw boundaries between the two, in case after case for some 200 years.

Another point that the Iranians will need to understand is that the separation doctrine does not mean that the American government is impervious to the importance of religion to government. There is a consensus emerging in America today about ways in which Christian organizations and government can work together. Nor does the doctrine of separation mean that the American people are godless and immoral. In fact, the American people are one of the most God-fearing, churchgoing, and honest peoples in the Western world. America is a nation that still stamps "In God We Trust" on its currency. As a matter of fact, at the dawn of the new millennium, the American concern with the evil consequences of blind globalization and the indiscriminate ideology of the free market has heightened ethical sensibilities. For example, Richard Tarnas, the philosopher and author of *The Passion of the Western Mind*, tells us, "The great danger of our time is that the quest [for technology] has not been matched by a moral and psychological awareness of our limits."

In this kind of thinking Americans can learn from Iranians. The Iranian-Islamic civilization fuses spiritual and worldly concerns. Annemarie Schimmel says, "Hafiz is perhaps the first poet in the Persian-speaking world who perfectly realized the unity of the mundane and the spiritual sphere." I believe that we will need the acuteness of vision and the mental eye of Hafiz to dare to gaze into the new millennium to speculate about the role of Iran.

In closing, I would like to emphasize what the three fundamental conditions are under which Iran could play an even more significant role in the world in the future than at present. First, the government and people will need to realize that Iran's strategic importance is not in and of itself sufficient to control the nation's destiny at home and abroad. Second, the government and people will need to arrive at a reasonable degree of consensus on prioritizing the three principles of independence, freedom, and Islam, which underpin what I call the ideal of Islamic democratic peace. Third, and most important, the government and people will need to create appropriate structures and procedures in order to implement effectively these principles, for I believe there can be no durable political order without equitable justice under the law and no justice without liberty.

INDEX

Assad, Hafez al-, 97–98, 105
Assembly of Experts (Iran), 36, 40, 343
authoritarianism, 343, 355
authority: centralization of, 17–18, 22;
    consolidation of, 44–45, 153; by divine
    right, 355; establishing, 24; of the
    faqih, 134, 151, 242; of religious leaders,
    157, 338; Shah's problem of, 58–59, 67
AWACS, 87, 88, 96
"axis of evil," 5, 193, 199, 313, 335, 347, 348
Azerbaijan: and Armenia, 169; and Iran,
    116, 170; Party, 19; and Soviet influence,
    1, 53, 54, 59, 129, 139; uprisings in, 41,
    169, 181n44
'Azizi, Ahmad, 89

Ba'athist regime: in Iraq, 85, 87, 97, 104,
    106, 225, 248–51, 253, 275, 278–79; in
    Syria, 322
Baghdad, 24, 85, 96, 103, 104, 130, 251.
    See also Iraq
Baghdad Pact, 21, 55, 218, 321, 322.
    See also CENTO (Central Treaty
    Organization)
Bahrain: Iranian influence in, 268, 269;
    Iran's claim to, 82, 107, 130; relations
    with Iran, 155, 224, 237; secular
    nationalism in, 273; Shia in, 4, 97, 240,
    241, 255–60, 261, 274, 356; terrorism
    in, 88, 104, 118, 139, 265, 271, 279; and
    the United States, 168
Baker, James, III, 168
Baluchistan, 42, 98, 103, 220
Banisadr, Abulhassan: challenges to, 44,
    72–74, 75–77, 90, 278, 310; foreign
    policy of, 115–17, 130–32; and Kurds,
    37; and revolutionary reforms, 36, 38,
    42; views of, 45, 46
Baradei, Mohamed El-, 202
Barzun, Jacques, 344
Basij, 85, 270
Batatu, Hanna, 249–50
bazaari forces, 35, 41, 63, 64, 272, 339
Bazargan, Mehdi: challenges to, 36, 43–
    44, 71–74, 76, 114–15, 131, 278, 309–10;

and foreign policy, 72, 101, 112–16,
    129–30, 248, 251–52, 256, 310; and the
    hostage crisis, 36, 43, 67, 72, 74, 108,
    130, 143, 310; as a revolutionary leader,
    36, 58, 62, 64, 72, 117, 124, 131, 216
Begin, Menachem, 329, 333
Beheshti, Muhammad, 36, 41, 42, 72–73,
    75, 117
Bekaa Valley, 97
Berri, Nabih, 98
Bible, 165, 185, 191, 197, 205, 337. *See also*
    Christians
Bin Laden, Osama, 350
Bozeman, Adda B., 133, 146n16, 184, 205,
    337
Brown, Harold, 115, 216–18, 220–21, 227,
    235, 310
Browne, E. G., 19
Brzezinski, Zbigniew, 43, 72, 115, 216
Bush, George H. W., 125, 156, 168, 289
Bush, George W., 5, 192–93, 194,
    199–201, 307, 313–14, 335, 346–50

Cairo, 322–24, 326. *See also* Egypt
Canada, 102, 121, 143
Carter, Jimmy: and the Arab-Israeli
    conflict, 328; and arms sales, 57,
    113–14, 219; Carter Doctrine, 95, 276;
    and the hostage crisis, 5, 44, 74, 115,
    156, 192, 310, 335; and human rights,
    51, 63, 65, 82; as an idealist, 196; and
    the Persian Gulf, 215, 216, 217, 230,
    235, 238–39
Caspian Sea, 158, 167, 169, 359
CENTCOM, 95, 276
CENTO (Central Treaty Organization), 55,
    113, 129, 217, 218. *See also* Baghdad Pact
Central Asia, 139, 167, 193, 198, 208, 312,
    349
Cheney, Dick, 349
China: compared to the Persian empire,
    185, 133, 337; and Iran, 105, 109, 166;
    in P5+1, 201, 204, 357; and the United
    States, 50, 99, 110; and world culture,
    124

Christians, 133, 162, 210, 240, 259, 330, 361, 364. *See also* Bible

church: in Latin America, 9; relation to state, 10, 12, 156, 177

Churchill, Winston, 209, 307

CIA (Central Intelligence Agency), 5, 54–55, 129, 150, 162, 276, 341, 346, 360

Civil Code (Iran), 19, 30n13

clergy (Islamic): as political faction, 24, 40, 42, 45–46, 166, 189, 338–40; power of, 13, 36, 46, 61, 78, 89, 100, 338; and the state, 9, 11–13, 242, 342–43. See also *ulama*

Clinton, Bill, 150, 153, 156–57, 175, 192, 209, 314, 346–47

Clinton, Hillary Rodham, 203

Colburn, Forrest D., 360

cold war: among Arab countries, 321; between Iran and Egypt, 321; between Iran and Saudi Arabia, 251, 260; between Iran and the United States, 111; between the Soviet Union and the United States, 54, 167, 297, 341, 349

communism: conception of democracy in, 25; factions in Iran, 2, 24, 30, 37, 42, 51–53, 64, 76, 91, 103, 130, 252, 268, 308, 340–41; influence of, 216–17, 219, 238, 321; and Iranian foreign policy, 53, 83, 152, 251, 323; regimes, 1, 59, 82, 134, 216, 243; and U.S. foreign policy, 218, 260, 341

Constituent Assembly, 40, 89

Constitution (U.S.), 177, 363

Constitutionalism, Revival of, 25, 340

Constitutional regime, 45, 47, 188

Constitutional Revolution (1905–11, Iran): causes of, 11, 17, 134; factionalism in, 308, 341; goals of, 5, 18–20, 25, 29, 163, 188, 206; as popular domestic uprising, 27, 33–35, 338–39, 340

Constitution of Iran (1906), 11, 42, 52–53, 55, 77, 339

Constitution of Iran (1979): adoption of, 40, 42, 117; amending, 38, 42, 166; and

the Assembly of Experts, 36, 40; and the *faqih*, 40–41, 73, 151–52, 156–57, 171, 177, 207, 241, 355; influence of, 89, 116, 170; principles of, 1, 108, 131, 132, 135, 136–38, 140, 171, 178, 210, 246, 343, 358, 361–63

Cook, Robin, 174, 193, 199, 313

Council of Guardians, 123, 198–99, 344

Cuba, 217, 238, 266, 325, 360

Cuellar, Javier Perez de, 123, 164, 287–88, 300n13, 311

culture: Iran's, 15, 111, 124, 129, 154, 201, 310, 336, 348, 353, 361 (*see also* heritage of Iran); —, political, 4, 17, 20, 91, 114, 131, 133–34, 136, 336, 339, 342–43, 345, 350, 354 (*see also* diplomatic culture); shared, 170, 198; Western, 141, 154, 162, 172, 353 (*see also* Western civilization); world, 124, 223

Cyrus the Great: foreign policy of, 184–85, 188, 193–94, 205, 319, 336–37; and the Shah, 56, 189, 342

Damascus, 97–98, 105, 122, 326, 349. *See also* Syria

D'Amato, Alphonse, 150; D'Amato Act, 155–56

Darius I, King, 133, 185

Dastghayb, Sayyid Abolhussain, 41

Dawa, Al- (party), 122, 249–51, 260, 263–64, 274–75, 278–79

Declaration of Independence (American), 176, 339, 350

Declaration of Rights of Man (French), 188, 336

democracy: challenges of, 20, 264, 339–40; Islamic form of, 5, 39–40, 116, 136, 151–52, 188, 198, 336, 342–46, 361, 363; Persian form of, 345; and pro-democracy movements, 335, 338, 343, 345–51; quest for, 61, 148, 178, 192, 193, 210, 259, 340, 356, 363; under the Shah, 26; spread of, 150, 157, 337, 363; types of, 25–26, 39–40; Western model of, 64, 128, 158, 172, 345–46

Democratic Party of Iran, 19

democratic peace: Islamic type of, 364; Khatami's idea of, 148, 151–56, 171, 346, 362; thesis of, 158n6, 181n51

democratization: in Iran, 51, 65, 171; in the Middle East, 349

Desert Storm, 168. See also Persian Gulf War (1991)

Dewey, John, 206

diplomatic culture: definition of, 5, 205, 354; in Iran, 205–8, 354, 357

domestic politics: in Iran, 33–34, 46, 52, 91, 129, 131, 154, 209; and relationship with foreign policy, 16–17, 28, 52, 71, 76, 111, 142, 179n4

Dulles, John Foster, 55

Eastern Mediterranean, 95, 217, 238, 356, 359

Ebadi, Shirin, 185, 336

Ebtekar, Massoumeh, 308, 314

Economic Cooperation Organization (ECO), 104, 109, 169

economy (Iran): Islamisation of, 39; and oil, 34, 56–57, 91, 189, 221, 325; problems of, 38–39, 55, 56, 62, 100, 173; reconstruction of, 39, 42, 46, 121, 140, 167, 361; reforms to, 28, 340

Egypt: and the Arab-Israeli conflict, 225, 233, 251, 320–21, 323, 325, 326–32; comparison with Iran, 208, 222, 336; and the Persian Gulf, 215–20, 251; relations with Iran, 141, 155, 192, 225, 321, 324–32; and the Soviet Union, 321, 323; and terrorism, 265; and the United States, 216–20. See also Cairo

Eisenhower, Dwight D., 55, 218; Eisenhower Doctrine, 55–56, 218

elections (Iran): for a Constituent Assembly, 40; of Khatami, 5, 148–49, 150, 171, 174, 345, 346, 361; laws, 28; and the Majlis, 27, 45, 117, 344, 345; for the president, 42, 109, 117, 200, 314, 344, 356; provincial/township, 27, 345, 362

factionalism, problem of, 2, 4, 25, 37, 114–16, 131–32, 142–44, 164, 308, 341–43, 345, 355. See also under names of political factions and parties

Fadallah, Mohammad Hussein, 105

Fahd, Prince of Saudi Arabia, 79, 251

Faisal, King of Saudi Arabia, 215, 251

Fanon, Franz, 35

faqih (fuqaha): and the Iranian Constitution, 5, 166, 171, 177, 207, 343; in Khomeini's philosophy, 134, 136, 139, 242–43, 245, 345; leadership of, 73, 77, 79, 152; power of, 5, 41, 46, 151, 354; rule of, 112, 115–16, 120, 163

fatwa: concerning Salman Rushdie, 142, 164, 174, 193, 199, 313; concerning the tobacco monopoly, 11

Fedayan-e Khalq: alliances of, 37, 62; views of, 40, 42, 51, 76, 308

Fedayan Islam, 11–12

Ferdowsi, 208

Ford, Gerald, 216

Fordou, 202, 204

foreign policy: of Iran (see under names of countries and Iranian leaders); in relation to domestic policy, 16–17, 28, 52, 66, 71–77, 91, 111, 129–30, 142, 154, 160–61, 165, 179n4, 209

Foroughi, Muhammad Ali, 53

Forouhar, Dariush, 40, 58

Fox, Annette Baker, 353

France: Iranians exiled in, 35, 75; nuclear negotiations with Iran, 200–203, 357; relations with Iran, 115, 121, 141, 143, 168, 174, 175; revolution in, 128, 135, 188, 336; terrorism against, 118, 122, 139, 263, 264

freedom: attempts at Iranian, 2, 5, 25, 26, 178, 210, 340, 344, 356, 360–61; versus the clergy, 12, 171, 343–45, 347, 363; as ideal of the Iranian Revolution, 1, 150, 163, 178, 339, 343; as inseparable from independence, 1, 66, 171, 178, 210, 343, 358, 360–61, 362, 363; of Iran from domination, 91, 150, 188, 309;

and Khatami, 148, 151, 170–72, 192, 198, 344; for political participation, 150, 198; versus security, 279, 281; as universal value, 210, 363

Friedman, Thomas, 346

Frum, David, 348

Frye, Richard N., 184–86, 336–37

Gates, Robert M., 204

Germany: under the Nazis, 1, 53; nuclear negotiations with Iran, 200–201, 357; relations with Iran, 102, 121, 143, 150, 174, 197, 339; and terrorism, 118, 122, 266

Gorbachev, Mikhail, 135–36, 144, 163, 190, 197

Great Britain: control over Iran, 1, 2, 17, 34, 178, 338–39, 360; influence on U.S.-Iranian relations, 53–56, 60, 117, 177, 215, 276; Iranian independence from, 18–19, 55, 113, 129, 134; Iranian opposition to, 12, 34, 320, 338; and Iran's oil nationalization dispute, 2, 20, 34, 46, 54, 134, 188–89, 321, 340–41, 360; nuclear talks with Iran, 200–201, 357; and the Persian Gulf, 107, 236, 249, 275, 325; relations with Iran, 45, 47, 53, 55, 75, 121, 143, 174, 288 (see also Rushdie, Salman)

Great Satan, 66, 72, 84, 87, 101, 135, 165, 191, 197, 243, 253, 277, 280, 308, 346. See also United States

Greece, 151, 172, 174, 185, 337

Green Movement in Iran, 355

Gulf Cooperation Council (GCC), 88, 96, 105–6, 108, 118, 155–56, 167–68, 173, 257–58, 263, 271, 277, 279–81

Gulf of Oman, 230, 325

Hafiz, 111, 355, 361, 364

Hajj: conceptions of, 255; Iranian political activity during, 79, 88, 118, 167; violence during, 121, 164, 190, 198

Hakim, Mahdi al-, 249, 274

Hakim, Muhammad Baqir al-, 250, 260

Hakim, Muhsin al-, 249, 274

Hamas, 193

Harriman, Averell, 341

Hashemi, Mehdi, 121, 138, 165

Hassan, Haj Mirza Mohammad, 11

heritage of Iran, 15, 157, 185, 210, 335–36, 354. See also culture: Iran's

Herodotus, 185, 205, 337

Hezbollah, 95, 98, 100, 105, 118, 139, 193, 240, 269–70, 356

Hidden Imam. See Twelfth Imam

Hodgson, Marshall G. S., 187, 338

Horn of Africa, 216, 224, 325

hostages, American: in Lebanon, 105–6, 118, 122, 139, 144, 165, 191, 264, 288–89, 312, 346 (see also Iran-Contra Affair); on TWA Flight 847, 109, 281

—in Iran (1979): after the capture of, 76, 90, 102, 165; background of, 114, 117, 130, 296, 307, 335; causes of taking, 42–44, 66–67, 77, 111; consequences of taking, 33, 44–45, 46, 67, 72–74, 101, 174, 278, 289, 311; influences in resolving crisis of, 74, 84, 117–18; and international legitimacy, 5, 307–15; prior to, 3; and the "second revolution," 131, 143, 165–66. See also American Embassy: in Tehran

human rights: international law of, 363; Iran's heritage concerning, 185, 205, 210, 336; Western pressure on Iran about, 3, 51, 63–65, 82, 342, 348, 350

Hussein, Imam, 36, 133–34, 253, 259

Hussein, King of Jordan, 332

Hussein, Saddam: invasion of Kuwait, 349; and the Iranian Revolution, 85; in the Persian Gulf, 168, 225, 248; and war with Iran, 95, 118, 137, 166–67, 250, 270, 274, 289–90, 292–94, 357; and war with the United States, 349

Hutson, James H., 177

IAEA (International Atomic Energy Agency), 199–204, 307

ideology: in foreign policy, 164, 194, 207;

ideology (continued)

    Islamic type of, 36, 83, 84, 85–86, 87, 101, 102, 170; of Khomeini, 84, 86–87, 90, 97, 120, 137, 163, 240, 241, 252, 268, 269, 308; —, export of, 81, 116, 131, 137, 244–46, 247–49, 261; and national interest, 168, 190–91, 193; political form of, 76, 85, 87, 308; versus pragmatism, 4, 46, 47, 166, 184–87, 190, 194, 205, 207; Shii type of, 10, 134, 254, 260; of the Soviets, 103, 135; and terrorism, 265; of the West, 364

imams, 134, 139–40, 142, 163, 247

independence: challenges to Iran's, 1, 2, 112, 114, 125, 167, 360, 362; efforts to ensure Iranian, 16, 17, 53, 77, 83, 134, 340–41, 356; goal of Iranian national, 18, 19, 20, 23, 25, 29, 30n14, 163, 166, 188, 350, 354, 355, 357, 361; as ideal of Iranian Revolution, 1, 91, 120, 150, 152, 163, 171, 178, 210, 309, 339, 343, 362, 364; as inseparable from freedom, 1, 66, 171, 178, 210, 343, 358, 360–61, 362, 363; Iran's assertion of, 1, 2, 19, 154, 208, 342–43, 348; Iran's winning of, 18, 25; legal, 86, 355; through nonalignment, 113, 114, 129; power as means of, 54, 58, 355; and security in the Persian Gulf, 167, 217, 222–23, 227, 229, 242, 243, 256, 259, 268, 281, 293

India, 16, 76, 91, 120, 141, 173, 216, 265, 266, 320, 325, 329

Indian Ocean, 56, 96, 115, 216–17, 221, 229, 235, 236–39, 310, 325

Indonesia, 230, 346

International Court of Justice, 74, 119, 291, 296, 311

Iran. See army (Iranian); economy (Iran); elections (Iran); military (Iran); monarchy (Iran); nuclear program (Iranian); students (Iranian); women (Iranian); workers (Iranian); youth (Iranian); and entries beginning with Iran or Iranian

Iran-Contra Affair, 84, 165, 191, 312

Iran Freedom Movement, 62

Iranian Nation Party, 40

Iranian Revolution: causes of, 4, 59, 111, 129, 135, 218, 258, 272, 363; challenges to, 46, 108; characteristics of, 89, 124, 177, 192, 222, 342, 360; claims of, 67; effects and impact of, 33, 95, 99–100, 104, 217, 235, 268, 271, 274, 277, 361; events leading to, 60–61, 64, 134; ideals of, 1, 91, 120, 150, 152, 163, 171, 178, 210, 309, 339, 343, 362, 364; implications and lessons of, 125–25, 128, 184, 219, 220, 225, 227, 235, 239, 249, 256; stages of, 71–76, 149, 185; support for, 85; views toward, 97

—foreign policy of: export of, 4, 46, 129, 140–41, 142, 145; independence as priority in, 354, 357; open-door, 109; and the Persian Gulf, 4, 167, 173, 217, 219, 220, 225, 227, 229, 232, 235, 237, 239, 249, 251, 256, 258, 268, 271, 274, 277, 280; religion in, 184–85; spiritual pragmatism in, 196; and the United States, 2, 3, 58, 335, 346, 357

Iranian Revolutionary Organization of the Masses of the Islamic Republic, 117, 130

Iranians' Party, 27

Iran-Iraq War: and the Algiers Agreement, 303n51; attacks on civilians, 304n57, 304n59; causes of, 5, 167, 287; and the Iranian Revolution, 250, 274; and Iran's foreign policy, 73, 74, 109, 166, 248; prisoner of war issues, 289, 298, 301n22; prolonging of, 191; and radicalism, 95, 118, 277, 281; reconstruction after, 198; U.N. report on, 288–91

Iran Liberation Front, 113

Iran-Libya Sanctions Act, 175

Iran-Novin Party, 26–27

Iran's Atomic Energy Organization (AEOI), 203

Iraq: and the Arab-Israeli conflict, 320, 322; invasion of Kuwait by, 168, 287,

289, 290, 295, 296, 311, 349; 1958
revolution in, 21, 56, 85, 274, 322; and
oil, 56, 101, 123, 221, 230–31; and the
Persian Gulf, 94–95, 98, 106–8, 117,
167–68, 173, 215, 221, 224, 237, 249,
251, 255–56, 258–59, 261, 263; Shia in,
223, 225, 240, 241, 248–51, 252–53,
255, 257–59, 263, 274–75, 278, 356;
and the Soviet Union, 103, 118, 223,
231, 325; and Syria, 97; and the United
Nations, 5, 75, 107, 164, 168, 173,
287–99, 311–12; and the United States,
96, 106, 107, 118, 123, 156, 166, 175,
192, 193, 199, 209, 281, 311, 313, 314,
346, 347, 349, 352n24. See also Baghdad
—and Iran: and Khomeini, 77, 87, 97, 98,
112, 143, 260; relations between, 130,
155, 174, 185, 208, 209, 224–25, 237,
248, 250, 252–53, 274, 337, 350, 356;
tensions between, 33, 37, 84, 107, 117,
122, 141, 167, 173, 257, 263, 279. See
also Iran-Iraq War
Islam: challenges to, 142, 165, 247,
249, 272, 322; as compatible with
modernism, freedom, and democracy,
36, 172, 188, 336, 344, 346; defending
the interests of, 84, 86, 90, 97, 128–29,
137, 243, 245, 251; and extremism,
177–78, 251, 267, 310, 343–44; ideal of
Iranian Revolution, 1, 91, 120, 150, 152,
163, 171, 178, 210, 309, 339, 343, 354,
361, 362, 363, 364; and the Iranian
Constitution, 62, 135, 171, 241, 362;
Khomeini's, 71, 76–77, 79–81, 85–90,
105, 113, 116, 119, 140–41, 163, 171,
196–98, 225, 240–41, 243–45, 248,
251–52, 254–55, 260; as part of Iranian
identity, 337, 354; in the Persian Gulf,
223, 225, 240–60; and pragmatism,
166, 191, 198, 207; resurgence of, 35,
79, 222, 240, 272; as source of power,
14, 85–86, 95; Sunni (see Sunnis;
Wahhabism); as a "third way" or the
"right way," 36, 39–40, 136, 140, 165;
Twelver Shii (see Shia; Shiism); and the

United States, 60, 77, 252–53; values
and universality of, 14, 81, 83, 85, 95,
105, 113, 116, 133–35, 140–41, 144, 163,
189–90, 196–97, 210, 310, 312, 336, 357
Islamic civilization, 47, 153, 364
Islamic Conference Organization (ICO),
142, 245
Islamic Front for the Liberation of
Bahrain, 88, 132, 256
Islamic Jihad Organization, 263–64,
283n6
Islamic Republican Party (IRP):
assassinations, 75; in elections, 45;
political relations, 36–37; power of, 36,
41, 72–73, 101; views of, 45, 77
Islamic Revolution. See Iranian Revolution
Islamic Revolutionary Guard Corps. See
Revolutionary Guard
Islamic Revolution Movement of the
Arabian Peninsula, 132
Ismail, Shah, 10, 186, 337–38, 343
Israel: and Arab-Israeli conflict, 153–55,
219–20, 224–25, 227, 233, 234, 251,
276, 281, 288; Iranian protests against
Israel, 87, 255, 268; Iranian views on
Arab-Israeli conflict, 321–31, 333; and
Khomeini, 78, 83, 88, 102, 253, 268,
308; and Lebanon, 98, 105, 139, 261,
356; as nuclear power, 173; and Persian
Gulf, 227, 233, 234, 253; relations
with Iran, 5, 43, 72, 154–55, 193, 225,
319–20; and Soviet Union, 320–23,
326, 333; threats with Iran, 3, 95, 200,
204, 208, 333; and United States, 153,
165, 191, 217, 218–20, 277, 308, 326. See
also Iran-Contra Affair

Jaleh Square, 57–58, 64
Japan, 47, 91, 94, 102, 109, 120–21, 215,
226–27, 230–31, 312
Jefferson, Thomas, 177, 350, 359, 363
Jerusalem, 83, 118, 154, 185, 268, 328, 330
jihad: definition of, 139, 245; financial,
123; on Qavam, 12; against terrorism,
199, 347

Johnson, Lyndon, 60
Jordan: relations with Iran, 192, 323, 326–27, 332; relations with the United States, 216–17, 218, 219, 220; and terrorism, 265; threats to, 95
Judaism: and fundamentalism, 240; and Jewish state, 200, 276, 320, 326; and Jewish suffering, 261; in pre-Islamic Iran, 185, 205, 337; and Shiism, 319
June 1963 crisis, 3–4, 9, 12–15, 21, 35, 61, 111, 129
justice: demand for, 151, 210; and durable order, 178, 315, 345, 364; as ideology, 185, 253; under Islam, 40, 116, 133, 135, 136, 163, 190, 196, 345; and liberty, 178, 315, 345, 364; as part of Persian culture, 133, 345; as part of world culture, 124, 223; as a revolutionary promise, 135, 314, 361; in Shii Islam, 133–34, 222, 241, 253, 260, 261

Kalali, Manuchehr, 27
Karbala, 118, 133, 248; Karbala-5, 122
Karzai, Hamid, 193, 199, 313, 350
Kashani, Sayyid Abolghassem, 12, 35, 341
Kayhan, 27, 142
Kazemi, Baqer, 61
Kennedy, John F., 3, 21, 61, 65, 342
Kenya, 115, 310
Khalid, King of Saudi Arabia, 87, 251, 254, 255
Khalilzad, Zalmay, 348, 350
Khalkhali, Sadeq, 73
Khamenei, Ali: as ayatollah, 149, 166, 355; and export of the revolution, 138, 144–45, 154–55; foreign policy of, 101, 120, 198; and Iran-Iraq War, 121, 294; and nuclear negotiations, 201, 202; as president of Iran, 75, 81, 83, 123; and the United States, 154, 199, 201, 203, 347, 348
Khan, Mirza Taqi (Amir Kabir), 113, 129
Khan, Mirza Yousef (Mostashar Dowleh), 188, 336

Kharrazi, Kamal, 152, 172, 174, 193, 199, 313, 362
Khatami, Mohammad: foreign policy of, 4, 148–58, 170–78, 192–94, 198–201, 209–10, 312–15; and Islamic democracy, 5, 198, 336, 343–47; as president of Iran, 148, 343, 353–54, 359
Khoeiniha, Mohammad Mousavi, 72, 309, 310
Khomeini, Ruhollah: challenges to, 75–77, 123; and domestic policy, 38, 39–46, 252, 278, 309–10, 314, 343; and ideals of the revolution, 1, 135, 150, 178, 210, 314, 343, 354, 361; ideas of, 4, 35, 113, 116, 240, 277, 308–9, 312; and the Iranian Constitution, 40–42, 52, 166, 171, 248, 268–70, 343, 361; Khomeini line (Khatti Imam), 116, 120, 165, 197, 259–60, 308; in opposition to the Shah, 9, 35, 36, 39, 58–60, 62, 64, 111, 162, 189, 342; and terrorism, 104–5, 250–51, 263, 265, 274, 279; and Velayat-e Faqih, 41, 79, 112, 134, 240–42, 243–44, 342
—foreign policy of: and export of the revolution, 80–81, 87, 88, 108, 116, 128–44, 163–64, 174, 176, 245–47, 250–51, 252, 260–61, 268, 309; and the hostage crisis, 5, 44–45, 50, 101, 114–15, 117, 131, 308–10, 335; impact of his ideology on, 4, 71–91, 163–65, 189–94, 196–98, 209, 243; and Iran-Iraq War, 76, 85–86, 97, 100, 106, 122, 143, 248–49, 290; and Iran's isolation, 101–3, 119, 124–25, 148, 312; with Iraq, 77, 87, 97, 98, 112, 143, 260; "Neither East nor West," 63, 66, 83, 84, 116, 120–21, 131, 136, 144, 163, 165, 190, 198, 243, 269, 309, 312; and the Persian Gulf, 167, 241–55, 259–61, 277; and the United States, 3, 36, 77, 99, 108–9, 112, 134, 156, 216, 277, 310, 335, 342; and the U.N. Security Council, 107
Khorramshahr, 76, 137, 165
Khosravani, 'Ataollah, 27

Khuzistan, 23, 37, 322
Kissinger, Henry, 56, 57, 99, 207, 260, 328, 330
Kurdish Democratic Party (KDP), 37
Kurdistan: Democratic Party of Kurdistan in Iran, 158n5; as part of Iran, 38; as Soviet-supported regime, 1, 53, 59
Kurds: as challenge to Iran, 37–38, 46, 114; demands for autonomy by, 38; Iranian violence against, 150; as political faction, 40; rebellions of, 23, 66, 168
Kuwait: and export of the Iranian revolution, 139, 237; Iraqi invasion of, 168, 287, 289, 290, 294, 295–96, 311, 349; and oil, 221, 230; and Persian Gulf security, 257; relations with Iran, 95, 98, 107, 168, 269, 281, 356; Shia in, 240, 273, 274, 356; and terrorism, 104, 108, 118, 139, 256, 263–65, 271, 273, 274, 279, 281, 282nn3–5

Laingen, Bruce, 3
law: under Cyrus the Great, 185, 337; D'Amato, 155; as essential to political order, 198, 315, 345, 364; in the international arena, 77, 114, 130, 137, 154, 172, 178, 245, 280, 287, 289, 292–94, 296–99, 309, 310–11, 363; under the Iranian Constitution, 2, 27–28, 170, 339; and the Iranian Revolution, 36, 73, 78, 314; under Islam, 11, 132, 309, 339–40 (see also Sharia); rule of, 25, 151, 172, 188, 192, 295, 344; of the sea, 221, 236; under the Shah, 13
Lebanon: independence of, 16; Iranian relations with, 95, 97, 98, 104, 117–18, 128–29, 130–31, 139, 141, 192; and Israel, 139, 193, 261, 265, 320, 323; radical groups in, 78, 95, 98, 104, 105, 118, 122, 132, 139, 144, 165, 191, 193, 260, 261, 263–64, 265, 288, 312, 346; and the United States, 218, 260
Ledeen, Michael, 349
lesser Satan, 103, 191, 243. See also Israel; Soviet Union

Liberation Front for Bahrain, 257
Liberation Movement of Iran, 124
Libya, 175, 230, 265, 266, 268
London. See Great Britain

Machiavelli, Niccolò, 56
Madison, James, 363
Magi (majus), 185, 186, 337,
Mahdi. See Twelfth Imam
Majlis: clerical supervision of, 78, 339; decisions of, 12, 18, 19, 37, 44, 117, 188; divisions within, 46, 122, 314, 344; elections of, 27–28, 45, 117, 343; establishment of, 339; and nationalization of oil, 2, 20; powers of, 17, 73, 339, 341; and the Shah, 53, 64
Maoism, 36
Mardom Party, 27
martyrdom, 36, 85, 100, 133, 222, 250, 253, 259
Marxism, 36, 135, 280, 360
Matindaftari, Hedayat, 40
McFarlane, Robert, 121
McHenry, Donald F., 296, 305n74
Mecca, 74, 87, 164, 190, 223, 252, 254–55, 265
Medina, 223, 252
Middle East: Arab-Israeli relations in, 154, 227, 326, 327–28, 332, 333; and the Iranian Revolution, 80, 97, 108, 115; Iran's position in, 28, 118, 135, 208, 246, 332, 335, 356; and Islam, 9–10, 152, 346; role of Persian Gulf in, 221, 246, 276; and Russia, 55, 322–23, 324, 333; and Shiism, 240, 241, 260–61; terrorism in, 95, 263, 265–66; and the United States, 66, 94, 108, 153, 208, 209, 216, 217–18, 227, 235, 260, 263, 310, 335, 349, 353; wars and arms in, 104, 209, 218, 220, 227, 233, 248, 276, 353
military (Iran): agreements with the Soviet Union, 144, 166, 217, 312, 324; agreements with the United States, 21, 35, 43, 54, 55–56, 57, 59–61, 84, 112,

military (Iran) (*continued*)
114, 125, 189, 218, 226–27, 229, 233, 276–77; and Iraq, 274, 292–93; and Khomeini, 137–40, 246; and liberty, 279; mobilization of, 85, 185–86, 191; and nuclear program, 201; power of, 28, 60, 189, 215, 225, 247, 278, 307, 325, 342, 355; reconstruction of, 39, 46, 114, 166–67, 198, 361; restraint of, 96, 97, 100, 279; setbacks of and challenges to, 37, 38, 82, 123, 219, 290; and the Shah, 3, 23, 38, 53–54, 59–60, 64, 65, 125, 161–62, 189, 217–19, 225, 342, 355

Millspaugh, Arthur, 18, 59

mini-Satan, 243, 253

Mobilization Force, 85, 270

modernization: as alienating force, 36, 63, 272; challenges to, 9, 19, 20, 22, 29, 36, 61–63; versus the clergy, 13, 15; of the economy, 62–63, 65; effects and implications of, 15, 24–26, 34, 112, 273; and the Iranian Constitution, 17, 18; Iran's goal of, 19–20, 21, 23–24, 29; military strength as prerequisite to, 54; and national independence, 19–20, 29, 54; in the Persian Gulf, 222; socioeconomic forms of, 17–18, 20, 21–25, 29; and the White Revolution, 20, 21, 23–25

Mohtashemi, Ali Akbar, 122, 141

monarchy (Iran): demands for constitutional, 11, 26, 134, 339; and the military, 38; opposition to, 12, 39, 77, 112, 161, 252, 361; and the *ulama*, 10, 13, 77–78

Montazeri, Hussein-Ali, 117, 121, 130, 131, 138, 140, 166, 246

Montazeri, Muhammad, 117, 130

Montreux Convention, 232, 236

Morgenthau, Hans J., 176, 307

Mosaddegh, Mohammad: and the clergy (*ulama*), 11–12, 13, 35; failures of, 45–46, 47; followers of the Mosaddegh Path (*rah-e Mossadegh*), 116, 308; and

nationalizing Iran's oil industry, 2, 20, 31n15, 134, 188–89, 321, 340–41; overthrow of, 5, 9, 12, 20–21, 45, 54, 111–12, 129, 150, 175, 192, 276, 321, 341, 346, 360; —, as cause of the Iranian Revolution, 111, 129, 309. *See also* Anglo-Iranian Oil Company (AIOC); National Front; nationalists
—foreign policy of: compared to Khomeini's, 134; with Israel, 321; national interest in, 188–89; and "negative equilibrium" (nonalignment), 83, 113, 115–16, 129, 130, 243; with the United States, 45–46, 54–55, 59, 175, 192, 309, 340–41, 346, 360

Moscow: and Egypt, 324; influence on Iranian foreign policy, 53, 55, 144; Iranian relations with, 53, 91, 99, 103, 114, 118–19, 169, 231, 268, 322; and the Persian Gulf, 223, 227, 268; and the United States, 216, 217, 227, 238

Mottaki, Manoucher, 202–4

Mousavi, Mir-Hossein, 79, 81, 82, 83, 109, 121, 131–32, 210

Mubarak, Hosni, 105, 328

Muhammad (Prophet), 36, 88, 128, 134, 140, 142, 163, 165, 197, 255

Mujahadeen-e-Khalq, 130, 143, 199, 249–50, 279, 308

Mujahadeen Islam (party): definition of, 11–12; views of, 40, 42

Mulk, Khajeh Nizam al-, 162, 360

Musandam Peninsula, 221, 233

Muslim People's Republican Party (MPRP), 37, 41

Nabavi, Behzad, 73, 74

Najaf, 112, 248

Nasser, Gamal Abdel, 55, 92n1, 321–24, 338

Natanz, 199–200, 202

National Democratic Front, 40, 76, 308

National Democratic Party, 40

National Front: alliances of, 12, 35, 39,

Oman (*continued*)
  agreements, 257; Iranian relations
  with, 225, 232, 233, 236, 325; Iraqi
  relations with, 237; Saudi support of,
  215; Shia in, 240, 274; and the Soviet
  Union, 277; and the Strait of Hormuz,
  221, 230, 231–34, 236
OPEC (Organization of Petroleum
  Exporting Countries), 56, 94, 96–97,
  273, 230–31
Organization of the Islamic Conference
  (OIC), 74, 86, 148, 173, 296, 311
Ottoman Empire, 10, 134, 162, 187, 206,
  338, 357

Pahlavi, Mohammad Reza Shah:
  alienating policies of, 4, 34, 37, 58,
  60, 61–62, 63–65, 71, 111–12, 123, 129,
  272 (*see also* June 1963 crisis; White
  Revolution); attempted assassination
  of, 2, 34; and the Constitution, 42, 53,
  55; fall of, 36, 38, 39, 43, 51, 65, 71,
  115, 131, 148, 268, 335; and the hostage
  crisis, 3, 43; and modernization,
  20–25, 29n1, 34, 61–63, 65; opposition
  to, 34–37, 52, 58–65, 76, 111–12, 115,
  129, 226, 241, 308, 342; power of,
  20–21, 24, 52, 59, 63; reforms led by
  (*see* reforms: under the Shah); and
  relations with the *ulama*, 11–12, 13–15,
  36, 52, 62, 269; supporters of, 12, 27,
  62; and use of religious symbols, 14,
  62, 354; views of on political systems,
  25–27, 31n22
—foreign policy of: and the Arab-Israeli
  conflict, 5, 225, 319–33; and domestic
  politics, 52, 58–60, 66–67, 314; and
  Egypt, 55, 321, 322–32; and ensuring
  dynastic interests, 58, 162, 189; and
  Great Britain, 53, 55; and Jordan, 332;
  and nationalization of Iran's oil, 56–57;
  and oil trade, 56–57, 60, 62, 112; as
  opposed to Khomeini's, 83–87, 90–91,
  103–4, 111–14, 162, 225, 229, 234, 243–
  44, 314; and overthrow of Mosaddegh,

12, 34, 54–55, 59, 162, 341; positive
  nationalism of, 243, 321; and relations
  with the United States, 2–4, 18, 34–35,
  51–63, 65–67, 71, 87, 112, 125, 162, 189,
  229, 308–9, 322, 328–30, 342, 361 (*see
  also* Baghdad Pact; CENTO [Central
  Treaty Organization]); —, military aid
  and trade with, 54, 55–56, 57, 59–60,
  61, 65, 112, 114, 189, 217–18, 226, 354;
  and security in the Persian Gulf, 51, 56,
  87, 112, 129, 162, 189, 217, 225, 229,
  234, 244, 247, 248, 251, 256, 342, 356;
  and the Soviet Union, 53–54, 55, 59,
  61, 114, 224–25, 321, 322, 323; and the
  White Revolution, 23
Pahlavi, Reza Shah (Reza Khan):
  abdication of the throne by, 1–2, 52; as
  "architect of independent Iran," 18, 19,
  340; foreign policy of, 18, 19, 189, 340;
  and the Iranian Constitution, 11, 42;
  and Khomeini, 77, 90; modernization
  under, 13, 18, 19, 30n12, 340 (*see
  also* Civil Code [Iran]; Trans-Iranian
  Railway); policies of, 18–19, 340; and
  political participation, 25; relations
  with the *ulama*, 11, 13 (*see also* Tobacco
  Protest [1891–92]); and the Soviet
  Union, 114
Pahlavi dynasty, 13, 58, 87, 160, 277, 342,
  361
Pakistan, 16, 76, 89, 91, 94, 103, 130, 141,
  173, 220, 265, 325
Palestine Liberation Organization (PLO),
  225, 330–32
Palestinian state, 95, 155, 266, 268, 276,
  331; Gaza, 276; West Bank, 276, 330
Parliament (Iran). *See* Majlis
Parsons, Anthony, 296
Pasdaran. *See* Revolutionary Guard
peasantry: and alienation from the Iranian
  regime, 14, 272; as constituency, 24;
  and land reforms, 14, 18, 21–22, 61, 342
Pentagon, 34, 60, 134, 189, 193, 233, 342,
  347, 348
perestroika, 125, 135

Perle, Richard, 348

Persian Empire, 133, 185, 205, 337, 356

Persian Gulf: extremism in, 104, 107,
164, 190, 234, 246, 250–51, 256–58,
263–66, 267–68, 271, 275–76, 277–82;
military aid and intervention in, 33, 96,
166, 168, 229, 232–36, 238–39, 260,
276–77, 281, 310, 349 (see also Persian
Gulf War [1991]); navigation in, 107,
158, 169 (see also straits by name); oil
in, 95, 221–22, 226, 229–39, 272–73,
276, 280, 325; relations within,
221–27, 236–38; security in, 4, 60,
86–87, 94–98, 115, 136, 167–68, 174,
208–9, 215–27, 229–39, 248, 295,
325, 356; Shii politics in, 4, 95, 222,
223, 240–41, 247–48, 250–51, 253–61,
263–65, 268–70, 274–75, 281, 356;
societal problems in, 270–74, 280–81;
and the Soviet Union, 99, 217, 223,
224, 232–35, 238–39, 325; and the
United States, 95–96, 99, 115, 118, 155,
168, 208, 215–21, 222–23, 226–27,
232–35, 238–39, 260, 276–77, 280–82,
310, 349. See also Persian Gulf countries
by name

—and Iran: and export of the revolution,
104, 107, 128–29, 139, 247, 248–49,
256, 260–61, 356; and Iran-Iraq War,
94–99, 104, 107, 166, 274, 277–79,
281; Khomeini's conception of security
in, 242–47; relations between, 98,
104–5, 107, 155–56, 167–68, 190, 198,
225, 247, 256, 312, 322, 356; role and
influence of Iran in, 23, 28, 87, 99, 168,
208, 216, 235, 248, 257, 258, 268–70;
and Shah as policeman of, 51, 112, 129,
162, 189, 244, 342

Persian Gulf War (1980–88). See Iran-Iraq
War

Persian Gulf War (1991), 96, 99, 104, 106,
168, 289, 295, 312, 346

P5+1, 201–2, 357. See also IAEA
(International Atomic Energy Agency);
nuclear program (Iranian)

Phalangists, 139, 243

Philippines, 104, 141, 162, 189, 265, 268,
341

Polk, William R., 353

Popular Front for the Liberation of Oman
and the Arabian Gulf (PFLOAG), 233

Popular Front for the Liberation of
Palestine (PFLP), 265, 332

pragmatism: versus ideology, 4, 46, 47,
184, 210; in Iranian foreign policy, 194,
196, 199, 205; spiritual form of, 196,
197–98, 205–6, 210

progress: of democracy in Iran, 350;
in Islamic civilization, 78, 140; on
peace in the Middle East, 108, 122; in
socioeconomic areas, 25, 341; in the
West, 361, 362

Pye, Lucian W., 170, 207, 228n2

Qabus, Sultan of Oman, 233

Qaeda, al-, 199, 209, 349

Qajar dynasty, monarchs of the, 10, 34,
338, 339, 340, 360

Qasemlu, Abdolrahman, 37

Qatar: expatriates in, 271; oil in, 230;
security agreements with, 168, 257;
Shia in, 240, 274; terrorism in, 265

Qavam, Ahmad, 12, 19, 30n14, 53

Qom, 9, 257; attacks in, 41; nuclear
program in, 202; the Shah's speech in,
14, 62; uprisings in, 4, 57, 58, 64

Qotbzadeh, Sadeq, 115–16, 117, 130–32,
310

Quran: ideas based on, 206, 243; precepts
of, 86, 108, 245

Rafsanjani, Akbar Hashemi: foreign
policy of, 102, 105–6, 108–9, 119–22,
124, 144, 152, 164, 166–70, 175, 191,
197, 198–200, 209–10, 312, 346; and
Gulf Security, 155, 244, 290; on the
Iranian Revolution, 140, 143, 144–45;
as a revolutionary leader, 73, 113, 117,
131, 132, 149

Rajai, Mohammad-Ali: and export of the

Satan. *See* Great Satan; lesser Satan; mini-Satan

Satanic Verses, The (Rushdie), 128, 141–42, 164, 174, 193, 199, 313

Saud, Saud al-Faisal al-, 98, 105, 106

Saud, House of, 97, 251, 252, 254, 277

Saudi Arabia, Kingdom of: and the Arab-Israeli conflict, 225, 234, 320, 324, 326, 328, 332; and Bahrain, 88; economic development in, 221–22, 226, 271, 273, 277; oil in, 94, 220–21, 230; and Persian Gulf security, 215–25, 234, 257–58, 261, 277, 349; political system in, 273, 275, 279; Shia in, 4, 223, 240, 241, 251–55, 257, 261, 274–75, 356; terrorism in, 265, 281, 350, 356; and the United States, 87, 88, 96, 215–20, 226, 234, 253, 277, 349. *See also* Riyadh

—and Iran: comparison between, 252–53, 260; and disputes with Khomeini over Hajj pilgrims, 87, 118, 121, 138, 164, 167, 190, 198, 254–55; and export of the revolution, 139, 254–55, 260, 269, 356; positive relations between, 173–74, 192, 198, 224, 251, 324; tense relations between, 87–88, 95–96, 98, 104–5, 107, 117–18, 130, 155, 225, 251–53, 257–58, 260

SAVAK (Iranian security police), 24, 63–64, 65

Savory, Roger M., 187, 205, 338

Schimmel, Annemarie, 364

September 11, 2001, 193, 199, 347, 349, 352n24

Shahanshah, 59

Sharia, 11, 132, 309, 339. *See also* law: under Islam

Shari'ati, Ali, 35, 47n6, 308

Shariatmadari, Ayatollah, 39, 41, 42, 171

Sharif-Emami, Jafar, 64

Sharjah, 108, 225

Shatt al-Arab, 224, 237, 293

Shayegan, Dr. Ali, 2, 6n1

Shia: in Afghanistan, 139; in Azerbaijan, 170; in conflict with Sunnis, 134, 162, 187, 251, 252, 270, 320, 338, 356; in contrast with Sunnis, 222–23, 275; cooperation with Sunnis, 249, 251, 320; as the deprived (*mahrumin*), 4, 134, 249, 275; and the Iranian Revolution, 95, 97, 222, 249–50, 261, 269; in Iraq, 95, 97, 168, 223, 225, 241, 246, 248–51, 258, 274–75, 278–79, 356; in Lebanon, 78, 95, 98, 105, 139, 260, 261, 263–64; as majority, 4, 37, 95, 97, 223, 225, 240, 248–49, 255, 259, 261, 274; as minority, 4, 134, 240, 253, 254–55, 261; as oppressed (*mustaz'afeen*), 253, 269; in the Persian Gulf, 4, 240–41, 247–48, 250–51, 253–61, 263–65, 268–70, 274–75, 281, 356; radicalism and extremism of, 11, 35, 88, 97, 106, 240, 249–50, 256, 257–60, 263–65, 273–75, 278, 288

Shiism: appeal and politics of, 4, 72, 247–49, 254–61, 274; aspects of, 36, 133, 134, 208, 222, 240, 241, 243, 248, 259–61, 275, 354; as imposed ideology, 10, 186–87, 194, 338; and Iran's foreign policy, 187, 194, 205, 225, 242–43, 260, 319; Khomeini's interpretation of, 14, 78, 79, 90, 137, 139, 163, 171, 241, 242, 245, 248, 259, 268, 269; and leadership of the *faqih*, 134, 139, 171, 242, 243, 245, 269; as official creed of Iran, 10, 11, 42, 134, 240–41; as sociopolitical movement, 241, 247–51, 253–54, 255–61, 281, 356; and the *ulama*, 9–10, 11, 72, 134, 274, 342–43

Shirazi, Rabbani, 41

Shush-Dezful, 85, 137

Shuster, Morgan, 18, 19, 188, 339, 360

Sinai II Agreement, 326, 329

socialism: as faction in Iran, 2; versus Khomeini's ideology, 76, 85, 116, 243, 249; and oil, 226, 231; and the Soviet Union, 128

Somalia, 115, 310

South Asia, 208, 220, 325, 356

Soviet Union: disintegration of, 165, 167,

States, 4, 5, 57, 101, 102, 105, 108, 109, 111, 125, 165, 174, 191, 192, 289, 328, 335, 349, 358, 362. *See also* American Embassy: in Tehran

Tehran Declaration, 53, 155

Tel Aviv, 3, 322, 324, 326

terrorism: against Americans, 199, 260, 263–64, 265, 347, 350; explanations and causes of, 266–68, 271, 275, 278–79; global war on, 209, 349; as international issue, 157, 174, 210, 263, 265–66; involvement of youth in, 271; during Iranian Revolution, 4, 71, 75, 149, 308, 332; during Iran-Iraq War, 66; Iran's alleged support of, 88, 104, 105–6, 109, 139, 153, 164, 190, 193, 246, 257, 274–75, 313, 347–49; Iran's denouncements of, 199, 274–75, 347; and Israel, 154; means of coping with, 234, 279–82; in the Persian Gulf, 4, 104, 105–6, 234, 263–65, 271, 275, 279–82

Third World, 103, 231, 266, 270, 276, 277; leaders, 38; nations, 29, 76, 83, 91, 104, 160, 362; peoples of, 2; phenomenon of, 240; policies concerning, 91, 130; society, 160

Thornburg, Max, 61

Tobacco Protest (1891–92), 11, 210, 338

Tocqueville, Alexis de, 176

Transcaucasia, 167, 312, 338

Trans-Iranian Railway, 19, 30n12

Truman, Harry, 341

Tudeh Party: alliances of, 19, 37; as a challenge to Khomeini's ideology, 76; destruction of, 103, 268; influence of, in Iran, 91, 341; opposition to, 21, 62; Soviet support of, 53; as a supporter of the hostage-taking, 130, 308; views of, 42, 49n26, 51, 341

Turkey: Iran's economic relations with, 76, 91, 103–4, 109, 130; Iran's political relations with, 103–4, 121, 141, 166, 187, 197, 208; and secularism, 13, 222; views of, 94

Turkish Straits, 232, 236, 238

Turkmenistan, 129, 139

TWA (Trans World Airlines) hijacking crisis, 98, 105, 109, 281

Twelfth Imam, 40, 48nn17–18, 78, 134, 163, 187, 205, 241–42, 261, 343

"twin revolution," 71, 92n1, 111, 162

two Tunbs, 56, 155, 225

ulama: as exporters of the revolution, 141, 246–47; as a political group, 12, 124, 134, 269; relation to state, 9–14, 134, 222, 269; role of, in Iranian society, 9, 15, 269. *See also* clergy (Islamic)

umma, 153, 189, 355

United Arab Emirates (UAE): disputes with Iran, 155, 167, 173, 192, 198; expatriates in, 271; oil in, 230; relations between, 108, 155–56, 277; security agreements with, 257; Shia in, 240, 274; and the Soviet Union, 277; and terrorism, 265, 274

United Nations: and the Arab-Israeli conflict, 320, 326, 329–31; Charter, 86, 137, 245, 292–93, 294, 298, 311; General Assembly, 199; membership in, 50, 163, 294; and the Persian Gulf, 236, 270, 280, 289; and rule of law, 295–97

—and Iran: and the Anglo-Iranian Oil Company dispute, 340; and dialogue among civilizations, 172, 199, 313; and the hostage crisis, 44, 77, 117, 310; and human rights, 64, 158, 298, 344, 345, 359; and Iran-Iraq War, 75, 106–7, 118, 173, 288, 290, 292–93, 294, 295–96, 298; and Khatami, 198, 313, 315, 347; and praise for Iran, 168, 169, 312

—secretary-general: Kofi Annan, 200, 313; Boutros Boutros-Ghali, 169; Javier Perez de Cuellar, 123, 164, 287–88, 300n13, 311; and Iran-Iraq War, 5, 287–95; and promoting dialogue among civilizations, 199, 313; Kurt Waldheim, 295, 300n13

White Revolution: analysis of, 16–29, 29n1; causes of, 61; failure of, 4, 342; implications of, 4, 23–24; and the Shah's priority of socioeconomic modernization, 20, 21, 23, 35. *See also* reforms: under the Shah

Wiesehofer, Josef, 185

Wolfowitz, Paul, 349

women (Iranian): as a constituency, 14, 148, 343, 361; emancipation of, 15, 26, 149; enfranchisement of, 26; as equal, 152, 171; and the Iranian Revolution, 123, 270, 344; rights of, 151, 152; among the youth, 23, 148, 150, 335, 347, 361

workers (Iranian): as a constituency, 24, 35, 62; in the oil industry, 220, 253; reforms concerning, 22, 26, 39, 62, 100; the Shah's support of, 14, 22, 26, 62; and terrorism, 258; well-being of, 22, 62

World Trade Organization (WTO), 314

World War II, 1, 2, 50, 54, 59, 77, 207, 217, 238, 289

Xenophon, 185, 337

Xerxes I, 185

Yazdi, Ibrahim, 42, 43, 72, 82, 113, 115, 116, 132

Yazid, 36, 85

Yemen, 320, 323; North, 215, 216, 218; South, 215, 325

youth (Iranian): demands of, 210; and education, 23, 150; expectations of, 12, 149, 280; and the Iranian Revolution, 85, 150, 308; —, exporting of, 80; and Khatami and pro-democracy movements, 148, 151, 335, 347, 361; and media, 150, 272; and terrorism, 24, 258, 270–71, 272, 280, 347; views of, 62, 148–50, 347

Zakaria, Fareed, 345

Zionism, 37, 41, 84, 142, 267, 277

Zoroastrian, 133, 186, 205, 208, 337, 338, 355

OTHER BOOKS BY R. K. RAMAZANI

AUTHOR

The Middle East and the European Common Market (1964)

The Foreign Policy of Iran: A Developing Nation in World Affairs, 1500–1941 (1966);
   awarded first prize by the American Association of Middle East Studies

The Northern Tier: Afghanistan, Iran and Turkey (1966)

The Persian Gulf: Iran's Role (1972)

Iran's Foreign Policy, 1941–1973: A Study of Foreign Policy in Modernizing Nations
   (1975)

Beyond the Arab-Israeli Settlement: New Directions for U.S. Policy in the Middle East
   (1977)

The Persian Gulf and the Strait of Hormuz (1979)

The United States and Iran: The Patterns of Influence (1982)

Revolutionary Iran: Challenge and Response in the Middle East (1986)

The Gulf Cooperation Council: Record and Analysis (1988)

EDITOR

Iran's Revolution: The Search for Consensus (1990)

Iran at the Crossroads (coeditor, 2001)

The Future of Liberal Democracy: Thomas Jefferson and the Contemporary World
   (coeditor, 2004)

Religion, State, and Society: Jefferson's Wall of Separation in Comparative Perspective
   (coeditor, 2009)